MODELS FOR IMPLEMENTING
RESPONSE TO INTERVENTION

Models for Implementing Response to Intervention

TOOLS, OUTCOMES, AND IMPLICATIONS

Edited by

Edward S. Shapiro
Naomi Zigmond
Teri Wallace
Doug Marston

THE GUILFORD PRESS
New York   London

© 2011 The Guilford Press
A Division of Guilford Publications, Inc.
72 Spring Street, New York, NY 10012
www.guilford.com

Last digit is print number: 9   8   7   6   5   4   3   2   1

Library of Congress Cataloging-in-Publication Data
Models for implementing response to intervention : tools, outcomes, and implications / edited by Edward S. Shapiro . . . [et al.].
   p. cm.
   Includes bibliographical references and index.
   ISBN 978-1-60918-124-6 (hardcover : alk. paper)
   1. Remedial teaching—United States.   2. Slow learning children—Education—United States.   3. Learning disabled children—Education—United States.   4. Effective teaching—United States.   5. Response to intervention (Learning disabled children)   I. Shapiro, Edward S.
   LB1029.R4M62 2011
   371.9′043—dc22
                                                          2010032228

About the Editors

Edward S. Shapiro, PhD, is Director of the Center for Promoting Research to Practice and Professor in the School Psychology Program at Lehigh University, Bethlehem, Pennsylvania. He is the 2006 winner of the Senior Scientist Award given by the Division of School Psychology of the American Psychological Association in recognition of a senior member of the field who has provided a sustained program of outstanding theoretical and research activity. Dr. Shapiro is a past Editor of *School Psychology Review,* the official journal of the National Association of School Psychologists. Best known for his work in curriculum-based assessment and nonstandardized methods of assessing academic skills problems, he has written numerous books and other publications in the areas of curriculum-based assessment, behavioral assessment, behavioral interventions, and pediatric school psychology, his latest books being *Academic Skills Problems: Direct Assessment and Intervention, Fourth Edition,* and *Academic Skills Problems Fourth Edition Workbook,* both published by The Guilford Press. Among his many projects, Dr. Shapiro has recently completed a federal project focused on the development of a multi-tiered, response-to-intervention (RTI) model in two districts in Pennsylvania. He has been working as a consultant to facilitate the implementation of RTI with the Pennsylvania Department of Education as well as with many individual school districts across the country. Dr. Shapiro also codirects a training grant from the U.S. Department of Education to train preservice school psychologists as facilitators and developers of RTI implementation.

Naomi Zigmond, PhD, is Distinguished Professor of Education at the University of Pittsburgh. She has been an active special education researcher and teacher for more than 40 years, with a focus on the organization of special education services for students with disabilities in elementary and secondary schools and the impact of program organization on student achievement. Dr. Zigmond's work has concentrated on the various roles of the special education teacher (consultant, co-teacher, resource teacher, self-contained class teacher, etc.) and how best to improve academic and social outcomes for students with disabilities in public schools. For the past decade, she has also led a team of researchers and practitioners in the development, production, distribution, scoring, reporting, and validation of the Pennsylvania Alternate System of Assessment, the statewide alternate assessment for students with significant cognitive disabilities. Dr. Zigmond has published many articles, book chapters, and books, and is a past Editor of *Exceptional Children.* In 1997, she received the Research Award from the Council for Exceptional Children in recognition of research that has contributed significantly to the body of knowledge about the education of exceptional children and youth. In 2008, Dr. Zigmond was awarded the highest honor that can be bestowed on a University of Pittsburgh faculty member: promotion to the rank of Distinguished Professor of Education, the first faculty member in the 100-year history of the School of Education to achieve this rank.

Teri Wallace, PhD, is Associate Professor in the College of Education at Minnesota State University, Mankato. Prior to her current position, she served as Principal Investigator for several state and federal projects through the University of Minnesota's Institute on Community Integration. Dr. Wallace also served as graduate faculty in the Department of Educational Psychology at the University of Minnesota. Her research interests include general outcome measurement development for students with significant cognitive disabilities, RTI, the use of data for decision making, and implementing co-teaching in teacher preparation programs. In addition, she is interested in the continuous improvement of teacher education.

Doug Marston, PhD, is Administrator for Research, Evaluation, and Assessment for the Special Education Department of the Minneapolis Public Schools, where he is responsible for teacher training in assessment and data utilization, grant writing, program evaluation, and implementation of the problem-solving model and the RTI model. In addition, Dr. Marston is an adjunct faculty member in the Special Education Program at the University of Minnesota, where he has taught classes in assessment and has been Co–Principal Investigator with the University of Minnesota faculty for several federally funded grants. He has published more than 35 journal articles and 10 book chapters in the areas of curriculum-based measurement, student progress monitoring, reading interventions for students with mild disabilities, the problem-solving model, and RTI, and coauthored *Classroom-Based Assessment: Evaluating Instructional Outcomes*. In 2006, Dr. Marston received the Ysseldyke Distinguished Best Practices Award from the Minnesota School Psychology Association and was also named one of the "100 Distinguished Alumni" of the College of Education, University of Minnesota. He currently serves on the National Advisory Board for the National Research Center on Response to Intervention.

Contributors

Julie Alonzo, PhD, is a research associate at the University of Oregon's Behavioral Research and Teaching center, where her work focuses on developing assessments appropriate for students from diverse backgrounds. A National Board–certified teacher, she taught high school for 12 years prior to pursuing her career at the University.

María Almendárez Barron, MA, is a doctoral candidate in Reading Education at the University of Pittsburgh. She served as a research associate for Project MP3 and provided direct onsite support to the schools participating in the grant.

Renée Bradley, PhD, works in the Office of Special Education Programs for the U.S. Department of Education in Washington, DC.

Ann Casey, PhD, is a long-time employee of the Minneapolis Public Schools in a variety of positions. She was very involved in the initial development of the Minnesota Public Schools problem-solving model and also in implementation at the building level. She is the former Director of the Minnesota Response-to-Intervention Center and currently works with the RTI Action Network as lead mentor for their leadership network.

Nathan H. Clemens, PhD, is Assistant Professor of School Psychology at Texas A&M University. His research interests include the assessment and measurement of reading skills in early elementary school, early identification of learning disabilities, and the implementation of RTI models in schools. He previously served as a school consultant on Project MP3 at Lehigh University.

Yvonne Curtis, DEd, is Superintendent of the Forest Grove School District in Oregon, where she works to transform the district into a coherent school system that ensures that every student graduates with the knowledge and skills necessary for college, careers, and citizenship. She taught elementary school for 15 years before moving to school and district administration, where she focuses these systems on educational equity.

Grace Zamora Durán, EdD, works in the Office of Special Education Programs for the U.S. Department of Education in Washington, DC.

Karen L. Gischlar, PhD, is Assistant Professor in the Department of Graduate Education, Leadership, and Counseling at Rider University in Lawrenceville, New Jersey. She has 19 years of experience in the public schools as a kindergarten teacher and school psychologist. Dr. Gischlar served as a consultant to the schools on Project MP3 at Lehigh University.

Alexandra Hilt-Panahon, PhD, is Assistant Professor in the Department of Special Education at Minnesota State University, Mankato. Her research interests are focused on school-based academic and behavioral interventions, including RTI. She served as the Coordinator of Project MP3 at Lehigh University.

Elizabeth M. Hughes, MEd, is a doctoral student in the Department of Curriculum and Instruction at Clemson University, with an emphasis in special education. Her research interests include inclusive education, policy, and the academic achievement of students with disabilities.

Amanda Kloo, PhD, is Research Assistant Professor of Special Education in the Department of Instruction and Learning at the University of Pittsburgh. She served as Codirector of Project MP3 at the University of Pittsburgh.

Matthew Lau, PhD, NCSP, works in the Minneapolis Public Schools as a bilingual school psychologist. He provides training and support to general and special education staff on the problem-solving model.

Phyllis Levine, PhD, is Director of the Office of Special Education Programs' Model Demonstration Coordination Center and education researcher at SRI International's Center for Education and Human Services.

Kimy Liu, PhD, is Visiting Assistant Professor at the University of Portland's School of Education, where her work focuses on preparing preservice teachers serving children with diverse learning needs in inclusive classrooms. She taught English as a second language in Taiwan and elementary school in Boston, where she developed a math curriculum. As a research assistant in the University of Oregon–4J RTI Project, she developed the RTI assessment rubric and provided support to schools.

Charles D. Machesky, PhD, is Superintendent of the Uniontown Area School District in Pennsylvania. He was trained as a special educator and special education supervisor before earning a doctorate in Educational Administration and assuming a leadership role in his district.

Doug Marston, PhD. *See* "About the Editors."

Paul Muyskens, PhD, is a school psychologist in the Minneapolis Public Schools. He provides training and consultation on curriculum-based measurement, RTI, and alternate assessment.

Edward S. Shapiro, PhD. *See* "About the Editors."

Eileen St. John, PhD, is a consultant at the Pennsylvania Training and Technical Assistance Network in Pittsburgh. She served as a research associate for Project MP3 and provided direct onsite support to the schools participating in the grant.

Kathleen Stanfa, MEd, is Assistant Professor in the Department of Special Education at Kutztown University in Kutztown, Pennsylvania. She is also a PhD candidate in the Special Education Program at the University of Pittsburgh and served as a graduate student researcher and data manager for Project MP3.

Larry Sullivan, PhD, is Director of Educational Support Services for the Eugene, Oregon, School District 4J. In the area of school psychology, he has been a school psychologist, Assistant Executive Director of the National Association of School Psychologists, and a member of the graduate faculty at the University of Dayton.

Jane Thompson, MSW, EdS, has been a principal for 11 years in the Minneapolis Public Schools and worked in the district for over 30 years. Her interest is in developing effective and efficient systems for accelerating student achievement.

Renáta Tichá, PhD, is a research associate at the Institute on Community Integration in the College of Education and Human Development at the University of Minnesota. She is interested in general outcome measure development for students with significant cognitive disabilities.

Gerald Tindal, PhD, is the Castle–McIntosh–Knight Endowed Professor of Education at the University of Oregon, where he serves as Area Head in the Department of Educational Methodology, Policy, and Leadership and Director of Behavioral Research and Teaching, a research center housing federal and state grants and contracts.

Mary Wagner, PhD, is Codirector of SRI International's Center for Education and Human Services and Principal Investigator of the Office of Special Education Programs' (OSEP) Model Demonstration Coordination Center. Her work in that role builds on her earlier experience as Principal Investigator of OSEP's National Behavior Research Coordination Center.

Teri Wallace, PhD. *See* "About the Editors."

Naomi Zigmond, PhD. *See* "About the Editors."

Preface

The Individuals with Disabilities Education Improvement Act, the 2004 reauthorization of the Individuals with Disabilities Education Act (IDEA), included groundbreaking provisions for revising the procedures that local education agencies (LEAs) use to identify students with specific learning disabilities (SLD). Response-to-intervention (RTI) procedures have been included in IDEA not only to improve the identification of and services to students with SLD but also because the three-tiered model of service delivery (Fuchs, 2003; National Association of State Directors of Special Education [NASDSE], 2005) that is necessary to implement RTI has implications for improving the delivery of effective instructional programs to all students in general and special education in particular (Vaughn, Wanzek, Woodruff, & Linan-Thompson, 2007).

Over the past few years, there has been a proliferation of research and conceptual articles, books, and position papers describing the methods, processes, and outcomes of RTI models. Although these publications have provided a strong and workable framework for implementing RTI, the outcomes of real-life, broad-based implementation in schools have been far less evident. Indeed, Glover, DiPerna, and Vaughn (2007), in a special series in *School Psychology Review*, point out that we need substantially more examples, descriptions, and detailed discussions of the outcomes of implementation of RTI models. In particular, there is a need for on-the-ground examples of RTI and all of its components, including tools used for implementation, as well as a full discussion of outcomes and issues, challenges and successes, the expected sequence of events leading to schoolwide change, what to predict when implementing RTI models, and what is not predictable.

In 2006, the Office of Special Education Programs of the U.S. Department of Education funded three model/demonstration projects focused on the use of progress monitoring within the implementation of models of RTI. These types of projects take well-developed and empirically supported models of change and put them in place in everyday school experiences. The model/demonstration projects then examine the nature of the process of implementation, the context in which the implementation occurs, and the effects of implementation on student performance outcomes. The projects funded in 2006 represented four different sets of schools across multiple districts in very different geographical regions of the United States (one project included implementation in two distinctly different districts).

The purpose of this volume is to provide a full discussion of the implementation of these four models of RTI. These models represent efforts to put schoolwide change process in place and to evaluate in depth the outcomes of the implementation. The book shares the experience of implementation, what it took to put these models in place, tools that were developed to facilitate implementation, and the outcomes of each implementation.

We begin with a brief overview and history of the concept of RTI and, specifically, how progress monitoring plays such a key role, underlying many of the decisions made through the model. Chapter 1 is authored by key leaders in the Office of Special Education Programs of the U.S. Department of Education, who have been at the front of the effort to put RTI models and processes in place nationally.

Five parts follow the introductory chapter. Each of the first four sections comprises three chapters with a similar framework that relate to one of the projects in which an RTI model was put in place with progress monitoring as a key underlying process. The first chapter provides the context and content of the model, the second chapter describes the processes used for implementation, and the third chapter discusses the outcomes of implementation. Each model provides tools used for implementation that were developed and field tested by each of the models.

We conclude the volume with a chapter by members of a consulting group (SRI International) whose job it was to coordinate the efforts of all projects. The authors reflect on the implementation of these models from the perspective of an outside organization that watched, listened to, and supported all the project implementation, while recognizing their need to report outcomes to the U.S. Department of Education, with which they were contracted. The volume represents the collective efforts of all of the principal investigators and their respective staffs across projects and offers readers a chance to experience and understand the intricacies, successes, and challenges of implementing models of RTI in elementary school buildings.

EDWARD S. SHAPIRO

REFERENCES

Fuchs, L. S. (2003). Assessing intervention responsiveness: Conceptual and technical issues. *Learning Disabilities Research and Practice, 18*(3), 157–171.

Glover, T. A., DiPerna, J. C., & Vaughn, S. (2007). Service delivery systems for response to intervention: Core components and directions for future research. *School Psychology Review, 36,* 526–540.

National Association of State Directors of Special Education. (2005). *IDEA 2004 and response to intervention: Policy considerations and implementation.* Alexandria, VA: Author.

Vaughn, S., Wanzek, J., Woodruff, A. L., & Linan-Thompson, S. (2007). Prevention and early identification of students with reading disabilities. In D. Haager, J. Klingner, & S. Vaughn (Eds.), *Evidence-based reading practices for response to intervention* (pp. 11–29). Baltimore: Brookes.

Contents

MODELS FOR IMPLEMENTING
RESPONSE TO INTERVENTION

CHAPTER 1

Progress Monitoring
SUPPORT AND PRACTICE IMPLEMENTATION FROM THE FEDERAL LEVEL

Grace Zamora Durán
Elizabeth M. Hughes
Renée Bradley

OVERVIEW OF PROGRESS MONITORING

Progress monitoring is a formative instructional design that allows teachers to supervise student progress by recording student performance on short assessments over time. The traditional alternative is a culminating assessment that judges student knowledge based on a single performance at the end of a given unit or extended period of time. In athletics, the final score of a game will let us know only which team or individual won; knowing the final score does not necessarily indicate how the game was played. A good coach will watch the game and call specific plays or make changes as they are required throughout the game based on the continuous or changing performance of the players. The coach does not wait until the game is over to make the necessary performance changes. Progress monitoring is similar in the sense that, rather than waiting to determine whether a child has failed (e.g., performance on end-of-chapter test, standardized tests) before making educational decisions, teachers are able to make instructional decisions based on current student performance and trajectory of student successes. Progress monitoring can be used for students both with and without disabilities and may be implemented in a variety of ways.

1

One type of progress monitoring that has an established body of research to support validity and reliability is curriculum-based measurement (CBM; Deno, 1985). CBM uses frequent but brief probes that assess student knowledge and task fluency on general outcome measures. The results of the probes are graphed and analyzed by teachers to determine improvement in student performance, or lack thereof, as a result of receiving instruction. Teachers who use CBM data to make instructional decisions are more aware of the impact of their teaching on student achievement and student outcomes (Fuchs, Deno, & Mirkin, 1984). Consequently, student achievement has been shown to increase at a greater rate when teachers use CBM data to guide instructional decisions based on the needs of the student, as opposed to not making instructional adjustments based on CBM data (Stecker & Fuchs, 2000). CBM data provide teachers with formative assessment that indicates when students are benefiting from instructions.

Progress monitoring is also a key component within a response-to-intervention (RTI) framework. RTI is a systematic process that closely monitors students' performance as they receive quality, evidence-based instruction. Although RTI was initially identified in the Individuals with Disabilities Education Improvement Act (IDEA; 2004) as an alternative means of identifying students with a specific learning disability (SLD), many institutions have extended RTI as an early intervention program for students who may be at risk of having an SLD or a behavioral disability. Legislation allows school districts to use alternative methods grounded by evidence-based instruction, such as RTI, to identify students with SLD. The current law allows states to interpret or implement the law as they deem appropriate for the students served in their educational systems. Consequently, states and school districts have implemented various forms of RTI. Although RTI has been widely interpreted, there are universal components that are fundamental to an RTI system. By design, RTI incorporates assessment and intervention at various stages of intensity within a multi-tiered system. The key elements of RTI include (1) universal screening of students and identifying low performers, (2) monitoring student progress, (3) implementing research-supported instruction and interventions, and (4) intervening as necessary based on monitored student performance.

As a key component within an RTI framework, progress monitoring may result in early identification of children with SLD. In turn, early identification may result in lower referral rates for special education services or for less intense services throughout a child's school years. Thus a seamless progress monitoring system allows educators to systematically track students' performance and growth as students move from one skill to the next, one year to the next, one curriculum to the next, and one setting to the next (Wallace, Espin, McMaster, Deno, & Foegen, 2007). The use of progress monitoring also helps address the difficulty in appropriately and efficiently identifying school-age children with SLD.

PROGRESS MONITORING AND THE DEFINITION
OF LEARNING DISABILITIES

Progress monitoring and learning disabilities (LD) have had a long history. The University of Minnesota was home to one of the five original LD Research Centers funded in 1977. This center was focused on two primary goals: (1) definitional issues for identification of students with LD and (2) curriculum-based assessment (Hallahan & Mercer, 2002). This early work laid the foundation for progress monitoring as a means of improving both instruction and learning.

It has been estimated that approximately 5% of school-age children have an SLD, making up almost half of all students who receive special education services (U.S. Department of Education, National Center for Education Statistics, 2009). Remarkably, these numbers do not include students who have not yet been identified with a disability or those who chronically struggle in academics but do not qualify for special education services. Compounding these issues is the challenge for educators to differentiate between students who have an SLD and chronic low performers, as both groups often demonstrate similar behaviors and academic low achievement, especially in the absence of high-quality instruction.

Prior to the reauthorization of IDEA in 2004, students who qualified for special education services under the diagnosis of SLD were identified by what is typically referred to as the discrepancy model. In the discrepancy model, student performance had to demonstrate that there was a severe difference between academic achievement (i.e., student outcomes) and intellectual ability (i.e., IQ). Critics claim that the discrepancy model is fraught with problems (Scruggs & Mastropieri, 2002). The standard assessment often used to measure intellectual ability, an IQ test, has been criticized for conceptual and measurement problems, specifically its lack of precision, consistency, and accuracy in identifying struggling students who may have SLD (Fletcher et al., 1994; Francis, Fletcher, Shaywitz, Shaywitz, & Rourke, 1996; Vaughn & Fuchs, 2003) and its tendency to discriminate against select populations. The discrepancy model has been known to allow students to struggle and fail in school prior to a determination of eligibility for services. Unfortunately, once a child academically falls behind grade level, the chances increase that the child will remain behind grade-level performance (Downer, Rimm-Kaufman, & Pianta, 2007).

In 2004, states were allowed to use different criteria to determine whether a child was eligible to receive special education services under the disability category of SLD. The definition of an SLD remained unchanged, but new criteria adopted established that the state

> Must not require the use of a severe discrepancy between intellectual ability and achievement for determining whether a child has a specific learning disability, as defined in 34 CFR 300.8(c)(10);

Must permit the use of a process based on the child's response to scientific, research-based intervention; and

May permit the use of other alternative research-based procedures for determining whether a child has a specific learning disability, as defined in 34 CFR 300.8(c)(10).

The changes in the law do not require states to use an alternative method to identify SLD, nor do they specify how states must execute alternative-based procedures to identify students with SLD, outside of requiring scientifically supported instruction and interventions. Since the changes in the law, the alternative identification method has increased in popularity, and many states have already adopted alternative procedures.

Two important components of the current law for alternative identification of SLD are early monitoring of student progress and early intervention for students who do not respond as expected in academics. As indicated earlier, one of the criticisms regarding the discrepancy model is late identification of SLD, which allows the student to consistently fail in academics before the discrepancy is large enough to be identified. Under the previous identification model, a student who struggled with reading throughout early elementary school might not be recognized for special education services until the child fell far enough behind in academics to be noticed by the teacher. If the student falls too far behind, the likelihood that the child will catch up to grade level decreases. Therefore, the best chances of increasing student success, aside from prevention (i.e., evidence-based practices), may be early detection and early intervention. Early detection and intervention is designed to identify the early warning signs that may indicate an academic or behavioral disability before the child fails or falls substantially behind grade level. Progress monitoring provides the practices teachers need to gather and analyze data critical to identifying early warning signs. Perhaps even more important, research has demonstrated that when teachers base their instructional programs on data, teachers are more effective, and children learn more (Fuchs et al., 1984).

FEDERAL SUPPORT FOR PROGRESS MONITORING

IDEA funds have contributed to the development of progress monitoring since the 1970s. In addition to the initial investments into LD research centers, this topic has received considerable support throughout the years through the model demonstration authority. The history of model demonstration projects for children with disabilities began in 1966 with the establishment of the Bureau of Education for the Handicapped (BEH) within the U.S. Office of Education. One of the main functions of the BEH was to administer and support model demonstration projects focused on the education of children with disabilities. Many of the first model demonstration projects focused on stimulating innovate practices and model programs in the education of young children with disabilities.

The mid-1970s saw the passage of Public Law 94-142, known today as the IDEA, which mandated a "free appropriate public education" for children with disabilities. Education became a federal department in 1980, and the BEH became the Office of Special Education Programs (OSEP). To aid in the implementation of Public Law 94-142 and its reauthorizations, OSEP funded hundreds of model demonstration projects throughout the 1980s and 1990s on topics such as instructional strategies, secondary transition, inclusive education, literacy, behavior, and early intervention. These projects were viewed as a fundamental strategy for moving policy and research in special education into practice to improve our nation's schools and early childhood programs and to support the implementation of IDEA. Findings from model demonstration projects served as the foundation for the IDEA Part C program for infants and toddlers and the IDEA Part B preschool program. Consequently, these findings eventually led to the development of widely used assessments for progress monitoring and a model for school-wide positive behavior support programs, among many other innovative practices and products.

In 2000, OSEP began work on what became known as the LD Initiative. This effort, although focused on LD definitional issues, again highlighted the critical importance of progress monitoring. Efforts from this initiative resulted in the funding of the National Center on Student Progress Monitoring. This center was instrumental in furthering the knowledge base and understanding of progress monitoring as a critical evidence-based practice to improve the instructional delivery and decision-making practices for all educators. The center compiled and distributed useful information, including program descriptions and research bibliographies.

In 2007, OSEP funded the National Center on Response to Intervention (NCRTI). This center combined the work of the previous Progress Monitoring Center, along with other efforts to provide broad support for widespread implementation. Numerous services and supports are available for interested parties through centers such as the NCRTI (*www.RTI4success.org*) and the Technical Assistance Center on Positive Behavioral Interventions and Supports (PBIS Center; *www.pbis.org*). The websites for both of these centers provide a variety of supports to assist school districts with the successful implementation of multi-tiered frameworks. Neither center endorses any one particular model but instead provides information that has been evaluated by experts in the field on a variety of topics and procedures relevant to RTI and PBIS as implementation frameworks. Online resources include electronic libraries, training modules, newsletters, and opportunities to hear experts discuss relevant trends and issues. The NCRTI provides peer-reviewed information regarding assessment and intervention tools, including what is available for universal screening of students, as well as continued progress monitoring.

PROGRESS MONITORING MODEL DEMONSTRATION GRANTS

In 2005, OSEP funded three model demonstration projects to identify, develop, and refine exemplars of progress monitoring. Most of these models were implemented within a multi-tiered framework (e.g., RTI) in most instances. Model demonstrations provide a vehicle for bridging the gap between existing research and practice at the school and program levels. The model demonstrations supported by OSEP provide a set of existing evidence-based intervention practices and implementation strategies that have social validity and that improve child or system outcomes. The models influence the knowledge of the internal participants, such as teachers, administrators, and other adults with whom the students interact. In addition to changing the knowledge of participants, the models essentially change the structural frameworks that organize and support the newly adopted changes. The models must develop and strengthen partnership with external stakeholders and essentially establish a system that can be sustainable beyond federal funding. These progress monitoring model demonstrations were implemented in Minnesota, Pennsylvania, and Oregon. Details of the challenges and successes of these implementations follow in later chapters in this book.

OSEP funded this cohort of three projects with the purpose of conducting demonstrations across sites so that initial scientific support could be further defined relative to effective implementation and sustainability in typical settings. The lessons learned and positive outcomes achieved from funding multisite projects, including previous models and model groups, were applied to these projects. A primary requirement of these projects was collaboration and communication with one another and with the Model Demonstration Coordination Center (MDCC), the role of which was to coordinate the activities across projects, among other responsibilities. The collaboration and communication that occurred across sites during the 4 years of funding contributed to the success of these projects. During regularly scheduled sessions, the project personnel took the opportunity to update one another and learn from one another. These sessions would result in adjustment of practices or approaches as necessary. The strategic adjustments to their approaches related to their practices, interactions with school staff, or other factors improved the implementation of their model, which, in turn, resulted in improved teacher practices, student outcomes, and, in some instances, improved policies. Although the sometimes forced collaboration among projects resulted in additional challenges, that effort pales in comparison to the lessons learned from each of the projects about implementing progress monitoring, about how to push ourselves to do more than we often think we can, and, most important, about the *how* of implementing evidence-based practices in real schools, with real teachers and real resources.

The lessons that have been learned and applied throughout the years concerning progress monitoring have been reinforced and enhanced through the work completed by the model demonstration projects described in this book. The practice of progress monitoring is emerging as a critical element of good instructional planning and delivery, not only for students with disabilities but also for all students. The impact of progress monitoring has yet to be fully realized. As this practice expands beyond elementary schools and into middle and high schools and expands its focus from early reading to math and other content areas, progress monitoring is destined to become a valuable mainstay in schools across the country. In addition, when used within a multi-tiered framework, progress monitoring can achieve powerful outcomes across student populations, educators, and systems. The increased use of progress monitoring across school levels and topic areas reinforces the notion that progress monitoring is a viable tool and resource that teachers can implement with fidelity to more effectively and efficiently deliver and assess instruction to achieve better results for all students within the education system.

AUTHOR'S NOTE

Grace Zamora Durán and Renée Bradley participated in this chapter as former teachers, consultants, administrators, association personnel, and clinical professors. Opinions expressed herein are those of the authors and do not necessarily reflect the position of the U.S. Department of Education, Office of Special Education Programs, and no official endorsement should be inferred.

REFERENCES

Deno, S. L. (1985). Curriculum-based measurement: The emerging alternative. *Exceptional Children, 52*, 219–232.

Downer, J. T., Rimm-Kaufman, S. E., & Pianta, R. C. (2007). How do classroom conditions and children's risk for school problems contribute to children's behavioral engagement in learning? *School Psychology Review, 36*(3), 413–433.

Fletcher, J. M., Shaywitz, S. E., Shankweiler, D. P., Katz, L., Liberman, I. Y., Stuebing, K. K., et al. (1994). Cognitive profiles of reading disability: Comparisons of discrepancy and low achievement definitions. *Journal of Educational Psychology, 86*(1), 6–23.

Francis, D. J., Fletcher, J. M., Shaywitz, B. A., Shaywitz, S. E., & Rourke, B. P.

(1996). Defining learning and language disabilities: Conceptual and psychometric issues with the use of IQ tests. *Language, Speech, and Hearing Services in Schools, 27*(2), 132–143.

Fuchs, L. S., Deno, S. L., & Mirkin, P. (1984). Effects of frequent curriculum-based measurement and evaluation on pedagogy, student achievement, and student awareness of learning. *American Educational Research Journal, 21*, 449–460.

Hallahan, D. P., & Mercer, C. D. (2002). Learning disabilities: Historical perspectives. In R. Bradley, L. Danielson, & D. Hallahan (Eds.), *Identification of learning disabilities: Research to practice* (pp. 1–67). Mahwah, NJ: Erlbaum.

Individuals with Disabilities Education Improvement Act of 2004, Public Law 108-446, 20 U.S.C.

Scruggs, T. E., & Mastropieri, M. A. (2002). On babies and bathwater: Addressing the problems of identification of learning disabilities. *Learning Disability Quarterly, 25*(3), 155–168.

Stecker, P. M., & Fuchs, L. S. (2000). Effecting superior achievement using curriculum-based measurement: The importance of individual progress monitoring. *Learning Disabilities Research and Practice, 15*, 128–134.

U.S. Department of Education, National Center for Education Statistics. (2009). Digest of Educational Statistics, 2008 (NCES 2009-020). Retrieved from *nces.ed.gov/fastfacts/display.asp?id=64*.

Vaughn, S., & Fuchs, L. S. (2003). Redefining learning disabilities as inadequate response to instruction: The promise and potential problems. *Learning Disabilities Research and Practice, 18*(3), 137–146.

Wallace, T., Espin, C. A., McMaster, K., Deno, S. L., & Foegen, A. (2007). CBM progress monitoring within a standards-based system. *Journal of Special Education, 41*(2), 66–67.

PART I

Monitoring Progress
in Pennsylvania Pupils
PROJECT MP3 AT LEHIGH UNIVERSITY

Introduction to Part I

Project MP3 (an acronym for Monitoring Progress in Pennsylvania Pupils) located at Lehigh University focused on the implementation of a response-to-intervention (RTI) model in a large school district (by Pennsylvania standards) located outside a city in central Pennsylvania. The district with which the project partnered had an RTI-type model that had been fully implemented in one high-need elementary school for 3 years prior to the project's beginning and was committed to implementing RTI across all elementary schools in the district over the subsequent years. Opportunity to expand the district's partnership to include a strong university partner, alongside the existing relationship with the regional state-supported group that provided technical assistance to the district, offered an exciting and inviting way for the district to improve the performance of struggling schools.

Three schools selected for Project MP3 represented high-need schools whose students had struggled with attaining reading proficiency over many years. Although the district had been engaged in conducting universal screening data in reading (Dynamic Indicators of Basic Early Literacy Skills [DIBELS]) for several years, the use of the data for purposes of instructional planning was inconsistent at best.

9

The U.S. Department of Education model/demonstration project awarded to Lehigh University was focused on the role of progress monitoring within an RTI model in improving the reading outcomes of students in grades K–5. The specific RTI model used in Pennsylvania was selected by the project and involved a three-tiered model of intervention support. Consistent with Pennsylvania's perspective of RTI, special education was treated as a service delivery model that would be embedded within the three tiers of support. Although typically students with identified special education needs in the area of reading were found to have needs consistent with a Tier 3 level of intensive support, a small percentage (approximately 10–15% across schools) were found to have needs more consistent with a Tier 2 level of strategic support. Additionally, Pennsylvania advocates the use of a standard protocol model of RTI, so MP3 used this model of support.

The three chapters describing Project MP3 first provide the context of the implementation with detailed descriptions of the district, the levels of support provided to the district, and the structure of the model itself. A number of the tools and materials used to develop the model are provided. Next, the process through which the model was implemented is fully described, examining how the model planned for sustainability and continuation once the funding support ended. Finally, student outcomes reflective of the impact of the model are provided in detail.

CHAPTER 2

The Structure and Content of the RTI Model

Alexandra Hilt-Panahon
Edward S. Shapiro
Nathan H. Clemens
Karen L. Gischlar

Response to intervention (RTI) is defined as "the practice of providing high-quality instruction and intervention matched to student needs and using learning rate over time and level of performance to make important educational decisions" (Batsche et al., 2005). The National Association of State Directors of Special Education (NASDSE) outlines four overarching principles that guide the implementation of RTI. First, there is a belief that all students can learn if effectively instructed. If students are not learning, then the instruction provided must be addressed. Effective instruction is considered the foundation of an effective RTI model and the basis for all decision making. Second, early intervention is the key to improved academic achievement for students, and early intervention should be provided within the context of a multi-tiered model of service delivery. Third, the delivery of instruction within the multi-tiered model must use research-based, scientifically validated interventions. Fourth, data must drive the decisions made related to instruction in both the core curriculum and tiered interventions. Although these principles must be the conceptual basis of any model of RTI, each district can apply these principles in a manner that suits the context of that particular district.

Prior to the implementation of RTI in a district, the consensus for supporting the model, as well as for establishing the infrastructure that will be the basis for implementation, must be built (Kurns & Tilly, 2008). Each component of the model must be clearly defined. All RTI models include the basic components of universal screening for all students, research-based tiered intervention with increasing support and intensity dependent on student needs, documentation of the fidelity of intervention delivery, a team-based decision-making process to drive instructional decisions, and progress monitoring to evaluate the effectiveness of instruction and student response to intervention (Elliot & Morrison, 2008). These components can be implemented in a variety of ways, but they must all be present in order to successfully implement RTI (Jimerson, Burns, & VanDerHeyden, 2007).

The specific model used in the district in which Project MP3 was implemented incorporated all of the components just discussed to create an effective and sustainable model of RTI. Figure 2.1 provides an overview of implementation components of the model that are described in this chapter. When designing the model, one of the key factors that were considered was the need for long-term sustainability of the model. It was particularly important to actively plan for the maintenance of the model given that grant funding was limited. One key to the success of the project from the perspective of our staff and district administration was that whatever was put into place must have the potential to be continued after additional monies and resources were no longer available. As such, the model was designed with existing resources and personnel in mind. This was vital to the success of the project. If an RTI model had been implemented that required additional staff, resources, or materials, it would have been unlikely that the district could have maintained implementation after the project (and funding) ended. By working within the existing budget and structure of the schools, we were able to create a model that would be viable for years to come.

Along with the careful consideration regarding the existing strengths and resources in the district, we found that it was vital to include key stakeholders in the decision-making process as the model was being developed. The planning and implementation process is discussed in full in Chapter 3, but the model described in this chapter was developed in conjunction with the Lehigh University research team, the Pennsylvania Training and Technical Assistance Network technical support personnel (PaTTAN, the state educational liaison), and district-level administrators who supported the implementation of RTI at the district level. Given that an RTI model requires systemic change in order to be successful, it was necessary to include in the process all those that had the power and authority to facilitate and maintain change. Although individual schools may be able to successfully implement RTI models in isolation, we believe that schools will have greater success when they are operating within a system that actively supports that change.

Start of School
- All students instructed in core reading program
- Ensure that all students receive core instruction
- Ensure that instruction is differentiated

Mid to End of September
- Fall benchmark (second or third week of September)
- Identify data SWAT team
- Notify teachers of testing dates
- Collect data
- Enter data into database
- Organize data in spreadsheet for grouping/data-based decision making

End of September
- All relevant data are gathered and entered into spreadsheet
- Core team meets to determine tier placement and initial intervention groupings
- Data team meets to review groupings/student placements
- Groups revised based on data team input
- Grade-level teams meet to review grouping/student placements
- Groups revised based on grade-level team input
- Final groupings are distributed prior to start of intervention groups

September to October
- Prepare for and begin intervention groups
- Identify interventions that will be used
- Identify teachers for each intervention group (occurs simultaneously with student grouping)
- Provide training for teachers in relevant intervention
- Prepare all necessary materials for intervention implementation
- Develop schedule including rooms for groups
- Begin interventions by third week of October

October to January
- Monitor student progress (October–January)
- Train data collectors in progress monitoring measures
- Identify personnel to monitor progress
- Create spreadsheets for tracking Tier 2 and Tier 3 student data
- Monitor all Tier 2 students once every 2 weeks
- Monitor all Tier 3 students once per week
- Grade-level teams meet monthly to discuss student progress and to make appropriate instruction changes

Mid-January
- Winter benchmark (mid-January)
- Repeat all steps above for winter-to-spring period

FIGURE 2.1. Implementation outline from beginning to middle of school year.

13

SCHOOL CONTEXT

RTI was implemented in three elementary schools in the district that participated in the MP3 Project. All three schools were elementary level, serving students in kindergarten through fifth grade. All grades in the schools participated in RTI. Although the three schools were similar in many aspects, each was unique in its own way and presented with its own set of challenges. The MP3 model implemented RTI only in the area of reading.

Participating Schools

The three elementary schools were in a school district of 11,018 students located in east central Pennsylvania. The district is considered large across the 501 districts of the Commonwealth and has a mixed urban, rural, and suburban student population. A total of 1,230 students in the district (12.5%) have individualized education plans (IEPs). The district consisted of 14 K–5 elementary schools ranging in size from 242 students to 731 students. The three schools that participated in the project ranged in size from 257 students to 318 during the first year of implementation. The percentage of students receiving free or reduced-price lunch was 32% in two of the schools and 50% in the third. A large portion of the population at all three schools was minority (30–55%). See Table 2.1 for details of school demographics.

School A served more than 300 students of varied ethnic and linguistic backgrounds. The teaching staff of School A included 17 classroom teachers (K = 2, first = 3, second = 4, third = 3, fourth = 3, fifth = 2), 1.5 special education teachers, one teacher of English language learners (ELLs), one instructional support (intervention specialist) teacher, and one reading specialist. In addition, there was one special education and one ELL paraprofessional who assisted in providing services to students in the classroom.

School B was the smallest of the three MP3 schools, serving 257 students. The teaching staff at School B included 13 classroom teachers (K = 1, first = 2, second = 3, third = 3, fourth = 2, fifth = 2), one special education teacher, one instructional support teacher, and one reading specialist. In addition, there was one special education paraprofessional who assisted in providing services to students in the classroom.

TABLE 2.1. School Demographics

	A	B	C
Enrollment	318	257	302
% Requiring free/reduced-price lunch	32%	32%	50%
% Minority students	30%	45%	55%
% Third graders passing reading PSSA	48%	76%	77%

School C served over 300 students. The teaching staff of School C included 16 classroom teachers (K = 2, first = 3, second = 3, third = 3, fourth = 2, fifth = 3), 1.5 special education teachers, 1 ELL teacher, 1 instructional support teacher, and 1 reading specialist. In addition, there was one special education and one ELL paraprofessional who assisted in providing services to students in the classroom.

ASSESSMENTS

Several measures were used to evaluate students' response to intervention; they are described next. The application of these assessments will be discussed later in this chapter.

- *Dynamic Indicators of Basic Early Literacy Skills* (DIBELS; Good & Kaminski, 2002). The DIBELS are a set of measures designed to assess three of the "5 Big Ideas" of early literacy: phonological awareness, alphabetic principle, and reading fluency. These measures together have been found to be predictive of later reading proficiency.
- *Pennsylvania System of School Assessment* (PSSA; Data Recognition Corporation, 2009). This statewide assessment is a measure of academic standards and of the efficacy of school programs to prepare students to meet those standards. This assessment is given to students in grades 3–5 in March each year.
- *4Sight Benchmark Assessments* (Success for All Foundation, 2006). Modeled after the PSSA, this benchmark assessment enables schools to evaluate student progress in academic standards multiple times throughout the school year. The results of testing allow schools to predict performance on the statewide test. This measure is given three times per year to all students in grades 3, 4, and 5.
- *AIMSweb® Maze Passages* (AIMSweb, 2008). Designed as an additional measure to monitor student reading comprehension, these 150- to 200-word passages test comprehension of material read silently by requiring students to complete multiple-choice questions in a cloze task. These measures are given three times per year at benchmark for all students in grades 1–5.

OVERVIEW OF THE MODEL

Two broad types of RTI models are described in the literature: a problem-solving model (more appropriately called a problem-analysis model; Burns, Deno, & Jimerson, 2007) and a standard protocol model (Fuchs, Mock, Morgan, & Young, 2003). Although both of these models involve use of an extensive problem-solving process, the two models have particular distinguishing characteristics. Typically, standard protocols involve the delivery of evidence-based, multicomponent programs with a strong research basis focused on specific skill areas. The intervention has well-defined steps for implementation that, if followed as prescribed, have a high probability of producing improved outcomes for students (D. Fuchs & Fuchs, 2006). Standard protocols are designed to be structured and explicit in defining the needed steps for implementation and are able to be delivered to small groups of children. Groups are identified by examining the general nature of student problems and matching them to the particular protocol. For example, on the basis of the data collected through universal screening, a determination would be made regarding which students needed more focus on fluency and which on vocabulary building and comprehension. The group to which the student is assigned would then be matched to that protocol. Because the steps of the intervention are well defined, the evaluation of the integrity of implementation is straightforward and can be determined by establishing a checklist of the critical steps for implementing the intervention. Following each step of the defined protocol is essential so that one is sure that the intervention is delivered as it was designed.

Standard protocols can be developed as packaged commercial programs designed to focus on an area of the student's problem. For example, in reading, programs such as Six-Minute Solution (Adams & Brown, 2003) are designed to focus primarily on the area of developing fluency. Other programs, such as Soar to Success (2008), are aimed more at developing vocabulary and comprehension, whereas programs such as Ladders to Literacy (O'Connor, Notari-Syverson, & Vadasy, 2005) are focused more on the development of phonemic awareness and alphabetic principle. Third-party evaluation of such packaged, multicomponent programs offers support for their empirical base (e.g., Florida Center for Reading Research). In addition to packaged programs, standard protocol models of RTI might include structured partnered reading activities, direct instruction of phonological or phonics skills, or reinforcement of skills through computer programs (Case, Speece, & Molloy, 2003; VanDerHeyden, Witt, & Gilbertson, 2007). A key feature of standard protocol models is that instruction/intervention protocols are used without an in-depth analysis of the deficit skill and are delivered in moderate-sized groups (6–10 students; e.g., Peer-Assisted Learning Strategies) (Fuchs, Fuchs, Mathes, & Simmons, 1997; McMaster, Fuchs, Fuchs, & Compton, 2005).

In contrast to standard protocol models, problem-solving models (problem-analysis models; Burns et al., 2007) emphasize individualized interventions that derive from the analysis of instructional/environmental conditions and skill deficits (Tilly, Reschly, & Grimes, 1999). The RTI problem-solving model is guided by a systematic analysis of instructional variables that is designed to isolate target skill/subskill deficits and shape targeted interventions (Barnett, Daly, Jones, & Lentz, 2004). As illustrated in Figure 2.2, common to all problem-solving models is a four-step process that systematically conceptualizes a problem, analyzes factors that contribute to the problem, implements targeted or individualized interventions to address the problem, and evaluates the effectiveness of the interventions (Allen & Graden, 2002). Interventions developed in this model are well matched to the individualized needs of the targeted student. Examples include the functional assessment of academic skills (Daly, Lentz, & Boyer, 1996; Daly, Martens, Hamler, Dool, & Eckert, 1999; Daly, Witt, Martens, & Dool, 1997) and curriculum-based evaluation (CBE; Howell & Nolet, 2000). The model has a long history of implementation in programs such as the Heartland Area Education Agency 11 in Iowa (Ikeda et al., 2007), the Minneapolis Public Schools (Marston, Lau, & Muyskens, 2007), and the St. Croix River Education District in Minnesota (Bollman, Silberglitt, & Gibbons, 2007).

One of the primary advantages of standard protocol models is the opportunity for quality control (Fuchs et al., 2003). Students are grouped based on a general area of concern (i.e., the areas of skill in need of inter-

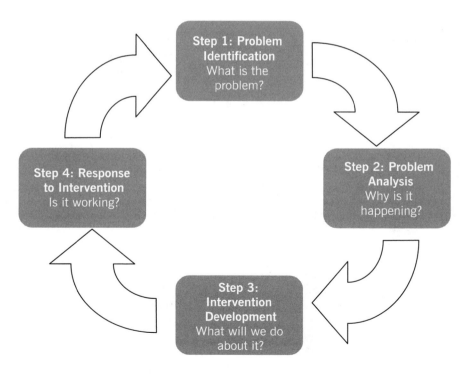

FIGURE 2.2. Problem-solving model.

vention in reading are primarily fluency or vocabulary/comprehension and phonemic awareness/alphabetic principle) and instruction can be delivered in groups (up to about 10) with high degrees of fidelity. Another advantage is the opportunity for a school to identify a small set of effective intervention strategies that can be applied broadly across many students who in general have the same skill needs. This advantage makes possible a highly efficient use of resource allocation and allows larger numbers of students to be accommodated in tiered interventions. A third and related advantage is that schools may already have materials available and, if not, bulk purchasing of materials can sustain many years of implementation. Additionally, because many teachers have already had extensive training with these protocols, they offer a built-in training resource for sustaining the protocol into the future as new teachers join the school staff.

Despite these advantages, standard protocol models present a challenge to addressing the unique learning needs of children who are experiencing more severe deficits (Fuchs et al., 2003). Although a standard protocol approach may match children's needs *in general* to the identified deficits, children with more complex and/or severe deficits may not fit easily into the general skill-deficit areas of the protocol. Also, at times the selection of the standard protocol intervention may not be closely aligned to the core instructional program. In other words, the approach taught to students in the intervention protocol may not be the same as the way the skill is taught within the core reading program. As such, students may show some confusion in not being able to transfer learning from the intervention setting back to the core instructional program.

In considering the two models of RTI, Project MP3 chose to implement a standard protocol model. Given the efficient use of resources evident in a standard protocol model and the relatively large numbers of students likely to need supplemental instruction, the choice of the standard protocol model was the most logical for the situation facing the implementation of Project MP3.

Like RTI models described in the literature and consistent with the recommendations of the Pennsylvania Department of Education, the model in the MP3 schools involved a three-tiered approach to intervention. All students were provided reading instruction in the core reading program with additional instructional time devoted to specific skill instruction through standard protocol interventions based on student needs. Universal screening was conducted three times per year, and students were assigned to interventions based on the results of the screening, along with other measures of student performance. Students below benchmark were monitored on a regular basis, data were regularly reviewed, and instructional changes were made based on students' response to instruction. Data-based decisions regarding instruction were made by school-based teams. The process of data-based decision making will be discussed in detail in Chapter 4.

Core Reading Instruction

The foundation of any RTI model is the implementation of a research-based core reading program in which all students participate (Denton, Vaughn, & Fletcher, 2003). According to the National Reading Panel (2000), effective instruction includes five essential components necessary for students to learn to read. These include phonemic awareness, phonics, fluency, vocabulary, and comprehension. Effective curricula weave these five elements, known as the "5 Big Ideas" in reading, together to provide a comprehensive program. This core reading program serves as a foundation for Tiers 2 and 3.

Before a multi-tiered model of intervention can be put in place, several questions need to be asked related to the effectiveness of the instruction in the core reading program being provided within the general education setting. First, it is important to determine whether the core program being implemented is sufficient. Are most students exposed to the core program learning at the expected rate? If the current core program is found to be sufficient, then implementation of additional tiers to support those students not served sufficiently through the core is appropriate. If, however, the core program is found to be insufficient, then it is important to determine why it is not effective. What aspects of instruction are ineffective, and how can those needs within the core be addressed (Kurns & Tilly, 2008)?

The schools participating in Project MP3 had established strong Tier 1 instruction prior to the start of the project. Core reading instruction occurred in 90-minute blocks daily for all students. With the implementation of RTI, all students were provided instruction within the general education classroom. Prior to RTI, students with IEPs or those who received ELL services were excluded from the general education setting for reading and instructed separately in the special education or ELL classroom. With the implementation of RTI, it was decided that these students would best be served within an inclusive model. As a result, ELL and special education teachers began to move into the general education classrooms to provide services for students during core instruction.

Prior to the implementation of RTI, the district had adopted the Houghton-Mifflin Reading Curriculum, which was used at all grade levels at all elementary schools. Teachers had been trained by representatives of the publishing company to implement the reading program and had been using it for several years before RTI was put in place. Given the importance of core instruction within a RTI model, establishing a strong core program is vital (Denton et al., 2003). Simmons and Kame'enui (2003) provide practitioners with guidelines to evaluate potential core reading programs. Specifically, consumers are advised to look for the following criteria when evaluating programs:

1. Is there evidence to support efficacy of the program established through experimental studies?
2. Does the program align with current reading research?
3. Does the program provide explicit instruction in phonemic awareness, phonics, fluency, vocabulary, and comprehension?
4. Was the program evaluated in schools or classrooms with similar demographic profiles?

Given these criteria, we felt that the district had a strong core reading program in place, which provided a strong foundation on which tiered intervention could be built.

Typical core instruction consisted of whole-group instruction, as well as small-group flexible grouping to allow greater differentiation within the classroom. Each classroom teacher was assigned a support person (e.g., reading specialist, special education paraprofessional) at least 15 minutes a day to assist with differentiation during flexible-group time. In addition, teachers met with the special education and ELL teachers periodically to plan and implement instruction.

Universal Screening

Universal screening occurred three times per year at all three schools. Prior to the start of Project MP3, the district had adopted the use of the DIBELS for ongoing universal assessment. In addition to the DIBELS measures and beginning with the start of Project MP3, all students in grades 1–4 were given the Maze assessment as a measure of reading comprehension. As described earlier, the AIMSweb Maze Passages require students to answer multiple-choice questions in a cloze format in order to assess reading comprehension. This measure was added as part of the research study but was valued by teachers as a means of monitoring students' comprehension. Screening occurred in mid-September, mid-January, and late May each year.

All universal screening data were collected by a specially formed team that consisted of specialists from the district, retired teachers hired by the district to assist with data collection, and Lehigh project staff. All data collectors were required to participate in training in the implementation and scoring of all assessment measures prior to administering assessments to students. Training consisted of didactic instruction on the use of the measures, as well as opportunities to practice administration and scoring. All data collectors needed to be able to implement and score assessments with accuracy before administering them to students. Project staff assessed all trainees to ensure that probes were administered and scored with at least 95% accuracy prior to actual administration with students.

Assigning Students to Tiers

After universal screening data were collected, these data were used in conjunction with other sources of data to determine to which tier students were assigned. The process of assigning students was a team effort, using existing data and knowledge about students to place them in the most appropriate tier. After DIBELS data were collected, all scores were entered into the AIMSweb database, and DIBELS recommendations for placement were obtained. All student data were organized on data sheets (see Figure 2.3) according to the DIBELS recommendation. In addition to the current benchmark period's DIBELS scores and instructional recommendations, the team analyzed as much information as possible to make the appropriate instructional placement. As such, numerous sources of additional data were included in the placement process. These data were summarized on the spreadsheet. Additional data included: DIBELS data from the previous benchmark period; the instructional recommendation from the previous benchmark period; the placement decision and intervention group the student was currently placed in; progress monitoring rate of improvement (ROI) for students currently placed in Tier 2 or 3; Maze scores (for grades 1–5); PSSA scores (for grades 3–5) from the previous school year; and available 4Sight scores (grades 3–5). These additional data helped team members to make the most informed decision regarding the best instructional placement for the student.

Assignment of Students to Intervention

After tier placement was determined for students, the task of identifying the most appropriate intervention for each student began. To do this, the data team evaluated students' needs based on the existing data, as well as information from the classroom teacher and support staff. Once the needs of the student were established, the intervention that best matched those needs was selected from those available in the school. Students with similar deficits in reading were grouped together. Additional criteria used to make tier placement decisions included the number of professionals available to teach skill groups and the size of the existing intervention group. The tier placement and intervention assignment processes are described in detail in Chapter 4.

The Structure of Tiered Intervention

As discussed previously, all students in each of the three schools received some level of tiered intervention. Each grade level was assigned 30–45 minutes of reading intervention time. This block, focused specifically on intervention, was referred to as "skill group" time and was given in addition to

Students at Strategic at Fall of Year	Fall DORF Score	Winter DORF Score	Reached Winter Benchmark Target of 92	Reached Winter Strategic Target of 67	Progress Monitoring ROI (12/19)	Winter Maze Score	4 Sight Baseline Total	4 Sight Test 2 Total	Decision

FIGURE 2.3. Data organization sheet. DORF, DIBELS Oral Reading Fluency.

the 90-minute reading instructional block. A consistent time block was utilized for each grade level in order to maximize the number of skill groups that could be run at one time. For example, at School A, all kindergarten and first-grade classrooms had skill-group time from 9:20–9:50 A.M. Second- and third-grade classes had skill groups from 10:15–11:00 A.M., and fourth and fifth grades from 1:35 to 2:15. All students in a particular grade were assigned to within-grade skill groups, meaning that groups were not formed based on individual classrooms but were formed across all students within a grade. Some cross-grade groups were also formed at the upper grades when appropriate. For example, students in fourth and fifth grade may have been placed in the same skill group if similar deficits and intervention needs were identified.

During skill-group time, teachers were responsible for teaching whichever students were assigned to their group, regardless of whether or not the students were in their classes for core reading instruction. In addition to the classroom teachers, all available support staff was utilized to lead skill groups. This allowed anywhere from 8 to 12 intervention groups to be conducted during a given intervention block. For example, at the K–1 level at School A, there were two kindergarten teachers and three first-grade teachers. This allowed five skill groups to be formed across the two grades. In addition, the reading specialist, instructional support teacher, special education teacher, and ESL teacher were also available during this time frame, allowing the formation of an additional four skill groups. As a result, the two grade levels could be divided into nine separate skill groups across all three tiers that focused on the specific needs of the students. An example of a skill-group schedule is provided in Figure 2.4. The structure and content of the skill groups by tiers are described next.

Benchmark Skill Groups

Students who met benchmarks for a particular assessment period were assigned to a benchmark group. These students were those who met the criteria set by DIBELS, as well as demonstrating proficiency in reading skills based on the additional data sources considered by the teams. Although these students' scores indicated that they were making adequate progress to meet end-of-year goals in reading, it was important to provide support and specialized instruction to maintain their progress. These groups were typically larger than the skill groups at the other tiers, given the students' success with reading. Typical group sizes ranged from 15 to 20. Although these groups were larger than those at Tier 2 or 3, they consisted of a homogeneous group of students who were performing at or above grade level. This allowed teachers to develop lesson plans that would advance the skills of the benchmark students. Activities and instructional practices implemented in these groups varied depending on the grade level but focused

Fall 2007 Intervention Schedule Grade K & 1 (Days 1-4) 9:20-9:50										
Activity: Road/Ladders		**Activity:**		**Activity:**		**Activity:** Project Read		**Activity:** Project Read	**Activity:** Project Read	
Teacher: Ms. S		**Teacher: Ms. C**		**Teacher: Ms. P**		**Teacher: Ms. G**		**Teacher: Ms. S**	**Teacher: Ms. W**	
Group: Benchmark K		**Group: Benchmark 1**		**Group: Benchmark 1**		**Group: Strategic 1**		**Group: Strategic 1**	**Group: Intensive 1**	
Karmyn	Jacqueline	Lauren	Austin	Rachel	Rinesa	Matthew	Samantha	Fabian	Madison	Jared	Jonathan
Nicholas	Dale	Madeline	Amya	Brooke	Nicole	Tyler	Rachael	Michael	Argyle	Logan	Kevin
Mauricette	Brendan	Joshua	David	Antonio	Jacob	Christopher	Michael	Kenneth	Shelby	Elvyn	
Samantha	Prince	Anthony	Alvaro	Dominick	Samantha	Mariarae	Makayla	Emalee	Zeliana		
Zack	Dillon	Misha	Darryl	Victoria	Nadia			Tyler			
Durrell	Megan	Carson	Ariana	Cole	Matthew						
Jonathan	Abby	Makenna	Camden	Michael	Jose						
Alexis	Chayla	Tia	Julian	Chanise	Jalen						

Activity: Ladders to Literacy		**Activity: FCRR/** Scott Foresman				**Activity:** Project Read		**Activity:** Scott Foresman	**Activity:** Project Read	
Teacher: Ms. H		**Teacher: Ms. I**				**Teacher: Ms. U**		**Teacher: Ms. F**	**Teacher: Ms. M**	
Group: Strategic K		**Group: Intensive K/1**				**Group: Intensive 1**		**Group: Intensive 1**	**Group: Intensive 1**	
Ojibway	Amy	Jan	Nathaniel			Kayla	Obiazi	Noah	Nadeline	Jordan	Isabella
Tyshawn	Logan	Artrim	Morgan			Tearra	Brian	Miles		Gwendeline	Aaron
Raihan	John	Shannon	Diana			Christian				Melody	Kevin
Mateo	Kelvin	Alex	Faina								
Christian	Ethan	Ashlynn	Lorenzo								

FIGURE 2.4. Skill-group schedule example.

on improving students' skills. For example, at the fourth- and fifth-grade teachers often used literature books to promote oral reading fluency, as well as to improve comprehension and writing skills. These groups were typically conducted by the classroom teachers at each grade level, given their familiarity with working with larger classes and with on-grade-level students.

Strategic Skill Groups

Students assigned to Tier 2 received intervention in groups ranging in size from 5 to 15 students, with an average of 10–12. Group size depended on several factors, including the number of students in need of a specific intervention and the number of teachers available to run groups, but was decided primarily based on the intervention chosen. Interventions chosen for strategic groups typically focused on specific skills such as decoding or reading fluency, depending on student needs. These groups were typically run by the classroom teacher, a paraprofessional, or a specialist, depending on the intervention and staff availability.

The type of standard protocol model used in Project MP3 used commercially available, empirically supported programs. A range of programs was selected for each grade level in order to provide programs that tend to focus on phonics, fluency, or comprehension. Table 2.2 shows the specific interventions by grade used for students assigned to Tier 2.

All teachers were provided training in these interventions prior to being asked to implement an intervention, so there was high fidelity regardless of the teacher assigned to a group. Intervention fidelity is discussed in detail later in this chapter.

Intensive Skill Groups

Students in Tier 3 received the most intensive intervention. These interventions were typically more comprehensive than those at the other two tiers, addressing all of the "5 Big Ideas" in reading. Table 2.2 provides a list of interventions used for students assigned to Tier 3. This list includes all interventions that were used during skill groups. A complete list of all interventions available in the district can be found in Chapter 4. Although any of the available interventions may have been used for individual students to supplement intervention, the interventions listed in Table 2.2 were those used for group intervention. These groups were typically run by the specialists in the school, including the instructional support teacher, the

TABLE 2.2. Interventions Used for Students Assigned to Skills Groups

Grade	Tier 2 interventions	Tier 3 interventions
K	Road to the Code Ladders to Literacy Scott Foresman—My Sidewalks	Scott Foresman—My Sidewalks Language for Learning
1	Project READ PALS	Project READ Scott Foresman—My Sidewalks
2	Project READ PALS Six-Minute Solution	Project READ Scott Foresman—My Sidewalks
3	PALS Report Form Read Naturally Soar to Success Rewards Six-Minute Solution	Scott Foresman—My Sidewalks Corrective Reading
4	PALS Report Form REWARDS Six-Minute Solution	Project READ Corrective Reading
5	PALS Report Form Read 180	Corrective Reading

reading specialist, and the ESL or special education teacher because of their expertise in the instruction of students functioning below grade level.

Progress Monitoring

All students in Tiers 2 and 3 were monitored periodically to assess progress within the curriculum and to inform instruction. Students assigned to Tier 2 were monitored once every 2 weeks, whereas students at Tier 3 were monitored weekly. Progress monitoring was conducted using the DIBELS progress monitoring passages for all students in grades K–5. All Tier 2 students were monitored on grade level. For students at Tier 3, a survey-level assessment was conducted to determine the highest instructional level (Shapiro, 2011; Shinn, Shinn, Hamilton, & Clarke, 2002). Students at Tier 3 were monitored anywhere from at grade level to 3 years below.

Each student was tested individually with a teacher according to the progress monitoring schedule. After each benchmarking period, each teacher was provided with a spreadsheet that included all students in the class who needed to be monitored, the dates on which monitoring should occur, and space to record scores after each monitoring session. An example of the spreadsheet is provided in Figure 2.5.

In order to ensure that progress monitoring (PM) was conducted consistently, specific times were allotted in the weekly schedule to complete all testing. Initially, this occurred 1 day a week during skill-group time. Unlike the other 4 days of the week, on Day 5 core reading instruction was

Teacher: Mrs. S Support: Mrs. F	Progress Monitoring Record Sheet							
Student	Level	18-Oct	25-Oct	1-Nov	9-Nov	16-Nov	28-Nov	5-Dec	12-Dec
Ted	3rd								
Shane	3rd								
Andy	3rd								
Jake	3rd								
Hannah	3rd								
Isaiah	3rd								
Laura	4th	■		■		■		■	
Briana	4th		■		■		■		■
Daniel	4th	■		■		■		■	
Dion	4th		■		■		■		■

FIGURE 2.5. Sample progress monitoring spreadsheet. *Note.* Black boxes indicate student does not need to be monitored that week.

extended for 30 minutes. Students remained in their homerooms and participated in core instruction while PM was conducted with individual students. In order to maximize instructional time, each teacher was assigned a support person to assist with PM. Support persons included the reading specialist, the special education teacher, and paraprofessionals. The teacher and support person worked together to decide the best way to complete PM, typically employing one of three options. The first option was to have the support person conduct a lesson with the whole class while the classroom teacher conducted PM. Often, the classroom teacher wanted to administer the PM probes in order to evaluate the students' performance firsthand. In addition, this provided support staff members such as the reading specialist with the opportunity to work with a large number of students. The second option was to have the classroom teacher conduct the lesson and the support person conduct PM. This was beneficial because it provided the teacher with an additional 30 or more minutes a week to address core instruction. The final option was for the teacher to assign an independent or small-group activity to the class while both teachers administered PM probes simultaneously. This option was efficient, allowing assessment of a whole class to be completed in less than 10 minutes. As stated earlier, the teacher and support person decided what method would work best for the particular needs of the class.

Although scheduled PM time was necessary during the initial months of implementation, it was found that, as PM became part of the culture of the school, it was no longer necessary to schedule time. Once teachers realized the value of the information the data provided, students were monitored consistently, even if time was not scheduled to do so. For example, at each of the schools it was decided either that students at particular grades or the entire student body would benefit from additional intervention. As a result, skill groups were extended to 5 days per week. When this occurred, teachers determined times at which they could monitor the students in their classes outside of a scheduled period. Given the time constraints placed on teachers, this action demonstrated the value that teachers placed on PM and the information they gained from the process.

During testing, a student would be called to the designated area for testing, given the 1-minute probe, and then asked to return to the group. The teacher would then score the probe immediately and enter the score into the spreadsheet described earlier. After all testing was completed, the classroom teacher would then enter all scores into the AIMSweb database. Classroom teachers were responsible for monitoring the data of the students in their classes.

Data Team Meetings

Data teams were formed at each school. The data teams consisted of a core group of teachers who served as data managers and facilitators of RTI within their respective schools. The data teams were responsible for, among other activities, completing the initial data analysis and grouping the students into tiers and skill groups.

The first task of the data team was to begin the process of assigning students to tiers and intervention groups within tiers, as described previously. Due to the large number of team members at School A (18), it was decided that a core team would be formed that would conduct the initial grouping. In the fall this team consisted of five members, including two project staff members, one PaTTAN staff member, the principal, and a district administrative representative. In the winter this group was expanded to include, in addition to those just listed, the reading specialist, instructional support teacher, special education teacher, and one classroom teacher. The teams at the other two schools consisted of eight and nine members, including the instructional support teacher, reading specialist, intervention specialist, PaTTAN staff members, two project staff members, and selected classroom teachers.

Once students were grouped and skill groups were formed, the data team was responsible for setting grade-level and schoolwide goals, as well as overseeing the implementation of the model. Figure 2.6 provides the protocol, developed by project staff, used by the data team during goal-setting meetings. The form offers a sequenced set of prompts for the team to follow at the meeting. Beginning with a review of the DIBELS data, measurable goals for the next benchmarking period were set for each grade. Team member concerns were recorded regarding the meeting of grade-level goals. Next, the team would conduct a brief brainstorming session (no more than 5–10 minutes), identifying grade-level instructional strategies, needed supports, materials, training, or services necessary to achieve the grade-level goals that were set. A few strategies were then selected, and an implementation plan was put in place.

The members of this team were seen as leaders in the school and assisted others in maintaining the integrity of the model. As the project progressed, the role of the project staff began to be reduced in order to ensure sustainability. As the roles of project staff lessened, the members of the data teams at each school took on those responsibilities. For example, initially project staff gathered, organized, and distributed all data necessary for grouping students into skill groups. Once school staff became comfortable with the use of data and how data were organized, the responsibility of data management was shifted to members of the data team. This occurred *before* the end of the project, prior to project staff exiting the buildings. This allowed the school staff ample time to adjust to these new responsibilities and to consult with project staff about any concerns. This model was effective in supporting independence of model implementation by the schools.

(text resumes on page 33)

Date: _____   School: _____

Data Reviewed (circle one):   Fall   Winter   Spring

Grades Reviewed: K   1   2   3   4   5

Meeting Attendees	Position

Please print the following data prior to the meeting:

1. School comparative performance for oral reading fluency and maze comprehension (FALL: Grades 2–5, WINTER/SPRING: Grades 1–5)
   a. COMPOSITE: AIMSweb Aggregate Growth (preferred) or Pennsylvania
   b. TARGETS: DIBELS Benchmarks
2. Early Literacy achievement percentages (K–2 only)
3. Grade-level histograms
4. Instructional recommendations by grade level for scheduling and reviewing quality of data
   a. Early Literacy for grades K–2 (includes Reading CBM)
   b. Reading CBM and Maze for grades 3–5

(cont.)

FIGURE 2.6. Data team meeting protocol.

1. **DATA REVIEW**: Complete the chart below using the Early Literacy achievement percentages and grade-level histograms. Circle the greatest areas of concern.

Grade	Measure	Intensive (Deficient) GOAL: < 5–10%	Strategic (Emerging) GOAL: 15–20%	Benchmark (Established) GOAL: > 75%
Kindergarten	ISF			
	LNF			
	PSF			
	NWF			
Grade 1	LNF			
	PSF			
	NWF			
	ORF			
Grade 2	NWF			
	ORF			
	Maze			
Grade 3	ORF			
	Maze			
Grade 4	ORF			
	Maze			
Grade 5	ORF			
	Maze			
AVG % TOTALS				

Note. ISF, initial sounds fluency; LNF, letter naming fluency; PSF, phoneme segmentation fluency; NWF, nonsense word fluency; ORF, oral reading fluency.

(cont.)

FIGURE 2.6. *(cont.)*

2. **GOAL SETTING**: Create a measurable goal or goals at each grade level to achieve by next review.

3. **BARRIERS**: Summarize the team's areas of concern.

4. **BRAINSTORMING:** Brainstorm strategies, supports, materials, training, or services needed to achieve goal(s) for 5–10 minutes. List all suggestions below.

Analyze each suggestion above. Consider those that are evidence-based, practical, and feasible within the given time frame. Circle those that meet these criteria.

(cont.)

FIGURE 2.6. *(cont.)*

5. **IMPLEMENTATION PLAN:** From the list above, select the strategies, supports, materials, training, or services the team will implement and complete the chart below.

Strategy, support, materials, training, or service	Location	Additional resources needed (materials, staff, time, etc.)	Date of implementation	Person(s) responsible and role	Comments

The implementation plan should be reviewed monthly until next benchmark period. The DDM team may choose to make changes to the implementation plan during these meetings.

Review date:_____

Review date:_____

Review date: _____

FIGURE 2.6. *(cont.)*

Grade-Level Teams

Although the data team focused primarily on the RTI process at the school-wide level, the focus of the grade-level teams was on evaluating the progress of individual students, as well as the grade as a whole. The grade-level teams consisted of the classroom teachers at each grade (range = 2–4 teachers), as well as support personnel, such as the reading specialist, the ESL teacher, the principal, the intervention specialist, and so forth. Grade-level teams met once a month to review individual student data and assess instruction. All meetings were held during a 45-minute period before the start of school. The principals devoted this time to teaming rather than to the traditional faculty meetings that had been held prior to the start of RTI. All grades met together in the same room at the same time, with each grade level working independently. Support personnel circulated around to all grade levels as needed. Prior to each meeting, classroom teachers would print PM graphs for each student in their classes who was being monitored (Tiers 2 and 3). Data for each student were reviewed, and decisions were made regarding the need for instructional changes. Team decisions were recorded on the grade-level team meeting record form (see Figure 2.7). A more detailed description of the process of these meetings is provided in Chapter 4.

Parent Involvement

One important component of the RTI model was parent involvement. It was important to involve parents in the process of their child's education, as well as to inform them of student progress. Although it is widely accepted that this is a valuable, and some would argue necessary, component of high-quality instruction, schools continue to struggle with the best ways to get parents involved. In order to address this need, a Parent Advisory Board was formed as part of the project. Three parents from each of the participating schools were invited to participate in this group designed to identify the best ways to inform and involve parents in the RTI process. In order to ensure diversity and a representative sample, the parents invited to participate were carefully selected by the school. Parents of students at each tier were represented. In addition, at least one parent from each school had a child with an IEP, and there were several parents of students of color. In total, six parents participated in the advisory board meetings across a 2-year period. Meetings were held in the evening for 90 minutes at one of the three participating schools. In addition to the parents, the principals from the three schools, district administrators, and project staff members were involved.

The meetings all followed a similar format, which included a brief overview of the goals and objectives for the evening, a breakout session

Student	Tier	Progress	Decision	Comment
	☐ Strategic ☐ Intensive	☐ Above Target ☐ Near Target ☐ Below Target	☐ Continue ☐ Raise Goal ☐ Instructional Change/ Modification	
	☐ Strategic ☐ Intensive	☐ Above Target ☐ Near Target ☐ Below Target	☐ Continue ☐ Raise Goal ☐ Instructional Change/ Modification	
	☐ Strategic ☐ Intensive	☐ Above Target ☐ Near Target ☐ Below Target	☐ Continue ☐ Raise Goal ☐ Instructional Change/ Modification	
	☐ Strategic ☐ Intensive	☐ Above Target ☐ Near Target ☐ Below Target	☐ Continue ☐ Raise Goal ☐ Instructional Change/ Modification	
	☐ Strategic ☐ Intensive	☐ Above Target ☐ Near Target ☐ Below Target	☐ Continue ☐ Raise Goal ☐ Instructional Change/ Modification	
	☐ Strategic ☐ Intensive	☐ Above Target ☐ Near Target ☐ Below Target	☐ Continue ☐ Raise Goal ☐ Instructional Change/ Modification	
	☐ Strategic ☐ Intensive	☐ Above Target ☐ Near Target ☐ Below Target	☐ Continue ☐ Raise Goal ☐ Instructional Change/ Modification	

FIGURE 2.7. Grade-level team meeting record form.

in which small groups worked together on a problem or task, and then a whole-group sharing session in which the work of the small groups was shared. Finally, a brief review of the outcomes of the meeting was provided, and the goals and objectives of the next meeting were introduced.

Across the entire project a total of five meetings were held with the Parent Advisory Board. The topics covered in these meetings varied, but all centered around the goal of making the RTI process and student progress more accessible to parents. The group began by developing a letter to be sent home to parents to introduce the process of RTI (see Figure 2.8). The team also collaborated on a letter for parents explaining the benchmarking results and intervention placement (see Figure 2.9). The team spent a great deal of time identifying ways to present data to parents that would be meaningful and useful as they evaluate their children's progress. Finally, the team discussed ways that parents could be involved in the educational process through at-home reading activities. The parents involved had varied backgrounds and educational levels, which was helpful in determining the best way to present information that would be meaningful for all parents. At the end of the project, it was decided by the district and the participating parents to continue the advisory board as a way of making progress toward greater parent involvement across the district.

Fidelity Checks

One vital component of a successful RTI model is the fidelity of the interventions that are implemented, as well as the integrity with which the model itself is implemented. In order to ensure that treatment fidelity was high, all skill groups were evaluated at least once between benchmark periods to determine the level of implementation fidelity. Fidelity checklists provided by the publisher of the specific intervention were used whenever possible. If none was available, a checklist was developed by project staff that delineated the steps of the intervention. An example of a fidelity checklist is provided in Figure 2.10. Project staff observed teachers while they implemented the intervention and provided feedback on performance after the observations.

Outcomes of fidelity checks are discussed in detail in Chapter 5, but overall fidelity was very high, exceeding 90%. If a teacher was not performing at this level, project staff would meet privately with the teacher to review the observation and discuss areas for improvement. A second observation was then scheduled to ensure that changes had been made. If, after the second observation, no improvements occurred, the principal would have been notified that there was a concern about fidelity to that particular intervention; however, this did not occur during the course of the project.

(text resumes on page 40)

Dear Parents/Guardians,

The purpose of this letter is to update you about the process that we are using schoolwide (K–5) called "Response to Intervention," or RTI. We were selected as one of three schools in Central Dauphin School District to work with Lehigh University and the Pennsylvania Training and Technical Assistance Network (PaTTAN) in this effort, which is funded by the U.S. Dept. of Education.

What is RTI? RTI is a multistep approach to providing high-quality instruction and interventions to students who struggle with learning. The whole idea is to prevent students from developing serious academic problems in reading, as well as to enhance instruction for those students who are doing well. All students will be assessed several times during the year. Every student will receive the core language arts curriculum in the regular education setting. The progress of a student is monitored and the results used to make decisions about the need for further research-based instruction and/or targeted interventions. The interventions will occur in small groups which are taught by trained teachers.

By using an RTI process, our school can potentially reduce the time a student waits before receiving additional instructional assistance; increase the number of students who succeed within the general education program, and limit the amount of unnecessary testing that is not related to instruction. The RTI project in Central Dauphin is called MP3 (Monitoring Progress of Pennsylvania Pupils). Your involvement in the educational decision making for your child is critical. *If* your child is identified as being in need of any targeted interventions, you will be informed and kept informed throughout the process.

This is a wonderful opportunity to help our students become more successful readers, and we have begun the process during the month of October.

Sincerely,

School Principal

FIGURE 2.8. Introductory parent letter.

From *Models for Implementing Response to Intervention: Tools, Outcomes, and Implications*, edited by Edward S. Shapiro, Naomi Zigmond, Teri Wallace, and Doug Marston. Copyright 2011 by The Guilford Press. Permission to photocopy this figure is granted to purchasers of this book for personal use only (see copyright page for details). Purchasers may download a larger version of this figure from the book's page on The Guilford Press website.

Dear Parent or Guardian,

We have recently completed the benchmark testing that is required by the Response to Intervention program. This assessment is designed to identify whether your child is ready to read on grade level (Tier 1) or whether your child needs additional and/or more intensive reading instruction (Tier 2 or Tier 3). All students in the school will be placed into a skill group in Tier 1, 2, or 3 for a minimum of 4 cycle days a week. The results of the benchmark testing indicate that your child would benefit from placement in:

_____Tier 1: REGULAR CURRICULUM + enrichment activities

_____Tier 2: REGULAR CURRICULUM + additional instruction

_____Tier 3: REGULAR CURRICULUM + additional, more intensive support

Your child will be placed in a _____ skill group starting on _____. This group will work on the following skill(s):

_____ **Early Literacy Skills:** This means the skills needed to begin to learn to read. This includes knowing the names and sounds of letters, understanding rhyming, and recognition of the beginning sounds in words. These skills are important because they are necessary before children can learn to read.

_____ **Decoding:** This means being able to recognize and sound out words. This is important because it is the foundation of reading.

_____ **Fluency:** This means reading quickly with few mistakes. This skill is important because students need to be able to read fluently to help them understand what they read.

_____ **Comprehension:** This means understanding what was read. This skill is important because the main purpose of reading is to comprehend.

_____ **Enrichment Activities:** This means activities that enhance the regular curriculum and expand on information and skills already mastered. This is important for students who have met grade-level goals so that they continue to improve and learn.

During the school year the staff will continue to monitor the progress of your child, and you will be notified of the results and recommendations. If you have any questions about this assessment or the recommendation, kindly contact me. Thank you for your continued interest in your child's school success.

Sincerely,

Your Child's Teacher

FIGURE 2.9. Skill group parent letter.

Soar to Success

Revisiting	Yes	No	N/A	Comments
Students reread, alone or with partner, previously read Soar to Success (STS) books				
Teacher works with individual students to take a retelling, conduct an oral reading check, or coach their reading				
OR				
Teacher and students hold a group conference on independently read books				
Teacher spends 5 minutes on revisiting				Start: End:
Reviewing				
Students summarize previous day's reading, using graphic organizers				
Students and teacher discuss strategies used and share examples of their use beyond STS				
Teacher spends 5 minutes reviewing				Start: End:
Rehearsing				
Do a quick text walk, guided preview, cooperative preview, or independent preview of text to be read				
Students may predict, question, or start a KWL chart				
Teacher spends 5–10 minutes rehearsing				Start: End:

(cont.)

FIGURE 2.10. Fidelity checklist.

Revisiting	Yes	No	N/A	Comments
Reading and Reciprocal Teaching				
Students silently read a meaningful chunk of text to verify predictions or answer questions				
Reciprocal teaching is employed with students and teacher taking turns assuming the role of the teacher to model these four strategies:				
Summarize				
Clarify				
Question				
Predict				
Teacher spends 10–15 minutes				Start: End:
Responding/Reflecting				
Students do one or more of the following:				
Make a written response after discussing their reflections				
Complete graphic organizers				
Reflect on strategies				
Discuss and share				
Teacher spends 5 minutes responding/reflecting				Start: End:

FIGURE 2.10. *(cont.)*

In addition to monitoring the integrity of intervention implementation, the fidelity of the model was also assessed in several ways. First, all components of the model were monitored by project staff, the principal, and the data team. Teachers were held accountable for conducting daily skill groups, collecting PM data, and participating in the data-based decision-making process. The structure of the model served to ensure accountability for individual teachers, which facilitated fidelity. For example, the cross-class and within-grade grouping of students provided a structure that reduced the likelihood that teachers would fail to implement intervention groups. If a teacher had an activity planned for the students in her or his class, she or he could choose to complete that activity or not, depending on time or interest. However, once skill groups were established, students from multiple classrooms were grouped together. A teacher could not easily cancel or skip intervention on a given day because that would affect not only his or her class but also the students and teachers in other classes. If a teacher did not conduct a skill group for any reason, it was known by the other teachers in that grade. Likewise, the fact that PM was scheduled and that each teacher had assistance from a staff member outside the classroom helped to ensure that it was consistently completed.

In addition to the naturally occurring fidelity checks already described, formal fidelity checks of team meetings were completed periodically throughout the course of the project to ensure that teachers were maintaining high integrity of the model. An example of a team meeting fidelity checklist is provided in Figure 2.11. Results of these assessments showed that teachers maintained a high level of fidelity throughout the course of the project, with an average of 95% of components completed.

CONCLUSION

This chapter describes the structure and content of the Project MP3 RTI model implemented in three elementary schools in a single district in Pennsylvania. The model included all the necessary components of an RTI model, including high-quality core instruction, multi-tiered intervention, and data-based decision making. As this model was being planned and implemented, it was important to consider not only what was included within the model but also how the model was implemented to make it successful.

As Kurns and Tilly (2008) describe, several factors will enhance the efficacy and sustainability of any RTI model. Specifically, it is important that there be supports in place for those individuals involved in the implementation of the model. RTI involves systems change, and those experiencing that change need support. Part of that support includes extensive professional development for teachers to ensure that they have the knowledge

Level of Implementation Scale

Data Analysis	Not Relevant	Not Evident (0 pt)	Partially Evident (1 pt)	Fully Evident (2 pt)
1. Student data are prepared for the meeting in a teacher-friendly format and sent to teachers in advance. Principal decides who is the session facilitator and arranges the meeting logistics. *Facilitator:* ___				
2. Attendees include principal, all data team members, and others. *Designated Attendees:* ___				
3. Data team sets measurable goals for each grade level presented in terms of specific percentages of students reaching proficiency on screening assessments (a specific number is stated for each goal, e.g. *"Right now we have 70% of our first graders at benchmark on the DIBELS Phoneme Segmentation Fluency subtest. By January, 80% of first-grade students will be proficient."*): *Specific goals:* ___				
4. Data team identifies barriers to meeting goals by designated time. Addresses all concerns.				
5. Data team brainstorms ideas to address concerns. Strategies are discussed, and the team identifies those that are most beneficial/feasible to implement.				

(cont.)

FIGURE 2.11. Team meeting fidelity checklist.

Data Analysis	Not Relevant	Not Evident (0 pt)	Partially Evident (1 pt)	Fully Evident (2 pt)
6. Data team plans the logistics of implementing agreed-upon strategies in all classrooms in that grade level (at least one specific strategy is discussed for scheduling, intervention implementation, and/or sharing progress monitoring data).				
Strategy discussed:_____				
7. Data team schedules a time to review the progress of students in follow-up meetings to determine the efficacy of implemented strategies (a specific time and date are set for the follow-up meeting).				
Follow-up meeting date/time:_____				
8. Data team discusses how to monitor the fidelity of the intervention (at least one strategy is discussed)				
Strategy discussed:_____				
9. Data team monitors the student's progress.				
10. Data team finetunes the strategies.				

TOTAL = _____ / _____ : _____ % Implementation

FIGURE 2.11. *(cont.)*

42

and skills necessary to implement RTI with success. Professional development drives effective instruction and allows ongoing data collection and data-based decision making. All of these aspects of RTI implementation are discussed in detail in Chapter 4.

The RTI model described in this chapter was implemented at three elementary schools in one district in Pennsylvania as part of a federally funded model demonstration project examining PM within an RTI model. The model incorporated the essential components of RTI (e.g., universal screening, tiered intervention, data-based decision making, and progress monitoring) while addressing the unique needs of the district and the individual schools. From the initial planning stages of the model, decisions were made that would enhance sustainability of the model after external funding and support were removed. The process for developing and implementing this model, as well as outcomes at the school and individual student levels, is described in detail in later chapters, but generally this model resulted in an effective process for implementation that led to positive outcomes for students. The results, along with the design of the model, which maintained pre-RTI staffing and resources within the schools, allowed long-term sustainability of the model. The success of this model highlights the potential of RTI to lead to positive change within our schools.

REFERENCES

Adams, G. N., & Brown, S. M. (2003). *The six-minute solution: A reading fluency program*. Frederick, CO: Sopris West.

Allen, S. J., & Graden, J. L. (2002). Best practices in collaborative problem solving for intervention design. In A. Thomas & J. Grimes (Eds.), *Best practices in school psychology IV* (pp. 565–582). Washington, DC: National Association of School Psychologists.

Barnett, D. W., Daly, E. J., Jones, K. M., & Lentz, F. E. (2004). Response to intervention: Empirically based special service decisions from single-case designs of increasing and decreasing intensity. *Journal of Special Education, 38*(2), 66–79.

Batsche, G., Elliot, J., Graden, J. L., Grimes, J., Kovaleski, J. F., & Prasse, D. (2005). *Response to intervention: Policy considerations and implementation*. Alexandria, VA: National Association of State Directors of Special Education.

Bollman, K. A., Silberglitt, B., & Gibbons, K. A. (2007). The St. Croix River Education District model: Incorporating systems-level organization and a multi-tiered problem-solving process for intervention delivery. In S. R. Jimerson, M. K. Burns, & A. M. VanDerHeyden (Eds.), *Handbook of response to intervention: The science and practice of assessment and intervention* (pp. 319–330). New York: Springer.

Burns, M. K., Deno, S. L., & Jimerson, S. R. (2007). Toward a unified response to intervention model. In S. R. Jimerson, M. K. Burns, & A. M. VanDerHeyden

(Eds.), *Handbook of response to intervention: The science and practice of assessment and intervention* (pp. 428–440). New York: Springer.

Case, L. P., Speece, D. L., & Molloy, D. E. (2003). The validity of a response-to-instruction paradigm to identify reading disabilities: A longitudinal analysis of individual differences and contextual factors. *School Psychology Review, 32*(4), 557–582.

Daly, E. J., III, Lentz, F. E., Jr., & Boyer, J. (1996). The instructional hierarchy: A conceptual model for understanding the effective components of reading interventions. *School Psychology Quarterly, 11*(4), 369–386.

Daly, E. J., III, Martens, B. K., Hamler, K. R., Dool, E. J., & Eckert, T. L. (1999). A brief experimental analysis for identifying instructional components needed to improve oral reading fluency. *Journal of Applied Behavior Analysis, 32*(1), 83–94.

Daly, E. J., III, Witt, J. C., Martens, B. K., & Dool, E. J. (1997). A model for conducting a functional analysis of academic performance problems. *School Psychology Review, 26*(4), 554–574.

Data Recognition Corporation. (2009). Technical report for the 2009 Pennsylvania System for School Assessment. Retrieved March 3, 2010, from *www.portal. state.pa.us/portal/server.pt/community/technical analysis/7447.*

Denton, C. A., Vaughn, S., & Fletcher, J. M. (2003). Bringing research-based practice in reading intervention to scale. *Learning Disabilities Research and Practice, 18*(3), 201–211.

Elliot, J., & Morrison, D. (2008). *Response to intervention blueprints: District level edition.* Alexandria, VA: National Association of State Directors of Special Education.

Fuchs, D., & Fuchs, L. S. (2006). Introduction to response to intervention: What, why, and how valid is it? *Reading Research Quarterly, 41*, 93–99.

Fuchs, D., Fuchs, L. S., Mathes, P. G., & Simmons, D. C. (1997). Peer-assisted learning strategies: Making classrooms more responsive to diversity. *American Educational Research Journal, 34*(1), 174–206.

Fuchs, D., Mock, D., Morgan, P. L., & Young, C. L. (2003). Responsiveness-to-intervention: Definitions, evidence, and implications for the learning disabilities construct. *Learning Disabilities Research and Practice, 18*(3), 157–171.

Good, R. H., & Kaminski, R. A. (Eds.). (2002). Dynamic Indicators of Basic Early Literacy Skills (6th ed.). Eugene, OR: Institute for the Development of Educational Achievement. Available at *dibels.uoregon.edu.*

Howell, K. W., & Nolet, V. (2000). *Curriculum-based evaluation: Teaching and decision making* (3rd ed.). Belmont, CA: Wadsworth/Thomson Learning.

Ikeda, M. J., Rahn-Blakeslee, A., Niebling, B. C., Gustafson, J. K., Allison, R., & Stumme, J. (2007). The Heartland Area Education Agency 11 problem-solving approach: An overview and lessons learned. In S. R. Jimerson, M. K. Burns, & A. M. VanDerHeyden (Eds.), *Handbook of response to intervention: The science and practice of assessment and intervention* (pp. 279–287). New York: Springer.

Jimerson, S. R., Burns, M. K., & VanDerHeyden, A. M. (2007). Response to intervention at school: The science and practice of assessment and intervention. In S. R. Jimerson, M. K. Burns, & A. M. VanDerHeyden (Eds.), *Handbook of response to intervention: The science and practice of assessment and intervention* (pp. 3–9). New York: Springer.

Kurns, S., & Tilly, W. D. (2008). *Response to intervention blueprints: School building level edition.* Alexandria, VA: National Association of State Directors of Special Education.

Marston, D., Lau, M., & Muyskens, P. (2007). Implementation of the problemsolving model in the Minneapolis Public Schools. In S. R. Jimerson, M. K. Burns, & A. M. VanDerHeyden (Eds.), *Handbook of response to intervention: The science and practice of assessment and intervention* (pp. 279–287). New York: Springer.

McMaster, K. L., Fuchs, D., Fuchs, L. S., & Compton, D. L. (2005). Responding to nonresponders: An experimental field trial of identification and intervention methods. *Exceptional Children, 71*(4), 445–463.

National Reading Panel. (2000). *Teaching children to read: An evidence-based assessment of the scientific research literature on reading and its implications for reading instruction* (NIH Publication No. 00-4754). Washington, DC: U.S. Government Printing Office.

O'Connor, R. E., Notari-Syverson, A., & Vadasy, P. F. (2005). *Ladders to literacy: A kindergarten activity book* (2nd ed.). Baltimore: Brookes.

Shapiro, E. S. (2011). *Academic skills problems: Direct assessment and intervention* (3rd ed.). New York: Guilford Press.

Shinn, M. R., Shinn, M. M., Hamilton, C., & Clarke, B. (2002). Using curriculumbased measurement in general education classrooms to promote reading success. In M. R. Shinn, H. M. Walker, & G. Stoner (Eds.), *Interventions for academic and behavior problems: II. Preventive and remedial approaches* (pp. 113–142). Washington, DC: National Association of School Psychologists.

Simmons, D. C., & Kame'enui, E. J. (2003). *A consumer's guide to evaluating a core reading program grades K–3: A critical elements analysis.* Eugene, OR: Institute for the Development of Educational Achievement.

Soar to Success. (2008). New York: Houghton Mifflin.

Tilly, W. D., III, Reschly, D. J., & Grimes, J. (1999). Disability determination in problem solving systems: Conceptual foundations and critical components. In D. J. Reschly, W. D. Tilly, & J. P. Grimes (Eds.), *Special education in transition: Functional assessment and noncategorical programming* (pp. 221–251). Longman, CO: Sopris West.

VanDerHeyden, A. M., Witt, J. C., & Gilbertson, D. (2007). A multi-year evaluation of the effects of a response to intervention (RTI) model on identification of children for special education. *Journal of School Psychology, 45*(2), 225–256.

CHAPTER 3

The Process of Implementation and Design for Sustainability

Karen L. Gischlar
Alexandra Hilt-Panahon
Nathan H. Clemens
Edward S. Shapiro

Recent legislation, including The No Child Left Behind Act (NCLB; 2002) and the Individuals with Disabilities Education Improvement Act (IDEIA; 2004), calls for increased accountability in our nation's schools. NCLB requires schools to implement high-quality, evidence-based instruction and intervention and to demonstrate adequate student achievement. Similarly, IDEIA requires that a student receive evidence-based, effective instruction prior to consideration for special education and related services (Kaiser, Rosenfield, & Gravois, 2009). This legislation sets the stage for school districts to implement multi-tiered instructional plans, or response-to-intervention (RTI) models. As described throughout the chapters in this text, RTI models include evidence-based instructional practices that are designed to meet the individual needs of learners. Student progress is monitored over time, and instruction is differentiated for students as needed (Mercier-Smith, Fien, Basaraba, & Travers, 2009). It is expected that implementation of a multi-tiered system of instruction will reduce overrepresentation of students in special education who are experiencing difficulties because of inadequate instruction and not because of true learning disabilities (Fletcher, Coulter, Reschly, & Vaughn, 2004; Klinger & Edwards, 2006; Walker-Dalhouse et al., 2009). Furthermore, RTI should benefit culturally diverse students because instruction is individualized to meet student needs (Klinger & Edwards, 2006; Walker-Dalhouse et al., 2009).

ASSESSING READINESS FOR CHANGE

This chapter describes the process of implementing an RTI model, which was the basis of Project MP3: Monitoring Progress of Pennsylvania Pupils. Three elementary schools from a school district in central Pennsylvania participated in the project. In selecting the three schools, the university staff and district administration determined which schools had the greatest need and were ready for schoolwide change. Dean Fixsen and colleagues at the National Implementation Research Network (*www.fpg.unc.edu/~nirn/ default.cfm*) have written and studied extensively the process of implementing systemic change and of specifically facilitating school change. Fixsen, Blasé, Horner, and Sugai (2009, p. 1) defined "readiness" as "a developmental point at which a person, organization, or system has the capacity and willingness to engage in a particular activity." Readiness of the schools was determined by considering several aspects. A first task was to demonstrate a clear need for change that was validated with data and consensus among stakeholders (Fixsen et al., 2009). District administration and university staff agreed that a need for change was evident in student performance indicators. The three schools selected serviced at-risk students who were performing below expectations on both statewide and district-level reading assessments, despite the use of reading labs and the presence of an instructional support teacher. In addition, the principal in each building voiced commitment to participation in the project, and willingness to engage was identified by Fixsen and colleagues as a necessary component in the process.

Second, key issues were identified (Fixsen et al., 2009). Generally, the district was using the Dynamic Indicators of Basic Early Literacy Skills (DIBELS; Good & Kaminski, 2002) for benchmarking purposes, but the progress monitoring (PM) feature of the assessment was not utilized systematically for decision making. Furthermore, the identified schools had "reading labs" for struggling students and/or used a phonics-based reading program, but it was unknown to what extent these programs were implemented with integrity. Finally, all three schools had a prereferral process in place, the instructional support team, through which struggling students were identified and remediation attempts were made. At the outset, administrators agreed that existing practices were not as effective in increasing student reading achievement as they would have liked.

The third component considered in assessing readiness was the ability of the schools to implement the proposed change model. In other words, the remediation plan needed to be feasible (Fixsen et al., 2009). To determine feasibility, the university staff and administration surveyed current school practices to determine components already in place that would facilitate implementation. First, the core reading curriculum was reviewed. In an RTI model, instruction in the general education core curriculum is perceived as primary prevention. When a child fails to respond to instruction in the universal core program, more intensive, individualized instruction is provided (Fuchs & Fuchs, 2006). The very premise of RTI is that students are receiving evidence-based instruction at each tier, including universally. In this district, the reading series from Houghton Mifflin Harcourt School Publishers was utilized across elementary schools. The What Works Clearinghouse (U.S. Department of Education Institute of Education Sciences [IES], 2008) reviewed nine studies published between 1985 and 2007 that utilized Houghton Mifflin Reading. IES (2008) reported that these studies did not meet intervention standards, and thus no conclusions could be drawn from the research regarding the effectiveness or ineffectiveness of the program. However, according to the publisher (Houghton Mifflin Harcourt, 1995–2007), their curriculum across grade levels includes instruction in oral language, comprehension, phonemic awareness, decoding skills, fluency, writing, spelling, and grammar. Furthermore, the publisher claims that the series is grounded in the research base in reading. Staff from Project MP3, in conjunction with the school district administrators, examined the teacher manuals across grade levels for evidence of the "5 Big Ideas" in reading: (1) phonemic awareness, (2) alphabetic principle, (3) fluency with text, (4) vocabulary, and (5) comprehension (National Reading Panel, 2000) within the themes and individual lessons.

Second, along with the content of the curriculum, an important aspect to consider was instructional fidelity. Fidelity can be defined as the delivery of instruction in the manner in which it was intended (Johnson, Mellard, Fuchs, & McKnight, 2006). In an RTI model, one cannot state for certain that a student has not responded to instruction if the degree of fidelity is unknown. The Houghton Mifflin Harcourt School Publishers reading series includes checklists for observation of fidelity of implementation. Prior to the start of Project MP3, principals conducted both formal observations and informal "walk-throughs" during reading instructional periods, but they did not use the checklists. The tool was introduced to the principals and suggested for use.

Finally, in assessing feasibility of MP3 implementation, preexisting interventions were inventoried and are included in Table 3.1. To start, interventions were categorized by the skill or skills addressed based on the National Reading Panel's (2000) "5 Big Ideas," or essential skill areas, in reading. Once the available interventions were categorized, they were evaluated for efficacy by consulting resources such as the What Works Clearinghouse (*ies.ed.gov/ncee/wwc*), the Best Evidence Encyclopedia (*www.*

TABLE 3.1. Existing Interventions Preimplementation

Targeted skill area	Tier 1	Tier 2	Tier 3
Phonological awareness and alphabetic principle	• Phonology K–2	• Language Circle phonology or linguistics • Peer-Assisted Learning Strategies (PALS)	• Glass analysis intensive linguistics • Corrective Reading • REWARDS
Comprehension	• Interactive read-alouds	• Language Circle story and/or report form • Soar to Success • PALS	• Lindamood–Bell Visualizing and Verbalizing • Language Circle story and/or report form • Corrective Reading Comprehension
Vocabulary	• Interactive read-alouds • Word walls		• Language for Learning • Language for Thinking • REWARDS
Fluency		• PALS • Read Naturally	

bestevidence.org), and the Florida Center for Reading Research (*www.fcrr. org*). Furthermore, gaps in available resources were identified. Grant funds were used to purchase additional intervention packages for the participating schools to fill these gaps. The additional programs and assessments purchased are included in Table 3.2. Interventions purchased were evaluated for research support by the same organizations used for existing programs. Finally, principals were asked to identify teachers who had previous training and experience with particular interventions to ensure that personnel resources would be utilized proficiently.

TABLE 3.2. Materials Purchased through Grant Funds

Intervention programs and materials	Assessments
Scott Foresman My Sidewalks Six-Minute Solution (Adams & Brown, 2003) Ladders to Literacy (O'Connor, Natari-Syverson, & Vadasy, 2005) Road to the Code (Blachman, Ball, Black, & Tangel, 2000)	AIMSweb Stanford Achievement Test, 10th Edition

IMPLEMENTATION ACTIVITIES

Within a systemic change process, an innovation is a program or practice that has a strong research base and that could have potential benefits for consumers (i.e., students; Fixsen & Blasé, 2009). According to Fixsen, Naoom, Blasé, Friedman, and Wallace (2005), implementation of a schoolwide change model is a process and not a one-time event. These authors describe a series of stages through which an organization progresses as change is implemented, but they concede that not much research exists on the process. The stages include: (1) exploration and adoption; (2) program installation; (3) initial implementation; (4) full operation; (5) innovation; and (6) sustainability (Fixsen et al., 2005). Activities conducted in the district as a function of Project MP3 are applied to these stages in the following sections. (See Figure 3.1.)

Exploration and Adoption

Before a schoolwide change initiative such as Project MP3 can be developed and implemented, a district must engage in exploration and adoption (Fixsen et al., 2005). In this stage, the primary focus is on diffusing information about the proposed program and on assessing the match between the school's needs, the program, and resources. At the outset, it is vital not only to evaluate a district's or school's readiness to adopt a program but also to identify potential barriers. Once informed, a district can make a decision to proceed with implementation activities or not (Fixsen et al., 2005).

Chinman, Imm, and Wandersman (2004) suggest a set of questions to be asked prior to considering implementation (see Table 3.3). Although their work was primarily with mental health service providers, the questions apply directly to implementation of large-scale change programs in the schools. Within the questions posed by Chinman and colleagues, the word *community* can be changed to *district* or *school*. The questions are comprehensive and are designed to address the organization's readiness to adopt an accountability model of service delivery, which in the schools would include systems such as RTI.

Kraft, Mezoff, Sogolow, Neumann, and Thomas (2000, as cited in Fixsen et al., 2005) conceptualized this primary stage as "preimplementation." They suggested that tasks in this phase include: (1) identifying the need for intervention considering the available data; (2) acquiring information via communication among stakeholders; (3) assessing the fit between the organization (e.g., district or school) and the suggested program; and (4) preparing personnel by mobilizing training and support (Kraft et al., as cited in Fixsen et al., 2005). In this district, the first preimplementation activity involved university staff meeting with district administration to identify a need for intervention. Data had already shown that student

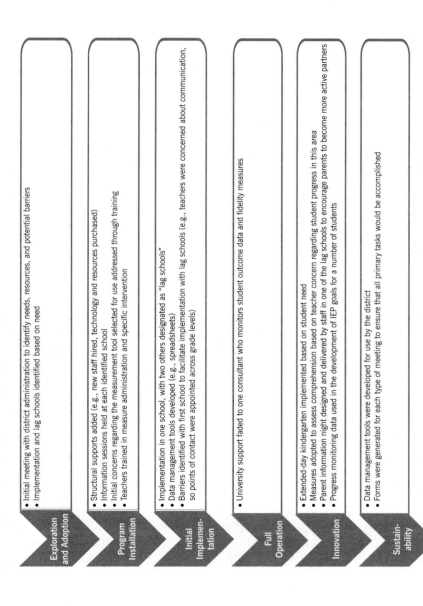

Exploration and Adoption
- Initial meeting with district administration to identify needs, resources, and potential barriers
- Implementation and lag schools identified based on need

Program Installation
- Structural supports added (e.g., new staff hired, technology and resources purchased)
- Information sessions held at each identified school
- Initial concerns regarding the measurement tool selected for use addressed through training
- Teachers trained in measure administration and specific intervention

Initial Implementation
- Implementation in one school, with two others designated as "lag schools"
- Data management tools developed (e.g., spreadsheets)
- Barriers identified with first school to facilitate implementation with lag schools (e.g., teachers were concerned about communication, so points of contact were appointed across grade levels)

Full Operation
- University support faded to one consultant who monitors student outcome data and fidelity measures

Innovation
- Extended-day kindergarten implemented based on student need
- Measures adopted to assess comprehension based on teacher concern regarding student progress in this area
- Parent information night designed and delivered by staff in one of the lag schools to encourage parents to become more active partners
- Progress monitoring data used in the development of IEP goals for a number of students

Sustainability
- Data management tools were developed for use by the district
- Forms were generated for each type of meeting to ensure that all primary tasks would be accomplished

FIGURE 3.1. Stages in the change process. From Fixsen, Naoom, Blasé, Friedman, and Wallace (2005), Louis de la Parte Florida Mental Health Institute, University of South Florida. Adapted by permission.

51

TABLE 3.3. The 10 Accountability Questions

1. What are the underlying needs and conditions in the district or school? (needs/resources)
2. What are the goals, target populations, and objectives (i.e., desired outcomes)? (goals)
3. Which evidence-based models and best-practice programs can be useful in reaching the goals? (best practice)
4. What actions need to be taken so the selected program "fits" the district or school context? (fit)
5. What organizational capacities are needed to implement the plan? (capacities)
6. What is the plan for this program? (plan)
7. How will the quality of the program and/or initiative implementation be assessed? (process evaluation)
8. How well did the program work? (outcome evaluation)
9. How will continuous quality improvement strategies be incorporated? (CQI)
10. If the program is successful, how will it be sustained? (sustainability)

Note. From Chinman, Imm, and Wandersman (2004). Copyright 2004 by RAND Corporation. Adapted by permission.

reading achievement was below expected levels, despite district attempts at intervention (e.g., reading labs and a phonology program). The university staff described RTI, and more specifically Project MP3, to administrators and assessed the fit of the model to the schoolwide needs by evaluating readiness, as previously described. The district made the decision to adopt the model in three schools. It was decided that one school would begin implementation in the first year and that the remaining two schools would begin implementation in the second year.

Program Installation

Planning Stage

Structural supports include the financial resources needed for implementation, human resource strategies, policy development, reporting frameworks, and outcome expectations. Specific activities in this stage may include realigning current staff, hiring new staff, purchasing technology, and providing initial information (Fixsen et al., 2005). Once the decision to adopt the MP3 model was made, tasks that define the program installation stage were undertaken in the 8 months prior to implementation in the first school. In this second stage of implementation, structural supports were put into place (Fixsen et al., 2005). In the district, the structural supports put into place concerned personnel, technology and other resources, and information dissemination. To start, the elementary staff development specialist was assigned the added responsibility of overseeing the implementation of Project MP3 in the three selected schools. The specialist's tasks included attending meetings at the three schools and supporting staff in data analysis, ensuring that teachers were adequately trained in reading interventions, monitoring progress toward school-level goals, and serving as an onsite consultant. Further changes in personnel included the district's hiring of an interventionist at each school using Title I funds and the formation of teams focused on data-based decision making. The interventionist in each building was responsible not only for delivering interventions with small groups of students (for a complete list of intervention groups, see Chapter 2) but also for data management and consultation. Formation of teams required all teachers to serve on grade-level teams, but service on the data team was voluntary, as it required time outside contractual obligations (see Chapter 2 for a full discussion of the formation of teams).

Because Project MP3 required activities that were beyond the typical expectations within the district, a small stipend from the project was paid directly to the elementary staff development specialist. In addition, it was important to secure the district's full cooperation for an extended period of years as the project was implemented, and having a member of the district staff partially supported by project funds provided the needed incentives for district "buy in."

To assist the schools with data management, grant funds were used to purchase an AIMSweb subscription (AIMSweb, 2008). AIMSweb is a benchmark and PM system that enables teachers to collect and organize benchmark screening data, to identify at-risk students, and to monitor student progress and determine response to intervention. The system provides the needed assessments and data analysis tools and generates reports that can be shared with other professionals, parents, and students. The teachers were taught to use the system and to interpret and report assessment results during professional development sessions that are described later.

Finally, during the months prior to implementation in the first school, information about the model was directly disseminated at meetings held in individual schools to avoid miscommunication about the project. Guldbrandsson (2008) noted that there is a clear distinction between "diffusion" and "dissemination" of information. Diffusion is a process by which information travels through certain channels over time via the members of a social system (Guldbrandsson, 2008), such as a faculty. Dissemination, on the other hand, is a planned and active process that is designed to increase the level and rate of adoption of a new program beyond what may have been achieved through diffusion alone (Guldbrandsson, 2008). To ensure that the model, the rationale, and roles and functions were clearly defined, information was deliberately presented by project personnel to teachers.

According to the National Association of State Directors of Special Education (NASDSE, 2008a), an early task in RTI implementation is to provide information to primary stakeholders (i.e., teachers and parents) in the following areas: (1) the definition of RTI; (2) components of the model; (3) benefits to implementing an RTI model; (4) potential barriers; (5) expected changes; (6) required commitments and resources; and (7) provision of exemplars of RTI models. The early sessions in the district focused on explanation of RTI, specifically the MP3 model, RTI and reading research, and data-based decision making. Initial response to these sessions was mixed; some teachers were very positive about implementation of the model, but many were apprehensive about changes that would be made in classroom instruction and procedures. In fact, a few teachers expressed concern that RTI was the "next thing in education" and that in a few years they would be asked to do "something else." These concerns were met with understanding and patience from university staff, but research was continually presented in support of implementation of the model and to emphasize data collection and analysis as "best practices."

During these initial overview sessions, teachers often asked questions about implementation and responsibilities during the process. Questions could be asked directly of university project staff and district administrators or through use of a "parking lot." The parking lot was a piece of paper attached to the wall on which teachers could apply questions written on Post-it Notes to ensure anonymity. One question that was consistently asked regarded the use of DIBELS (Good & Kaminski, 2002) as the indicators to measure student progress. A number of teachers suggested that the DIBELS were a poor measure to use because they promoted "faster, not better" reading. Teachers were concerned that fluency measures would not provide an accurate picture of a student's reading ability. Indeed, these are concerns and arguments that have been raised in the reading literature base (Pressley, Hilden, & Shankland, 2005; Samuels, 2007). In response, professional development specifically on CBM and reading was designed and delivered at the outset of the project. For example, professional development training described the history of CBM and the development and rationale of oral reading fluency as a research-validated *indicator* of overall reading achievement. Professional development in this area sought to promote a better understanding of CBM and why simple fluency-based measures are reflective of skills within a general academic domain. Project personnel deemed this to be an important aspect of initial training because the teachers needed to have confidence in the measurement system on which decisions would be made for the system to work as intended. These trainings were presented at the individual buildings, and concepts were reiterated at the first summer institute that occurred prior to the start of the project in the first school. (See Figure 3.2 for an overview of professional development sessions.)

Professional development design and delivery were fully supported by the Pennsylvania Training and Technical Assistance Network (PaTTAN), the state educational liaison. As noted, a number of PaTTAN consultants had developed a previous relationship with the district across various ini-

Data-Based Decision-Making Models	Instruction and Intervention in Reading	Assessment
• Overview of the MP3 model • Question and answer sessions • Using data to inform instruction	• "5 Big Ideas" • Intervention programs • Differentiating instruction in the core curriculum	• Administration of measures • Teaming roles and responsibilities • Use of data management tools and programs

FIGURE 3.2. Professional development process.

tiatives. The consultants who worked with the university in the implementation of Project MP3 had extensive knowledge and experience in both RTI models and reading instruction and intervention, including work with struggling readers. As consultants, they had worked with individual teachers and also had a wealth of experience designing and delivering professional development sessions. Finally, the consultants were well versed in data-based decision making and had access to district-level data that were useful in the planning stages.

Summer Institute

After the initial school-level meetings during the spring prior to project implementation, a summer institute was held. The purpose of the summer institute was to provide training in reading and interventions through such sessions as "From Phonics to Fluency to Proficient Reading" and to allow time for planning related to the RTI model project. Prior to this institute, the principal in each building, with the support of the university staff, formed a team responsible for providing leadership on RTI implementation and data-based decision making (i.e., "data team"). According to NASDSE (2008b), a vital step in implementing an RTI model is to establish a leadership team. This team should include: (1) a data mentor who has expertise in data collection, organization, display, analysis, and interpretation and who can train and support teachers in these tasks; (2) a content specialist who has the capacity to train faculty in intervention packages and strategies; (3) a facilitator whose responsibility is to oversee and support functioning through setting meetings, developing agendas, facilitating communication, and determining the effectiveness of the process; (4) a staff liaison person who is responsible for communication with school personnel who are not members of the core leadership team; and (5) an instructional leader, specifically the principal, whose primary responsibility in an RTI model is to support the staff by communicating openly, by building culture, and by creating specific routines and procedures. Additional members of the MP3 schools' data teams in the district included grade-level teachers who were selected by building principals because of their perceived leadership abilities and knowledge about reading instruction and data-based decision making. Participation on the data team was voluntary because it required teacher attendance at additional meetings beyond the contractual agreement. These key people in each building attended the summer academy.

In addition to the data teams, in attendance were Lehigh University staff, including the co-principal investigator, project coordinators, and district staff, including the director of curriculum, the director of pupil services, the director of special education, the elementary staff development specialist, a district school psychologist, and select grade-level representatives. Also, three consultants from PaTTAN, who had expertise in reading instruction and intervention and RTI models, attended. These attendees formed the leadership team, which was identified as a necessary component by NASDSE (2008b) in implementing an RTI model.

At the summer academy, the school-level leadership teams considered basic questions in establishing an action plan for their respective buildings. A first step was to review school-level data to determine whether the core reading curriculum was sufficient by considering the percentage of students performing in the low-risk or proficient status ranges on standardized measures (NASDSE, 2008b). For example, one school noted that a particular strength for fourth graders was "open-ended questions" on reading assessments, which suggested to them strong instruction at the previous grade levels. After strengths were identified, the next step was to determine needs that were indicated through data analysis. The same school noted that a substantial number of students had not met kindergarten DIBELS benchmarks for phoneme segmentation. Because this skill has been shown to predict future reading proficiency, this area was targeted as a building-level need. In addition to identifying the areas of need, the team also considered factors that may have been contributing to performance. The school in the example noted that direct instruction in phonological awareness and PM were not occurring in kindergarten. As the final step in this part of the action planning process, the school developed a strategy for addressing needs. For example, in kindergarten, the plan was to train the teacher in instructional methods and PM and to monitor fidelity of instruction during reading. The plan included the target area to be addressed, the resources and activities required in plan implementation, the name of each person or persons responsible for carrying out activities, and the date by which each component was to be completed. Initial responsibility for monitoring the plan was left to the principals, but university staff also monitored.

The next task for the team in developing the action plan was to identify screening measures (NASDSE, 2008b). As stated, the district was administering the DIBELS benchmark assessments to all students three times per year, but the data were not used in the decision-making process. At the summer institute, other assessments also were identified that could offer support in making instructional decisions for both grade levels and individual students. These included DIBELS PM probes, AIMSweb Maze assessments, the 4Sight benchmark reading assessments (Success for All Foundation, 2005–2006), and Houghton Mifflin Harcourt School Publishers' reading theme tests. The recommended schedules for administration were followed for the benchmark assessments. For PM probes, the leadership teams decided to administer probes weekly to students receiving intervention at Tier 3 and every other week to students placed in Tier 2 intervention groups. NASDSE (2008b) also states that a function of the team during action planning is to establish cut points for measures in placing students into instructional tiers. Because the district was using the DIBELS (Good & Kaminski, 2002), the tier placement suggested by the system was used as a guideline; additional information, including reading series tests and 4Sight scores, was used to support decisions.

The final step in completing the action plan was to determine what additional skills and training were needed to be able to implement the plan. The team was asked to identify topics for professional development that were aligned with training needs identified through the action plan. Furthermore, the team was instructed to set time in the schoolwide calendar for staff collaboration and reflection on teaching practices and student learning. An example of an identified training need was differentiated instruction. The team believed that teachers needed more training in meeting the needs of diverse learners during the core instructional period, and thus a session was developed for this purpose. (For a sample action plan outline, see Figure 3.3.)

NASDSE (2008b) recommends that another task during action planning should be to collect and organize data. At the summer institute, the teams worked to develop plans that included school- and grade-level goals. These goals were developed by considering current data and then determining percentages of students who could possibly move into Tier 1, or the benchmark group. Furthermore, the teams developed a yearlong calendar of events. The calendars included dates for benchmark assessments, professional development sessions, and data team, intervention grouping, and grade-level meetings. The calendars also noted which university- or school-level personnel were responsible for completion of each task. A copy of the calendar for each building was distributed to core team members and district administrators. The primary responsibility for ensuring that dates on the calendar were met was left to the building principals, but university staff closely monitored the schedules. Finally, a person in each building was designated to serve as the data manager. This person was trained directly by university staff to enter and interpret data and to serve as an onsite consultant for teachers.

(text resumes on page 65)

✒ **What you need to do**

- As a team, discuss strengths and concerns about student achievement highlighted by the data.
- Summarize the student achievement Areas of Strength.
- Summarize the student achievement Areas of Concern.
- Brainstorm causes.

Through discussion, describe your fact-based *observations and questions about student progress.* All *observations must be supported by data. Encouraging diverse points of view will lead to better diagnosis and greater ownership of the current state of student learning and achievement.*

FORMATIVE ASSESSMENTS of Student Progress: DIBELS/AIMSweb	What do you SEE in the data? What do the data SAY?		Causes: What is happening or not happening?
	Areas of Strength	Areas of Concern	
Whole school			
Kindergarten (focus—PA, letter recognition, beginning phonics, vocab, comp)			
First Grade (focus—phonics, prior skills not mastered, automaticity, vocab, comp)			
Second Grade (focus—advanced phonics, automaticity, fluency, skills not mastered, vocab, comp)			

(cont.)

FIGURE 3.3. Sample action plan.

From *Models for Implementing Response to Intervention: Tools, Outcomes, and Implications*, edited by Edward S. Shapiro, Naomi Zigmond, Teri Wallace, and Doug Marston. Copyright 2011 by The Guilford Press. Permission to photocopy this figure is granted to purchasers of this book for personal use only (see copyright page for details). Purchasers may download a larger version of this figure from the book's page on The Guilford Press website.

| | What do you SEE in the data? What do the data SAY? | | Causes: What is happening or not happening? |
	Areas of Strength	Areas of Concern	
Third Grade (focus—morphology, fluency, prior skills not mastered, vocab, comp)			
Fourth Grade (focus—morphology, fluency, prior skills not mastered, vocab, comp)			
Fifth Grade (focus—morphology, fluency, prior skills not mastered, vocab, comp)			
FORMATIVE ASSESSMENTS • of Student Progress 4Sight			
Whole School			
Third Grade (proficiency, subskills)			
Fourth Grade (proficiency, subskills)			
Fifth Grade (proficiency, subskills)			

FIGURE 3.3. *(cont.)*

(cont.)

59

FORMATIVE ASSESSMENTS of Student Progress Houghton Mifflin Theme Tests	What do you SEE in the data? What do the data SAY?		What QUESTIONS do the data raise? What questions do you have about what you see?
	Areas of Strength	Areas of Concern	
Whole School			
Kindergarten			
First Grade			
Second Grade			
Third Grade			
Fourth Grade			
Fifth Grade			

FIGURE 3.3. *(cont.)*

(cont.)

WHOLE SCHOOL

*"Where do we want to go next?"—Identify and describe below **2 to 4 research-based** or promising strategies that you will implement. Emphasize strategies that enhance standards-aligned instructional practices; build capacity of teachers, staff, and administration; and are within your power to accomplish successfully.*

School Team:	Lead Person(s):	Date:

Student Achievement Improvement Target (OR Area of Concern to be addressed): READING

1.			
2.			
3.			
4.			

*This step is repeated for each grade level independently, as related to school-level goals.

"How are we going to get there?"—Complete the "What needs to be done" column for each promising strategy described above. Next, complete the remaining columns for the strategy. Use additional sheets, as needed.

(cont.)

FIGURE 3.3. *(cont.)*

What needs to be done?	When?	By Whom?	With What?	Resources, etc., needed to complete:	Done? ✓
Schoolwide Data Team members (volunteer) determined					

For each data source : _____
  • how often it will be administered
  • by whom it will be administered
  • who will enter the data					

For each data source : _____
  • how often it will be administered
  • by whom it will be administered
  • who will enter the data					

For each data source : _____
  • how often it will be administered
  • by whom it will be administered
  • who will enter the data					

For each data source : _____
  • how often it will be administered
  • by whom it will be administered
  • who will enter the data					

For each data source : _____
  • how often it will be administered
  • by whom it will be administered
  • who will enter the data					

For progress monitoring:
  • how often it will be administered
  • by whom it will be administered
  • who will enter the data
  • who will monitor PM data (timely, entered, red flags)					

FIGURE 3.3. *(cont.)*

(cont.)

What needs to be done?	When?	By Whom?	With What?	Resources, etc., needed to complete:	Done? ✓
Who will determine what the focus of each data/grade-level team meeting is and what data are needed?					
Who will gather and prepare the data packets for • whole school? • grade-level team meetings?					
How often will the schoolwide data team meet and what will be the purpose?					
How often will the grade-level teams meet and for what purpose?					
Who will model data use for staff?					
Who will facilitate the schoolwide data team meetings?					
Who will facilitate grade-level team meetings (leading group through analysis to instructional decisions)?					
Data calendar developed (enter in calendar:) • Schoolwide data team meetings (beginning, middle, end, or more often?) • Grade-level team meetings (at least monthly) • Administration of each data source (before data and grade-level team meetings)					

(cont.)

FIGURE 3.3. *(cont.)*

63

"What additional skills/training/capacity-building do we need?"—Describe the professional development, etc., needed to successfully carry out the tasks outlined in Step 3. Align the focus of your professional development to the needs identified in your plan. Set aside on <u>calendar</u> the "sacred time" reserved explicitly for staff collaboration and evidence-based reflection on teaching practices and student learning.

School Team:	Lead Person(s):	Date:

Date/Time *When?*	Participants *For whom?*	Topic/Focus/Purpose *What?/Why?*	Delivery Format *How?*	Facilitator/Provider *By whom?*	Application *How? When? Who?*

Consider:
- 2-hour-delay days
- Full day
- Coaching
- Short times (20–30 minutes) before school, after school, part of staff meetings (very focused topic)

FIGURE 3.3. *(cont.)*

An additional planning task that NASDSE (2008b) lists as primary is to determine how and by whom supplemental instruction will be delivered. At the summer institute, each school-level group considered how building-level personnel could be used effectively to facilitate implementation of the model. The principal for each building reviewed teachers' preservice training, professional development records, and experience with interventions to determine how staff should be assigned to skills groups. Those with specialized training (i.e., special education or reading) were assigned to the most intensive intervention groups.

Finally, the planning teams worked to develop a daily schedule for each school. The goal was to have a 90-minute block of reading time for each classroom that was uninterrupted by other activities, such as lunch or fine arts periods. Additionally, it was necessary to schedule the intervention group periods for certain grade levels (e.g., fourth and fifth) during the same block of time to enable children to attend intervention groups that best addressed their needs. During reading instructional periods, students were not removed from the classroom for any therapies (e.g., speech and language), and the principals tried not to schedule activities, such as assemblies, during these "sacred" instructional periods. (See Chapter 2 for a sample intervention group schedule.)

Professional Development

As described, select staff participated on the data team, but every teacher was expected to serve as a member of his or her respective grade-level team. According to NASDSE's (2008b) blueprint for RTI implementation, a key step in model implementation is to organize a team structure for ongoing data-based decision making. Although NASDSE suggests that not every teacher, nor even grade level, needs to be represented within a decision-making team, the MP3 model included the larger data team and smaller grade-level teams. The addition of the smaller grade-level teams ensured that every teacher participated in the process of collecting, analyzing, and interpreting data. The decision was made to include all teachers on a grade-level decision team because the measure of instructional effectiveness is student response to instruction and/or intervention (Olson, Daly, Andersen, Turner, & LeClair, 2007). It was believed that requiring teachers to examine student data regularly would result in reflective teaching practices and would increase "ownership" of the model. Thus professional development sessions in data collection and analysis and instructional practices were designed and delivered to all teachers. Professional development sessions were offered throughout the school year on dates previously built into the calendar by district administration and during faculty meetings at the respective schools.

High-quality professional development can significantly influence teachers' classroom instructional practices and positively affect student achievement (Danielson, Doolittle, & Bradley, 2007). In an RTI model, high-quality professional development is a key component because teachers' use and knowledge of evidence-based practices are central to implementation (Gettinger & Stoiber, 2007). Kratochwill, Volpiansky, Clements, and Ball (2007) suggested that there are two key areas in which educators require professional development in RTI. First, teachers need to understand the conceptual, methodological, and practical aspects of RTI models. Second, training in the systematic change factors that influence the process of implementing a new initiative is needed. Specific areas for training in an RTI model include assessment administration and interpretation, prevention and intervention activities, and the systemic skills that will enable the school to adopt, implement, evaluate, and sustain the model (Kratochwill et al., 2007).

Professional development experiences must be ongoing and include coaching and feedback, rather than a "one-shot" training session (NASDSE, 2008). Based on these research findings, training sessions were developed by the university staff in conjunction with school administration, including the elementary staff development specialist and the building principals. At the outset of the project, preliminary data were collected from the three participant schools through surveys. First, surveys were distributed to teachers, which assessed their level of skill and experience in teaching reading and in PM. The surveys also asked teachers to provide demographic information, such as years of experience and level of educational attainment. These surveys were developed by SRI International, evaluators of the funded U.S. Office of Special Education Programs model demonstration projects, and the purpose was to obtain baseline information about the sites prior to implementation. Results of the surveys indicated that the majority of teachers (range = 82.9–93.1%) reported receiving training across the "5 Big Ideas" in reading: (1) phonemic awareness; (2) alphabetic principle; (3) fluency with text; (4) vocabulary; and (5) comprehension. However, only 67.5% of the teacher respondents indicated training in the identification of scientifically based interventions. This suggested that, although teachers were aware of the "5 Big Ideas," they may not have known how best to intervene on behalf of struggling students. Furthermore, 88% of teachers reported that they had received training in using data to make decisions, but only 66.7% reported training in evaluating instructional effectiveness. When asked how often they used data to make decisions for students, 57.3% reported weekly, 26.5% reported monthly, 9.4% reported several times per year, and 2.6% reported rarely. When teachers were asked specifically about the use of reading PM, 43.6% reported use with most students, 32.5% reported use with some students, 3.4% reported use with few students, and 18.8% reported that they did not use PM at all.

The results of the survey were used in conjunction with district- and school-level information to design professional development sessions. First, as previously discussed, early preimplementation sessions focused on the definition of RTI, the components of the model, and the expected change process (as suggested by NASDSE, 2008a). After the initial overview sessions, trainings were developed in specific areas crucial to implementation, including the "5 Big Ideas" in reading, PM, data-based decision making, and the individual interventions. Some sessions were delivered to all three schools simultaneously, whereas others were designed to meet the individual needs and thus were delivered at school-level meetings. (See Figure 3.2.)

Teachers across grade levels in all three schools attended each of five sessions devoted to the "5 Big Ideas" of reading instruction. It was anticipated that this training would increase the dialogue across grades in best practices in reading instruction. Because NASDSE (2008a) suggests that "one shot" training is not effective, after the initial trainings in reading, university- and district-level staff served as consultants, providing resources and direct feedback to teachers in the areas of reading instruction and intervention.

Teachers in each building also received direct training in PM. During the initial professional development session, university staff demonstrated administration and scoring of PM probes, then teachers scored probes as they watched videos of children completing tasks. Practice continued until teachers were proficient and comfortable with PM administration. Beyond this training, university staff monitored PM administration through conducting periodic spot checks.

In addition to administration of the probes, teachers were instructed in the use of AIMSweb. Teachers practiced entering data for example students at these trainings, then were taught to access graphs needed for grade-level meetings. Additionally, teachers were instructed how to read the graphs and how to share results with parents and other professionals. A separate training in AIMSweb was conducted for the data team in each building, who was responsible for using schoolwide data to set goals and to group students for interventions. This training was ongoing, as university staff participated in every data and grade-level team meeting for the first 3 years of the project to ensure that data were being interpreted and used proficiently.

According to Kratochwill and colleagues (2007), teachers need to understand the conceptual, methodological, and practical aspects of RTI models. Because data-based decision making is at the very core of RTI models, ongoing training was offered in the skills that make up this area. During early training sessions, the university staff displayed examples of data and led discussion about decisions that could be made about instruction both at the grade and individual-student levels. After this initial practice, data were displayed and teachers worked in small groups to make decisions. For example, teachers were given individual student PM graphs, and they were asked to decide whether to continue instruction for the student, to change instruction, or to collect more data before a decision could be made. After these initial experiences, ongoing training was provided at data and grade-level team meetings as university staff modeled the decision-making process and supported teachers as they assumed responsibilities.

Initial Implementation

Generally, change does not occur evenly or simultaneously within an organization or school. Changes in skills, capacity, and culture take time to develop fully. During the initial stage, there is likely to be an air of fear and inertia as an organization struggles to adopt and internalize new practices (Fixsen et al., 2005). With an understanding of this process, Project MP3 was implemented in one school during the first year, with implementation occurring in the other two schools the following year. To determine which school would be the first, several factors were considered. To start, the first school was deemed neediest when adequate yearly progress (AYP) indicators were considered. Second, the teachers in this building seemed most resistant to the project when compared with the teachers in the other two identified schools. The university team and district administration decided that this would be the best place to start because staff in this school would most likely need the extra support from the university before becoming independent.

This design allowed the identification and remediation of barriers with the first school, which facilitated implementation in the two remaining schools (termed "lag" schools based on their time-lagged implementation). For example, during initial implementation in the first school, teachers expressed concern about receiving complete information from the data team meetings. To address this concern, three "point of contact" (PoC) people from the data team were assigned to disseminate information to specific grade levels. When the model was implemented in the lag schools, PoCs were assigned at the outset to avoid a similar problem. A second area of concern identified by the first school regarded procedures and expectations for "push-in" support. This concern was addressed by having the principal observe during push-in support lessons and provide direct feedback. Also, a feedback form was developed to help teachers communicate more effectively with support teachers. These procedures were put in place in the lag schools at the beginning of the school year to facilitate their transition into the model. The designation of the PoC and development of the feedback system were in line with the NASDSE (2008b) guidelines for RTI implementation that suggest that a plan for ongoing communication with all stakeholders needs to be established at the beginning of model implementation.

Finally, the lag school model enabled the teachers from the first school to serve as a resource when the project moved to the full implementation stage. During the second summer academy, teachers from the initial school had the opportunity to share their experiences within the MP3 model with teachers from the lag schools, who were about to enter the project. They were able to discuss some of the challenges encountered, but also the success stories.

During the second year of the project, the two lag schools adopted the model. Although barriers were identified and addressed with implementation in the first school, this second year was still considered to be the initial implementation phase (Fixsen et al., 2005). All three schools remained dependent on university support. MP3 university staff continued to lead data team and grade-level meetings, coordinate data collection, entry, and analysis, and conduct fidelity checks. During this phase, procedures for fidelity were developed—which are discussed later in the chapter—but primary responsibility for overseeing the model lay with the university.

Full Operation

Full operation of the model occurs when the new practice becomes integrated into the system across practitioners, the organization, and the community (Fixsen et al., 2005). At this point, the new system is operating according to plan, with practitioners working proficiently and skillfully. The program has become accepted practice, and the organization has fully adapted, with processes and procedures fully recognized as routine (Fixsen et al., 2005). As this volume goes to press, the district is in its fifth year of implementation (i.e., fifth year at the initial school and fourth year in the two lag schools). University support is limited this year to one consultant who monitors implementation primarily through review of student outcome data and fidelity measures primarily through periodic e-mail contact. Furthermore, the consultant is available to answer questions and offer support, as needed. Otherwise, the three schools have adapted the model and are operating independently, with the principal in each building serving as the instructional leader; a change of principals occurred in one of the lag schools during the last year of Project MP3 involvement. The district has moved the RTI process into all 14 of its elementary schools and is one of only a handful of districts in the state that have been approved for use of the RTI model for eligibility decisions on specific learning disabilities (SLD).

Innovation

As a school or system implements a new practice, the opportunity for learning occurs (Fixsen et al., 2005). Staff learn more about the program itself and also the conditions under which it can best be implemented with fidelity and have positive effects. Because each school differs in both its student body and staff composition, implementation also affords the opportunity to refine and expand practices to fit unique needs. A valid change to the "standard model" can enhance outcomes for a particular school. However, caution should be exercised in changing or adding elements to ensure that practice is not drifting from the intended program and threatening fidelity of implementation (Fixsen et al., 2005).

In the district, several innovations were added to the existing model as teachers adapted and internalized the RTI model. First, the data team in two of the buildings noted that kindergarten students in the intensive tier were not making the expected progress. In an effort to promote achievement, an extended day program was offered to these students. Typically, kindergartners attended school for 2.5 hours per day. Students in the extended day program attended general education kindergarten in the morning, then participated in the extended day program after school. Instruction in the afternoon focused on early literacy skills. This initiative was conceived and implemented solely by the district, which evidenced their movement toward independence in the RTI process. Data teams independently identified an area of need and devised a plan for remediation. However, at the time this volume went to press, no data were available to document the effectiveness of this practice.

Second, as the project progressed, teachers requested a PM measure for comprehension because they believed that the fluency probes were not adequate for a small number of students who were not performing well on classroom tasks and tests. This request led to the addition of the AIMSweb Maze measure, a proxy for reading comprehension, as well as using the theme tests that were a part of the reading series used for core instruction.

As the third innovation, the teachers in one of the lag schools took the initiative to conduct an RTI parent information night. Core members of the data team, specifically the instructional support teacher, intervention specialist, and reading specialist, presented detailed components of RTI and explained how PM probes were scored and administered. The presenters also explained to parents how to interpret PM graphs and allowed time for practice with examples. After the presentation, the parents were invited to review the interventions used across the tiers. The teachers had made colorful poster board displays and were available to discuss specific interventions and to answer questions. Parents who attended were able to select a book to take home for each of their children. Although parent attendance was low, this session was very informative. The faculty in this building is currently working to brainstorm ideas to increase participation in the future. Some ideas include providing dinner and babysitting services for parents wishing to attend.

Finally, the staff in each building began to use PM data for multidisciplinary evaluations and in the development of IEP goals, although they were not directly instructed in these areas. Analysis of IEPs across the three schools for students who had reading goals suggested that faculty in each building began to incorporate PM into development of the goals on a limited basis. The criteria for rating the IEPs are included in Figure 3.4. The rating scores across schools ranged from 1 to 1.8 during their first years in the project. The only exception was a rating of 2.4 in one of the buildings, which included end-of-the-year oral reading fluency (ORF) in long-term goal development.

By the second year of MP3 in each building, the three schools moved toward partial or suggested evidence in the following areas that were evaluated in the IEPs: (1) PM data were used for eligibility decision making and included in the evaluation report; (2) the present level of performance (PLOP) statement included the students' current ORF; (3) the goals were based on the end-of-year benchmarks for ORF; and (4) long-term goals included the expected end-of-year ORF. These ratings suggested that the faculty in the schools began to incorporate the data into the special education eligibility process and into goal setting for students.

Sustainability

The goal during the final stage of implementation is the long-term survival and continued effectiveness of the program. As personnel and funding sources change, procedures must be in place that allow the program to endure (Fixsen et al., 2005). For Project MP3, steps were taken throughout the implementation process to ensure that responsibilities within the model could be shifted easily to district personnel from the university. First, university staff worked with the district to develop data management tools to facilitate the data collection and analysis processes. (See Chapter 3 for samples of data management tools developed.) A spreadsheet was developed that enabled school personnel to compare student data across measures. A university staff member sat with the data team in each building and instructed them in the use of the spreadsheet. Additionally, a spreadsheet was developed for calculating goals. Teachers had been taught the manual procedure for calculating the number of students at each benchmarking period who could be expected to move from one tier to the next by the subsequent benchmark. After learning and applying the mechanics, the teachers were provided with a spreadsheet that did the calculations. In addition to this spreadsheet, the schools were provided with spreadsheets for intervention groups and tier movement to aid them in tracking students. Finally, the schools were given instruction sheets for using AIMSweb and decision-making goals and all forms that had been used during meetings, including the grade-level data-decision form on which teachers recorded decisions made for individual students after data review. Development of these tools enabled responsibilities for data collection and analysis to be gradually handed to school personnel.

Indicators	Ratings*
Progress monitoring data were used for eligibility decision making and included in the evaluation report.	
The present level of performance (PLOP) statement included the expected oral reading fluency (ORF) benchmark for the student's grade level.	
The PLOP statement included the student's current ORF.	
The goals were based on the end-of-year benchmarks for ORF.	
The goals relied on the normative slope of improvement.	
The goals relied on a 1.5 times increase in slope over baseline.	
Long-term goals included the expected end-of-year ORF.	
Short-term objectives included expected gain in ORF.	
The progress monitoring data for several points across the year were compared with PLOP scores.	
The progress monitoring data were graphed.	
The rate of improvement for progress monitoring was compared with the goal at monthly intervals.	
End-of-year goals were adjusted based on trend lines.	
Instruction/services were modified to reflect the data.	
Computerized systems were used to provide student skills profiles.	
Skills profiles were used in instruction planning and/or modification.	

* 1 = no evidence; 2 = suggested/partial evidence; 3 = clear evidence.

FIGURE 3.4. Rating criteria for IEPs.

To further support long-term sustainability, forms were generated for each meeting type (i.e., data team, grade-level, and intervention grouping meetings) that detailed who was to attend, the responsibilities of faculty, and goals for each meeting. At the start of the project, Lehigh University staff members led the meetings and completed the paperwork in an attempt to model for the faculty and principal, who was designated as the building-level leader in the process. With time, meetings were handed to the principals to lead, with university personnel observing and providing feedback. The forms served as guides to meeting structure and content. In addition to modeling for the principals, the university also demonstrated to teachers how to interpret student and grade-level data and to set appropriate instructional goals. At the start of the project, a university staff member or district administrator led this process with teachers, but with time, support was faded.

Prior to the start of the project, the majority of teachers in each building had a limited knowledge base, skill set, and direct experience with RTI models, PM, and data-based decision making, as evidenced on their responses to the initial survey. By the end of the first year in each building, the faculty had assumed most of the responsibilities for implementation. During the second year, the principal in each building led meetings and monitored progress toward grade- and building-level goals independently. Furthermore, the teachers took full responsibility for analyzing student and grade-level data, setting goals, and determining interventions. Although university staff continued to attend the intervention grouping meetings that occurred after each benchmarking period, the faculty in each building took responsibility for forming groups and matching interventions.

The personnel in each building became much more independent during their second year of model implementation, but there remained areas in which support from the university was needed. The district had decided at the outset to take a team approach to benchmark assessments because of the concern about teachers administering the measures in a standardized fashion to their own students. However, the district faced challenges in finding enough evaluators to cover all grade levels. Retired teachers were called to help, but through the final year of implementation, university staff also administered benchmark assessments. Also, principals required help completing all intervention integrity checks when this responsibility was handed to them. This was a second area in which the university offered continued support.

SUMMARY

Project MP3 was a federally funded model demonstration project in which university staff trained and supported a district implementing RTI models in three of their schools with the hope of moving to full district implementation. Prior to the start of the project, the university assessed the district for readiness. Key indicators of readiness included willingness, ability, and feasibility. Once the district was deemed ready for the implementation, the university assisted the district in choosing three schools to pilot the model and was responsible for training, modeling, and monitoring at the outset. With time, the university developed tools and procedures for sustainability purposes and gradually faded support. This model was grounded in the research (e.g., Fixsen et al., 2005; NASDSE, 2008a, 2008b) that suggests systematic implementation with clearly defined tasks at each stage, including: (1) exploration and adoption; (2) program installation; (3) initial implementation; (4) full operation; (5) innovation; and (6) sustainability.

As the process unfolded, several strengths and challenges to implementation were noted. A strength was the district administration's commitment to the project. As the literature has suggested (e.g., Fixsen et al., 2005; NASDSE, 2008a, 2008b), a systematic change process cannot be implemented without strong leadership, including a clear vision for implementation, process, and outcomes. In addition, administrators at the district level worked not only to identify buildings with high need but also principals whom they believed had the knowledge base and skills to serve as instructional leaders. In addition to leadership, other noted strengths included the teachers' willingness to participate and assume new roles and tasks; existing resources, including intervention programs; and the preexisting relationship with PaTTAN.

During the process, several challenges to implementation also were noted. The first concerned resources. To supplement materials, the university purchased several reading intervention packages for the buildings. Further university grant funds were used to supplement the salary of the district's elementary staff development specialist, as she was assigned extra duties in conjunction with implementation of the model project. For districts wishing to implement a system without university and/or grant support, districts need to consider how reallocation of resources can provide the needed financial support for materials and personnel. Another challenge during implementation was faced when teachers raised concerns about the measures selected for use. The importance of ongoing professional development and coaching became clear as the implementation process unfolded.

The outcomes of the design and implementation process directly influenced the structure and content of the RTI model, as discussed in the next chapter. The action plan developed during the summer prior to the first year of implementation is clearly evident in the tasks undertaken by the first school. Because the plan served to focus attention on primary goals and related tasks and also identified key personnel, it helped to keep the first school on track. Thus similar plans were developed for the lag schools in the ensuing years. Although much planning and preparation went into developing the model before it was implemented with the initial school, lessons were learned along the way, and adjustments to the plan were made as needed.

REFERENCES

Adams, G. N., & Brown, S. M. (2003). *The six-minute solution: A reading fluency program.* Frederick, CO: Sopris West.

Archer, A. L., Gleason, M. M., & Vachon, V. (2000). *REWARDS: Reading excellence: Word attack and rate development strategies.* Frederick, CO: Sopris West.

Blachman, B. A., Ball, E. W., Black, R., & Tangel, D. M. (2000). *Road to the code: A phonological awareness program for young children.* Baltimore: Brookes.

Chinman, M., Imm, P., & Wandersman, A. (2004). Getting to outcomes 2004: Promoting accountability through methods and tools for planning, implementation, and evaluation. Santa Monica, CA: Rand Corporation. Retrieved March 30, 2010, from *www.rand.org/pubs/technical_reports/2004/RAND_TR101.pdf.*

Danielson, L., Doolittle, J., & Bradley, R. (2007). Professional development, capacity building, and research needs: Critical issues for response to intervention implementation. *School Psychology Review, 36,* 632–637.

Fixsen, D. L., & Blasé, K. (2009). Implementation: The missing link between research and practice. *Implementation Brief, 1.* Retrieved December 22, 2009, from *www.fpg.unc.edu/~nirn/resources/publications/NIRN_brief_1_2009.pdf.*

Fixsen, D. L., Blasé, K. A., Horner, R., & Sugai, G. (2009, February). Readiness for change: Scaling up brief 3. Retrieved December 22, 2009, from *www.fpg.unc.edu/~sisep/docs/SISEP_Brief_3_Readiness_2009.pdf.*

Fixsen, D. L., Naoom, S. F., Blasé, K., Friedman, R. M., & Wallace, F. (2005). *Implementation research: A synthesis of the literature* (FMHI Publication No. 231). Tampa: University of South Florida, Louis de la Parte Florida Mental Health Institute, National Implementation Research Network.

Fletcher, J. M., Coulter, W. A., Reschly, D. J., & Vaughn, S. (2004). Alternative approaches to the definition and identification of learning disabilities: Some questions and answers. *Annals of Dyslexia, 54,* 304–331.

Fuchs, L. S., & Fuchs, D. (2006). A framework for building capacity for responsiveness to intervention. *School Psychology Review, 35,* 621–626.

Gettinger, M., & Stoiber, K. (2007). Applying a response-to-intervention model for early literacy development in low-income children. *Topics in Early Childhood Special Education, 27,* 198–213.

Good, R. H., III, & Kaminski, R. A. (2002). *Dynamic Indicators of Basic Early Literacy Skills* (6th ed.). Eugene, OR: Institute for the Development of Educational Achievement.

Guldbrandsson, K. (2008). From news to everyday use: The difficult art of implementation. Östersund, Sweden: Swedish National Institute of Public Health. Retrieved March 22, 2010, from *www.fhi.se/PageFiles/3396/R200809_implementering_eng0805.pdf.*

Johnson, E., Mellard, D. F., Fuchs, D., & McKnight, M. A. (2006). *Responsiveness to intervention (RTI): How to do it*. Lawrence, KS: National Research Center on Learning Disabilities.

Kaiser, L., Rosenfield, S., & Gravois, T. (2009). Teachers' perception of satisfaction, skill development, and skill application after instructional consultation services. *Journal of Learning Disabilities, 42*, 444–457.

Klinger, J. K., & Edwards, P. A. (2006). Cultural considerations with response to intervention models. *Reading Research Quarterly, 41*, 108–117.

Kratochwill, T. R., Volpiansky, P., Clements, M., & Ball, C. (2007). Professional development in implementing and sustaining multitier prevention models: Implications for response to intervention. *School Psychology Review, 36*, 618–631.

Mercier-Smith, J. L., Fien, H., Basaraba, D., & Travers, P. (2009). Planning, evaluating, and improving tiers of support in beginning reading. *Teaching Exceptional Children, 41*, 16–22.

National Association of State Directors of Special Education. (2008a). *Response to intervention: Blueprints for implementation* (District Level). Alexandria, VA: National Association of State Directors of Special Education.

National Association of State Directors of Special Education. (2008b). *Response to intervention: Blueprints for implementation* (School Level). Alexandria, VA: National Association of State Directors of Special Education.

National Reading Panel. (2000). Teaching children to read: Report of the National Reading Panel. Retrieved April 1, 2010, from *www.nichd.nih.gov/publications/nrp/smallbook.pdf*.

O'Connor, R. E., Notari-Syverson, A., & Vadasy, P. F. (2005). *Ladders to literacy: A kindergarten activity book* (2nd ed.). Baltimore: Brookes.

Olson, S. C., Daly, E. J., III, Andersen, M., Turner, A., & LeClair, C. (2007). Assessing student response to intervention. In S. R. Jimerson, M. K. Burns, & A. M. VanDerHeyden (Eds.), *Response to intervention: The science and practice of assessment and intervention* (pp. 117–129). New York: Springer.

Pressley, M., Hilden, K., & Shankland, R. (2005). *An evaluation of end-grade-3 Dynamic Indicators of Basic Early Literacy Skills (DIBELS): Speed reading without comprehension, predicting little* (Technical Report). East Lansing: Michigan State University, Literacy Achievement Research Center.

Samuels, S. J. (2007). The DIBELS tests: Is speed of barking at print what we mean by reading fluency? *Reading Research Quarterly, 42*, 563–567.

Success for All Foundation. (2005–2006). *Pennsylvania Reading* (2nd ed.). Baltimore: Author.

U.S. Department of Education Institute of Education Sciences. (2008, September). Houghton-Mifflin Reading. Retrieved March 22, 2010, from *www.ies.ed.gov/ncee/wwc/reports/beginning-reading/houghton/index.asp*.

Walker-Dalhouse, D., Risko, V. J., Esworthy, C., Grasley, E., Kaisler, G., McIlvain, D., et al. (2009). Crossing boundaries and initiating conversations about RTI: Understanding and applying differentiated classroom instruction. *Reading Teacher, 63*, 84–87.

CHAPTER 4

Student Achievement Outcomes

Nathan H. Clemens
Edward S. Shapiro
Alexandra Hilt-Panahon
Karen L. Gischlar

Response to intervention (RTI) is considered to have two key purposes: (1) to provide a system of prevention and intervention to improve student academic skills or behavior and (2) as an alternative approach for identifying students with disabilities (Fletcher & Vaughn, 2009; Fuchs & Deschler, 2007). Although the ideas behind RTI are not new (e.g., screening to identify at-risk students, progress monitoring, delivery of research-supported interventions, among others), schoolwide and widespread implementation of RTI is still in its infancy.

The literature base of studies reporting outcomes of RTI implementation is growing rapidly, and published evaluations of RTI implementation have varied with regard to the data reported to reflect outcomes of the RTI process. For example, Bollman, Silberglitt, and Gibbons (2007) evaluated RTI outcomes with regard to increases in student achievement and reduction of the incidence of learning disabilities. VanDerHeyden, Witt, and Gilbertson (2007) evaluated the outcomes of an RTI model with regard to changes in rates of referrals for special education evaluations, percentage of students who qualified for services, and other factors related to special education identification. Peterson, Prasse, Shinn, and Swerdlik (2007) evaluated an RTI model along a range of outcome indices, including student achievement, delivery of special education services, referral and eligibility evaluations, and teacher and parent satisfaction with the model.

Shapiro and Clemens (2009) proposed a set of indicators that could be used to evaluate the impact and outcomes of RTI implementation. Several of the indicators were designed for use shortly after implementation of the RTI model to gather preliminary data on effectiveness. These indicators included the percentage of students identified for each tier across benchmark assessments, rates of improvement of students between benchmark assessments, the degree to which students "moved" to more or less intensive tiers between benchmark periods, rates of improvement on progress monitoring (PM) within tiers compared with targeted growth rates, and the percentage of students referred for evaluations who actually qualified for services. Because the key purposes of RTI are broad and could potentially involve a host of indices on which to evaluate the impact of RTI, investigations will likely continue to vary with regard to the outcomes reported.

As a system of prevention and intervention, improvement in achievement for all students within a school system represents one of the most important potential outcomes associated with RTI. Improvements to instruction, as well as the ways in which students at risk for failure are identified and provided with targeted intervention, form the basis on which other outcomes, such as reductions in the rates of referrals to special education, would occur. Indeed, one should not expect a great deal of change in referrals and identification of students with the most intense levels of problems if the foundation and instruction for *all* students has not been improved first. Thus changes in student achievement may arguably be the most important initial outcome observed following the implementation of an RTI model.

The purpose of this chapter is to provide a preliminary overview of some of the outcomes in student achievement observed through the implementation of the Project MP3 RTI model in Pennsylvania. Specifically, the data presented in this chapter describe differences or changes in student reading achievement observed following the implementation of the model and over the course of several years of implementation. In evaluating the data, the following broad outcome evaluation question guiding the analyses was used: *Does the implementation of an RTI model result in increased student achievement in reading, and does longer implementation (i.e., longer student exposure to the model) result in better outcomes?*

The RTI model being described here was implemented in kindergarten through fifth grade across a 3-year period. Space does not allow an examination of student reading outcomes across all of the grades in which the model was applied. Instead, data analyses presented in this section were limited to third grade in order to focus evaluation on a select grade level. Third grade was selected for several reasons. First, given the setup of the project and the assessments collected by the school district, key data sources were available for third graders; among those, two measures were selected for analyses in this chapter: (1) the Pennsylvania System of School Assessment (PSSA) and (2) Oral Reading Fluency (ORF) from the Dynamic Indicators of Basic Early Literacy Skills (DIBELS; Good & Kaminski, 2002). The PSSA is the state-mandated high-stakes assessment and is administered starting in third grade, thus providing an indicator of overall reading achievement. ORF data were selected for these analyses to provide an index of basic skills in passage-reading fluency. Additionally, because ORF was administered at the fall, winter, and spring benchmark assessments beginning in the winter of first grade, it provided a measure that could be used to evaluate rates of improvement over time.

Second, using third grade as the grade of analysis provided the opportunity to evaluate the cumulative impact of the RTI model following consecutive years of implementation. Making comparisons across cohorts of students with regard to their achievement in third grade afforded the opportunity to compare the achievement of students who had experienced between 1 and 3 years of the RTI model. One might expect students who received consecutive years of tiered instruction to demonstrate higher achievement than students who received tiered instruction for shorter periods.

It is acknowledged that a main thrust of RTI is to prevent academic skills problems through early identification and intervention. Early intervention is almost always recommended, especially for reading problems, as evidence indicates that the impact of reading interventions declines after first grade (National Reading Panel, 2000). Studies of RTI processes have often utilized populations in kindergarten and first grade (e.g., McMaster, Fuchs, Fuchs, & Compton, 2005; Simmons et al., 2008; Vellutino, Scanlon, Zhang, & Schatschneider, 2008). Therefore, one would expect that the greatest improvements might be observed in early grades, before skills problems become more entrenched. Although our use of third grade as the evaluation point might suppress intervention effects that might be observed, we were interested in the potential for end-of-third-grade achievement to summarize how students had acquired skills from kindergarten through third grade, to provide an indication of performance at a critical time when students are typically administered high-stakes tests, and to show how exposure to tiered instruction affected achievement levels observed at the end of third grade.

MEASURES

DIBELS ORF

ORF (Good & Kaminski, 2002) is a curriculum-based measure (CBM) of oral reading. Each ORF probe consists of a passage of text aligned to grade-level difficulty. The analyses described here utilized ORF data collected in the fall, winter, and spring of the school year. Each benchmark assessment involved the administration of three ORF probes with students on an individual basis, each timed for 1 minute, from the standard set of DIBELS Sixth Edition benchmark assessment materials (Good & Kaminski, 2002). A median score of words read correctly per minute was derived from the three probes. The ORF passages have demonstrated a median alternate-form reliability of .94 (Good, Kaminski, Smith, & Bratten, 2001). CBM ORF holds an extensive history of demonstrating validity in reflecting overall reading achievement (e.g., Reschly, Busch, Betts, Deno, & Long, 2009; Shinn, Good, Knutson, Tilly, & Collins, 1992).

Pennsylvania System of School Assessment

The PSSA is a criterion-referenced standards assessment for the state of Pennsylvania. The test is administered for reading and math starting in third grade and provides, in addition to scaled scores, the level of proficiency attained by the student in the academic area. According to these levels, students scoring within the "Proficient" or "Advanced" levels would be considered to have met the standard, and students scoring within the "Basic" or "Below Basic" levels would be considered below standard. The analyses described here used third-grade student scaled scores from the total reading battery of the PSSA, as well as level of proficiency. The technical information available indicated that the reading form of the third-grade PSSA had an overall reliability coefficient (Cronbach's alpha) of .91 (Data Recognition Corporation [DRC], 2008). A modified bookmark procedure was used to establish the performance cut points for PSSA (DRC, 2008). The performance levels set for the third-grade reading PSSA test were as follows: Advanced/Proficient = 1235 or above standard score; Basic = 1168 to 1234 standard score; Below Basic = < 1168 standard score (DRC, 2008). Successful performance on the PSSA is considered as Proficient or above.

INTERVENTION FIDELITY

The degree to which the Tier 2 and Tier 3 interventions were implemented with fidelity was measured across the course of the project implementation. Intervention fidelity data were collected via direct observation by university support staff, which at that time included three of us (N. H. C., A. H. P., K. L. G.). Observations were conducted during the fall and spring semesters. Data were collected using checklists consisting of important steps or characteristics in the implementation of the intervention. Several of the packaged interventions provided fidelity checklists with the materials, and these were used whenever possible. Intervention fidelity was summarized as the percentage of steps completed. Data indicated that intervention fidelity was high across the years of implementation. Following the fidelity observations, verbal and written feedback were provided to all teachers regarding their implementation. The average fidelity score across schools, grades, and intervention groups was 98% for the 2006–2007 school year (school A only), 93% for the 2007–2008 school year (all schools), and 94% for the 2008–2009 school year (all schools). Follow-up consultation was provided to teachers for whom fidelity was below 85%.

ANALYSIS FRAMEWORK

The data presented in this section primarily compared third-grade student achievement across schools and cohorts. Descriptive data are presented to examine trends within schools, particularly changes in performance across cohorts *within* schools, not between schools. In most cases, data were available for a 4-year period, from the 2005 school year through the 2008 school year, allowing the comparison of scores across several cohorts of third-grade students. This provided the opportunity to examine changes in student achievement as a function of RTI implementation over time. Longer implementation of RTI in a school means that students will receive tiered instruction beginning at an earlier age and for longer periods of time. In the case of the MP3 model, RTI was not implemented in any of the schools during the 2005 school year. The RTI model was introduced to School A at the beginning of the 2006 school year, and data were available for the subsequent 2 school years (2007, 2008). RTI was implemented in Schools B and C starting in the 2007 school year, and data were available for the following school year. The delay in implementation for Schools B and C meant that the 2006 school year could be used as a pretreatment comparison. Table 4.1 summarizes the implementation of the RTI model in the three schools.

The analyses did not include spring ORF scores for the 2005 cohort in Schools B and C. Project MP3 research staff were less directly involved in training staff and coordinating the data collection at these schools dur-

TABLE 4.1. RTI Implementation Schedule for Project MP3 Schools

	School year			
	2005	2006	2007	2008
School A		X	X	X
School B			X	X
School C			X	X

Note. X indicates that the RTI model was being implemented during that school year.

ing this year, and due to concerns about the reliability of the data, ORF data for the 2005 cohort were excluded from this and subsequent analyses. PSSA data from the 2005 cohort, on the other hand, were included across all three schools because the standardized nature of the assessment and the controls that schools must adhere to when administering the measure provided confidence in the reliability of the data.

If tiered instruction is indeed effective in preventing academic problems and improving achievement for all students, one would expect that students in later cohorts, who were exposed to tiered instruction for longer periods of time starting in earlier grades, would demonstrate greater achievement over students from earlier cohorts, who were exposed to tiered instruction for less time. This method of comparison was used in the analyses described subsequently. Patterns of student achievement and growth over time were examined with regard to the changes in achievement following RTI implementation and after longer implementation of RTI, as well as whether these changes were observed across schools. Students who moved in or out of the schools during the course of the project were not included in the analyses because they would not have experienced tiered instruction for the same amount of time as other students who had been at the school from the start of implementation.

RESULTS

ORF Data

Table 4.2 displays descriptive statistics for third-grade spring ORF and PSSA scores observed across schools and cohorts. Figure 4.1 displays these data in box plots, permitting examination of changes in the score distributions over time. For ORF scores, a modest increasing trend is observed following RTI implementation for Schools B and C, whereas an increasing trend is not evident for School A. Of interest is the change in the lower percentiles over time, particularly for Schools B and C. In the box plots, the lower edge of the shaded rectangle represents the 25th percentile for the distribution, and the bottom tail of the lower whisker represents the 10th percentile. A tighter distribution in the data is also observed in later cohorts for Schools B and C. Students at the lower end of the distribution would most likely be those students receiving Tier 2 and 3 interventions. Therefore, increasing trends observed at these percentiles provide an indication of increasing scores at lower ends of the distribution, a preliminary indicator of possible success of tiered instruction.

This pattern is confirmed by the data in Figure 4.2, which displays the percentage of students scoring within the "Low Risk" and "At-Risk" levels on spring ORF. According to DIBELS benchmark targets, students reading 110 or more words correctly per minute at the end of third grade are

TABLE 4.2. Means and Standard Deviations for Third-Grade Spring ORF and PSSA Scores by School across Cohorts

		Cohort							
		2005		2006		2007		2008	
		M	SD	M	SD	M	SD	M	SD
School A	Spring ORF	114.56	34.80	86.86	36.67	111.03	38.82	104.75	33.01
	PSSA Scale Score	1357.15	211.89	1270.41	157.42	1318.69	148.55	1301.84	111.55
School B	Spring ORF			102.68	29.69	113.53	38.53	118.12	26.29
	PSSA Scale Score	1304.51	189.76	1314.32	114.30	1291.87	136.14	1324.88	102.83
School C	Spring ORF			97.76	36.41	109.61	36.79	110.23	29.68
	PSSA Scale Score	1305.57	191.79	1316.59	144.62	1361.37	109.39	1339.94	123.07

Note. The dashed line indicates RTI implementation; data to the left of the dashed line were collected during year(s) in which RTI model was not in place; data to right of dashed line were collected during years in which RTI model was in place.

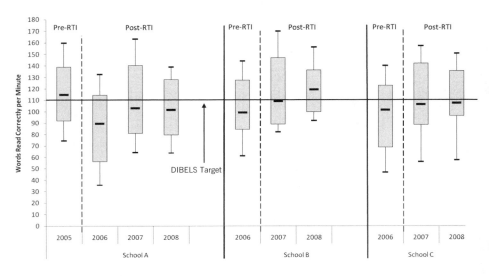

FIGURE 4.1. Box plots of third-grade spring ORF scores by school and cohort. Bottom tail of the lower whisker represents the 10th percentile. Rectangle represents the 25th to 75th percentiles. Bold line within rectangle represents the 50th percentile. Top tail of upper whisker represents the 90th percentile. Horizontal line indicates the DIBELS benchmark target for the spring of third grade (110). Dashed lines indicate when RTI model was implemented. Later cohorts were exposed to the RTI model for longer periods of time, starting in earlier grades.

considered likely to meet benchmark ORF targets in fourth grade and to be at *low risk* of future reading failure. Students reading fewer than 80 words in the spring of third grade would be considered *at risk* of failing to meet benchmark targets the following year. The remainder of students (reading between 80 and 109 words) are considered to be at *some risk* of failing to meet future reading targets. These risk levels are designed as instructional recommendations, and in our model they served as preliminary guides for the placement of students into intervention tiers (e.g., *low risk* suggested Tier 1 placement, *some risk* suggested Tier 2 placement, and so on). In addition to DIBELS data, intervention placement decisions included other data sources, such as 4Sight Benchmark Assessments (successforall.org), AIMSweb CBM Maze (*www.aimsweb.com*), and teacher judgment. Thus actual student tier placement was often consistent with the DIBELS instructional recommendations but was not strictly dictated as such. As evident in Figures 4.1 and 4.2, increases in average ORF scores across cohorts for Schools B and C were associated with an increasing percentage of students achieving the spring benchmark target (i.e., low risk) across cohorts and with a decreasing percentage of students classified as at risk across implementation years. This trend was not observed for School A, however, which

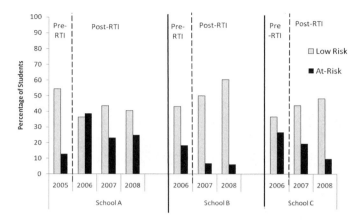

FIGURE 4.2. Percentage of third-grade students scoring within "Low Risk" and "At-Risk" levels on spring ORF. Dashed lines indicate when RTI model was implemented. Later cohorts were exposed to the RTI model for longer periods of time, starting in earlier grades.

is not surprising given the lack of positive change observed in average scores over time.

PSSA Data

Figure 4.3 displays box plots of third-grade standard scores on the PSSA test across schools and cohorts. Similar to changes in ORF data, cohorts in Schools B and C generally demonstrated higher scores following RTI implementation over previous cohorts at the same school. This trend is not evident for School A.

Data that are perhaps more relevant to schools concerned about making adequate yearly progress are the percentage of students who score within proficient levels on the test. The percentages of students scoring within proficient or advanced levels on the PSSA are summarized in Figure 4.4. For Schools B and C, in general, higher percentages of students met proficiency for cohorts following RTI implementation (2007 and 2008 cohorts).

Evidence of Effectiveness of Tiered Instruction

Rate of Improvement within Tiers

An assumption in implementing increasingly intensive interventions for students at risk is that students will demonstrate faster rates of growth over typical instruction without the supplemental intervention layers. One index for evaluating whether tiered intervention has resulted in the desired effect

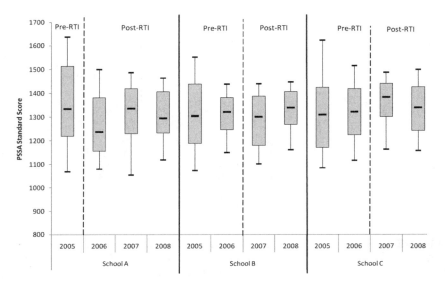

FIGURE 4.3. Boxplots depicting third-grade PSSA scores by school and cohort. Bottom tail of the lower whisker represents the 10th percentile. Rectangle represents the 25th to 75th percentiles. Line within rectangle represents the 50th percentile. Top tail of upper whisker represents the 90th percentile. Dashed lines indicate when RTI model was implemented. Later cohorts were exposed to the RTI model for longer periods of time, starting in earlier grades.

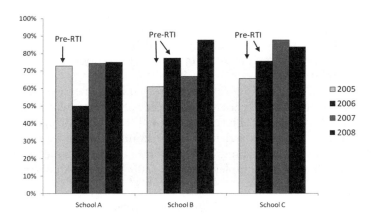

FIGURE 4.4. Percentage of third-grade students scoring "proficient" or above on the third-grade PSSA test across schools and cohorts.

of increased rates of growth is to evaluate rates of improvement demonstrated by students within each of the three tiers.

Figures 4.5, 4.6, and 4.7 display the average rates of improvement (ROI) on third-grade ORF between the fall and winter benchmark assessments according to the level at which students scored in the fall of the school year. ROI (calculated by subtracting the fall score from the winter score and dividing by the number of weeks between assessments, yielding number of words gained per week) can be compared across cohorts to indicate whether RTI implementation, or longer implementation of RTI over time, results in increased ROI in ORF. The fall-to-winter time period was selected because evidence indicates that estimates of within-semester (e.g., fall to winter or winter to spring) growth are more reliable than estimates of growth across the full year and that more growth is often observed across grade levels between fall and winter as opposed to between winter and spring (Ardoin & Christ, 2008). In addition, because intervention tier placement could change for students across a school year and because these changes often took place at the winter benchmark assessment, using growth from one semester increased the likelihood that students received intervention within a specific tier for that semester.

Figure 4.5 displays the average ROI for students who scored within the low-risk range in the fall of the school year. Across schools, an increasing trend was observed, such that ROI increased across cohorts. Examining Schools B and C in particular allows ROI comparisons between (1) cohorts

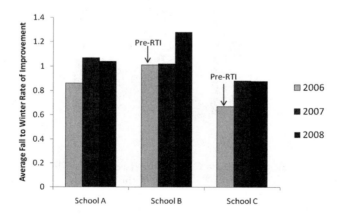

FIGURE 4.5. Average third-grade ORF ROI between fall and winter benchmarks for students scoring within low-risk range in the fall of the school year. ROI, rate of improvement. School A began RTI implementation in 2006, and Schools B and C began RTI implementation in 2007. Later cohorts were exposed to the RTI model for longer periods of time, starting in earlier grades.

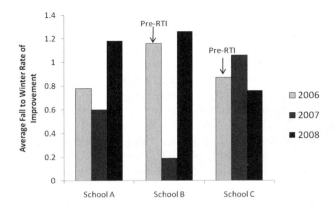

FIGURE 4.6. Average third-grade ORF ROI between fall and winter benchmarks for students scoring within the some-risk range in the fall. ROI, rate of improvement. School A began RTI implementation in 2006, and Schools B and C began RTI implementation in 2007. Later cohorts were exposed to the RTI model for longer periods of time, starting in earlier grades.

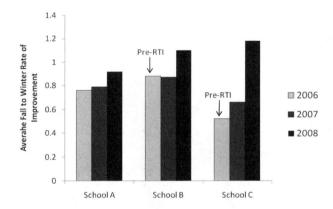

FIGURE 4.7. Average third-grade ORF ROI between fall and winter benchmarks for students scoring within the at-risk range in the fall. ROI, rate of improvement. School A began RTI implementation in 2006, and Schools B and C began RTI implementation in 2007. Later cohorts were exposed to the RTI model for longer periods of time, starting in earlier grades.

that did not receive tiered instruction (2006 cohort), (2) the cohort that received tiered instruction during their third-grade year (2007 cohort), and (3) the cohort that received tiered instruction across both their second- and third-grade years (2008 cohort). Highest ROI was observed for the 2008 cohort, for School B. This pattern is encouraging because it suggests that rates of growth did not suffer for students who were likely not to receive more intensive Tier 2 or Tier 3 intervention and, in fact, showed increased ROI following implementation of RTI. Under the MP3 model, students in Tier 1 engaged in reading enrichment activities while their lower achieving peers received Tier 2 and Tier 3 interventions.

Figure 4.6 displays the average fall-to-winter ORF ROI for students who scored within the some-risk level at the start of third grade. For these students, no clear pattern emerges across schools or cohorts. The students from the 2008 cohort in School A (during the third year of RTI implementation at this school) demonstrated the highest ROI compared with previous cohorts in the same school. Schools B and C demonstrated inverse patterns of each other, such that ROI during the first year (2006 cohort, pre-RTI) was nearly the same as the 2008 cohort (following two years of RTI). These results may suggest that the interventions provided to the students within this skill category were not intensive enough to result in increased ROI over time.

Figure 4.7 displays the average fall-to-winter ORF ROI for students who scored within the at-risk level in the fall. These students would be in need of the most intensive level of interventions. The data indicate an increasing trend across cohorts for all three schools, with the 2008 cohort (students who received tiered instruction the longest) demonstrating the highest ROI. Of interest is the 2008 cohort in School C, which demonstrated an average ROI that was more than double the ROI observed for the 2006 cohort (pre-RTI). In general, the data suggest that interventions implemented for students within this category, which were usually Tier 3 interventions during RTI implementation years, were successful in increasing ORF ROI between the fall and winter benchmark periods.

Cumulative Impact of Tiered Instruction?

A compelling question under RTI pertains to whether longer implementation of tiered instruction has a cumulative impact (i.e., a "snowball effect") on student achievement over the long term. In other words, if RTI is implemented at earlier ages, and if students receive tiered instruction across consecutive grade levels, would increasingly higher levels of achievement be observed over time? Although examining ROI can provide information toward answering this question, level (i.e., scores from one point in time) must be considered as well. The analyses presented in Figures 4.8 and 4.9 attempted to provide a preliminary evaluation of this question.

Figures 4.8 and 4.9 display the average ORF scores between second and third grades for students who scored within the some-risk (Figure 4.8) and at-risk (Figure 4.9) levels in the fall of second grade. In the interest of clarity, only data from Schools B and C are presented because the RTI model was implemented at the same time in both schools. Two cohorts were contrasted: students who were enrolled in third grade in the 2007 school year and students enrolled in the third grade during the 2008 school year. RTI was implemented in these schools during the 2007 school year. Therefore, students in the 2007 cohort in Schools B and C would have received tiered instruction in third grade *only*. Students in the 2008 cohort in these schools would have received tiered instruction in both second *and* third grades. If cumulative years of tiered instruction lead to higher achievement over time, one would expect the 2008 cohort, having received more years of RTI, to demonstrate higher levels of achievement over the 2007 cohort.

In general, the data displayed in Figures 4.8 and 4.9 are consistent with this hypothesis. The cohorts generally start second grade at similar mean levels across the two schools. Across second and third grades, however, some separation in scores is apparent. In general, students in the 2008 cohort finished second grade, started third grade, and finished third grade at higher levels than the previous cohort. As in previous analyses, these data can be taken as preliminary evidence of the effectiveness of tiered

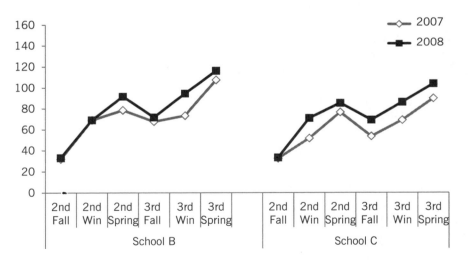

FIGURE 4.8. Mean ORF scores by cohort between second and third grade for students scoring within the some-risk level in the fall of second grade. Schools B and C began RTI implementation in 2007. Therefore, the 2007 cohort was exposed to RTI during third grade only, and the 2008 cohort was exposed to RTI during 2007 and 2008.

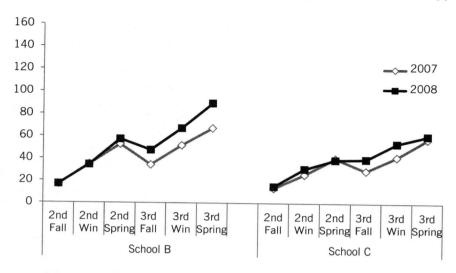

FIGURE 4.9. Mean ORF scores by cohort between second and third grade for students scoring within the at-risk level in the fall of second grade. Schools B and C began RTI implementation in 2007. Therefore, the 2007 cohort was exposed to RTI during third grade only, and the 2008 cohort was exposed to RTI during 2007 and 2008.

instruction and are suggestive of a potential cumulative effect of long-term implementation of RTI.

Summary of Student Achievement Outcomes

This outcome domain examined changes in student achievement following implementation of the RTI model. In examining the data for third-grade students across the schools, of primary interest was whether increased student achievement was observed as a function of RTI implementation and whether student achievement increased if students were exposed to tiered instruction for longer periods of time. In general, the data are suggestive of positive increases in student achievement, although the results are mixed between schools. For Schools B and C, modest increasing trends were observed for spring ORF scores following RTI implementation, as well as an increasing percentage of students achieving DIBELS spring benchmark goals (i.e., low risk) with a corresponding decrease in the percentage of students falling within the at-risk range. Although changes in PSSA scores were more subtle, a slight increasing trend was observed with regard to the percentage of students achieving proficiency on the test. These patterns were generally not observed for School A, in which student achievement gains appeared to be more variable, without an apparent trend in a positive direction. Possible reasons for these differences between schools are discussed later.

Interesting patterns were observed across schools when examining fall-to-winter rates of improvement on the ORF measure (Figures 4.5, 4.6, and 4.7). For students who scored within low-risk (Figure 4.5) and at-risk (Figure 4.7) levels in the fall of the third grade, rates of improvement tended to increase across years of implementation, as well as following introduction of the RTI model (Schools B and C). These results are important because they suggest that (1) the increasing trend in rates of growth for students with the lowest ORF scores in the fall—those who would generally be considered for the more intensive levels of interventions within a three-tiered approach—suggests that instruction delivered across this time frame was effective in increasing rates of growth for students over time, and (2) introduction of a model of tiered instruction did not appear to have a negative impact on the rates of growth for students who would not typically receive these additional supports (i.e., Tier 1 students). Both outcomes are important for RTI implementation.

Changes in rates of growth for students with ORF scores within the some-risk level in the fall, on the other hand, were more variable (Figure 4.6), with no clear pattern of increasing growth. These data may suggest that the interventions or groups implemented in this tier may not have effectively addressed these students' skill deficits.

Perhaps more telling when examining changes in rates of growth for students falling within risk levels in the fall is to consider the comparison mean scores at benchmark data collection points across two separate cohorts of students followed from second to third grade. As shown in Figures 4.8 and 4.9, exposure to tiered instruction across 2 full years, during both second and third grades (see 2008 cohort in Figures 4.8 and 4.9), tended to be associated with higher rates of growth and higher mean scores at benchmark periods over students who were exposed to tiered intervention during third grade only (see 2007 cohort in Figures 4.8 and 4.9). Of particular interest is that this effect was replicated across two schools. These data provide preliminary evidence of a "snowball" effect of RTI, such that longer exposure to targeted interventions may result in increased rates of growth and higher average scores, two elements critical for students who must close the gap between their performance and that of their typically performing peers.

Although we can only speculate, there are several possible reasons why students in School A did not demonstrate positive trends in student achievement over the course of RTI implementation. Anecdotal evidence suggests that leadership at the building level, training, cohort-specific differences, and teacher abilities and attitudes may have affected outcomes for students at School A. A detailed discussion of these points is provided next.

GENERAL SUMMARY

The aim of this chapter was to summarize preliminary data investigating outcomes of the MP3 RTI implementation. The analyses focused on outcome domains specific to student achievement, intervention implementation, and patterns of referral and eligibility evaluation decisions.

Data suggested improved student achievement for third-grade students following RTI implementation in two out of the three schools. In the two schools that demonstrated improvements (Schools B and C), the following trends were observed across school years: (1) increasing mean scores on year-end ORF, (2) an increasing number of students with ORF scores within the low-risk range and a corresponding decrease in the number of students with ORF scores within the at-risk range, (3) increasing rate of improvement in fall-to-winter ORF for students in the at-risk range in the fall of third grade (with stable rates of improvement for students in the low-risk range), and (4) an increasing number of students scoring within the proficient range on the third-grade PSSA. These data are preliminary and descriptive, and we are currently analyzing the data more thoroughly. But the observed trends provide encouraging evidence that implementation of tiered instruction should result in reducing the number of students at risk for academic failure in later grades and in improved student achievement overall.

The absence of these positive trends observed for School A points to important factors in the implementation of RTI. Anecdotal information suggests that critical features of RTI extend beyond effective interventions, universal screening, and PM. First, building leadership appeared to play an important role in the impact of the model. The principal at this school had a leadership style that was self-described as "collaborative." This translated to teachers having a great deal of power in the decision-making process related to RTI implementation. Although it is important for staff to have ownership of the development of the model, there were many times in the first year of implementation when decisions made related to RTI implementation were ignored, changed, or discarded due to staff protest. In other words, if teachers did not want to do something, it was not implemented, regardless of the potential positive outcomes for students. For example, it was suggested at the beginning of the first year of implementation that skill group time be increased for the third grade due to high levels of students in tiers 2 and 3 following fall benchmark screening. Despite evidence for the need for increased support, this additional intervention time was not implemented because of teacher protest.

Another factor that may have had a significant impact on the outcomes for students at School A was the effect of individual cohort differences. Specifically, the 2006 third-grade cohort at School A began third grade an average of 30 words below benchmark. Evidence of the lower achievement of this cohort relative to others can be observed in Figures 4.2–4.4. This cohort as a whole was significantly behind and therefore needed greater gains than their peers. However, the low achievement by this cohort does not explain the persistent lack of gains observed with subsequent cohorts under RTI. Instead, the persistent lack of improved achievement observed in School A may be indicative of inadequate reading instruction in kindergarten through second grade, instruction that resulted in students who were less well prepared for the challenges of third-grade reading material and test content.

The training and skills of the teachers at School A may have played a role in suppressing intervention effects. Specifically, training for School A was less intensive and was provided closer to the start of implementation than it was for Schools B and C. Although it was believed at the time that the training provided was adequate, anecdotal reports from the teachers at the end of the first year indicated that they did not feel as prepared as they would have liked prior to the start of implementation. As a result of this feedback, training for Schools B and C was conducted the year prior to implementation, and all teachers were provided with additional supports as needed. This additional training likely influenced the impact of intervention.

Finally, the attitudes of the staff related to implementing RTI may have had a significant impact on intervention effects. Anecdotal evidence indicated that there had been a long history at School A of teachers making decisions independently, and systemic change did not often occur. Given the radical change that was necessary related to instructional practices, teaming, and scheduling, not all teachers were supportive of RTI in the initial stages of implementation. This lack of support likely had a significant impact on how teachers delivered intervention and how RTI was adopted within the school. Although we saw some resistance at all three schools when RTI was initially implemented, the level of discontent at School A was substantially greater than at the other two schools. It should be noted that once teachers began to see positive effects for individual students, RTI was more accepted within the school. Despite this, the extent of impact the initial resistance may have had on outcomes for students at School A is unclear.

UNANSWERED QUESTIONS

As this was only a preliminary investigation, several unanswered questions remain. First, conclusions regarding the magnitude of achievement improvement should be considered tentative because student gains were assessed based on trends in descriptive data, not statistical analyses. The analyses of ORF growth between benchmark assessments must be considered in light of evidence indicating a lack of equivalence across some of the DIBELS ORF passages (Francis et al., 2008). Additionally, without experimental control, conclusions regarding the causal impact of the RTI model on achievement are speculative. For example, improvements in PSSA test scores may have been more related to teachers getting better at teaching to the test than to effects of the tiered intervention model. More well-controlled studies should be better able to determine the causal role of an RTI model in improving achievement.

The second unanswered question relates to the fact that the analyses described in this chapter were limited to third grade. We chose third grade because of its importance for schools in high-stakes testing and accountability, but in the relatively brief time frame under investigation, the effects on student achievement were likely less evident at third grade than at kindergarten, first, or second grades. We are currently undertaking analyses investigating effects of RTI at younger grades. Preliminary findings indicate a greater impact on student achievement in kindergarten and first grades (Shapiro et al., 2010), consistent with research indicating that reading intervention is most effective when it is implemented prior to second grade (National Reading Panel, 2000). Future research should continue to investigate which interventions are associated with the greatest improvements, as well as other teacher or instructional factors that influence student growth.

Third, we provided only anecdotal evidence for the lack of gains in student achievement observed in School A compared with Schools B and C, and our conclusions on why this occurred were speculative. Future research might investigate systemic factors related to leadership and systemic change processes as critical factors in improving student achievement even when tiered instruction is in place. As described by Fixsen, Naoom, Blasé, Friedman, and Wallace (2005), implementation consists of coordinated change at system, organization, program, and practice levels. Research has shown that in order for implementation of large-scale system change to be effective, several factors must first be in place: (1) The practitioners who carry out the change must be carefully selected and undergo comprehensive training, coaching, and performance feedback; (2) the organization (e.g., school, agency) must provide the means for training, coaching, and feedback to occur; (3) practitioners and consumers must be fully involved in the process of developing and implementing change; and (4) implementation and sustainability of programs must be supported through policies, regulations, and funding at the state and federal levels. There was anecdotal evidence to suggest that all of these variables played an important role in implementation outcomes. Future research might evaluate these factors more systematically.

Fourth, this 3-year period (with RTI in place for only 2 years in two of the three schools) was a relatively brief time frame from which to evaluate outcomes. Additionally, university involvement was present for the years described in this chapter. We plan to continue to analyze data from these schools in subsequent years to examine long-term changes and whether outcomes observed were sustained after university support ended. Other research should continue to collect data well beyond the initial implementation of RTI in investigating sustained effects of tiered instruction.

Finally, the analysis described in this chapter examined primarily the changes that occurred between benchmark periods on the measures collected as universal screening measures (the DIBELS ORF measure). Shapiro and Clemens (2009) describe several other indices that can be used to reflect impact of RTI models. Included are the nature of movement of students between tiers (how many students moved from Tiers 3 to 2 to 1 versus from 1 to 2 to 3), as well as the movement within tiers that is reflected through rates of improvement evident in PM. Given the effort at systemwide change in these schools, it is very possible that changes such as tier movement and changes within tiered intervention processes would reflect positive outcomes for the RTI model, including changes in school A, where universal screening data alone did not reflect strong changes. Given that we know RTI is a multiyear change process and that most researchers speak about a 3- to 5-year change process (e.g., Chard et al., 2008; Simmons et al., 2008), it is possible that changes in the desired direction were occurring at School A, albeit slower than desired and not entirely tapped by the approach to the data analysis reported here. Subsequent studies are under way to analyze the data using tier movement.

CONCLUSIONS

The data presented in this chapter should be encouraging for those interested in whether RTI can improve student outcomes. RTI is aimed at systemic changes and reforms to school processes, but improvement in student achievement can be viewed as a critical first indication of the impact of an RTI model. Other anticipated outcomes, such as reductions in the rates of students referred to special education or improvements in the referral process of students for eligibility evaluations, would be expected to follow subsequent to improvements to instruction and intervention overall. Although more work is needed, we feel as though the implementation of the RTI model in the schools described in this chapter resulted in positive effects in student achievement. Although RTI may be a relatively new term, it is in fact a collection of practices (e.g., early prevention and intervention, intervention aimed at specific skill deficits, empirically supported instruction, progress monitoring, data-based decision making) that have been known be effective for quite some time. With successful and effective implementation of these components, coupled with strong leadership and effective handling of the school system and change process, there is reason to think that improved outcomes for students can be achieved.

REFERENCES

Ardoin, S. P., & Christ, T. J. (2008). Evaluating curriculum-based measurement slope estimates using data from triannual universal screenings. *School Psychology Review, 37*, 109–125.

Bollman, K. A., Silberglitt, B., & Gibbons, K. A. (2007). The St. Croix River Educational District model: Incorporating systems-level organization and a multi-tiered problem-solving process for intervention delivery. In S. R. Jimerson, M. K. Burns, & A. M. VanDerHeyden (Eds.), *Handbook of response to intervention: The science and practice of assessment and intervention* (pp. 319–330). New York: Springer.

Chard, D. J., Stoolmiller, M., Harn, B. A., Wanzek, J., Vaughn, S., Linan-Thompson, S., et al. (2008). Predicting reading success in a multilevel schoolwide reading model: A retrospective analysis. *Journal of Learning Disabilities, 41*, 174–188.

Data Recognition Corporation. (2008). Technical report for the Pennsylvania System of School Assessment, 2007 Reading and Mathematics Grades 3, 4, 5, 6, 7, 8, and 11. Available at *www.portal.state.pa.us/portal/server.pt/community/technical_analysis/7447*.

Fixsen, D. L., Naoom, S. F., Blasé, K. A., Friedman, R. M., & Wallace, F. (2005). *Implementation research: A synthesis of the literature* (FMHI Publication No. 231). Tampa: University of South Florida, Louis de la Parte Florida Mental Health Institute, National Implementation Research Network.

Fletcher, J. M., & Vaughn, S. (2009). Response to intervention: Preventing and remediating academic difficulties. *Child Development Perspectives, 3*, 30–27.

Francis, D. J., Santi, K. L., Barr, C., Fletcher, J. M., Varisco, A., & Foorman, B. R. (2008). Form effects on the estimation of students' oral reading fluency using DIBELS. *Journal of School Psychology, 46*, 315–342.

Fuchs, D., & Deschler, D. D. (2007). What we need to know about responsiveness to intervention (and shouldn't be afraid to ask). *Learning Disabilities Research and Practice, 22*, 129–136.

Good, R. H., & Kaminski, R. A. (Eds.). (2002). Dynamic Indicators of Basic Early Literacy Skills (6th ed.). Eugene, OR: Institute for the Development of Educational Achievement. Available at *dibels.uoregon.edu*.

Good, R. H., Kaminski, R. A., Smith, S., & Bratten, J. (2001). *Technical adequacy of second grade DIBELS Oral Reading Fluency (D-ORF) passages* (Technical Report No. 8). Eugene, OR: University of Oregon.

McMaster, K. L., Fuchs, D., Fuchs, L. S., & Compton, D. L. (2005). Responding to nonresponders: An experimental field trial of identification and intervention methods. *Exceptional Children, 71*, 445–463.

National Reading Panel. (2000). *Teaching children to read: An evidence-based assessment of the scientific research literature on reading and its implications for reading instruction* (NIH Publication No. 00-4754). Washington, DC: U.S. Government Printing Office.

Peterson, D. W., Prasse, D. P., Shinn, M. R., & Swerdlik, M. E. (2007). The Illinois flexible service delivery model: A problem-solving model initiative. In S. R. Jimerson, M. K. Burns, & A. M. VanDerHeyden (Eds.), *Handbook of response to intervention: The science and practice of assessment and intervention* (pp. 300–318). New York: Springer.

Reschly, A. L., Busch, T. W., Betts, J., Deno, S. L., & Long, J. D. (2009). Curriculum-based measurement of oral reading as an indicator of reading achievement: A meta-analysis of the correlational evidence. *Journal of School Psychology, 47,* 427–469.

Shapiro, E. S., & Clemens, N. H. (2009). A conceptual model for evaluating systems effects of RTI. *Assessment for Effective Intervention, 35,* 3–16.

Shapiro, E. S., Clemens, N. H., Panahon, A. H., Gischlar, K. L., Devlin, K. T., & Bowles, S. A. (2010). *Outcomes of benchmark assessment across two years of RTI implementation in MP3 schools* (Technical Report No. 1). Bethlehem, PA: Lehigh University.

Shinn, M. R., Good, R. H., Knutson, N., Tilly, W. D., & Collins, V. L. (1992). Curriculum-based measurement of oral reading fluency: A confirmatory analysis of its relation to reading. *School Psychology Review, 21,* 459–479.

Simmons, D. C., Coyne, M. D., Kwok, O., McDonaugh, S., Harn, B. A., & Kame'enui, E. J. (2008). Indexing response to intervention: A longitudinal study of reading risk from kindergarten through third grade. *Journal of Learning Disabilities, 41,* 158–173.

VanDerHeyden, A. M., Witt, J. C., & Gilbertson, D. (2007). A multi-year evaluation of the effects of a response to intervention (RTI) model of identification of children for special education. *Journal of School Psychology, 45,* 225–256.

Vellutino, F. R., Scanlon, D. M., Zhang, H., & Schatschneider, C. (2008). Using response to kindergarten and first grade intervention to identify children at risk for long-term reading difficulties. *Reading and Writing, 21,* 437–480.

PART II

Implementing RTI in Low-Achieving, High-Need Schools

PROJECT MP3
AT THE UNIVERSITY OF PITTSBURGH

Introduction to Part II

The western Pennsylvania, University of Pittsburgh Project MP3 provided a unique opportunity to study the successes and challenges of implementing a PM model embedded within a response-to-intervention (RTI) framework for two reasons. First, while many school districts in Pennsylvania had already incorporated at least parts of this model within an RTI/PM initiative promoted by the Pennsylvania Department of Education, the school district selected for this model demonstration project had not. For the western Pennsylvania team, the 3-year model demonstration funding provided a unique opportunity to study a real-world adoption and application of the model from scratch. Second, the schools in which the project was housed were the lowest achieving elementary schools in the district, and the district faced enormous challenges: substantial proportions of minority students and students eligible for free or reduced-price lunch and an academic performance history indicating significant and persistent underachievement.

The MP3 model utilized by the University of Pittsburgh was embedded in a three-tiered framework for reading instruction, grades K–4. In Tier 1, all students were to be provided research-based grade-level reading instruction using the district adopted core curriculum and were to participate in universal screening three times per year as part of primary prevention. Supplemental Tier 2 intervention was to be provided for a subset of students who had not yet met grade-level benchmark goals, thereby demonstrating that Tier 1 core instruction alone was not sufficient for reading success. In Tier 2, students' reading skills were to be monitored at least twice per month. Tier 3 intervention was to be provided for a much smaller subset of students who were performing well below grade level and who appeared to need more intensive reading support. PM of these students' reading skills was to occur weekly. A standard protocol approach was implemented at both Tiers 2 and 3, in which an intervention teacher implemented a sequenced, scripted reading intervention to small groups of students homogeneously grouped according to screening results. Like most RTI models in the literature, this one was based on the premise that instructional group size would decrease and instructional intensity would increase as students "moved up" the three-tier pyramid in order to halt and reverse reading failure as quickly as possible. School-level data-based decision-making teams and grade-level teams of teachers met regularly (monthly and weekly, respectively) to review evidence of student progress in Tier 1, Tier 2, and/ or Tier 3 instruction and to recommend changes in grouping arrangements and instructional strategies.

In the University of Pittsburgh version of this RTI model, special education is not considered a separate tier. Given the state's strong commitment to inclusion, students with disabilities can receive specially designed reading instruction at any tier. However, students who are referred for special education services tend to have failed to adequately respond to either Tier 2 or Tier 3 interventions, or to both. Once referred, a multidisciplinary evaluation is conducted and eligibility for special education services determined. Students already eligible to receive special education and related services, as well as students newly placed in special education, still receive large-group grade-level Tier 1 core instruction. And they would still participate in instructional-level Tier 2 or Tier 3 interventions, with PM linked to their IEP goals.

CHAPTER 5

Context and Commitment

Amanda Kloo
Charles D. Machesky
Naomi Zigmond

In August 2006, a team of western and central Pennsylvania researchers launched Project MP3: Monitoring Progress of Pennsylvania Pupils, a model demonstration project funded through the U.S. Department of Education's Office of Special Education Programs to document and evaluate the implementation of a schoolwide progress monitoring (PM) model aimed at improving grades K–4 reading achievement and reducing unnecessary referrals to special education. Many school districts in Pennsylvania had already incorporated at least parts of this model within a response-to-intervention (RTI)/PM initiative promoted by the Pennsylvania Bureau of Special Education. For the western Pennsylvania team, the 3-year, model demonstration funding provided a unique opportunity to find a school district that had not yet adopted a PM framework and to study real-world adoption and application of the model from scratch.

The western Pennsylvania Project MP3 provided a unique opportunity to study the successes and challenges of implementing a PM model embedded within an RTI framework designed to improve K–4 reading achievement in struggling schools. In this chapter, we provide an overview of the context for model implementation in three of the district's low-achieving elementary schools. Next, we detail key administrative decisions that were fundamental to promoting systemwide school change. We highlight the necessary policy and practical innovations supported by the district's superintendent that helped to marry the lofty theoretical goals of RTI to the real-life burdens of capacity, resources, time, and school culture common to many low-performing districts across the country.

THE CONTEXT

The Model

The model was simple enough:

- Teach reading well the first time around.
- Monitor progress of all students several times each year to "catch" students falling behind.
- Provide daily interventions to students not making adequate progress within the core reading program; monitor progress of those students monthly.
- Provide even more intensive daily small-group interventions to students making minimal progress; monitor progress weekly for those students. Teach teachers to administer PM assessments, interpret data, and make instructional changes based on group and individual trends.

The model is based on a three-tiered framework for reading instruction for kindergarten through fourth grade (Reschley, 2005; Vaughn Gross Center for Reading and Language Arts, 2005).

Figure 5.1 provides a schematic of the MP3 model implemented in western Pennsylvania. In Tier 1, all students are provided research-based grade-level reading instruction, and all students are screened three times per year as part of primary prevention. Supplemental Tier 2 intervention is provided for the subset of students who have not yet met benchmark goals, thereby demonstrating that Tier 1 core instruction alone is not sufficient; those students' reading skills are monitored at least twice per month. Supplemental Tier 3 intervention is provided for a much smaller subset of students who are performing well below grade level and appear to need more intensive reading support. Like most RTI models in the literature, this one shows instructional group size decreasing and instructional intensity increasing as students' performance improves in order to halt and reverse reading failure as quickly as possible. In the Pennsylvania version of this RTI model, special education is not a separate tier. Given the state's strong commitment to inclusion, students with disabilities may receive specially designed reading instruction at any tier. Students who are referred for special education services tend to have failed to adequately respond to either Tier 2 or Tier 3 interventions, or to both. Once referred, a multidisciplinary evaluation is conducted and eligibility for special education services deter-

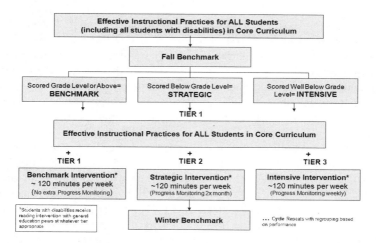

FIGURE 5.1. Schematic of MP3 progress monitoring model implemented in western Pennsylvania.

mined. In Pennsylvania, districts may choose to use an RTI approach to identify a specific learning disability (SLD) in lieu of an assessment to determine an ability–achievement discrepancy. Students already eligible to receive special education and related services, as well as students newly placed in special education, still receive large-group, inclusive, grade-level Tier 1 instruction. And they still participate in instructional-level Tier 2 or Tier 3 interventions, with PM linked to their IEP goals.

The implementation of this prevention-oriented policy initiative in three elementary schools in western Pennsylvania is the focus of this chapter. We describe the policy and practical decisions the district and the schools had to make to implement PM and RTI in a historically low-achieving school with a substantial population of students at risk for academic failure—characteristics that are common to many public schools across the nation.

The District[1]

There are 501 school districts in Pennsylvania. In searching for a school district in the western part of the state in which to implement Project MP3, several criteria were considered: The district had to have at least three elementary schools; its student population needed to include a substantial proportion of minority students and students eligible for free or reduced-price lunch; its performance history on the annual statewide accountability tests

---

[1]In this chapter and the two that follow, the name of the school district and the names of the three target schools in the district have all been replaced by pseudonyms.

had to indicate a pattern of significant underachievement; it could not be part of the state's Reading First initiative (in which PM and RTI-like activities were part of the implementation model); it could not have embraced the statewide training initiative to implement PM in special education and general education classrooms; and the superintendent had to be willing to commit the school district to a collaborative venture with university researchers. Alliance School District fit the bill (see Table 5.1 for demographic and achievement data for the Alliance School District). Alliance is a small school district with a kindergarten center, six elementary schools (two 1–8, two K–6, two K–5), one middle school (6–8), and one high school (9–12). The district superintendent saw Project MP3 as a useful way to accomplish needed schoolwide reforms and pledged "100% support of Project MP3, research-based reading instruction, and RTI practices." His relentless and very vocal support for systemwide changes in the district's reading program was a key factor in promoting administrator and faculty buy-in, fidelity of implementation, and sustainability of the model.

At early meetings with the superintendent in January 2006, he expressed concerns about the district's elementary-level reading program; his recent review of summative reading achievement data showed steady declines in scores over a 5-year period, particularly in third through fifth grades. Moreover, the percentage of students achieving proficiency on the state accountability assessment in reading varied widely across the six elementary schools in the district, from 87% of fifth graders scoring proficient or better in the top school to 13% of fifth graders scoring proficient or better in the bottom school. The superintendent volunteered the three lowest elementary schools to participate in Project MP3 across the 3-year implementation period. He hoped the project would help him build a stronger districtwide infrastructure to support systemwide instructional consistency, academic growth, and teacher expertise. He and his administrative team suggested that the project begin its work in the lowest achieving school, Larue Elementary, then introduce the model to the other two schools, Boyce Elementary and Washington Elementary, the following year and focus on sustainability and expansion in the final year of grant funding.

TABLE 5.1. Alliance School District 2006 Demographics and Achievement Data (Pre–RTI Implementation)

Enrollment	3,512
Minority	20%
% Receiving free/reduced-price lunch	53%
% Proficient on fourth-grade state test	55%
% Proficient on third-grade state test	56%

The three target schools shouldered many of the burdens common to public elementary schools across the country (Strizek, Pittsonberger, Riordan, Lyter, & Orlofsky, 2006). Teacher turnover was high, academic achievement was low, resources were limited, and morale was plummeting. Moreover, the teaching staffs had limited access to and scant familiarity with research-based reading instructional strategies and materials. In fact, interview and survey data collected at the three schools before model implementation revealed that *none* of the teachers had been exposed to or trained in the National Reading Panel's "5 Big Ideas" (National Institute of Child Health and Human Development [NICHD], 2000) of reading instruction. Nearly 80% of the teachers, and many of the central office staff members, had graduated from a local undergraduate teacher preparation program that was fiercely committed to a whole language–based approach to reading instruction. They sincerely believed that not only was it unnecessary to teach but also that they were prohibited from teaching phonics rules or explicit reading strategies because these practices conflicted with the whole-language ideologies of powerful district administrators. They believed that their students' deficient reading skills were inevitable, given the myriad of conditions over which teachers have no control (e.g., socioeconomic status, race, limited parental involvement, students' lack of motivation, behavior problems, poor attitude, cognitive deficits, etc.); teachers took no responsibility for the underachievement of their students and, in interviews, never mentioned instructional factors that they could manipulate as explanations. Moreover, only 20% of the teachers collected and systematically analyzed student achievement data to establish performance goals and inform their instruction. There were very few opportunities during the school day for classroom teachers to talk with one another either within a grade level or across grade levels. About 95% of teachers at Larue Elementary had been there fewer than 5 years, and 65% of Larue teachers were recent district hires. The majority of those new hires were openly looking for opportunities to transfer to other schools within the district or to neighboring "higher performing" districts as soon as vacancies arose.

Although the implementation context was not equally dismal at all three model demonstration sites, the data were strikingly similar and equally as concerning. The superintendent, building principals, and key district administrators agreed that an overhaul of the current reading instructional system was needed. They viewed Project MP3 as a useful and legitimizing resource for professional development and onsite support for the overhaul effort.

The Target Schools

Table 5.2 displays demographic and baseline reading achievement data on the Dynamic Indicators of Basic Early Literacy Skills (DIBELS; Good

TABLE 5.2. MP3 Model Demonstration Site Demographics and Achievement Data (Pre–RTI Implementation)

	Larue School (Grades 1–4)				Boyce School (Grades 1–4)				Washington School (Grades 1–4)			
Enrollment	252				236				173			
Minority	58%				9%				57%			
% Receiving free/reduced-price lunch	92%				54%				24%			
% Proficient/advanced on fourth-grade state test	21%				62%				57%			
% Proficient/advanced on third-grade state test	29%				54%				57%			
Grade	1	2	3	4	1	2	3	4	1	2	3	4
% Reaching grade-level ORF benchmarks on DIBELS	18%	10%	12%	2%	65%	28%	54%	8%	24%	43%	39%	11%
% Average/above average on Maze	—	21%	10%	13%	—	27%	15%	25%	—	27%	16%	13%

& Kaminski, 2002), the Reading Maze (Shinn & Shinn, 2002), and the Pennsylvania System of School Assessment (PSSA) Reading subtest for the three target elementary schools selected to participate in Project MP3. At Washington, fewer than 25% of first-grade students reached proficiency standards predictive of future reading success on the oral reading fluency (ORF) measure, and fewer than 50% of students at all subsequent grade levels met conventional end-of-year fluency benchmarks. Moreover, the percentage of students scoring in the average to above-average range on the Maze ranged from 13 to 27% across grades 1–4. Despite low scores on the screening measures, 78% of Washington's fourth graders met or exceeded state test reading proficiency thresholds on the end-of-year summative exam. Larue Elementary results showed fewer than 20% of students achieving at benchmark on the DIBELS ORF measure in first grade and only 2% achieving proficiency at the fourth-grade level. On the Maze measure, only 10% of third graders scored at average or above average. Larue's PSSA data were equally dismal, with the vast majority of third- and fourth-grade students scoring below the proficient level. Boyce's third- and fourth-grade PSSA scores were better, but DIBELS and Maze performance was depressed, with as few as 8% of fourth graders scoring at benchmark ORF on grade-level text and only 25% of fourth graders successfully completing the Reading Maze—an achievement pattern similar to Washington's.

To more fully understand the reasons for the apparent underachievement in these three schools, the MP3 staff interviewed district leaders, school principals, and lead teachers and observed classroom reading instruction over a period of 3 months in the spring of 2006. Six themes emerged, consistent across the three sites despite differences in achievement, student population, and school setting. Those overarching concerns were (1) narrow scope and limited skill focus of the extant reading curriculum; (2) wide variation in teachers' reading expertise and knowledge of reading instructional methodologies; (3) teachers' *and* administrators' superficial understanding of low-performing students' instructional needs and limited knowledge of how to meet those needs within the current curriculum; (4) lack of resources, materials, and time to support comprehensive reading instruction to academically diverse groups of students; (5) limited use of student data to inform and change instructional practice at the classroom, grade, and building levels; and (6) lack of systemwide collaboration between school and district leaders concerning reading achievement. Each of these is discussed in some detail next.

1. *Narrow scope and limited skill focus of current reading curriculum.* Curriculum staff described the district's reading program as being a "balanced literacy curriculum" in which instruction was centered on implementing guided reading (Fountas & Pinnell, 1991) to small groups or pairs of students using instructional-level material. The teachers supplemented

their guided-reading program with a supplemental introduction of the weekly (every Monday) focus skills outlined in the Harcourt *Trophies* reading series (Beck, Farr, & Strickland, 2003). Although the guided-reading framework seemed to be working successfully in some of the district's elementary schools, as evidenced by their high numbers of proficient students, the framework was not working at the three target schools.

Multiple classroom observations of reading instruction and interviews of reading teachers at each school and grade level revealed similar patterns of reading instruction despite variations in student ability and performance. Reading instructional times varied from 45 to 145 minutes per day across classrooms and school buildings, depending in large part on the number of small groups the teacher decided to organize and on the classroom management skills of the teacher in balancing small-group teacher-led instruction using leveled books with the rest of the class working independently at learning centers. Teachers reported that, often, reading groups would not receive any teacher-led reading instruction for days at a time because of the rotation schedule or schedule adjustments dictated by vacation days, snow days, special school events, or another group's level of need. When things went smoothly, the weekly focus skills were introduced on Monday, and reinforcement activities were assigned as homework or included as practice pages to be worked on at the learning centers for the rest of the week. In most weeks, however, no Monday focus-skills instruction was given. During the spring of observations and interviews at Larue, not a single teacher in first through fourth grade was observed (or, when interviewed, reported) teaching a focus-skill lesson as detailed in the *Trophies* manual. At Washington, explicit instruction using the *Trophies* was observed primarily in fourth grade. However, that instruction was mostly introductory. Students were given limited opportunities for directed practice and application of the skills introduced beyond independent practice on learning center activities and worksheets or homework assignments. Similar trends were observed at Boyce, where one second-grade teacher went so far as to ask the observer to refrain from telling her supervisor that she had devoted an entire class period to teaching decoding rules because she was "afraid" of word getting out that she was actually teaching phonics to her students. When discussing their limited use of *Trophies* materials, teachers explained that the materials did not support the guided-reading framework or the strong whole-language philosophy to which "powerful district administrators and influential Title One teachers" were committed.

It was rare to see any teacher engage the entire class in a reading activity. Few classrooms had a complete class set of *any* student books. Instead, a handful of student anthologies were available at the classroom listening center for students to listen to or read along with during small-group guided-reading rotations. Students were exposed to a variety of texts and encouraged to explore literature and discover concepts about print on their own in learning centers and independent reading activities. Code-based reading instruction and explicit strategy instruction occurred only incidentally.

2. *Wide variation in teachers' reading expertise and knowledge of reading instructional methodologies.* Teacher surveys and interviews revealed that most teachers had limited expertise in providing instruction in the five areas of reading identified as critical by the National Reading Panel (NICHD, 2000). Of the "5 Big Ideas," teachers had the most experience with supporting students' practice of oral reading fluency using guided reading and running records of students' reading accuracy and miscues. Instruction in the alphabetic principle and in phonemic awareness was rare, though more likely to occur (through workbook pages assigned at learning centers) in the upper elementary grades (3 and 4) than in the early elementary grades (1 and 2). Comprehension and vocabulary practice centered on oral retellings, answering of comprehension questions, vocabulary worksheets, and dictionary work, as well as story grammars and summaries. Six of the 15 upper-elementary teachers who were interviewed or observed reported having been trained in facilitating literature circles (Daniels, 2002). Two frequently included student-led literature circles as a guided-reading center. The other teachers reported that although they were enthusiastic about literature circles, they could not find the time to implement one nor to provide the adult supervision deemed necessary to promote active engagement of struggling readers in literature discussions of grade-level text. Moreover, 30 of the 36 grade 1–4 teachers in the three schools reported that they had not participated in any professional development workshops or trainings focused on explicit direct instruction of the "5 Big Ideas" or systematic assessment of those specific skills in the past 3 years. Of the six teachers who did attend such trainings, offered through the state's Reading First initiative, three reported that they found the information interesting but not applicable or relevant to their situations. The three others were "surprised" to learn how strong the evidence was for direct instruction of reading skills and saw "great potential" in adding some of the strategies they learned to their teaching repertoires. However, all three had difficulty conceptualizing how to do so and still conform to the district's curricular expectations. Finally, none of the classroom reading teachers and only a minority of the special education teachers had any familiarity with curriculum-based measurement (CBM) or RTI methodologies.

3. *Teachers' and administrators' superficial understanding of low-performing students' instructional needs and limited knowledge of how to meet those needs within the current curriculum.* Although both teachers and administrators acknowledged that the three target schools were underachieving, they did not seem to grasp the magnitude of the problem. As a result, the report by MP3 staff of spring baseline achievement data set in

the context of national norms was greeted with surprise and concern. The magnitude of the disparity between their students' benchmark attainment and that of "healthy" readers was shocking (see Table 5.2). One teacher commented:

> "I think I lost sight of what 'average' reading skill was. I've been so focused on supporting students' individual growth at their individual pace that I set the 'third-grade-level expectation bar' way too low. These results show that too, too few of my kids can successfully apply the skills that third-grade readers should before they leave my classroom. I never thought about their achievement in a big picture way like that before. I hyper-focused on individual student weaknesses instead of thinking about what I needed to change in third-grade reading instruction overall to build a better foundation of skills." (third-grade teacher, Washington Elementary)

The principal of Washington agreed that although their approach of "taking each student from where he or she is" was important, teachers needed a clearer vision of "where each student should be" to more accurately asses need and deliver instruction.

Many teachers did not consider instruction to be a reciprocal interaction. A student's failure to thrive in the classroom was attributed to his or her inability to learn, not to inappropriate or inadequate instruction. Special education personnel reported that many teachers simply wanted very low performing students "out" of their classrooms and relegated to special education, and, indeed, there was a relatively large number of first- through fourth-grade students referred for special education evaluation on the basis of deficient reading skills. In the year prior to model implementation at Larue, 26 students in grades 1–4 were referred for special education eligibility determinations because of reading difficulties, but only 12 of those students (46%) were determined eligible for special education services. At Boyce, the referral-to-placement rate was 62% (5 students found eligible out of the 8 students referred for reading difficulties), and at Washington, it was 56% (9 out of the 16 students referred for special education evaluation were found eligible to receive special education services). Teachers at all three schools appeared to lack ownership of students' reading struggles. Remediation and intervention were viewed as a "special education problem" for those lucky enough to qualify. Academic failure was viewed as a "kid problem," exacerbated by "home problems" (lack of parental involvement, limited opportunities for supervised reinforcement and practice of learned skills at home, chaotic home environments not conducive to instilling a motivation to learn and achieve, etc.).

Research has shown that practical execution of differentiated instruction designed to meet the needs of low-level students is far from thoughtfully and explicitly applied (Fuchs & Fuchs, 1998; O'Sullivan, Ysseldyke, Christenson, & Thurlow, 1990; Zigmond & Baker, 1996). Indeed, the lack of ownership of student underachievement of the teachers in our target schools appeared to be linked to their limited experience and expertise in providing the explicit, systematic reading instruction needed by students with significant reading difficulties. Even though many of the teachers had students with disabilities included in their classrooms during reading instruction and had access to a special education teacher who provided input and guidance on adapting and modifying assignments, classroom teachers reported feeling ill equipped to identify and meet the needs of students reading significantly below grade level. Furthermore, they questioned whether it was their responsibility to do so.

4. *Lack of resources, materials, and time to support comprehensive reading instruction to academically diverse groups of students.* As discussed earlier, in spring 2006 instructional resources to support core reading instruction to all students at a grade level were at a premium. All classrooms had multiple collections of leveled books to use in small-group teacher-directed guided-reading groups, as well as a variety of teacher-made or teacher-purchased learning materials for independent center work. For each grade level, there was a limited number of *Trophies* anthologies and supplemental resources such as phonics practice books or spelling books. However, teachers did not have classroom sets of any materials sufficient for whole-class instruction. Instead, teachers shared available copies of these books and resorted to making multiple photocopies of activity pages to assign as "worksheets" for homework, seatwork, or center work. As soon as any discussions of "differentiated instruction" and "differentiated interventions" surfaced as the MP3 model was introduced and explained, all stakeholders identified a lack of available resources as a serious concern.

There were also limited opportunities for teachers to collaborate or consult with each other. No matter the setting, there was little to no common planning time for grade-level teachers or specialized support staff (e.g., special educators, Title I teachers). As a result, curricular planning and delivery were variable across classrooms and inconsistent from grade level to grade level and building to building.

Finally, personnel available for reading interventions were at a premium. Prior to MP3 implementation, each of the three school sites had two Title I Reading Recovery teachers assigned to provide reading remediation to five to seven low-performing readers in first grade. Clearly, only a very few underachieving students were being served. The MP3 model called for providing Tier 2 or Tier 3 interventions to *all* students whose screening data indicated a need. The spring 2006 data quickly revealed that at Larue alone there were 65 first graders who failed to meet DIBELS benchmarks and were in need of daily secondary or tertiary intervention. In a traditional/theoretical RTI model, personnel would be needed to teach 14 "intensive" intervention groups of three ro four students each, three "strategic" intervention groups of five to six students, and one group of 10 students performing at benchmark in first grade alone. To do this would require 18 teachers to be available for group instruction at the same time. However, Larue had only seven teachers available to teach intervention groups—the four first-grade classroom teachers, the two Reading Recovery teachers, and a special education teacher serving primary-level students. The need was even greater at the upper elementary grades. Staffing seemed nearly impossible.

5. *Limited use of student data to inform and change instructional practice at the classroom, grade, and building levels.* Before MP3, teachers frequently collected running record data on students and conducted miscue analyses according to guided-reading guidelines, but they rarely "used" the data to move students from one reading group to another or to change the level of assigned reading texts. Teachers did not use the data to influence how they distributed their time or what they taught in the group lessons. Some teachers reported that the running record data collection was so time-consuming that they could feasibly assess only a handful of students each week. Furthermore, though the teachers felt very comfortable with coding student miscues, they were extremely uncomfortable interpreting these data to plan "what to do next" and "when and how to do it." Most student miscue inventories were simply filed away on a shelf somewhere as the class went on with its daily instructional life.

Principals reported having attended state-sponsored professional development workshops on analyzing and interpreting formative and summative state achievement data as a way to improve student performance on the annual accountability assessment. But the principals were still trying to figure out how to apply what they had learned in their schools; the data seemed disconnected from classroom practice and from the district's curriculum framework. One principal reflected:

> "It's often difficult to clearly see the relationship between students' 'movement' through guided-reading levels and their mastery of state standards. We work with teachers to map the focus skills and activities from *Trophies* to the standards, but evidence of student competency of those skills is limited to grades on weekly tests. Therefore, measuring progress is difficult. This creates a lot of stress with the PSSA looming over us each year."

6. *Lack of systemwide collaboration between school and district leaders concerning reading achievement.* School principals and faculty reported that despite having strong collegial relationships at the building level, communication and collaboration across buildings and with district adminis-

tration was difficult. Teachers reported that they rarely communicated with grade-level colleagues at other school buildings to plan for cohesive grade-level instruction. Moreover, they viewed communication with and classroom visits from district administrators as purely evaluative rather than supportive. Of greatest concern was their perception that district leaders had contrasting visions and goals for reading instruction in the district. It seemed to many that the "reading wars" were being waged throughout the district each day; the superintendent was committed to changing the core reading curriculum to emphasize the "5 Big Ideas" in reading, whereas the curriculum coordinator was still strongly committed to the whole-language instruction philosophy and to guided-reading methodologies.

Another very significant factor influencing collaboration among teachers and between teachers and administration was the very strong and contentious teacher union. Union representatives in each building scrutinized every request for teacher action, inside their classrooms and outside them, to guard against any breaches in the prevailing union contract. Teachers could not be required to stay a minute longer than the contract stipulated for a meeting or a professional development workshop. All extracurricular teacher activities were to be undertaken only by volunteers. Observations of teachers by Project staff members, whether for data collection or for coaching, required union approval. Grievances were commonplace, and though they were usually settled amicably, the school climate was adversarial.

It was in this climate and constraints that the MP3 staff sought to implement the PM/RTI model described in Figure 5.1, beginning first in Larue Elementary and, after 1 year, in Boyce and in Washington.

COMMITMENT

The literature base on school change is rich with data highlighting the importance of strong administrative and professional leadership in successfully implementing and sustaining early reading intervention models (Denton, Vaughn, & Fletcher, 2003; Hilton, 2007; Moore & Whitfield, 2009). Klingner, Vaughn, Hughes, and Arguelles (1999) describe these critical leadership qualities as "administrative backing." They found that successful, long-lasting instructional reform was "backed" by school leaders who were strongly committed to the initiative, who had a clear, consistent vision for change, and who established a stable support and resource system for teachers. Fortunately, the superintendent of the Alliance School District possessed these vital characteristics, without which it would have been impossible to undertake Project MP3. Immediately on hearing the rationale for model design and components, he committed himself and the district to its implementation, recognizing that it would require fundamental changes in his schools, in the district's reading curriculum, in the focus of academic instruction, and in the attitudes and expertise of both tenured and new teachers. His focus on widespread systemic change was grounded in what Fullan (2002) describes as "moral purpose," that is, "acting with the intention of making a positive difference in the environment" (p. 7). The goal of this intention is to foster systemwide sustainable improvement and ultimately close the gap between high- and low-performing schools and students (Fullan, 2002).

Facilitating Model Implementation

Through the superintendent's leadership and a collaborative partnership with the Project MP3 team, the district established an instructional system that not only successfully operationalized the RTI model to positively affect student growth but also successfully rebuilt the district's infrastructure to sustain school change. This restructuring was no easy undertaking. First steps focused on addressing the six themes the spring 2006 data identified as top priorities for change.

1. *Broaden the scope and skill focus of the reading curriculum.* The district's first task was to revamp Tier 1 by adopting a research-based core reading series. The superintendent worked closely with MP3 staff and state curriculum experts to strategically revamp the district's instructional materials budgets so that classroom sets of Harcourt *Trophies* could be introduced in all the elementary schools, K–6. An order was placed in July with a guarantee of delivery by August; boxes of materials arrived just days before schools reopened for the 2006–2007 school year. MP3 staff proposed that inservice training sessions on how to use the new reading series be scheduled over the summer, but union rules did not permit the superintendent to require that teachers work during the summer months. Instead, an orientation and training day on using the new reading series was scheduled for all elementary-level reading and language arts teachers on the first available district-wide inservice day in mid-September (after school had been in session for 3 weeks). Because Larue Elementary was the target school for piloting the MP3 model, teachers received somewhat more intensive training in the core series. As part of the financial support provided by MP3, teachers were invited to return to school 2 days prior to their contractual start date for more extensive preparation in research-based reading instruction and how to effectively use the new reading series for a whole class. Twelve of the 16 grade 1–5 classroom teachers, as well as the reading intervention teachers and the special education teachers assigned to Larue, volunteered to participate in the training (and were paid for participation from model development funds).

Now that teachers had the materials to provide research-based reading instruction to their students, daily schedules were modified to include 60-

to 90-minute blocks of uninterrupted core reading time across grade-level classrooms. Then, MP3 staff provided a set of sample lesson plans covering the first 4 weeks of school to help teachers structure both the time and instruction of each *Trophies* lesson. The objective was to have each block of core instruction time address the "5 Big Ideas" of reading, to provide opportunities for whole-group, small-group, and independent learning, and to include key elements of direct instruction, including teacher modeling, guided practice, independent practice, and reinforcement.

Of course, introducing a core reading program was only the first step in broadening the scope and focus of Larue's reading curriculum (see U.S. Department of Education, 2002). Tiers 2 and 3 of the MP3 model were introduced (Figure 5.1), and "intervention time" was built into the daily schedule for *all* students: those at benchmark, those below benchmark, and those at serious risk. The 60- to 90-minute core reading periods were supplemented each day by 45- to 60-minute "reading intervention periods" scheduled for *all* elementary-level grades. In this way, all students, all available teachers, and all available instructional spaces were reorganized for simultaneous reading interventions. MP3 funds were used to purchase reading intervention materials, and MP3 staff provided ongoing daily onsite coaching to Larue teachers implementing Tier 2 and Tier 3 interventions.

2. *Increase all teachers' reading expertise and knowledge of reading methodologies.* Research is clear that multifaceted, ongoing, professional development and training are critical to successful implementation of RTI models (Kratochwill, Volpiansky, Clements, & Ball, 2007). As part of their commitment to MP3, the district broke with tradition and established a professional development framework that included summer instructional institutes for teachers on intervention instruction; districtwide pre-school-year trainings on effective implementation of Tier 1 instruction, PM, and RTI methodologies; frequent inservice workshops on the "5 Big Ideas," and even weekend study sessions on CBM and data-based decision making. There were also specific workshops for the special education teachers on how to integrate PM data into IEP goal attainment. The superintendent also worked closely with the school board, building principals, and administrative colleagues to redefine expert reading teacher roles and create three "literacy coach" positions to strengthen the district's infrastructure and capacity for effective reading instruction, as well as to support the MP3 implementation and sustain the changes introduced by the model. The coaches received training and were certified as teacher trainers for all intervention programs implemented as part of the MP3 RTI model, as well as teacher trainers for the innovative technology tools used for data collection and management.

3. *Increasing understanding and ownership of low-performing students' needs and knowledge of how to meet those needs within the reading*

curriculum. As part of the multiple professional development opportunities available for teachers to increase their knowledge of reading intervention and assessment strategies with at-risk and special education populations, the Alliance director of special education developed a new framework for prereferrals and referrals aligned with the multiple tiers and decision gates of RTI methodology designed to improve the accuracy of teacher referrals for special education eligibility. Moreover, in an effort to improve service delivery and tiered reading instruction for students already identified for special education, the district revised IEP writing guidelines and purchased IEP writing software to integrate student PM and intervention program data into specially designed instructional plans, annual goal statements, and recommendations for accommodations and adaptations. Finally, both special and general educators were assigned to teach small-group interventions; the groups consisted of both special education and non-special education students. These groupings, coupled with the institution of sacrosanct shared planning and discussion time for grade-level classroom teachers, intervention teachers, and special education teachers, dramatically increased teacher collaboration and communication about students' needs. A general sense of "shared ownership" for all learners' reading achievement among all teachers was also quite evident (Murawski & Hughes, 2009).

Recognition and understanding of students' reading needs was also highly influenced by the implementation of the PM model itself. As teachers' familiarity with the multiple components of PM improved, so did their ability to use this information effectively to thoughtfully plan instruction to better target skill deficiencies. The model helped teachers establish and measure students' academic goals and clearly understanding their progress (or lack thereof) toward those goals. Teachers engaged students in goal setting, graphing, and discussions about individual growth and progress. The model promoted teacher accountability and reflection on the impact of instruction provided to *all* students (Deno et al., 2009; Deno, Fuchs, Marston, & Shinn, 2001; Stecker & Fuchs, 2000; Vaughn, Linan-Thompson, & Hickman, 2003).

4. *Allocating resources, materials, and time to support comprehensive reading instruction to academically diverse groups of students.* Building resource capacity and instructional and professional support and establishing a sound professional development framework were key to implementation success and laid the foundation for sustainability (Danielson, Doolittle, & Bradley, 2007; Hilton, 2007). But in addition, creative allocation and redistribution of district funds were required to meet the schools' burgeoning needs for instructional materials, technology tools, and personnel to support the MP3 implementation. To that end, district administrators rallied together to seek out combined funding sources of more than $50,000 to purchase core reading and, after the first year, small-group intervention materials to be used with *all* students regardless of entitlement sta-

tus. Thousands of additional dollars were spent on technology equipment, including personal digital assistants (PDAs) loaded with PM assessment software and linked to an online data-management system to improve the utility, efficiency, and accuracy of screening and PM of students. Building principals restructured teachers' schedules to include weekly common planning times so that grade-level teams could discuss and plan for instruction and examine student data. The rationale for assigning district Title I staff to teaching assignments was reconceptualized; instead of spreading resources equally across the elementary schools, personnel were allocated on the basis of "need," reevaluated each year based on achievement data. This flexibility allowed the superintendent to prioritize personnel resources for the highest need schools, such as Larue in Year 1.

5. *Encouraging use of student data to inform and change instructional practice at the classroom, grade, and building levels.* The district made both a financial and ideological commitment to establish a sound data-based decision-making process to evaluate student-level, class-level, grade-level, and building-level progress. Frequent, systematic review of student PM data and diagnostic assessment data at the student, classroom, and school levels provided the careful link between assessment and instruction that could positively influence academic growth overall (Capizzi & Fuchs, 2005; Fuchs, Butterworth, & Fuchs, 1989). In addition to the weekly grade-level team meeting schedules discussed earlier, school-level data teams—including teachers' representatives from each grade level, school guidance counselors, the building principal, reading intervention teachers, special education teachers, and a central administrator—convened monthly at each school site to analyze performance data and intervention impact data. Because these monthly meetings were not originally part of the teachers' "contractual obligations," the district set aside funds to pay the attendees for their time and effort. Eventually, as teachers and administrators more readily recognized the value and importance of these meetings, the superintendent worked with teachers' union representatives to refine the definition of teachers' professional responsibilities to include participation in both grade-level and school-level data teaming.

District-level data reviews were also initiated at monthly principals' meetings, at central administrative meetings, and at an annual school board meeting. MP3 staff modeled the development of quarterly achievement summaries for school board members, of district newsletters, and of school data reports. Assessment data that were once considered punishing, especially if student scores were low, came to be vehicles for conversation and collaboration in school-improvement planning, reflective practice, and diagnostic teaching to promote high standards and expectations for reading achievement of all students.

6. *Improving systemwide collaboration between school and district leaders concerning reading achievement.* At the start of the model dem-

onstration project implementation, the superintendent was the most vocal champion of the MP3 model. By relentlessly including other central office administrators (e.g., the Title I coordinator, director of curriculum, and director of special education) in planning and data review meetings with building principals and MP3 staff, resistance to change was diminished. The director of curriculum embraced both direct instruction in the five core elements of reading and differentiated instruction based on timely reviews of PM data. The Title I coordinator embraced the reallocation of resources to serve the most needy students and schools. The director of special education embraced the reconceptualization of special education referral and service delivery to focus on data-based decision making, goal setting, and instructional efficacy. The principals strengthened lines of communication among building-level and district-level personnel and shared knowledge, expertise, resources, and practices across buildings. Team presentations at regional and state conferences provided tangible evidence of this increased collaboration among the superintendent, director of curriculum, director of special education, literacy coaches, principals, and teachers.

DRASTIC Administrative Actions

Initiating school reform is a daunting, multifaceted, time-consuming, and often thankless undertaking (Bryk & Schneider, 2002; Fullan, 2003; Heifetz, 1994). Fullan, Bertani, and Quinn (2004) identify 10 crucial elements of effective leadership for change that result in building school capacity, increasing student achievement, and improving district functioning. These elements influenced changes in the leadership structure in the district and informed strategic plans for implementing and sustaining RTI districtwide. Of primary importance were: fostering a demanding school culture that requires collaboration and expects instructional excellence; adhering to a collective moral purpose vehemently committed to the vision for improvement; establishing the right infrastructure for change that promotes common direction and collective purpose; building capacity and financial investments to support internal growth; embracing productive conflict grounded in collaborative problem solving and reflective practice; building external partnerships to promote purposeful direction and build expertise; and engaging in ongoing learning grounded in professional knowledge building and disciplined inquiry (Fullan et al., 2004). In trying to explain to other school leaders how he engineered the required administrative actions to support change, the Alliance School District superintendent reported that it called for drastic moves (Kloo, Machesky, & Zigmond, 2008). The mnemonic DRASTIC reflected his belief that school reform is a daunting but doable task. The mnemonic is spelled out and elaborated in Figure 5.2. Each action is interdependent and assigned no specific priority.

Take **DRASTIC** Action

Promote *D*iplomatic decisions. Build consensus among all stakeholders. Foster a willingness to change (e.g., to abandon long-established "comfortable" practices if data indicate they are ineffective; to promote open-mindedness to learning and professional growth). Take professional risks in supporting school change. Promote shared ownership of student achievement throughout the district, not just at the classroom level. Celebrate improved achievement as a joint effort involving team problem solving and team collaboration. Encourage commitment to excellent instruction and educational accountability throughout the district.

Provide *R*elentless support. Show unwavering commitment to the success of the model. Communicate openly that this initiative is not a fad or an experiment but a powerful and practical tool for strengthening the district. "Personalize" the initiative. Making it "the superintendent's project" can promote buy-in from teachers, principals, and school board members. Foster public and vocal support from the school board to parents and the general public.

Demonstrate *A*dministrative leadership. Articulate a clear vision among school and district leaders. Focus not on the lofty theoretical goals of RTI of decreasing referrals to special education or improving eligibility decisions, but rather on ensuring that *all* students across the district are benefiting from effective, research-based reading instruction. "The first will come after the second has had time to take hold." Maintain a clear focus on "what is best for children" as competing initiatives or ideologies clash. Model open communications among district and school leaders, teachers, students, and parents. Encourage humility and reflective practice at all levels from administration to classroom. Have the courage to change practices and accept expert guidance.

Engage in *S*trategic planning. Allocate resources creatively and flexibly. Pool funds from different sources. Prioritize needs. Focus on the neediest schools first (because if the model "works" there, implementations at less needy schools can only be smoother, easier, and more positive). Create new positions or redefine professional responsibilities of existing positions to meet the needs of your learning community. Select personnel carefully to ensure shared vision, common goals, necessary expertise, and philosophical match. Focus on long-term sustainability; "keep your eye on the prize." Seek opportunities to build within-district capacity, expertise, and leadership in instructional practice, administration and policy, technology, and family partnerships. Encourage staff self-improvement through grant opportunities, professional certifications, instructional endorsements, postgraduate work, and so forth.

Be *T*hick skinned. Weather the inevitable storms. Be prepared for challenges and hurdles; the returns are well worth it. Become a public relations expert; promote good press for district academic achievements, great and small. Recognize and find solace in the fact that CHANGE TAKES TIME! Be the target for criticism to protect your staff and teachers to enable them to focus on students. Confront union/labor disputes head on with conviction and stay true to what is best for students.

(cont.)

FIGURE 5.2. Recommended administrative actions to facilitate model implementation.

Support Innovative practices. Support teacher and administrative ingenuity through grant writing, fundraising, and so forth. Provide accessible, parent-friendly data reports, newsletters, and performance updates. Build the home–school connection by creating opportunities for parents to attend teacher conferences and school events. "When parents see firsthand evidence of student achievement and school improvement, their support for the initiative, their desire to become more involved and invested in their child's school experience, and their pride and support of their child's school and school community is increased" (superintendent, Alliance School District).

Become a Consumer of research. Gone are the days of falling prey to educational fads and fashions. Instead, encourage research-based professional growth at all levels, and give it time. Embedding educational practice in research will have many payoffs. Elementary-level teachers will see their expertise grow and skills improve with each passing year of the project. Building principals will evolve from building managers to instructional leaders as they learn more and more about reading research and best instructional practices. The superintendent will grow from a political leader to a true educational leader who can thoughtfully communicate the educational mission of his or her school district by drawing on relevant research, empirical evidence, and data.

FIGURE 5.2. *(cont.)*

The marriage of the DRASTIC leadership model supporting district change and the MP3 model supporting instructional change significantly improved both student achievement and district functioning overall. Table 5.3 details achievement data for each of the model demonstration schools by the end of Year 3 of Project MP3.

Excitingly, more students reached grade-level goals for reading fluency and comprehension. Even more dramatic, however, were the increased number of students at Larue reaching proficient/advanced thresholds on the PSSA. After 3 years of RTI implementation, 44% of Larue's third graders met or exceeded grade-level standards on the state test, as did 33% of the fourth-grade class, as compared with 29% and 21%, respectively, in 2006. In fact, Larue Elementary met "adequate yearly progress" (AYP) goals in 2006 for the first time since state accountability testing began. District, school, and community members alike described the transformation in Larue's instructional and achievement context as "remarkable." Local newspaper reports congratulated district leaders, principals, and teachers for undertaking RTI implementation as part of their vision for school change (Oravec, 2009).

Implementing a PM/RTI model into the Alliance required drastic measures. It did not simply involve turning teachers around: teaching teachers how to administer and score curriculum-based assessments, to participate in data-based decision-making meetings, to teach reading well, and to use formative data to guide instructional groupings and plans. It required heroic and unswerving commitment from the superintendent in the face

TABLE 5.3. MP3 Model Demonstration Site Achievement Data (Post–RTI Implementation)

	Larue School (Grades 1–4)				Boyce School (Grades 1–4)				Washington School (Grades 1–4)			
% Proficient/advanced on fourth-grade state test	33%				70%				70%			
% Proficient/advanced on third-grade state test	44%				80%				94%			
Grade	1	2	3	4	1	2	3	4	1	2	3	4
% Reaching grade-level ORF benchmarks on DIBELS	46%	40%	28%	42%	69%	50%	69%	61%	67%	43%	63%	44%
% Average/above average on Maze	—	76%	56%	67%	—	91%	77%	80%	—	63%	77%	37%

of school board, administrative staff, and union skepticism. It required an unequal redistribution of resources in money, personnel, time, and attention to address needs of schools in which hopes for improving achievement had long been abandoned. It required a complete reorganization of the school schedule to allow for daily core reading instruction and tiered reading interventions in all four primary grades. It required the daily presence of MP3 onsite support staff to coach, commiserate, and cheer as principals and teachers tried and eventually succeeded in changing the attitudes and aspirations of colleagues, students, and parents toward school, learning, and achievement. And it required patience and persistence because changes did not occur overnight. It required top-to-bottom reform. But it demonstrated that incredible change could be accomplished and that a low-resourced, low-achieving school and school district can be turned around.

REFERENCES

Beck, I. L., Farr, R. C., & Strickland, D. S. (2003). *Trophies: A Harcourt reading/language arts program.* Orlando, FL: Harcourt.

Bryk, A., & Schneider, B. (2002). *Trust in schools: A care resource for improvement.* New York: Sage.

Capizzi, A. M., & Fuchs, L. S. (2005). Effects of curriculum-based measurement with and without diagnostic feedback on teacher planning. *Remedial and Special Education, 26,* 159–174.

Daniels, H. (2002). *Literature circles: Voice and choice in book clubs and reading groups.* Portland, ME: Stenhouse.

Danielson, L., Doolittle, J., & Bradley, R. (2007). Professional development, capacity building, and research needs: Critical issues for response to intervention implementation. *School Psychology Review, 114,* 632–637.

Deno, S., Reschly, A., Lembke, E., Magnusson, D., Callender, S., Windram, H., et al. (2009). Developing a school-wide progress-monitoring system. *Psychology in the Schools, 46*(1), 44–55.

Deno, S. L., Fuchs, L. S., Marston, D., & Shinn, J. H. (2001). Using curriculum-based measurement to establish growth standards for students with learning disabilities. *School Psychology Review, 30,* 507–524.

Denton, C., Vaughn, S., & Fletcher, J. (2003). Bringing research-based practice in reading intervention to scale. *Learning Disabilities Research and Practice, 18*(3), 201–211.

Fountas, I. C., & Pinnell, G. S. (1991). *Guided reading: Good first teaching for all children.* Portsmouth, NH: Heinemann.

Fuchs, L. S., Butterworth, J. R., & Fuchs, D. (1989). Effects of ongoing curriculum-based measurement on student awareness of goals and progress. *Education and Treatment of Children, 12,* 63–72.

Fuchs, L. S., & Fuchs, D. (1998). General educators' instructional adaptation for students with learning disabilities. *Learning Disability Quarterly, 21*(1), 23–33.

Fullan, M. (2002). The role of leadership in the promotion of knowledge management in schools. *Teachers and Teaching: Theory and Practice, 8*, 409–419.

Fullan, M. (2003). *The moral imperative of school leadership.* Thousand Oaks, CA: Corwin.

Fullan, M., Bertani, A., & Quinn, J. (2004). New lessons for districtwide reform. *Educational Leadership, 61*(7), 42–46.

Good, R. H., III, & Kaminski, R. A. (Eds.). (2002). Dynamic Indicators of Basic Early Literacy Skills (6th ed.). Eugene, OR: Institute for the Development of Education Achievement. Available at *dibels.uoregon.edu.*

Heifetz, R. (1994). *Leadership without easy answers.* Cambridge, MA: Harvard University Press.

Hilton, I. (2007). Response to intervention: Changing how we do business. *Leadership, 36*(4), 16–19.

Klingner, J., Vaughn, S., Hughes, M., & Arguelles, M. (1999). Sustaining research-based practices in reading: A 3-year follow-up. *Remedial and Special Education, 20*(5), 263–274, 287.

Kloo, A., Machesky, C., & Zigmond, N., (2008, April). *Rethinking traditional instruction: Defining administrative roles in the era of RTI.* Paper presented at the annual Council for Exceptional Children Conference, Boston.

Kratochwill, T., Volpiansky, P., Clements, M., & Ball, C. (2007). Professional development in implementing and sustaining multitier prevention models: Implications for response to intervention. *School Psychology Review, 36*(4), 618–631.

Moore, J., & Whitfield, V. (2009). Building schoolwide capacity for preventing reading failure. *Reading Teacher, 62*(7), 622–624.

Murawski, W., & Hughes, C. (2009). Response to intervention, collaboration, and co-teaching: A logical combination for successful systemic change. *Preventing School Failure, 53*(4), 267–277.

National Institute of Child Health and Human Development. (2000). *Report of the National Reading Panel: Teaching children to read: AR evidence-based assessment of the scientific research literature on reading and its implications for reading instruction* (NIH Publication No. 00-4769). Washington, DC: U.S. Government Printing Office.

National Research Council. (1998). *Preventing reading difficulties in young children.* Washington, DC: National Academy Press.

Oravec, A. (2009, October 5). Celebrating achievement: New approach changes school. *Herald Standard*, pp. A1–A2.

O'Sullivan, P. J., Ysseldyke, J. E., Christenson, S. L., & Thurlow, M. L. (1990). Mildly handicapped elementary students' opportunity to learn during reading instruction in mainstream and special education settings. *Reading Research Quarterly, 25*(2), 131–146.

Reschly, D. J. (2005). Learning disabilities identification: Primary intervention, secondary intervention, and then what? *Journal of Learning Disabilities, 38*, 510–515.

Shinn, M. R., & Shinn, M. M. (2002). Reading Maze—CBM. Eden Prairie, MN: Edformation. Available at *www.aimsweb.com.*

Stecker, P. M., & Fuchs, L. S. (2000). Effecting superior achievement using curriculum-based measurement: The importance of individual progress monitoring. *Learning Disabilities Research and Practice, 15*(3), 128–134.

Strizek, G. A., Pittsonberger, J. L., Riordan, K. E., Lyter, D. M., & Orlofsky, G. F. (2006). *Characteristics of schools, districts, teachers, principals, and school libraries in the United States: 2003–04 Schools and Staffing Survey* (NCES No. 2006-313 Revised). Washington, DC: U.S. Government Printing Office.

U.S. Department of Education. (2002). Guidance for the Reading First Program: Final guidance. Washington, DC: Author. Retrieved September 10, 2008, from *www.ed.gov/programs/readingfirst/guidance.pdf.*

Vaughn Gross Center for Reading and Language Arts at the University of Texas at Austin. (2005). *Introduction to the three-tier reading model: Reducing reading difficulties for kindergarten through third grade students* (4th ed.). Austin, TX: Author.

Vaughn, S., & Linan-Thompson, S. (2003). Group size and time allotted to intervention: Effects for students with reading difficulties. In B. Foorman (Ed.), *Preventing and remediating reading difficulties: Bringing science to scale* (pp. 275–298). Parkton, MD: York Press.

Vaughn, S., Linan-Thompson, S., & Hickman-Davis, P. (2003). Response to treatment as a means for identifying students with reading/learning disabilities. *Exceptional Children, 69*(4), 391–410.

Zigmond, N., & Baker, J. M. (1996). Full inclusion for students with disabilities: Too much of a good thing? *Theory Into Practice, 31*(1), 26–34.

CHAPTER 6

A Blueprint for Change

Amanda Kloo
María Almendárez Barron
Eileen St. John
Naomi Zigmond

Implementing change is never easy, but that was precisely the task ahead of us as soon as funding was received for Project MP3. As discussed by Kloo, Machesky, and Zigmond (Chapter 5, this volume), our charge was to implement a schoolwide progress monitoring (PM) model aimed at improving grades K–4 reading achievement and reducing unnecessary referrals to special education and to document and evaluate that implementation. Many school districts in Pennsylvania had already incorporated at least parts of this model within a response-to-intervention (RTI)/PM initiative promoted by the Pennsylvania Department of Education, Bureau of Special Education. But to fully understand the change process, we deliberately chose to partner with a western Pennsylvania school district that had not yet adopted a PM framework so we could experience and study a real-world adoption and implementation of our model from scratch.

The Alliance School District[1] needed to change. Three of the six elementary schools were struggling to meet the accountability requirements

---

[1]In this chapter, and Chapters 5 and 7, the name of the school district and the names of the three target schools in the district have all been replaced by pseudonyms.

of the No Child Left Behind Act (NCLB; 2001) and the Individuals with Disabilities Education Act (IDEA; 2004). In the more than 150 articles or editorials appearing in the local newspaper over the 3-year period before model implementation, headlines had proclaimed, "Local Teachers Fare Poorly on State Tests" (Schiffbauer, 2003); "[Alliance] Educators Probe Possible Cheating on State Test" (Ostrosky, 2004); "State Lists Schools That Failed to Reach Federal Guidelines" (Schiffbauer, 2005); and "[Larue] Students May Attend Another School" (Oravec, 2006). By 2006, Larue Elementary had been placed into Level 1 School Improvement status as a result of significantly depressed achievement and attendance schoolwide. A school improvement plan was required by the state, but, according to the superintendent, "the school atmosphere was negative and morale was low. The teachers at Larue were fixed in the belief that it was a failing school with very little or no hope of recovery. Members of the community had long ago given up on Larue." Everyone, from the school board to the school administrators to the teachers to the parents, bemoaned Larue's constant failure to achieve and spoke of parent frustrations and teacher failings.

Implementing systems change, whether within a classroom, a school, or a school system, is a daunting task. It requires a transformation, a cultural change (Reeves, 2009). For 3 years, we worked with Alliance administrators, teachers, and students to change behavior, attitudes, beliefs, and value systems of individuals and groups while we encouraged and supported dramatic shifts in pedagogy and curriculum. We worked "in the trenches," were a visible presence in the halls, in classrooms, in principals' offices, and in central administration. We learned a lot about what it takes to help an underachieving, underresourced school "turn around" and about what it takes to introduce and then institutionalize an RTI model. Implementation of the MP3 model in Alliance required total system reform at both macro and micro levels, ranging from redefining professional roles to modifying instruction and assessment practices to adapting daily schedules and classroom arrangements. In this chapter, we share what we have learned by detailing Alliance's complex journey through the readiness, supported implementation, and sustainability stages of piloting the MP3/RTI model.

STAGE 1: ACHIEVING READINESS FOR IMPLEMENTING MP3

Very early in the process of undertaking systemwide change, Alliance needed to assess its capacity to support such change. Research describes this as the "readiness" or "self-assessment" stage of implementation (Edl, Humphreys, & Martinez, 2009; Hall, 2008; Nastasi, Moore, & Varjas, 2004). During this stage, school leaders and teachers identify common goals and prioritize needs related to RTI implementation. At Alliance,

	• Develop functioning decision-making teams at district- school, and grade levels • Increase knowledge and skills of professional staff
Learn as a Professional Community	

	• Determine if the current reading program is working • Select and implement new reading program • Train and support with coaching and lesson plan templates ongoing learning of new reading program • Select, train, and implement new assessment systems
Evaluate Current Practice	

	• Overall assignment of personnel within the building • Flexible use of Title I staff • Flexible use of special education staff • Redefine instructional responsibilities of staff • Rebuild instructional schedules • Reallocate physical space • Purchase instructional materials for Tier 2 and Tier 3 interventions
Address Constraints of Capacity and Logistics	

	• Focus on rationale for implementation of the new model • Use research to support the model • Require attendance by all staff at professional development • Parent and community outreach program
Build Consensus and Network with Stakeholders	

FIGURE 6.1. Stage 1: Getting ready to implement MP3.

this process involved school administrators and teachers in a great deal of learning—learning about reading research, learning about measuring student achievement, learning about RTI methodology, and learning about interdependence. For the first time, the educators at Alliance embraced the idea of learning with each other and from one another. The Stage 1 readiness strategies we engaged in are outlined in Figure 6.1.

Learn as a Professional Community

Develop Functioning Decision-Making Teams

The first critical readiness step involved bringing sets of people together into district-level, school-level, and grade-level RTI teams. The *district-*

level leadership team was composed of key central administrators (i.e., superintendent; directors of curriculum, federal programs, and special education), the three project schools' principals, and the district literacy coach. The leadership team was to meet quarterly to collectively analyze district- and school-level achievement data, set goals, solve problems, and celebrate achievements.

Initially, MP3 staff facilitated the leadership team meetings and used the outlines provided in Figures 6.2 and 6.3 to structure the discussions. This outline helped MP3 staff guide leadership team members through comprehensive yet concise data reviews, first at the district level then at each school building. The facilitative role was eventually assumed by the district RTI coordinator, and the discussion structure was used to develop a variety of districtwide RTI reports, including quarterly school board reports, federal and state audit reports, and strategic planning reports. For each meeting, data sets were prepared to display district-level and school-level DIBELS benchmark data, Maze results, and 4Sight data. After a careful data review, team members raised concerns or challenges inherent in the data and generated district-level responses to those challenges. They also sought to locate at least one piece of data that warranted a celebration, and they generated ideas for how to celebrate the accomplishment.

School-level "data decision-making teams" (DDMTs) included the building principal, representatives from each grade-level teaching team, special educators, reading intervention teachers, guidance counselors, literacy coaches, central administrators, and related service personnel. These school-level teams gathered monthly to analyze grade-level data, set goals, reflect on instructional practice, plan for interventions, and discuss particular at-risk students. For each meeting, first an MP3 staff member, then the school-based literacy coach prepared the materials and data needed and facilitated the review. First, team members reviewed school achievement overall, then worked with a grade-by-grade review of the data. Then the DDMT made intervention grouping assignments and set progress goals for the next data collection period. The goal-setting process would help teams to identify, at the next data review, those students who were making better or worse than expected gains in correct words read per minute on the benchmarking tests (see Figure 6.4).

At each benchmark data review, DDMTs also determined who the "fly-up" students would be. These were students whose rate of improvement (ROI) was sufficient to propel them into the next lower level of risk; at the next benchmarking period, these students would be ready to "move up" to a less intensive tier of reading intervention (i.e., from Tier 3 to Tier 2, or from Tier 2 to Tier 1). Figure 6.5 provides the step-by step procedure DDMTs used to identify the "fly-up" students at each grade level.

(text resumes on page 136)

DISTRICTWIDE DATA REVIEW: Discuss districtwide achievement. Review all achievement data.

❖ Distribute and discuss the summary report and graphs (or display on PowerPoint, on overhead, on chart paper, etc.).

❖ Ask/think about . . . THE BIG PICTURE

  ○ What are our overall goals for achievement?

    ▪ What do we want our breakdown of DIBELS tiers and 4Sight performance ranges to be?

    ▪ Discuss and arrive at consensus about what challenging yet reasonable goals for district achievement and growth should be set given your achievement history, contextual fit, etc.

  ○ How are we doing overall?

    ▪ Review PSSA data (when applicable).

      • How many students in each grade/what percentage of students in each grade scored in the advanced, proficient, basic, and below basic ranges?

      • How does this compare with the past? (Review past performance if applicable.)

    ▪ Review DIBELS data.

      • How many students in each grade/what percentage of students in each grade fell into each tier?

      • How does this compare with the past? (Review past performance if applicable.)

    ▪ Review Maze data.

      • How many students in each grade/what percentage of students in each grade scored above average, average, below average, and well below average ranges?

      • How does this compare with the past? (Review past performance if applicable.)

    ▪ Review 4Sight data.

      • How many students in each grade/what percentage of students in each grade scored in the advanced, proficient, basic, and below basic ranges?

      • How does this compare with the past? (Review past performance if applicable.)

  ○ What do these data tell us together/overall?

  ○ What districtwide concerns do we have in response to these data? (Discuss three.)

    ▪ What can we do about those challenges? (Generate three ideas.)

    ▪ How should we follow up?

  ○ What can we celebrate in response to these data? (Discuss three.)

    ▪ How can we build on those strengths? (Generate three ideas.)

    ▪ How should we follow up?

    ▪ How should we communicate this to parents and our community?

FIGURE 6.2. Discussion outline for leadership team district-level data review.

SCHOOL-LEVEL DATA REVIEW

❖ Distribute summary report that provides a comprehensive yet concise picture of school achievement, including:

- Summary of overall school performance on PSSA (when applicable).
- Summary of district-level benchmark result reports/graphs displaying the total percentage and number of students at each tier by school.
- Summary of overall school performance on Maze.
- Summary of overall school performance on 4Sight.

o What concerns do we have in response to these data? (Discuss one concern for each school.)

- What can we do about those challenges?
- How should we follow up?

o What can we celebrate in response to these data? (Highlight one achievement for each school.)

- How can we build on those strengths?
- How should we follow up?
- How should we communicate this to parents and our community?

1. ACTION ITEMS

❖ What are our immediate concerns and greatest areas of needs in terms of . . .?

- Nominate three focus areas to discuss at this meeting:

  ☐ Curriculum

  ☐ Special education

  ☐ RTI (Intervention)

  ☐ Title I

  ☐ Personnel

  ☐ Materials

  ☐ Professional development

  ☐ Parent outreach/communication

2. OTHER?

Next meeting date _____

FIGURE 6.3. Discussion outline for leadership team school-level data review.

Date: _____ School: _____

Data Reviewed (circle one): Fall Benchmark   Winter Benchmark   Spring Benchmark

Grades Reviewed: _____ Facilitated by: _____

1. **DATA REVIEW**: Discuss schoolwide achievement. Review the DIBELS school-level benchmark result reports/graphs.

   ○ Distribute and discuss the graphs (or display on PowerPoint, on overhead, on chart paper, etc.).

   ○ Ask/think about . . . THE BIG PICTURE. (Follow same procedures for discussing DIBELS, Maze, 4Sight data, or other data.)

      ○ How did our students do overall?

      ○ How does this compare with last time?

      ○ What schoolwide concerns do we have in response to these data? (Discuss three.)

         ▪ How should we follow up?

      ○ What can we celebrate in response to these data? (Discuss three.)

         ▪ How should we follow up?

   ○ Also ask . . .

      ▪ Do other data sources tell us anything unique?

      ▪ Do the results "match"? Are the results "different"?

         ▪ What are the possible reasons for the differences? (Discuss three.)

2. **GOAL SETTING**: Consider breaking into small groups or grade-level groups to work on grade-level goal setting.

   a. Distribute and follow grade-level goal-setting (determining "fly-up" students) procedures.

   b. Share grade-level goals with whole group.

3. **INTERVENTION GROUPING:**

   ▪ Distribute grade-level benchmark reports displaying rank-order individual student scores and recommended tier assignments.

   ▪ Discuss/make note of intervention teacher assignments for the grade level. (Who is teaching what?)

(cont.)

FIGURE 6.4. Discussion outline for school-level data decision-making team (DDMT) data review.

- Create initial intervention-group rosters.
    - Examine distribution of student scores and assign the neediest students to intervention groups first to create initial intervention-group rosters.
        - Keep group size limits in mind. (intensive = no more than 6; strategic = no more than 12; benchmark = about 20–25)
        - Review lists of "fly-up" and "non-fly-up" students.
    - Consider other assessment data (Maze, 4Sight, other).
        - Do the results change the grouping arrangement in any way? (Make adjustments/changes based on consensus.)
- Review group breakdown.
    - Assign groups to teachers/intervention programs.
        - Consider "best fit" for
            - Student instructional and behavioral needs
            - IEP requirements
            - Teacher strengths
4. **LOGISTICS:** Reconvene as large group. Discuss/make note of any specific needs; plan how to address these needs:
    - Personnel
    - Space
    - Scheduling
    - Materials

FIGURE 6.4. *(cont.)*

1. NOTE "TYPICAL" ROI
   a. To set grade-level goals, use the ROI norm chart to find the normative rate of improvement (ROI) at the 50th percentile for the grade. This tells you the number of words (or sounds) "typical" readers gain each week.
   b. Fill in the typical ROI for each grade level applicable in the ROI Calculations Chart (below or in spreadsheet).

2. SET THE ROI ACCELERATOR
   a. Because we need some readers to grow faster than average in order to catch up to their peers, we would increase the rate of improvement. For example, we might accelerate the ROI by 1, by 1.5, or by 2 times the number of words gained by a typical reader to increase our expectations for growth.
   b. Discuss and decide as a group what accelerator you feel is challenging yet reasonable for your students based on the data you have; make adjustments to the accelerator as needed.
   c. Set the accelerator for each grade level in the ROI Calculations Chart (below or in spreadsheet).

3. CALCULATE GOAL ROI
   a. Solve the equation for each grade level in the ROI calculations chart to calculate the goal ROI for each grade level: TYPICAL ROI × ACCELERATOR = GOAL ROI (below or in spreadsheet).

Goal Rate of Improvement (ROI) Calculations Chart

Grade	Skill	Typical ROI	Accelerator	GOAL ROI
1	PSF	×	=	
1	NWF	×	=	
1	ORF	×	=	
2	ORF	×	=	
3	ORF	×	=	
4	ORF	×	=	

(cont.)

FIGURE 6.5. DDMT procedures for setting grade-level goals and identifying "fly-up" students. PSF, phoneme segmentation fluency; NWF, nonsense word fluency.

4. CALCULATE EXPECTED WORDS GAINED
   a. Once we know the rate at which we expect kids to improve each week at each grade, we can easily figure out how many words (or sounds) they will gain by the next benchmark period, which is our expected word gain (EWG).
   b. Multiply the GOAL ROI by the number of weeks between benchmarks in the EWG Calculations Chart to calculate the EWG for each grade level: GOAL ROI × Weeks = EWG (below or in spreadsheet).

Expected Word Gain (EWG) Calculations Chart

Grade	Skill	GOAL ROI*	Weeks	EWG
1	PSF	×	=	
1	NWF	×	=	
1	ORF	×	=	
2	ORF	×	=	
3	ORF	×	=	
4	ORF	×	=	

5. SET "FLY-UP" CUT SCORE for STRATEGIC TO BENCHMARK
   a. Now we can use the EWG to predict which kids will "fly up" to a less intensive intervention tier by the next benchmark.
   b. Let's begin with flying up from strategic to benchmark.
      i. First use the DIBELS Benchmark Goals sheet to find the target for each grade-level literacy skill to achieve benchmark status by the next benchmark period.
      ii. Fill in the target DIBELS goal for each grade level in the Fly-Up Calculations Chart (below or in spreadsheet).
      iii. Next, fill in the EWG for each grade level calculated above.
      iv. To make our prediction about "who" will fly up from strategic to benchmark, we calculate a cut score that tells us the minimum number of words current strategic students must be reading correctly to realistically move up to benchmark by the next testing period. BENCHMARK TARGET − EWG = FLY-UP CUT SCORE (solve below or in spreadsheet).

Fly-Up Calculations Chart . . . STRATEGIC to BENCHMARK

Grade	Skill	Benchmark Target WPM	EWG	"FLY-UP" SCORE
1	PSF	−	=	
1	NWF	−	=	

(cont.)

FIGURE 6.5. *(cont.)*

Grade	Skill	Benchmark Target WPM	EWG	"FLY-UP" SCORE
1	ORF		−	=
2	ORF		−	=
3	ORF		−	=
4	ORF		−	=

6. HIGHLIGHT "FLY-UP" Kids
   a. Finally, we examine our data reports to see which current strategic students met or exceeded that "fly-up score." Those are the kids we should expect to achieve benchmark by the next benchmark period.
   b. Highlight their names in green.
   c. Discuss who those students are and decide as a group if this "fly-up" goal is challenging yet reasonable for them based on the data you have. Discuss the instructional needs of those students.
   d. Make adjustments to "fly-up" list as needed.

7. SET GRADE-LEVEL GOALS FOR GROWTH
   a. Count the number of students highlighted in green.
   b. To calculate the goal number and percentage of students scoring in the benchmark range by the next testing period, add the green highlighted number to the CURRENT total number of students scoring in the benchmark range found on your Benchmark Results Report (below or in spreadsheet).

GRADE-LEVEL GOALS FOR TOTAL BENCHMARK STUDENTS

Grade	Skill	# Green Students	Current Benchmark	Total #/% Future Benchmark #	%
1	PSF	+	=		
1	NWF	+	=		
1	ORF	+	=		
2	ORF	+	=		
3	ORF	+	=		
4	ORF	+	=		

(Repeat steps 5–7 to set "fly-up" cut score for INTENSIVE to STRATEGIC.)

FIGURE 6.5. *(cont.)*

135

Grade-level teacher teams were composed of classroom teachers, special education teachers, and reading intervention teachers providing direct
support to target students in that grade. MP3 staff met weekly with those
teachers to discuss and plan both core instruction and Tier 2 and Tier 3
interventions, to explore research-based reading methodologies and materials, and to analyze and discuss individual student progress data. As time
went on and collaborative dialogue about reading achievement became
more commonplace, grade-level team meetings were facilitated by district
literacy coaches.

The most important feature of the grade-level meetings was the determination each week of which students were (or were not) responding to
reading instruction and, on the basis of that information, how instruction
needed to be changed. The data came from monitoring the performances
of students in Tiers 2 and 3 (see Figure 6.6 for the outline that guided those
data reviews).

Teachers found the process of setting individual student goals both
very challenging and very confusing. To make the process more "under-
standable" and less "number heavy," grade-level teams often abandoned
the idea of *individual* goal setting and decided instead to set the same goal
for all students in the strategic range, then to set a lower goal for all students
in the intensive range and perhaps an even lower goal for all students with
IEPs (with a few individual exceptions here and there). Teams also tended
to "round up," so that a goal of 0.9 words-per-week improvement would
be rounded up to a goal of 1 word-per-week improvement, just to make the
math a little more straightforward. Over time, however, teams fell into a
routine that guided them on the need to make instructional changes. They
adopted a four-step process to guide the decision making and the mnemonic IDEA[2] to remember the steps:

- I: Investigate data trends.
- D: Discuss possible reasons for the trend.
- E: Evaluate the effectiveness of instruction.
- A: Adjust the goal and/or adapt instruction.

They needed a form that walked them through each step of the data-based
decision-making process, and eventually settled on the one in Figure 6.7.

Of course, teaming was not without its challenges. Mixing together
personnel with different viewpoints was important to build consensus and
encourage shared learning, but this ideological diversity initially produced
rather contentious interactions and discussions. To build trust, an MP3

[2]This mnemonic was originally developed for an inservice workshop series created by
Zigmond, Shapiro, and Edwards as part of a progress monitoring initiative launched by
the Pennsylvania Training and Technical Assistance Network in May 2005.

Date: _____ School: _____

Data Reviewed (circle one):   Fall Benchmark   Winter Benchmark   Spring Benchmark PM

Facilitated by: _____

1. **PROGRESS REVIEW**
   o Sort student graphs by intervention group/tier level.
   o Visually scan for direction of trend line against aim line.
   o Sort again by "type of progress":
     ▪ ABOVE AIM LINE
     ▪ STEADY PROGRESS
     ▪ BELOW AIM LINE
     ▪ DECLINING
2. **PRIORITIZE NEEDS**
   o Discuss the neediest students first.
     ▪ Follow *IDEA* process.
   o Review "watch list."
     ▪ How are they doing?
     ▪ Next steps . . .
     ▪ 1. *IDEA* process low performers.
     ▪ 2. Consider possibility of referral to the student study team.
   o Review list of fly-up kids.
     ▪ Are they "flying up"?
     ▪ If not, discuss/follow IDEA process.
3. **CELEBRATE GROWTH**
   o Discuss high-performing students.
     ▪ Discuss/complete IDEA form.
4. **DDMT REVIEW**
   o Prioritize students to discuss at the next school-level DDMT.
   o Prioritize instructional needs/concerns to discuss at the next school-level DDMT.
5. **COLLABORATION/CONSULTATION**
   a. Plan for consultation with
      i. Literacy coach (Date)
      ii. Special education teacher (Date)
      iii. Reading intervention teacher (Date)
      iv. Other _____(Date)
6. **OTHER?**

FIGURE 6.6. Grade-level team procedures for review of progress monitoring data.

Teacher: _____   Date: _____

Student: _____

Describe the instructional intervention currently provided:

Intervention Group _____

Program _____

Lesson # _____

Specific Activities _____

Other _____

I: Investigate Data Trends: SCORES ____ ____ ____ ____ ____ ____

Are 2 out of 4 or 4 out of 6 data points above the aim line? (circle one)   YES   NO

Are 2 out of 4 or 4 out of 6 data points below the aim line? (circle one)   YES   NO

D: Discuss possible reasons for the trend

(If ABOVE aim line) Three skills the student is excelling with: _____

(If BELOW aim line) Three skills the student is struggling with: _____

Other considerations: _____

_____

E: Evaluate the effectiveness of instruction

Average fidelity rating: _____

Strengths of instructional program: _____

Limitations of instructional program: _____

Other considerations: _____

_____

A: Adjust goal and/or adapt instruction

(ABOVE aim line) Set new goal: ____ Median score ____ ÷ (ROI:____ × ____ weeks
until benchmarking) = NEW _____ wpm goal

(BELOW aim line) Note type of instructional change to occur (check one)*

**SIMPLE (no change to
existing instruction)**

**MODERATE (enhance
existing instruction)**

**EXTENSIVE (change existing
instruction)**

FIGURE 6.7. Grade-level team form for evaluating individual student progress.

From *Models for Implementing Response to Intervention: Tools, Outcomes, and Implications*, edited by Edward S. Shapiro, Naomi Zigmond, Teri Wallace, and Doug Marston. Copyright 2011 by The Guilford Press. Permission to photocopy this figure is granted to purchasers of this book for personal use only (see copyright page for details). Purchasers may download a larger version of this figure from the book's page on The Guilford Press website.

staff member facilitated meetings and refereed confrontations to model reciprocal learning, healthy debate, and open communication. Over time, defenses lowered, and Alliance's learning communities began to take shape. Eventually, RTI's biggest skeptics became its most vocal supporters as student achievement improved, teacher expertise increased, and professional collaboration strengthened.

Increase Knowledge and Skills of Professional Staff

In addition to learning to interact and communicate as an educational community, it was important for Alliance personnel to grow professionally. Kratochwill, Volpiansky, Clements, and Ball (2007) suggest that sustaining a successful implementation of RTI depends as much on the skills and knowledge of the professionals implementing the model as on the infrastructure of the system in which the model is implemented.

Survey data collected before MP3 implementation indicated that, historically, the professional development framework at Alliance involved three or four traditional "teacher inservice" workshops on various instructional topics during staff development days throughout the year. In addition, individual teachers periodically attended workshops and trainings offered by the state department of education or private consulting companies. Follow-up to the inservices (help in implementing new ideas, or sharing new ideas with others in the grade or school) was rare. More than 65% of the 36 teacher respondents reported that they saw little practical value in participating in district-mandated professional development. Fifty-eight percent indicated that recently attended workshops had "little" influence on their classroom practice. Most concerning were reports that only 6 of the 36 teachers had been trained in instructional strategies addressing the National Reading Panel's "5 Big Ideas" (National Institute of Child Health and Human Development [NICHD], 2000) of early literacy, and that only two of the six special education teachers reported familiarity with curriculum-based measurement (CBM) and RTI methodologies.

To combat this dearth of knowledge, MP3 staff surveyed and interviewed district personnel to identify the training content, frequency, and delivery structure (e.g., onsite vs. inservice, ongoing vs. intermittent, etc.) that would have the greatest potential to influence teacher practice. The resulting model of professional development included a combination of bottom-up and top-down activities: onsite consultation by university staff and district literacy coaches, after-school trainings at least every 2 months throughout the school year, teacher study group discussions during weekly grade-level team meetings, summer institutes with intervention experts, weekend workshops, and focused strands on assessment or instruction on districtwide inservice days. Because of a very strong teachers' union and specifically negotiated teacher work hours, participation in professional development opportunities scheduled outside of the regular school day was initially entirely voluntary, and both teacher participants and, when necessary, presenters were paid from project funds. Over time, as participating teachers recognized the value of the professional development and saw their own practice improve, they spread the word to colleagues. Soon participation increased—even on weekends! Ultimately, the response to professional development was so positive and the impact so great that the district took over organizing and providing professional development, as well as paying teachers for attending. This MP3 experience is consistent with the robust research base that supports comprehensive, ongoing, coherent professional development as one link to effective program implementation resulting in positive student outcomes (Connell, Turner, & Mason, 1985; Gingiss, 1992; Kratochwill et al., 2007; Mihalic, Irwin, Fagan, Ballard, & Elliott, 2004; Porter, Garet, Desimone, Yoon, & Bierman, 2000).

Evaluate Current Practice

The Core Reading Program

A basic premise of RTI is that *all* students receive high-quality, research-based instruction in the general education setting (Stecker, Fuchs, & Fuchs, 2008). Proponents of tiered reading instruction maintain that comprehensive core reading instruction (Tier 1) should successfully meet the learning needs of approximately 80% of the student population, leaving only 20% in need of more intense intervention (National Association of State Directors of Special Education [NASDSE], 2005). Before Alliance could implement an RTI framework and tackle systemwide change, they needed to come to terms with the effectiveness (or lack thereof) of their current reading program. Achievement data analysis and critical examinations of curricular and instructional practices at the three model demonstration schools underscored the need to strengthen Tier 1 reading instruction for all students. The district's reliance on guided reading (Fountas & Pinnell, 1991) as the basic curricular tool for all reading instruction was not working. Many students were in need of more explicit, direct, systematic instruction keyed into developmental reading skills and the NRP's "5 Big Ideas" in reading. For expedience (the district had a positive working relationship with the local sales representative), and because some of the teachers were already familiar with the focus skills introduced in the series, the superintendent decided to adopt Harcourt *Trophies* (Beck, Farr, & Strickland, 2003) as the core reading series districtwide. In Larue Elementary, the new core program would be implemented for 6 weeks before Tiers 2 and 3 were introduced; in the "lag schools" (Boyce and Washington), Tiers 2 and 3 would be introduced after a full year of implementing the new core program.

An order was placed in July with a guarantee of delivery of classroom sets of Harcourt *Trophies* books and teachers' manuals by the opening of school in late August. MP3 staff proposed that inservice training sessions on how to use the new reading series be scheduled over the summer, but union rules did not permit the superintendent to require that teachers work during the summer months. Instead, an orientation and training day, led by the publishers of the series, was scheduled for all elementary-level reading and language arts and special education teachers on the first available district-wide inservice day in mid-September (after school had been in session for 3 weeks).

Project MP3 staff could not wait. For the project activities to remain on schedule, Larue teachers needed to begin implementing the core reading series with some fidelity from the first day of school. To achieve that goal, the research staff developed a daily lesson plan template that could help even teachers with limited experience teaching reading to effectively organize the core reading block. The example shown in Figure 6.8 suggests five activities lasting 80 of the 90-minute core reading block, identifies the skills to be addressed in each activity (and the Pennsylvania Reading Content Standards to which they are aligned), the pages in the teacher's edition of the reading series on which to find the instructions for that portion of the lesson, and the student materials that will be needed. The core lesson plan template also helped make transparent the structure of reading instruction at each grade level and the alignment of lesson elements to the state standards, focused teachers on big ideas and prerequisite skills, helped to prioritize essential instructional activities, and balanced whole-group, small-group, and independent learning activities.

MP3 staff (and, after a few months, the school's literacy coach) also provided in-class support, modeling, and coaching in implementing the core program. During the first half of Year 1, we tried to provide new teachers at Larue with extensive daily support for core instruction, reducing it to 2–3 days per week in the second half of the year. Of course, with strong union protections, teachers had to volunteer to be supported, and support varied in frequency depending on teachers' desires. In Year 2 at Larue, because of a mass turnover of staff, support was offered as much as 4 days per week for the first half of the year, then 2 days per week in the second half. By Year 3, district literacy coaches, mentored by MP3 staff, took over supporting core instruction.

Formative Assessment

Current assessment practices also needed to be reevaluated. Teachers reported collecting running record data often but hardly ever using it to inform instruction. Moreover, they told research staff that although these

Grade: 1   Theme: 1   Story: "The Butterfly"   Date: September 5 (Day 1)

PA Standard Alignment: 1.1.C, 1.1.D, 1.1.E

Objectives: Teacher's Edition (TE) Page- 2A
    1. Students will generate short /a/ vowel patterns
    2. Students accurately and fluently read and spell short /a/ words
    3. Students will recognize high-frequency words in isolation and in context

Activity 1—Time: 20 minutes

Grouping: ✓ whole, ____ small, ____ pairs, ____ individual

Location: ✓ on carpet, ____ seats, ____ centers, ____ other: _____
- Sharing Literature: Rainbows   TE 2C
- Fluency: Modeled reading: "The Butterfly"
      -Listen and respond   TE 3B-C
- Phonemic Awareness:
      -Generate rhyming words   TE 4A
      -Focus on /a/   TE 4B

Activity 2—Guided Practice Time: 20 minutes

Grouping: ✓whole, ✓small, ____ pairs, ____ individual

Location: ____ on carpet, ✓seats, ____ centers, ____ other: _____
- Phonics:
      - Word blending and building TE 5A
      -Application: Practice book   Page 4
- Spelling:
      -Pretest   TE 5C
      -Application: Practice book   Page 5

Activity 3—Time: 25 minutes

Grouping: ✓whole, ✓small, ____ pairs, ____ individual

Location: ✓on carpet, ____ seats, ____ centers, ____ other: _____
- Vocabulary:
      -High-frequency words   TE 6C
      -Application: Pocket charts   TE 6C
- Comprehension:
      -Guided comprehension   TE 6C-7A
      -Retelling   TE 7A

Activity 4—Time: 10 minutes

Grouping: ____ whole, ____ small, ✓pairs, ____ individual

Location: ____ on carpet, ____ seats, ____ centers, ✓ other: Reading spots _____
- Fluency
      -Repeated reading: Segments of "The Butterfly"

(cont.)

FIGURE 6.8. Core lesson plan template (completed for grade 1 lesson).

Activity 5—Time: 5 minutes

Grouping: ✓whole, ____ small, ____ pairs, ✓individual

Location: ____ on carpet, ✓seats, ____ centers, ____ other: _____
• Review: /a/   TE 7A

Homework Intro: Take home book and read to family

FIGURE 6.8. *(cont.)*

data were useful in making level changes to students' individual guided-reading books, they were not useful in assessing student progress toward grade-level reading standards or "expected" skill milestones. In fact, one teacher revealed two filing cabinets "hidden" in the back of her room that literally overflowed with miscue analyses and classroom tests that she hadn't reviewed in months. She told researchers that her grade-level team collected whatever data the administration "mandated." When asked how they used these data, she seemed surprised and responded, "we were only told to do it . . . we don't know what to do *with* it."

Teacher interview data revealed that any new assessment system would need to be efficient, easy to use, relevant to instruction, and accurate and dependable. The MP3 PM framework fit the bill (see Figure 5.1 in Chapter 5, this volume). The model established a system of universal screening and skill benchmarking using the curriculum-based Dynamic Indicators of Basic Early Literacy Skills (DIBELS; Good & Kaminski, 2002) and the Reading Maze (Shinn & Shinn, 2002) with all students in grades 1–4 three times per year, with more frequent PM of low-performing students.

Address Constraints of Capacity and Logistics

Among the most significant factors affecting Alliance's capacity to implement RTI were staffing, scheduling, space, and "stuff." Baseline achievement data revealed that large numbers of students were performing below grade-level proficiency standards. In fact, only about 10% of students at Larue in grades 1–4 were able to reach grade-level reading benchmarks in the spring before the MP3 project was initiated. In fourth grade alone, students were reading 67 words correct per minute on average (i.e., 51 words correct per minute fewer than DIBELS end-of-fourth-grade oral reading fluency [ORF] benchmarks), and only 2% of the fourth-grade class had reached end-of-year fourth-grade ORF goals. In order to provide teacher-directed, small-group reading interventions to all below-benchmark students with the low student-to-teacher ratios recommended in the RTI literature, 18 adults would have to be assigned to provide skill-group intervention to the fourth graders alone (NASDSE, 2005; Vaughn & Linan-Thompson, 2003).

The data for the other grade levels were equally dismal. Larue simply did not have the time, the classroom space, or the number of adults needed for a "traditional" RTI implementation. As much as possible, district administrators and principals reassigned personnel and reconceptualized professional responsibilities to address highest priority needs (like those at Larue) first. This overhaul required creative and flexible use of Title I and special education staff, redefining classroom teachers' instructional responsibilities to include intervention teaching, as well as core reading instruction, retooling of daily schedules, and the creation of a new position, the school-based literacy coach. All these were major changes in the lives of Alliance schools and their staff members. Naturally, such dramatic changes sparked concern and contention among some staff members. Continuous problem solving, communication, collaboration, and a constant refocusing on student achievement were needed (and, after 3 years, is still needed) to address these concerns.

Instructional schedules were essentially built from scratch to balance time for core instruction and time for Tier 2 and Tier 3 intervention across grade levels. This was no small feat. Scheduling at each school was constrained by numerous variables: availability of shared spaces and staff with upper elementary and middle school classes; schedules and case loads of special education teachers and related service personnel; special subject personnel and class periods; lunch, recess, and dismissal rotations; contract-mandated teacher preparation time; school assemblies and events; and the need to allocate adequate instructional time to all academic content areas. Therefore, in order to provide up to 90 minutes of daily core instruction plus at least 120 minutes of small-group intervention time weekly, a block of "intervention time" was carved out in the daily schedule of each grade level. This arrangement resulted in predictable, consistent intervention time for struggling students, as well as enrichment time for their higher achieving peers. Flexibility and skillful negotiation were required when devising the schedules. Students' instructional needs, revealed by assessment data, drove the process, but contextual fit was just as important. That meant that, although daily schedules "looked" different across grade levels or schools in terms of allocated time, personnel rotation, and so forth, each grade-level schedule met the foundational RTI principle that all students receive grade-level core reading instruction and struggling students receive instructional-level reading intervention.

Physical space at each school would also significantly affect intervention delivery. To provide reading intervention to multiple small groups of students at multiple grade levels at multiple times each day required multiple instructional spaces. In some cases, this meant commandeering quiet nooks and crannies throughout the building; in others, it meant repurposing spaces formerly used for Reading Recovery, special education resource rooms, even storage closets. It also meant having as many as three intervention groups taught by three different teachers at a time in a single classroom space. Schools needed to rearrange classrooms, unearth additional furniture (desks, tables, chairs, etc.), and share instructional tools (projectors, screens, boards, charts, etc.). In all cases, teachers and students had to change their style of teaching and learning to adjust to space, location, and noise constraints. The circumstances were not ideal, but they were realistic.

The final major logistical issue involved securing the right "stuff" to implement MP3. As detailed in Chapter 5 of this volume, this was a model demonstration project in its truest form. The adoption of a core reading program was new. The establishment of multi-tiered interventions was new. The execution of PM and data-based decision making was new. Therefore, thousands of dollars of *new* instructional materials and technology tools were required to support the process. District departmental budgets were pooled to purchase the complete sets of the new Harcourt *Trophies* reading series for each K–6 classroom districtwide to support strong Tier 1. Project MP3 grant funds were used to purchase a preliminary set of standard protocol intervention materials for Larue. District personnel began to write grants to secure funds to purchase technology tools for data collection and data management. State and federal monies were allocated or reallocated to support intervention staffing and to compensate teachers for participation in professional development. Implementing the model was an expensive endeavor; it required that project staff and school district administrators communicate openly and often with the school board and parents to explain the magnitude of short-term financial investments and the expected long-term educational outcomes. District leaders evaluated and audited current spending practices to eliminate wasteful spending on ineffective practices and instead put money into sustainable endeavors such as ongoing professional development, research-based instructional and assessment practices, and centralized decision making (Grubb, 2010).

Build Consensus and Network with Stakeholders

Build Consensus

Consensus building is a crucial step to implementing any school improvement or instructional initiative (Fullan, Bertani, & Quinn, 2004; McIntosh, Filter, Bennett, Ryan, & Sugai, 2010; National Association of State Directors of Special Education [NASDSE], 2008). Building support for RTI at the school and district levels is essential to ensuring that instruction and services provided to students are of high quality and delivered with fidelity. Garnering support for the monumental changes required to implement the RTI model at Alliance was complicated. As Kloo and colleagues (Chapter 5, this volume) pointed out, the project's commitment to direct explicit instruction of reading was in conflict with the balanced-literacy curricular vision held by many whole-language supporters throughout the district. Moreover, many classroom teachers were troubled by the new district special education mandate to include *all* students with IEPs and significant learning and behavioral difficulties in general education core reading instruction.

The process of building support and consensus was slow and evolutionary. First, we focused on ensuring that all staff understood the rationale and the need for implementing RTI at Larue, Boyce, and Washington schools. Administrators, principals, and teachers joined MP3 staff in achievement data review meetings to highlight academic program strengths and identify areas of need. Then we introduced district personnel to RTI research that illustrated how Project MP3 elements had been used successfully in other settings. Finally, we relied on word of mouth and MP3 staff enthusiasm and conviction to change people's minds. The superintendent's relentless support of the initiative and vocal commitment to change were, of course, critical. Building principals attended statewide conferences and workshops to learn from and communicate with other schools engaged in RTI work. Classroom teachers talked with project staff about instruction, achievement, and professional goals.

As understanding of RTI increased, support for implementation grew. We encouraged individual supporters to rally their colleagues and build partnerships. Positive comments from influential teachers in the building were especially useful. However, broad-scale consensus did not occur until we saw even small positive changes in student data after the first year of implementation at Larue Elementary. Improved student performance and increased teacher expertise were surfacing slowly. End-of-year achievement data showed that RTI could positively influence change even in the neediest of schools. Skeptics proclaimed, "If RTI worked at Larue, it will work anywhere!"

Network with Stakeholders and Experts

The success of a school reform initiative, such as that involved in Alliance's implementation of the RTI model, hinges on strong, collaborative relationships among stakeholders. Teachers and administrators must share the same vision and the same knowledge base (Christenson & Peterson, 2006) if they are to set informed goals that will help sustain and grow the RTI effort. Parents and school board, and community members need to understand how tiered interventions affect students' instruction, achievement outcomes, and the eventual success of the entire school. Accomplishment of grade-level and school goals should be measured not only in student achievement gains but also in stakeholder buy-in and support.

The Alliance district's collaboration with university Project MP3 staff helped to promote this collective understanding. School principals and teachers at Alliance reported that, historically, family and community involvement with the districts' schools was limited, especially at the three model demonstration schools. Building a common purpose and avenues for communication took time and patience. MP3 partners and the district and school leadership teams forged a parent–community outreach plan that would gradually build understanding of RTI and foster support over time. The 6-point plan included: (1) annual pre- and post-school-year presentations about RTI and its impact on student achievement at open session school board meetings; (2) frequent communication with the local newspaper about academic innovations and improvement at the demonstration sites; (3) newsletters and reports for parents and guardians summarizing individual-student, grade-level, and school progress; (4) structured opportunities for parents to discuss students' progress in reading intervention and parent–teacher conferences; (5) multiple family and community school events celebrating literacy and learning; and (6) the creation of a parent advisory committee in each school dedicated to discussion of issues related to RTI implementation and instructional and behavioral issues affecting the school community at large.

As we tackled each component of the plan, we became increasingly aware that all shared information needed to be accessible and relevant to stakeholders. A common language about RTI was important. School faculty and parent advisors helped research staff refocus presentations and memos to be more concise and "parent-friendly" and less "academic." Schools partnered with local businesses to increase school attendance by offering family incentives, food, and children's activities at school events. Literacy coaches and MP3 staff helped teachers draft templates to facilitate discussions with parents about student progress using data reports and graphs. Continuous and relentless focus on student growth within the RTI model was key in building positive partnerships between the home, community, and school.

Networking with "expert" partners when undertaking system change is also valuable (Fullan et al., 2004). The faculty and staff at Alliance admitted that the external/university consultation and support offered by MP3 research staff was critical. Onsite consultation was frequent and intense (provided as often as daily) during the readiness and initial-implementation phases of MP3. To promote sustainability in the final phase of the project, however, MP3 staff support was systematically reduced to promote independence at each school and interdependence among schools.

Summary

Our experience implementing RTI clearly indicated that the school district, its personnel, and its community needed to get ready. They needed to increase their knowledge base and learn as a professional community; to critically evaluate their current instructional, curricular, and assessment practices; to address limitations in district and school capacity and logistics; to rally support among school board members, school administrators, teachers, parents, and community representatives to build consensus for changing the status quo; and to network with experts and stakeholders to build support and interdependence.

STAGE 2: IMPLEMENTING THE RTI MODEL WITH SUPPORT FROM MP3 STAFF

The 3 years of working in the Alliance school district taught us a great deal about the process of implementing an innovation. We experienced district politics, a strong union agenda, ideological conflicts, and personal animosities. But more important, we watched as the district worked through each challenge as it arose and taught us what needed to be done to put our model in place (see Figure 6.9).

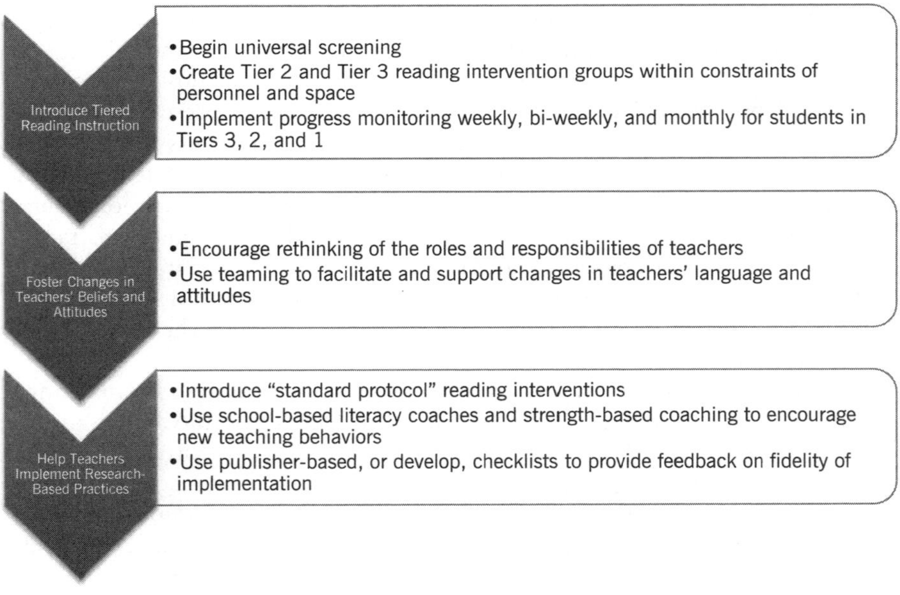

Introduce Tiered Reading Instruction
- Begin universal screening
- Create Tier 2 and Tier 3 reading intervention groups within constraints of personnel and space
- Implement progress monitoring weekly, bi-weekly, and monthly for students in Tiers 3, 2, and 1

Foster Changes in Teachers' Beliefs and Attitudes
- Encourage rethinking of the roles and responsibilities of teachers
- Use teaming to facilitate and support changes in teachers' language and attitudes

Help Teachers Implement Research-Based Practices
- Introduce "standard protocol" reading interventions
- Use school-based literacy coaches and strength-based coaching to encourage new teaching behaviors
- Use publisher-based, or develop, checklists to provide feedback on fidelity of implementation

FIGURE 6.9. Stage 2: Implementing the model with MP3 staff support.

Introduce Tiered Reading Instruction

Target Student Needs

Perhaps the most important feature of the Alliance implementation was their determination to keep everyone focused on student needs during the complex, multifaceted process of operationalizing RTI in the district. That meant, from Day 1, "fixing" the core reading program so that more students had a chance to succeed in learning to read and collecting student achievement data that could be used to guide instruction. We had sold the RTI model in simple terms: We were going to institute procedures that could catch students falling behind and could help them to catch up. We delivered a new core reading program and professional support to ensure that all students received the best possible basic (Tier 1) reading instruction and the tools of PM to help teachers systematically assess all students' reading skills and use the data in instructional decision making.

Denton, Vaughn, and Fletcher (2003) assert that high-quality general classroom instruction requires the coordinated efforts of teacher preparation, preservice and inservice training, researchers, legislators, and school systems. In short, it is multifaceted, time-consuming, and challenging. The challenge was even greater given the time line for implementation at Alliance.

To extend the core reading instruction training provided to teachers at Larue at the start of school, research staff and district literacy coaches provided daily, onsite, ongoing coaching to teachers during planning periods, team meetings, and faculty meetings and co-taught reading classes. Research staff walked teachers through detailed planning of the first month of core reading lessons using the structured lesson plan template detailed in Figure 6.8 to build familiarity with the new reading series and help target critical skills. This template was also a useful gauge of fidelity of implementation of Tier 1 instruction. Teachers were observed regularly to provide them with feedback on their progress and growth. At the beginning of the implementation process at Larue Elementary, the core reading instruction fidelity averaged 39% across grade levels. After 2 years of implementation, this statistic reached 88%.

Six weeks after introducing the new core reading program at Larue (and 1 year after introducing it at Boyce and Washington), Tiers 2 and 3 reading interventions were added. As described earlier (see Figure 5.1 in Chapter 5 of this volume), the MP3 tiered intervention model paralleled most RTI models detailed in the literature. Group instructional size would decrease and instructional intensity would increase as students "moved up" the pyramid. Each subsequent tier of intervention would be more focused and more explicit to target students' specific skill deficits. Triannual screenings of students' reading skills informed intervention grouping and instructional decisions. Students reaching DIBELS grade-level benchmarks would be assigned to large groups (10 or more students) of "benchmark" enrichment with no additional PM. Students scoring below average would be assigned to medium-sized (4–6 students) "strategic" intervention groups whose progress would be monitored twice per month. And the lowest achieving students would receive small-group (1–3 students) "intensive" support with weekly PM. We wanted to follow this model explicitly at Alliance. We discovered that you can't always get what you want. The large numbers of low-performing students made the theoretical RTI group sizes impossible to staff and house. Intervention group size and makeup would need to stray from the theoretical model in order to fit the real-world context of Alliance's struggling schools.

To responsibly address the most significant reading problems at each grade level, school DDMTs had to determine the number of staff members who could be allocated to provide Tier 2 or Tier 3 interventions, then work "from the bottom up" in assigning the neediest students to small-group intensive interventions first, then the higher performing needy peers to medium-sized groups. To begin, the DDMT compiled a list of the teaching staff members available to provide intervention instruction at each grade level; the list included classroom teachers, the Title 1 reading specialist(s), the special education teacher(s), and any other personnel not assigned to classroom instruction during the intervention time block. Next, students in all classrooms at each grade were combined and rank-ordered based on their most recent DIBELS scores. Working from the bottom of the list (i.e., the students with the lowest DIBELS scores), homogeneous instructional intervention groups were formed and assigned to available staff. Intensive-group sizes were held to 4–6 students (not the literature-prescribed 1–3), and strategic groups were held to 8–12 students (not the literature-prescribed 4–6). After all but one teacher were assigned to teach the neediest students, that one teacher was assigned the benchmark group, that is, "everyone else." Ultimately, intensive groups averaged approximately 6 students, strategic groups averaged approximately 12 students, and benchmark groups averaged approximately 20 students.

To illustrate the process, Table 6.1 provides a snapshot of the "grouping" decisions (and compromises) made that first fall at Larue Elementary. In the first grade, 43 students scored in the "seriously at risk" range, 16 students scored at the "strategic" level, and 10 students achieved benchmark or higher. In a theoretical RTI model, Larue Elementary would have created 14 intensive intervention groups of 3–4 students each, 3 groups of 5–6 students each for strategic instruction, and 1 group of 10 students performing at benchmark. To do this they would have needed 18 teachers available for group instruction at the same time. However, only 7 teachers were available to teach intervention groups—the 4 classroom teachers and 3 specialized staff members. So, instead of 14 intensive intervention groups, the data decision-making team arranged for 4, and instead of a

TABLE 6.1. Constraints and Outcomes of Intervention Group Decisions at Larue in Fall 2006

		Grade 1	Grade 2	Grade 3	Grade 4
Intervention level based on DIBELS cut scores		Number of students/ number of groups needed	Number of students/ number of groups needed	Number of students/ number of groups needed	Number of students/ number of groups needed
Benchmark 20–25 students		10 students/1 group	8 students/1 group	4 students/1 group	7 students/1 group
Strategic 4–6 students		16 students/3 groups	11 students/2 groups	15 students/3 groups	10 students/2 groups
Intensive 1–3 students		43 students/14 groups	44 students/15 groups	38 students/13 groups	48 students/16 groups
Available personnel					
Classroom		4	3	3	3
Title I		1	1	1	2
Special Ed.		1	1	1	1
Other		1	1	1	1
Total		7	6	6	7
Actual intervention groups based on capacity		Number of students/ number of groups possible	Number of students/ number of groups possible	Number of students/ number of groups possible	Number of students/ number of groups possible
(Benchmark + "high" strategic or benchmark + all strategic)	Benchmark 20–25 students	20 students/1 group	19 students/1 group	20 students/1 group	21 students/1 group
(Low strategic + "high" intensive or high intensive only)	Strategic 10–12 students	24 students/2 groups	25 students/2 groups	20 students/2 groups	20 students/2 groups
(Lowest intensive)	Intensive 5–6 students	24 students/4 groups	19 students/3 groups	17 students/3 groups	24 students/4 groups

151

maximum of 3 students per group, these were groups of 6. Instead of 3 strategic groups of 6 students each, the remaining 19 students who scored at the "intensive" level and 6 of the 16 students who scored at the bottom of the "strategic" level were organized into two instructional groups of 12 students each, and the remaining 10 "strategic" students became part of a benchmark group of 20 students. The same process was used in grades 2, 3, and 4. The circumstances were not ideal but were realistic and were markedly better than the previous instructional context.

Implement Routine PM

Teachers reported that the most powerful feature of the MP3 model was the systematic use of PM data to inform instructional decision making. PM data helped teachers, principals, and administrators to target both grade-level and individual students' needs and to set grade-level and individual goals for growth. However, it took time before teachers at Alliance recognized the feasibility and the utility of PM. When the model was piloted at Larue, the collection of PM data was viewed as a burdensome activity mandated by Project MP3, not part of teachers' contractual responsibilities and not a useful practice that should be embedded into everyday instruction. To protect teachers' time and respect the terms of their contract, union leaders recommended (required) that data collection should be voluntary, and, if teachers did not choose to collect PM data themselves, grant staff would have to do it instead. This union mandate significantly taxed grant funding, personnel, and time as MP3 staff added "progress monitoring of individual students" to their already long list of daily consultation services to Larue. We assessed all students in the hesitant teachers' intervention groups, entered those data, and provided progress reports to the teachers about students' growth. However, there was a bright side: Teachers had the opportunity to observe, inquire, and learn about PM gradually. By observing MP3 staff, they saw how efficient the assessment process was and how informative the data were. Slowly, more and more teachers volunteered to take on the data collection themselves. Eventually, after 10 weeks of university-led data collection, 18 of the 20 teachers providing intervention volunteered to attend a weekend training to learn how to do PM themselves and, even more important, how to use the results to inform instructional decision making. The seed was planted and began to take root.

As implementation continued and the value of frequent PM became more tangible to teachers, school and district partners explored ways to make the process more efficient to better promote sustainability (Gersten & Dimino, 2001). First, employment contract language was reworded to encompass the instructional and assessment responsibilities associated with RTI. Next, the district pooled funds to purchase, train, and provide every teacher responsible for reading intervention instruction at the three grant sites in grades K–4 with PDAs linked to an online PM assessment and data-management system. Classrooms were equipped with additional computers and technology resources so teachers could access and use the online system to generate student graphs, view data reports, and analyze data. Time for data review meetings was built into daily, weekly, and monthly calendars. And, most important, district administrators, school principals, and teacher leaders adopted and communicated the philosophy that PM was simply a "best practice" that was an integral part of reading instruction in the Alliance School District. Three times each year, Alliance K–4 teachers were expected to:

1. Gather baseline performance data using CBM.
2. Review data at grade-level and school-level team meetings.
3. Establish grade and individual goals for growth and progress.
4. Assign students to intervention groups.
5. Target student skill deficits through standard protocol interventions.

Then, at monthly grade level–school level team meetings they would:

6. Investigate data trends to determine students' levels and slopes of progress.
7. Discuss possible reasons for the trend.
8. Evaluate the effectiveness and fidelity of intervention instruction.
9. Adjust goals and/or adapt instruction to better meet student needs.

Alliance discovered that PM was a great idea, and streamlining the process by introducing PDAs linked to an online PM assessment and data-management system helped to increase its efficiency, promote its ease of use, and increase its utility.

Foster Changes in Teacher Beliefs and Attitudes

Research on educational reform and adult learning has established that effecting change in educational practice is extremely difficult, even in the best of situations (see Fullan & Stieglebauer, 1991; Reid, 1987; Sarason, 1990). At the start of the MP3 implementation, Alliance was certainly not at its best. Changing student achievement required first changing school and district cultures, professional roles, and community perceptions. A fundamental shift in thinking was required to establish the environment necessary to sustain any changes that might be accomplished (Senge, 1999). The first shift required administrators, principals, and faculty to rethink the role of "teacher."

In the past, teachers in Alliance schools, as well as most other schools, were validated for *perfecting* instruction and fostering achievement of *their own* students. Alliance teachers assumed the historical role of the "expert" who brings all knowledge to the classroom, whereas students were assumed to be "passive learners" (Flores & Day, 2006). Classroom walls were barricaded against outside influences, and closed doors promoted isolation. Teachers were experts in individual disciplines and specialty areas and leery of evaluation or criticism. The high-pressure environment of accountability exacerbated their fears. Reflective practice was rare.

MP3/RTI shattered these constructs. Teachers were expected to take responsibility for *all* students' reading achievement, including that of students with disabilities who had been previously segregated from the general student population. Instruction was to be *flexible* and *responsive* to student needs. Classrooms were to welcome academically diverse students and collegial collaboration with other professionals. Teachers were to embrace learning and to try new things. Such a transformation of roles required a transformation of professional identity. It was accomplished, according to the teachers, by putting in place support systems that validated teachers for being and feeling like professionals, for developing positive working relationships with literacy coaches, and for making use of opportunities for teaming within and across schools,

Strong support systems were fostered through grade-level and school team meetings. These sessions provided the safe forum in which to discuss both instructional successes and challenges overall and student successes and challenges in response to that instruction. Meeting agendas afforded time for professional learning, collaborative brainstorming, and problem solving. Teacher practice, teacher perceptions, even teachers' use of language began to change. Phrases such as "Antonio can't . . . " or "Antonio doesn't . . . " were replaced with "Antonio's data show that he is struggling with. . .". Academic failures began to be perceived as instructional failures instead of student failures. Conversations centered on how to *change instruction* rather than how to *change the student*.

Establishing professional teams within and across schools fostered shared intelligence and expertise (Elmore & Burney, 1999). Specialists and generalists supported mutual learning. Conversations were at times difficult for many teachers who, prior to RTI implementation, were trained only to teach reading in a whole-language framework, for those who relied extensively on worksheet drill and practice activities for skill application, and especially for those who had no explicit training at all in the teaching of reading. Many teachers were not ready to embrace recommended changes until they saw proof that the changes improved student performance data. Ultimately, the data helped them to overcome their own cognitive dissonance. Fullan (1993) sums up the belief of many that you can't *make* people change. So during the implementation phase, one purpose for collecting student data was to demonstrate to reluctant teachers that interventions were improving content skills and test scores of struggling students. Data provided the ammunition to shoot down the most pernicious self-fulfilling prophecy in education—defining academic difficulty as a result of individual inability rather than the result of inappropriate instruction and assuming that students who struggle in reading or math are simply unable or unwilling to do the work and will therefore never succeed.

Embracing change at Alliance meant becoming more optimistic about the schools' and the district's possibilities. We have learned that this is a critical feature of an RTI implementation. Low scores year after year demoralize teachers and students alike. Morale at a persistently low-performing school like Larue was very low, and the community's confidence in the school was even lower. Teachers blamed the students for failing to achieve, school leaders blamed the teachers for failing to get students to achieve, administrators blamed school leaders for failing to change their teachers, and the community blamed the administrators for tolerating repeated failure. The MP3 focus on formative assessment data helped teachers to see, concretely, the progress their students could make. The focus on team meetings and collaborative support helped teachers share, concretely, the effectiveness of their instruction and explore realistic alternatives to make instruction even more effective. As Alliance embraced the strategies of change, the positive possibilities began to seem endless.

Help Teachers Implement Research-Based Practices with Fidelity

Every facet of the MP3 model of RTI was grounded in an empirical research base, including the use of a standard protocol approach to Tier 2 and Tier 3 intervention. Standard protocol interventions are evidence-based remedial programs that have been tested and validated through experimental research. Lessons are structured and explicit and, when implemented correctly, have a high probability of resulting in student success. Fidelity of implementation is a crucial component because saying whether or not a student has "responded" to an intervention is contingent on whether that intervention was delivered as designed (Fuchs, 2003; Vellutino, Scanlon, Small, & Fanuele, 2006).

Standard Protocol Reading Interventions

The use of standard protocol interventions supported Alliance's operationalization of RTI by maximizing what McIntosh and colleagues (2010) describe as "the reality principle" of sustainable prevention models. That is, practices are feasible given teachers' other responsibilities and are easily integrated into daily practice. The "packaged" nature of the standard protocol lessons required little extra teacher planning or preparation, which allayed union representative concerns that intervention instruction would overextend teachers. Their efficiency was particularly appealing to teachers already engrossed in learning to implement the newly adopted core reading series. Moreover, standard protocol interventions were particularly well suited to teachers who had limited expertise in teaching reading. The sequenced, scripted lessons would ensure instructional integrity and student improvement when implemented with fidelity.

Despite these benefits, the institution of standard protocol interventions required substantial initial effort. Because no such programs had ever been used in the district before and because the direct-instruction nature of the programs was foreign to teachers trained in whole language and guided reading approaches, extensive onsite training and coaching had to be provided. Scores on fidelity of implementation checklists developed for each program began low but, with a combination of teacher self-monitoring and research team corrective feedback, soon hovered at 80–85%. For a small group of teachers, however, fidelity scores were particularly variable. These were teachers who found the "packaged" materials to be useful, practical, and efficient but also frustrating; they wanted to "own" the implementation of the standard protocol and make adaptations and modifications that were not sanctioned. These teachers frequently modified the standard protocols on their own, sharply decreasing their fidelity ratings despite PM data and colleagues who urged them to return to standard practices.

Coaching

Instructional coaching was critical to the success of the MP3/RTI implementation. The district created literacy coach positions to provide direct onsite daily support to teachers through what we came to describe as "strength-based coaching." Strength-based coaching is based on the cognitive coaching model for teaching excellence (Costa & Garmston, 2002). Unlike expert–novice coaching models, strength-based cognitive coaching establishes reflective-learning partnerships. Consultation is nonjudgmental and developmental, not dogmatic. Its fundamental assumption is that educators always do the best they can for students, based on the instructional expertise they have at that moment in time. If we wish to change what teachers do for children, we must help them enhance their expertise by embracing what research tells us about instructional practices. Strength-based coaching fit particularly well in Alliance, where teachers often felt overwhelmed and underprepared to take on so many new things.

Coaches helped teachers to reconceptualize instruction as a constant state of reflection and growth. Teaching of reading needed to be dynamic and flexible because the needs of students were dynamic and in flux. Instruction had to be sound in content, faithful in delivery, and responsive in design. Helping teachers to accomplish the first two requirements was relatively easy. Literacy coaches disseminated research-based practices through modeling, co-teaching, and professional development. They helped teachers measure instructional integrity using fidelity checklists and lesson protocols. However, promoting responsive instruction required a shift in teaching beliefs. Coaches had to inspire "learned optimism" (Seligman, 1998). Seligman (1998) suggests that an individual's thinking is shaped by the way he or she explains life's vicissitudes to him- or herself; individuals who attribute problems to ingrained personal failings and unchangeable conditions and who attribute successes to uncontrollable factors learn to expect failure and become pessimistic. Such were the perceptions of Alliance personnel at our three target schools. However, according to Seligman, individuals who attribute problems to correctable mistakes and controllable conditions and who attribute successes to their own hard work and good decisions learn to expect that things will turn out well, and they become optimistic. Building on Seligman's ideas, coaches helped teachers to recognize that student failure is a result of instructional failure—instruction that does not match students' needs or that does not result in students' progress.

The first step toward building this optimism focused on enhancing teachers' knowledge base through professional development and collaborative learning opportunities ranging from formal inservice workshops to minitrainings during team meetings to in-class modeling and consultation. Next, coaches engaged teachers in reflective practice, teaching them to analyze the extent to which their instructional plans matched their students' academic and behavioral data. A "positive–negative–positive" structure was adopted to guide teachers' self-reflection and build confidence in their skills and trust in the collaborative relationship with the coach. Within this structure, teachers first highlight one instructional success, then examine an instructional challenge, then highlight another instructional success. Afterward come collaborative brainstorming and problem solving. Coaches, teachers, and teacher teams generate lists of instructional adaptations and modifications that have the greatest potential to effect change. The menu of options is rank-ordered from the simplest to implement to the most involved. Finally, teachers choose one or two changes to apply and plan with the coach for implementation. Then the cycle is repeated. Ultimately, when teachers see the direct relationship between instructional change and student response, their confidence, optimism, and willingness to change increases. Using this structure, after a year of RTI intervention instruction, even initially resistant teachers were welcoming coach support, crediting intervention instruction for student growth, and taking responsibility for students' learning. One teacher commented that "knowing that my teaching helped my kids become better readers is the best motivator for me to persevere and improve!" Respecting teachers as professionals and individuals helped to avoid teachers' union disputes, to build trust among staff, and to open minds and classroom doors to innovative practices.

Develop Mechanisms to Provide Feedback on Fidelity of Implementation

As discussed earlier, measuring the fidelity of an intervention is essential to RTI success. However, measuring the fidelity at Alliance was no easy task. For one thing, it was district policy that peers could not "evaluate" peers. More seriously, teachers were very concerned about being "evaluated"; they feared criticism, humiliation, and degradation by peers and supervisors. These fears appeared to be rooted in teachers' instructional insecurities and their past negative experiences with evaluation. The whole idea of fidelity checks sparked suspicion and concern. Transparency and trust building were key factors in institutionalizing fidelity checks in such a guarded and adversarial environment.

This was a gradual process in Alliance. Teachers first had to have adequate time to hone core reading and intervention program instruction. They needed time to develop positive relationships with school leaders, literacy coaches, peers, and the MP3 staff. Above all, teachers needed to have the opportunity to "see" evidence of student learning. The climate had to be right to implement fidelity checks, lest the positive momentum of school change come to a screeching halt.

MP3 staff and district administrators developed a plan to roll out the fidelity checking process. First, detailed explanations about the purpose and intent of fidelity measurement were provided to teachers, principals, central administration, literacy coaches, and union representatives (see Figure 6.10). Copies of implementation fidelity checklists were provided for review and discussion. Where possible, the fidelity checklists were part of the Teachers' Manual, or the set of published materials provided with the reading intervention materials. In some cases the checklists were developed by MP3 staff and school-based coaches (see, e.g., Figure 6.10 for the checklist developed for implementation of the Harcourt *Trophies* Intervention Kit). The benefits and drawbacks of each were discussed and debated. The message was clear—fidelity checks were assessments of instructional integrity, not evaluations of individual teachers. To foster acceptance of this message, teacher volunteers were solicited to participate in the process and then reflect on the experience with peers. To emphasize the importance of the reflection phase, each checklist was subtitled "Feedback Form for Program Success." Once volunteers saw the value in the process, fidelity checks became less intimidating.

Teacher's Name: _____   Date: _____

Intervention Lesson #: _____   Group: _____

Location: _____   Start Time: _____

Literacy Coach: _____   End Time: _____

1. Physical Setup and Materials	Yes	No	NA	Comments
a. Materials are ready.				
b. Can students see the teacher and materials?				
c. Does the teacher monitor all students?				
2. Management Skills	**Yes**	**No**	**NA**	**Comments**
a. Begins lesson on time.				
b. Transitions smoothly.				
c. All students are engaged.				
3. Presentation Skills	**Yes**	**No**	**NA**	**Comments**
a. Teacher follows Before/After Core Story Lesson (see back).				
b. Teacher follows Directed Reading Intervention Story Lesson (see back).				
c. Teacher models prior to student practice.				
d. Teacher scaffolds instruction.				
e. Teachers corrects all errors (group and individual).				
f. Students use manipulatives to provide additional support when needed.				
g. Teacher moves quickly from one part of the lesson to the next.				
h. Teacher completes lesson in time allotted for interventions.				
i. Teacher has good pacing.				

(cont.)

FIGURE 6.10. Fidelity checklist for Harcourt *Trophies* Intervention Kit.

4. Monitoring Independent Work	Yes	No	NA	Comments
a. Students are on task and working independently.				
b. Students complete assignments in the time allotted.				
c. Work is neat and has few or no mistakes.				
d. Teacher monitors any paired or independent reading and reinforces good work.				

To Get Percent Score (Total # of "Yes" column) divided by (total # of applicable items) × 100=%

Lesson Sequence

1. Core Story Reteaching Lesson

Review phonics:
- Identify the sound
- Associate letters to sound
- Word blending
- Skill application

Vocabulary
- Preteach vocabulary
- Apply vocabulary strategies

Focus skill
- Follow lesson's particular preteach skill

Read core selection
- Preview selection
- Set purpose
- Model
- Reread and summarize

2. Intervention Story Lesson

Directed reading:
- Follow guided reading of story
- Model
- Summarize selection

Focus skill:
- Follow lesson's particular reteach skill (utilize skill cards)

Review phonics:
- Follow particular lesson's phonics skill practice

Fluency:
- Practice fluency

FIGURE 6.10. *(cont.)*

After initial exposure to the process, teacher leaders, literacy coaches, principals, and district leaders formalized the process. First, teachers completed self-checks by using the relevant implementation checklist to plan, and then reflect on, lesson delivery. Second, literacy coaches conducted "informal" checks; the coach completed a fidelity rating for an observed lesson, and the teacher completed a self-check on the same lesson. Differences in ratings and perceptions were discussed, and plans for fine-tuning the instruction were developed. Finally, "formal" fidelity checks were done, after which the coach and teacher analyzed the results and planned for supportive next steps. The goal was to achieve the standard protocol intervention program's fidelity threshold and move toward 100% fidelity of implementation. Before long, after multiple positive interactions, teachers embraced the process overall. By Year 3 of the project, the district officially endorsed fidelity measurement as an important aspect of quality assurance and a required step for RTI and eligibility determination.

Summary

Implementing MP3 at Larue Elementary was no easy task; implementing at Boyce and Washington 1 year later was just as challenging. But by all measures (teacher satisfaction, district approval, student achievement) the implementation was a great success (see Chapter 7, this volume). The most important factor in achieving the implementation was to keep everyone focused on the ultimate goal: increasing student achievement. Every change, whether in school organization, in planning, in assessment, or in instruction, was justified by its contribution to improving student achievement. Personnel in Alliance showed us that to be successful, they needed to target student needs, embrace change, adopt research-based practices, learn to work with coaches and to collaborate with each other, and strive for high standards of implementation fidelity.

STAGE 3: SUSTAIN THE INNOVATION

Because grant support for the MP3 implementation could be sustained for only 3 years, sustainability needed to be addressed from the very start. It became the primary focus of the work at Larue during the third year of the project. We learned quickly that sustainability and follow-through required that everyone in the district view himself or herself as "partners" in the school change process, not implementers of some outsiders' ideas. As the outsiders, we needed to facilitate that shift in responsibility and ownership to increase the probability that our collective hard work would become standard practice in this transformed district (Figure 6.11).

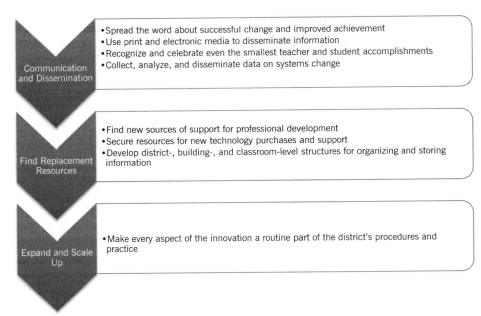

FIGURE 6.11. Stage 3: Sustaining the implementation.

Communication and Dissemination

Sustainability of school reforms and initiatives such as RTI depend on effective communication throughout a school district and widespread dissemination of innovations and results. The communication network for sustainability helps to build an enhanced knowledge base among all stakeholders. Only knowledgeable teachers and administrators can set the informed goals that will help sustain and grow the RTI model. Informed parents and school board and community members need to understand how tiered interventions have affected instruction and produced successful student outcomes. Therefore, grade-level and school goals must be measured not only in terms of student achievement but also in the understanding and support of every stakeholder interested in improving the academic success of the district. And only after getting feedback from these stakeholders should a school celebrate an achievement or revisit the work that was not entirely successful.

The most effective vehicles for communication at Alliance included newsletters, Wikis, school board reports, and conference presentations. An RTI newsletter was developed and distributed by the district literacy coach appointed RTI coordinator. A quarterly districtwide newsletter available in hard and electronic copies included logistical information for teachers (e.g., benchmarking dates, snow delay intervention schedules, etc.), district and school data summaries, upcoming professional development opportunities, instructional strategy recommendations, and highlights of innovative practices or notable successes throughout the district. The RTI Wiki was an internal district website displaying interlinked electronic folders and pages containing information about RTI. MP3 staff, district literacy coaches, the RTI coordinator, and technology personnel developed it collaboratively to serve both as a resource center and a communication forum for teachers, principals, and district administrators involved with RTI. The site took the place of large binders created to be hard-copy RTI implementation manuals at each school. Specific resources related to model components and district policies were easily accessible at the click of the mouse. Interactive discussion forums allowed users to post questions and answers about RTI or reading instruction in general.

The RTI coordinator drafted quarterly RTI summaries for the school board highlighting changes in achievement and academic growth at each of the three schools implementing RTI. Additionally, she made formal presentations about the impact of RTI on student achievement at open-session school board meetings at the start and end of each school year. Finally, district leaders and school personnel were invited to make presentations at state and national education conferences about their experiences with RTI and their journey to school change.

Developing these communication vehicles took a lot of time, effort, and modeling from MP3 staff because sharing information was not typical district practice prior to implementation. Teachers and principals had always been very "possessive," even secretive, about instructional practices and student outcomes in their schools, especially if the data were poor. They needed to experience and learn that being transparent and sharing data could help them sustain the district's investment in change.

Recognize and Celebrate Even the Smallest Accomplishments

Implementing RTI at Alliance took a lot of hard work, and a little positive reinforcement went a long way. It was very important to acknowledge small changes and to celebrate small successes as harbingers of the greater ones to come. We learned to acknowledge achievements at every step of the implementation process at Alliance, and so did school and district personnel. This positive momentum fostered positive interactions and built collegial relationships. It helped everyone to replace pessimism with optimism, to see possibilities not recognized before. For example, celebrating even small achievements of teachers and students helped to shatter the myth that Larue was and always would be a failing school with underachieving students and ineffective teachers. It helped to break the cycle of failure in the district's lowest performing schools.

Evaluating *student* growth is the foundation of RTI methodology. Evaluating *system* growth should be integral as well. Of course, simply collecting data is meaningless. The process of measuring growth is given life only when districts strive to make sense of the data and develop action plans in response to it (Earl & Fullan, 2003). To sustain and extend positive student achievement outcomes, the professional learning community in each school must use its data to reflect on and improve instructional practice. So, after the data-based decision-making process for student progress was well established, we turned our attention to strengthening the data-based decision-making process for district progress. Student achievement data were examined building by building and grade level by grade level to assess the "health" of elementary reading instruction overall. Goal attainment and instructional fidelity data were analyzed to determine the contextual fit and effectiveness of specific intervention programs. Longitudinal data were reviewed to highlight achievement trends and patterns for cohorts of students across the district. Although these quantitative analyses were informative, we found that qualitative stories of change in Alliance schools were even more powerful (see Chapter 7, this volume). Reflecting on teacher discussions during faculty meetings and workshops helped to capture shifts in instructional ideology. Reviews of teacher participation rates at volunteer professional development opportunities showed evidence of changes in professional learning. Newspaper articles about district achievement were collected to gauge changes in community perceptions of the quality of education provided in Alliance.

Sustaining RTI requires schools to become curious about progress on both macro and micro levels. Collecting and interpreting student achievement data is only the first step. Analyzing program efficacy, subgroup performance, costs versus benefits, and so forth, are the more sophisticated skills that evolve into true knowledge building and educational excellence.

Find Human and Financial Resources to Replace Those Covered by the Grant

Participation in Project MP3 brought substantial support and significant resources to Alliance. To sustain the change effort, the district needed to become independent of these resources. Together with MP3 staff, district personnel developed an action plan for long-term sustainability. Professional development, technology resources, and funding were identified as primary needs. To increase in-house capacity for ongoing professional development in reading and RTI-related expertise, the district appointed three literacy coaches to support reading instruction and RTI in the district's elementary schools. These positions required no new expenditures because they were simply reassignments or redefinitions of existing Title I positions. The appointments went to experienced teachers with advanced degrees in reading, curriculum, and administration. The coaches worked one-on-one with MP3 staff at the model implementation schools to hone coaching skills, as well as increase knowledge of RTI. The district also "promoted" the most experienced literacy coach (who had been a coach at Larue from the start of MP3) to the position of district RTI coordinator. She took over all coordination and organization responsibilities previously performed by MP3 staff so as to sustain RTI in grades K–4 at the target schools, extend the model in those schools to fifth and sixth grades, implement it at the three remaining elementary schools, and expand the model to the secondary level. The coaches were prepared to be trainers for the online data management system and to provide direct support and professional development to teachers and administrators in the use of technology tools for data collection and analysis. They were also trained in effective implementation of intervention programs. The RTI coordinator became certified as a trainer for Language Essentials for Teachers of Reading and Spelling (LETRS; Moats, 2008). Professional literature and texts were purchased for teacher learning libraries, and the RTI coordinator and literacy coaches participated in and supported teacher study groups. All of these efforts required initial financial backing from the district, but the investment helped save money in the long run by limiting the district's reliance on outside consulting support. And, in addition to these "in house" efforts, the district established strong relationships with state and university partners to take advantage of both free and grant-based training and professional development.

To ramp up technology support for RTI in the district, the RTI coordinator, literacy coaches, and district administrators actively pursued private, state, and federal grants to purchase computers, PDAs, software, and other tools. They reallocated and redistributed existing funds to purchase sustainable resources such as mobile computer labs and software libraries that were shared among teachers to maximize resources. Special education, Title I, and curriculum funds were pooled to buy licenses for Web-based intervention programs for individual-student, small-group, or large-group use. Best of all, they took advantage of free resources such as Wiki builders to create district Wiki spaces to share information about RTI. Teachers who were particularly computer savvy or passionate about data analysis collaborated to produce spreadsheet templates, PowerPoint presentations, and databases that were shared with colleagues to aid in analyzing data and reporting results.

Develop District-, Building-, and Classroom-Level Structures for Organizing and Storing Information

In large measure, the key to sustaining an RTI implementation is organization. Implementation required flexible scheduling, careful data management, thoughtful problem solving, creative resource allocation, multilevel communication—the list is endless. To keep all these elements working symbiotically requires coordinated effort and excellent organization. All stakeholders must have easy access to the materials necessary to support day-to day RTI operations. In the Alliance school district, these materials were initially gathered into file folders. The principal at each of the three target schools stored copies of intervention schedules, goal charts, and progress graphs. Teachers stored copies of PM materials, data decision-making guidelines, intervention protocols, student graphs, data summaries, and parent reports. Literacy coaches stored copies of lesson plan templates, fidelity checklists, intervention data, training materials, and assessment and instructional guides. District administrators stored copies of growth analyses, referral guidelines, strategic plans, and RTI research.

Soon, file folders were overflowing into drawers and drawers into cabinets. One RTI binder grew into two, then three, and so on. Ultimately, a district RTI Wiki was created to house anything and everything RTI-related. Wikis make information easily accessible to anyone in the district with Internet access. Principals can log onto the Wiki to locate materials and information related to leading an RTI effort at the school level. Teachers can locate and download PM guidelines. Literacy coaches can access links to training modules and webinars. Even substitute teachers can download intervention guides and PM procedures. Of course, some teachers will always rely on paper copies, disks, and even Post-it Notes for the exchange of information. Furthermore, accessing the Internet is sometimes impossible due to server errors, technology glitches, or limited computer availability. It is important to keep no-tech and low-tech options available, including Wiki information backed up on CDs, as well as stored in hard copy, by the RTI coordinator and distributed to staff as needed.

Expand and Scale Up

The research literature suggests that an innovation should be implemented gradually through a carefully planned, phased approach to give staff time to learn, problem solve, and develop the needed experience base (Fixsen, Naoom, Blasé, & Wallace, 2007). Instead, Project MP3 implementation was a whirlwind! After only a few months of planning and readiness preparation, the model was piloted in Larue Elementary; 1 year later it was replicated at Boyce and Washington. Years 1 and 2 focused on implementation; Year 3 focused on building sustainability. Nevertheless, in response to the dramatic impact the model had on student achievement and teacher practice at each of the target schools, the district decided to extend the model to the remaining three elementary schools and began planning for scaling up in the middle schools and high school. These plans reflected the confidence of Alliance personnel in the value of sustaining and scaling up the MP3 model.

Summary

Implementing an innovation is a challenge, sometimes complicated by and sometimes facilitated by an external agent. Sustaining an innovation rests solely on the shoulders of the implementer. The Alliance School District worked hard to institutionalize MP3. They developed and nurtured communication networks and vehicles. They learned to celebrate small and large successes. They monitored the growth and capacity of the district to sustain RTI as carefully as they monitored student achievement. They sought internal sources of support to maintain the professional and financial resources contributed by the external project funds. They got organized and set out to expand and scale up the MP3 implementation. They embraced MP3 and made it their own.

CONCLUDING COMMENTS

In the 3-year life of Project MP3, we covered a lot of ground. We recruited a school district to collaborate with us in an implementation of an RTI model. We collected baseline data to help us and the district evaluate current practices, resources, and student achievement. We prepared teachers and school administrators to adopt a new core reading program, implement tiered reading instruction, collect periodic assessments of students' reading skills, and use PM data to inform instructional groupings and interventions. We trained literacy coaches and helped them complete fidelity checks to ensure that new reading instruction met standards for fidelity. We watched the school district transform, the school culture change, student achievement improve, and the community become more positive about the futures of their children. We documented the readiness and implementation processes and deliberately focused the district's energies on ensuring sustainability. The school district had a very successful implementation, and we learned a great deal from the experience. The blueprint for change outlined in this chapter derives from that documentation and from those experiences.

REFERENCES

Beck, I. L., Farr, R. C., & Strickland, D. S. (2003). *Trophies: A Harcourt reading/language arts program.* Orlando, FL: Harcourt.

Christenson, S. L., & Peterson, C. J. (2006). *Family, school, and community influences on children's learning: A literature review.* Minneapolis: University of Minnesota Extension Service, All Parents Are Teachers Project.

Connell, D. B., Turner, R. R., & Mason, E. F. (1985). Summary of findings of the school-health education evaluation: Health promotion effectiveness, implementation, and costs. *Journal of School Health, 55*(8), 316–321.

Costa, A. L., & Garmston, R. J. (2002). *Cognitive coaching: A foundation for Renaissance schools.* Norwood, MA: Christopher-Gordon.

Denton, C. A., Vaughn, S., & Fletcher, J. M. (2003). Bringing research-based practice in reading intervention to scale. *Learning Disabilities Research and Practice, 18,* 201–211.

Earl, L., & Fullan, M. (2003). Using data in leadership for learning. *Cambridge Journal of Education, 33*(3), 383–394.

Edl, H. M., Humphreys, L. A., & Martinez, R. S. (2009). University–school collaboration for the implementation of a Tier III reading program for elementary school students. *Journal of Applied School Psychology, 25*(3), 221–243.

Elmore, R. F., & Burney, D. (1999). Investing in teacher learning: Staff development and instructional improvement. In L. Darling-Hammond & G. Sykes (Eds.), *Teaching as the learning profession: Handbook of policy and practice* (pp. 341–375). San Francisco: Jossey-Bass.

Fixsen, D., Naoom, S., Blasé, K., & Wallace, F. (007, Winter/Spring). Implementation: The missing link between research and practice. *APSAC Advisor,* pp. 4–10.

Flores, M. A., & Day, C. (2006). Contexts which shape and reshape new teachers' identities. *Teaching and Teacher Education, 22,* 219–232.

Fountas, I. C., & Pinnell, G. S. (1991). *Guided reading: Good first teaching for all children.* Portsmouth, NH: Heinemann.

Fuchs, L. S. (2003). Assessing intervention responsiveness: Conceptual and technical issues. *Learning Disabilities: Research and Practice, 18,* 172–186.

Fullan, M. (1993). *Change forces: Probing the depths of educational reform.* Bristol, PA: Falmer Press.

Fullan, M., Bertani, A., & Quinn, J. (2004). New lessons for districtwide reform. *Educational Leadership, 61*(7), 42–46.

Fullan, M., & Stieglebauer, S. (1991). *The new meaning of educational change.* New York: Teachers College Press.

Gersten, R., & Dimino, J. (2001). The realities of translating research into classroom practice. *Learning Disabilities Research and Practice, 16,* 120–130.

Gingiss, P. L. (1992). Enhancing program implementation and maintenance through a multiphase approach to peer-based staff development. *Journal of School Health, 62*(5), 161–166.

Good, R. H., III, & Kaminski, R. A. (Eds.). (2002). Dynamic Indicators of Basic Early Literacy Skills (6th ed.). Eugene, OR: Institute for the Development of Education Achievement. Available at *dibels.uoregon.edu.*

Grubb, N. (2010). Correcting the money myth: Rethinking school resources. *Phi Delta Kappan, 91*(4), 51–55.

Hall, S. (2008). *Implementing response to intervention: A principal's guide.* Los Angeles: Corwin Press.

Individuals with Disabilities Education Act Amendments of 1997, Public Law No. 105-7, 1997.

Individuals with Disabilities Education Improvement Act (2004), Pub. L. No. 108-446, 20 Stat.145.

Kratochwill, T. R., Volpiansky, P., Clements, M., & Ball, C. (2007). Professional development in implementing and sustaining multitier prevention models:

Implications for response to intervention. *School Psychology Review, 36*(4), 618–631.

Moats, L. C. (2008). *Language Essentials for Teachers of Reading and Spelling* (LETRS). Longmont, CO: Sopris West.

McIntosh, K., Filter, K. J., Bennett, J. L., Ryan, C., & Sugai, G. (2010). Principles of sustainable prevention: Designing scale-up of school-wide positive behavior support to promote durable systems. *Psychology in the Schools, 47*(1), 5–21.

Mihalic, S., Irwin, K., Fagan, A., Ballard, D., & Elliott, D. (2004). *Successful program implementation: Lessons from Blueprints* (No. NCJ 204273). Washington, DC: U.S. Department of Justice, Office of Justice Programs, Office of Juvenile Justice and Delinquency Programs.

Nastasi, B. K., Moore, R. B., & Varjas, K. M. (2004). *School-based mental health services: Creating comprehensive and culturally specific programs* (pp. 79–80). Washington, DC: American Psychological Association.

National Association of State Directors of Special Education. (2005). *Response to intervention: Policy considerations and implementation.* Alexandria, VA: Author.

National Association of State Directors of Special Education. (2008). *Response to intervention: Blueprints for implementation.* Alexandria, VA: Author.

National Institute of Child Health and Human Development (NICHD). (2000). *Report of the National Reading Panel. Teaching children to read: An evidence-based assessment of the scientific research literature on reading and its implications for reading instruction* (NIH Publication No. 00-4769). Washington, DC: U.S. Government Printing Office.

No Child Left Behind Act, Public Law 107-110, 15 Stat.1425 (2001).

Oravec, A. (2006, August 27). [Larue] students may attend another school. *Herald Standard*, pp. A1, A4.

Ostrosky, S. (2004, March 26). [Alliance] educators robe possible cheating on state test. *Herald Standard*, pp. B1, B4.

Porter, A. C., Garet, M. S., Desimone, L., Yoon, K. S., & Bierman, B. F. (2000). *Does professional development change teaching practice?: Results from a three-year study.* Washington, DC: American Institutes for Research in Behavioral Sciences.

Reeves, D. B. (2009). *Leading change in your school: How to conquer myths, build commitment, and get results.* Alexandria, VA: Association for Supervision and Curriculum Development.

Reid, W. A. (1987). Institutions and practices: Professional education reports and the language of reform. *Educational Researcher, 16*(8), 10–15.

Sarason, S. B. (1990). *The predictable failure of educational reform.* San Francisco: Jossey-Bass.

Schiffbauer, K. (2003, January 12). Local teachers fare poorly on state tests, results show. *Herald Standard*, pp. B1–B2.

Schiffbauer, K. (2005, December 31). State lists schools that failed to reach federal guidelines. *Herald Standard*, pp. B1, B5.

Seligman, M. E. P. (1998). *Learned optimism: How to change your mind and your life.* New York: Free Press.

Senge, P. H. (1999). *The dance of change: The challenges to sustaining momentum in a learning organization.* New York: Doubleday.

Shinn, M. R., & Shinn, M. M. (2002). Reading Maze—CBM Eden Prairie, MN: Edformation. Available at *www.aimsweb.com.*

Stecker, P. M., Fuchs, D., & Fuchs, L. S. (2008). Progress monitoring as essential practice within response to intervention. *Rural Special Education Quarterly, 27*(4), 10–17.

Vaughn, S., & Linan-Thompson, S. (2003). Group size and time allotted to intervention: Effects for students with reading difficulties. In B. Foorman (Ed.), *Preventing and remediating reading difficulties: Bringing science to scale* (pp. 275–298). Parkton, MD: York Press.

Vellutino, F. R., Scanlon, D. M., Small, S., & Fanuele, D. P. (2006). Response to intervention as a vehicle for distinguishing between children with and without reading disabilities: Evidence for the role of kindergarten and first-grade interventions. *Journal of Learning Disabilities, 39,* 157–169.

CHAPTER 7

Celebrating Achievement Gains and Cultural Shifts

Naomi Zigmond
Amanda Kloo
Kathleen Stanfa

Response to intervention (RTI) holds considerable promise as a method of early identification of students at risk, as a framework for providing quality reading instruction and targeted intervention, and as a catalyst for school change. The potential for RTI to effect positive change in both students and school systems lies within its multilayered structure, designed to provide a continuum of instructional support. RTI models seek to strengthen the effectiveness of literacy instruction for *all* students, to increase the intensity of targeted interventions for students at risk, and ultimately to prevent chronic school failure (Burns & VanDerHeyden, 2006). In order to achieve these ambitious goals, an RTI model requires the collection and utilization of reliable student performance data. This data-driven process improves instructional practices and academic progress. Research has demonstrated that when teachers apply progress monitoring (PM) methodologies, such as those embedded within multi-tiered RTI frameworks, student learning and growth improve, as do teacher decision making and instruction (Fuchs & Fuchs, 2002).

The MP3 model implemented in the Alliance School District[1] and described in Chapters 5 and 6 promoted exposure of all students in grades

---

[1] In this chapter, and Chapters 5 and 6, the name of the school district and the names of the three target schools in the district have all been replaced by pseudonyms.

1–4 to a research-based core reading curriculum and provision of empirically validated interventions to students who need them. Students' skills were continuously monitored to provide powerful evidence to guide teachers' instructional adaptations and modification when inadequate growth or "response" to intervention was detected in individual students. At the class or grade level, these data provided timely snapshots of cohort growth and efficacy data for Tier I grade-level reading instruction. At the teacher level, the MP3 model promoted teacher learning and professional growth around research-based reading instruction and assessment practices. At the district level, the MP3 model helped to create a dynamic, integrated instructional framework grounded in validated pedagogy and guided by outcome data. To evaluate these multiple layers of school-system change, the MP3 team tracked the "progress" of the RTI implementation just as they encouraged Alliance personnel to track the "progress" of individual students' learning to ensure that desired educational outcomes were being achieved. Successful implementation of RTI methodology was considered an evolving enterprise that required continuous evaluation and data-based modifications.

The goals for RTI in Project MP3 in the Alliance School District were simple: to increase reading success at the elementary grades in struggling schools and prevent student reading failure. We hoped to reduce the number of students at risk for reading problems, to "catch" students falling behind and introduce interventions that improved their reading growth, and to increase teachers' capacity to use data to make appropriate instructional changes in both their grouping decisions and their intervention strategies. Student achievement outcomes were used to evaluate the relative effectiveness of the instruction at each tier and overall. Teacher interviews, observations, and surveys were used to evaluate changes in teachers' knowledge and professional skills, as well as their beliefs in the capacity of their students to improve academically. In this chapter, we report the extent to which MP3 goals were accomplished. We begin with a discussion of student outcomes at each of the three implementation schools, follow with reports of teacher changes at each of the three sites, and conclude with an overall evaluation of the success of MP3 model implementation.

STUDENT OUTCOMES OF MP3 IMPLEMENTATION

Project MP3 was not designed as a research study with an experimental design. Instead, we developed a plan to systematically document the implementation of MP3 in each of the three schools in which we were working. Narrative note-taking was supplemented by student performance data on oral reading fluency (ORF) screening measures administered in fall, winter, and spring each year, as well as ORF PM data administered to particular students at varying frequencies based on student need. Student achievement data were collected at all three elementary schools each spring from 2006 through 2009. Intensive data collection began at Larue in the 2006–2007 school year and continued for 3 years. Intensive data collection began at Boyce and Washington 1 year later and continued for 2 years. Because each school was unique both with regard to the student body and the teaching staff and to their approach to model implementation, student outcomes are described for each school individually.

Measures of Student Achievement

Two types of student achievement data were used to examine the academic outcomes of model implementation: curriculum-based measures (CBM) and standardized test scores. CBM of reading performance for first through fourth graders included Dynamic Indicators of Basic Literacy Skills (DIBELS; Good & Kaminski, 2002) and the Reading Maze (Shinn & Shinn, 2002). Both were administered at regular intervals to provide indicators of improvement over time. Baseline CBM data were collected in the spring of 2006, prior to model implementation. During the 2006–2007 school year, universal screening data were collected three times (fall, winter, and spring) at each target school site. More frequent PM data were collected for students who scored below benchmark. For students whose CBM scores placed them in Tier 2 intervention, PM data were collected twice monthly. For students in Tier 3 intervention, CBM data were collected on a weekly basis.

CBM is considered a highly reliable overall indicator of a student's proficiency. In addition, CBM correlates strongly with high-stakes tests, including Pennsylvania's statewide accountability assessment (Shapiro, Keller, Lutz, Santoro, & Hintze, 2006). Because they repeatedly sample performance in the year-long curriculum, CBM tasks are ideal for measuring small gains toward long-range goals; CBM tasks allow teachers to predict in a short time whether an intervention is working or needs to be changed. With this information, instructional changes can be made as needed throughout the year. Moreover, CBMs are relatively easy and quick to administer, can be given repeatedly, and incorporate standardized methods for administration and scoring. For these reasons, CBM is well designed for instructional decision making in a tiered model.

It is important to recognize that CBM is designed to be an "indicator" of academic performance within a particular domain (Deno, 1985). Thus, although curriculum-based assessments provide useful information, they cannot tell us everything about a student's abilities. ORF measures are the most commonly used CBMs in reading for elementary students. They require students to read aloud from a passage for 1 minute. The number of words read correctly is scored. A robust research base has examined the technical adequacy of ORF measures. In a review of the literature, Wayman and colleagues report the findings of five studies that demonstrate test–retest reliability coefficients ranging from .82 to .97, with most above .90 (Wayman, Wallace, Wiley, Ticha, & Espin, 2007). Alternate-form reliability coefficients were likewise above .90. As far as validity, this review found 14 studies that related validity coefficients to criterion-related measures. The validity coefficients ranged from .63 to .90, with most above .80 when compared with published reading assessments. Correlations with basal series mastery tests ranged from .57 to .86. Additionally, ORF measures have been demonstrated to be sensitive to growth (Fuchs & Fuchs, 1992) and able to discriminate between skilled and less skilled readers. Hintze and Silberglitt (2005) assert that ORF accurately represents the overall level of competence in the domain of reading.

ORF measures show stronger correlations at the primary grades, decreasing at the intermediate level. In contrast, Maze correlations remain stable across grade levels. Correlations between the Maze and a 1-minute read-aloud in a random sample of elementary students across grades 3, 4, and 5 were .77, .86, and .86, respectively (Espin, Deno, Maruyama, & Cohen, 1989). Fuchs and Fuchs (1992) found that Maze scores were strongly correlated to a read-aloud ($r = .83$) and correlated to the Reading Comprehension subtest of the Stanford Achievement Test ($r = .77$).

In addition to these formative reading assessments, summative reading subtest scores were obtained from the annual statewide accountability assessment (Pennsylvania System of School Assessment [PSSA]) for third and fourth graders. The PSSA is a criterion-referenced assessment that assesses students' reading and math skills beginning in grade 3 (Pennsylvania Department of Education, 2003). The reading assessment portion of the PSSA covers five general skill areas. Students are required to read various passages and respond to them in ways that reflect different skills, including (1) reading independently; (2) reading critically; (3) reading, analyzing, and interpreting literature; (4) characteristics and function of the English language; and (5) research. Students' scaled scores correspond to one of four performance categories based on their scores: below basic, basic, proficient, and advanced. Scores at or above proficient are reported to be equivalent to the 43rd percentile performance on the PSSA. Scores at or above basic are equivalent to the 22nd percentile on the PSSA (Mead, Smith, & Swanlund, 2003).

Student Achievement at Baseline

The spring 2006 baseline benchmark offered a snapshot of the reading "health" of the three schools, an indicator of how students were performing prior to the implementation of MP3 (see Table 7.1). None of the schools was reaching an acceptable level of reading proficiency, but although all three schools were below average in ORF and Maze performance, one school in particular, Larue Elementary, was performing well below the others. Larue

TABLE 7.1. Baseline Means and Standard Deviations

Grade	Benchmark cut score	Larue		Washington		Boyce	
		Mean	SD	Mean	SD	Mean	SD
		2006 ORF					
1	40	21.7	21.02	28.9	23.46	56.4	30.85
2	90	42.6	30.65	78.5	78.49	75.0	35.01
3	110	83.3	27.93	97.7	36.22	111.5	28.68
4	118	66.9	25.98	87.2	27.72	87.3	25.86
		2006 Maze					
2	[a]	6.7	5.62	10.1	5.34	10.5	5.26
3	[a]	6.5	3.29	9.7	4.60	10.0	5.08
4	20	9.5	4.09	13.7	5.73	13.8	6.11

[a]Cut score indicating benchmark performance not yet established.

had an alarmingly high proportion of students who scored in the at-risk category (see Figure 7.1), about 50% more than the other buildings. It was for this very reason that Project MP3 began model implementation at Larue.

Larue Elementary after 1 Year of MP3 Implementation

During the 2006–2007 school year, MP3 staff worked closely and intensively with teachers at Larue to implement the new core curriculum, PM, and data-based instructional decision making. The work paid off. When we compared spring-to-spring benchmark scores (see Figure 7.2), it was clear that students at Larue were making progress, although not nearly

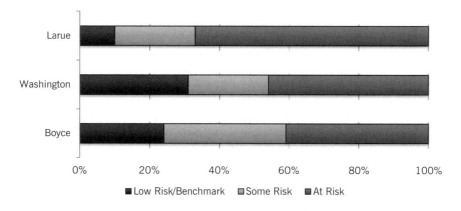

FIGURE 7.1. Distribution of DIBELS ORF scores at baseline.

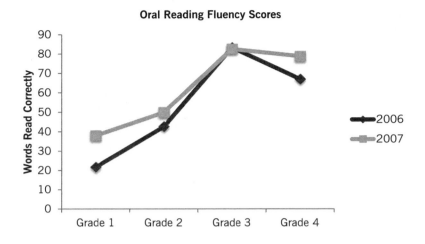

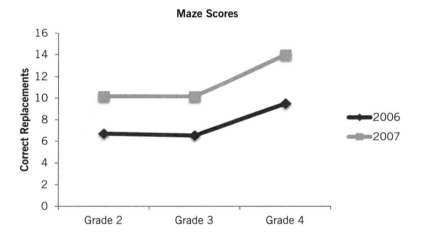

FIGURE 7.2. ORF and Maze scores for Larue students after 1 year.

the dramatic turnaround that we had hoped for. Each grade level (with the exception of grade 3, whose ORF scores were static) performed better at the end of the first year of MP3 than they had prior to implementing RTI. The most encouraging findings, the first-grade data, helped build momentum for model implementation.

The PM data also helped MP3 staff and teachers judge the impact of the tiered interventions. We compared the distribution of students among the tiers (based on the PM data) in the fall and in the spring, using movement of student placements from Tier 3 to Tier 1 as one indicator of success. For example, complete fall, winter, and spring data were available for

53 second graders and 45 third graders at Larue. Fall DIBELS scores indicated that 7 of the second graders achieved the fall benchmark, 10 scored in the "some-risk" range, and 35 scored in the "at risk" range. By spring, the distribution had shifted slightly, with 8 students achieving benchmark status, 13 students scoring in the "some-risk" range, and 31 students scoring in the "at-risk" range. In other words, there was a net loss of 4 students from Tier 3, a net gain of 3 students at Tier 2, and a net gain of 1 student in Tier 1. At third grade, there were 4 students who achieved benchmark status in the fall, 15 whose scores placed them at "some risk," and 26 whose scores placed them "at risk." By spring, those numbers had shifted to 7 students at benchmark, 15 students at "some risk," and 23 students "at risk." This meant a net loss of 3 students from Tier 3 and a net gain of 3 in Tier 1. Although the number of students in each grade who moved across tiers was small, the teachers were encouraged to see increases in the population of Tier 1 and decreases in the population of Tier 3. We allowed the third-grade teachers to celebrate their moderate successes, but closer inspection of the second-grade data led to a sobering reevaluation of interventions in all three second-grade tiers. Figure 7.3 illustrates graphically

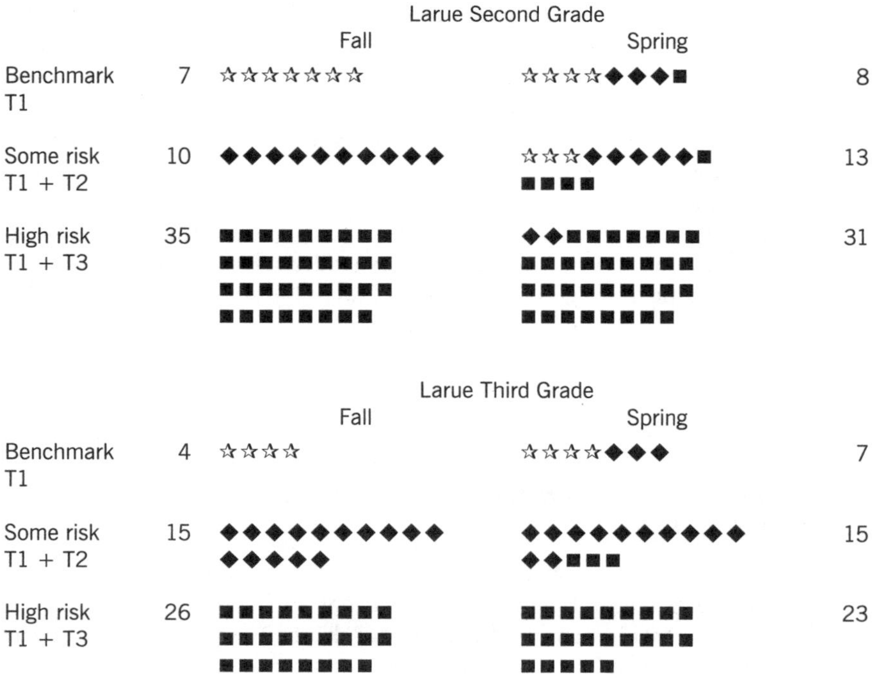

FIGURE 7.3. Movement of second- and third-grade students across tiers of instruction at Larue Elementary in the 2006–2007 school year.

the distribution of second and third graders into tiers in fall and spring of the 2006–2007 school year. Each star represents a student who achieved benchmark status in the fall testing and received the Tier 1 "enrichment" intervention, each diamond represents a student scoring at "some risk" in the fall and receiving Tier 2 intervention, and each square represents a student who scored in the "at-risk" range and received Tier 3 interventions. At third grade, all movement across tiers was in the hoped-for direction (i.e., from Tier 3 to Tier 2, or Tier 2 to Tier 1). At second grade some students moved up, but some also moved down the proficiency ladder. This detailed tracking of student movement demonstrated vividly the variability of student outcomes in each of the second-grade instructional tiers and suggested that celebration was premature.

These and other formative analyses of the achievement data also helped shape and focus MP3 staff efforts for Year 2. For example, we noticed considerable growth in Larue students' ORF DIBELS data for each grade level from fall to winter benchmark but then a flat line, or decreased growth, from winter to spring. Larue teachers reported that between January and April, considerable amounts of intervention time were lost, first from school cancellations/snow days, then from 2-hour delays in the start of school because of weather conditions (reading was taught first thing in the morning and was skipped when the start of school was delayed), and finally because class time was increasingly devoted to preparation for the statewide accountability assessments. Because interventions occurred intermittently, teachers were not following intervention programs with as much fidelity as they had in the fall. Momentum waned as the weather warmed and state testing grew near. In Years 2 and 3 of model implementation, we would have to deal with this issue.

Despite the imperfections of the first year of MP3 implementation, Larue ended the academic year with improved student achievement (see Figure 7.4). The percentage of students achieving grade-level benchmarks rose from 10 to 24%; the percentage of students scoring in the at-risk range decreased from 67 to 52%. With 1 year of RTI completed, Larue looked forward to assuming more and more responsibility for keeping RTI working in their building.

Achievement Outcomes after Washington and Boyce Come on Board

Teachers and administrators at Washington and Boyce Elementary saw the changes taking place at Larue and were eager to begin utilizing RTI in their buildings. During year 1 of the project, both Washington and Boyce had implemented the new core reading program that had been instituted at Larue. Data from these schools indicated that implementation of the core reading program alone in grades 1–4 was having a positive impact on stu-

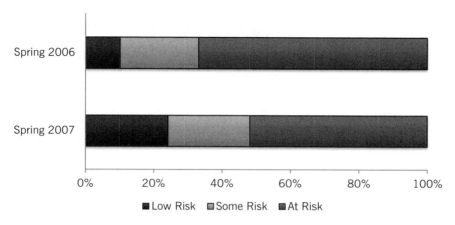

FIGURE 7.4. Changes in student achievement after 1 year of model implementation at Larue Elementary.

dent achievement. Each school looked forward to the value that implementing the MP3 model would provide.

As RTI took shape at Washington and Boyce, many of the support resources at Larue were shifted to the new implementation sites. Nevertheless, when the outcomes across all three schools in the second and third years were reviewed, even greater improvement trends were in evidence than those that had been experienced the first year at Larue. In each of the schools, the numbers of students achieving DIBELS benchmarks, reading at grade level, and requiring only Tier 1 instruction grew steadily.

Changes on the State Accountability Assessment

We begin with a close look at PSSA Reading scores for students in grades 3, 4, and 5 in each of the three buildings. In Table 7.2, we provide the percentage of students scoring at proficient or advanced (above approximately the 43rd percentile) levels on the state accountability measure in the spring of 2006 (i.e., before implementation of MP3) and in the spring of 2009 (i.e., after 3 years of Project MP3). The table also provides the percentage of students scoring below basic (i.e., below the 22nd percentile) on the PSSA. Improvements were remarkable at all three schools.

Changes in Reading Fluency Rates

Screening data collected three times per year also show a steady increase in CBM scores at all grade levels and across each of the project schools. During the baseline CBM data collection across the three schools in grade 3 in

TABLE 7.2. Percent of Students Scoring Proficient + Advanced and below Basic on PSSA before and after MP3 Implementation

School	Grade	Percent scoring proficient + advanced			Grade	Percent scoring below basic		
		2006	2009	Percent change		2006	2009	Percent change
Larue	3	26%	38%	+12%	3	48%	42%	−6%
	4	20%	31%	+11%	4	54%	40%	−14%
	5	10%	40%	+30%	5	69%	35%	−34%
Washington	3	78%	94%	+16%	3	11%	0%	−11%
	4	57%	70%	+13%	4	11%	15%	−4%
	5	57%	60%	+3%	5	23%	21%	−2%
Boyce	3	54%	80%	+26%	3	20%	6%	−14%
	4	62%	70%	+8%	4	20%	17%	−3%
	5	50%	53%	+3%	5	32%	34%	−2%

the spring of 2006, only 22% of students scored at the low-risk level. This meant that less than a quarter of students were reading at grade level. This number increased steadily over the next 3 years. By spring 2009, the percentage of students reading at grade level rose to 53% (Figure 7.5). Just over half of the students were reading successfully, on grade level! In the same time period, the percentage of third graders meeting the target grade-level score on the Maze test rose from 15.6% to 41.0% (Figure 7.6).

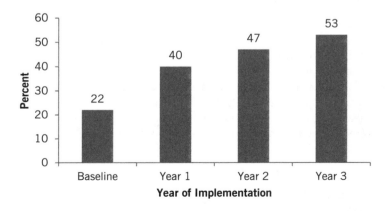

FIGURE 7.5. Percentage of students reading at grade level.

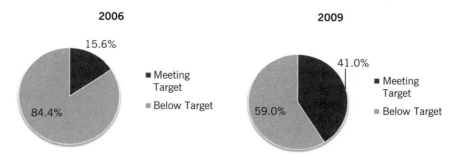

FIGURE 7.6. Percentage of students attaining Maze targets.

Growth within Tiers

One method of quantifying student growth in an RTI framework is to utilize the slope, or rate of improvement (ROI), on a frequently administered measure. Examining the average ROI within each tier of reading intervention provides an index both of student progress and of the effectiveness of instruction at that tier.

Measurement of growth for PM is based on the accuracy or reliability of the slope produced by multiple repeated scores. The slope represents the average unit gain over a specific period of time. For the ORF measure, a mean increase in the number of correct words read per week is used as an index of improvement. Similarly, an increase in the number of correct selections on the Maze can be used to quantify growth. Ideally, the slope is easy to compute and interpret and an accurate predictor of future performance; it can minimize the individual errors of prediction. The most common way of calculating slope uses the ordinary least squares method of linear regression.

So that reading CBM can be utilized as a valid and reliable index to student growth, standards for rates of growth have been proposed. First, empirical evidence demonstrates that growth on reading CBM tends to be inversely related to grade level; growth is more dramatic in the primary grades. Most standard growth rates in use today reflect this phenomenon. In an influential study, Hasbrouck and Tindal (2006) identified norms for students in grades 2–5 for the three annual performance benchmarks (fall, winter, spring) with a sample of more than 7,000 students over 9 years. Similarly, Fuchs, Fuchs, Hamlett, Walz, and Germann (1993) established weekly growth rates for ORF and the Maze task in grades 1–6. These are average rates of weekly improvement, or what can be expected of typical academic development.

For Project MP3 we relied on these accepted norms for grade-level targets, as well as individual rates of improvement. This simplified the data decision-making process, although its accuracy in predicting progress for students who have the most significant reading problems is not clear (e.g., Hintze & Silberglitt, 2005, have suggested that using growth rate estimates based on initial decile performance results in more accurate growth expectations). Nonetheless, we utilized the generally accepted targets in our data analysis. In practice, as teachers set their goals for the benchmark period, two words per week was considered an ambitious goal. For low-performing students and students with IEPs, the expectation was somewhat lower, but still relatively high, 1.5 words per week. Minimum targets would be set at the number of words needed to move to the next tier or, in the case of Tier 1, to progress to the next grade-level target on schedule. For students in Tier 3, setting the goal for a student to move up a tier was often unrealistic. Instead, for the lowest performing students, the goal was set to provide growth sufficient to narrow the gap between these poor readers and their more fluent peers.

The third-grade cohort of 2008–2009 had an average ROI of 0.9, slightly less than one word per week growth on the ORF measure. Fuchs and colleagues (1993) conclude that approximately one word per week is a realistic goal for a typical third grader; an ambitious goal might be 1.5 words per week gain. The ROI of 0.9 represents nearly average growth for typical students in the third grade. However, there were large numbers of struggling readers in the third grade. Only 49% of third graders scored in the benchmark range in the fall of 2008. More ambitious goals would be needed for these students to reach grade-level targets. Table 7.3 provides the mean ORF scores for each of the instructional tiers across each benchmarking period during the 2008–2009 school year and the mean ROI for each instructional tier. The target ROI of 0.9 is the minimum growth a low Tier 2 child would need in order to meet benchmark in the following period.

On average, students in each of the tiers of intervention made the expected ROI, and as a total group, the average ROI across all tiers, fall to spring, was 0.95. These averages, however, obscure the fact that some students in each tier made substantial progress, enough to move them to a less intensive level of intervention, whereas some students made meager progress or regressed. "Responders" to Tier 3 intervention (i.e., the 8 of 38

TABLE 7.3. Third-Grade Fluency Scores by Tier

	Tier 1			Tier 2			Tier 3		
Period	n	Mean	% of total	n	Mean	% of total	n	Mean	% of total
Fall	71	102.48	49%	36	64.61	25%	38	32.18	26%
Winter	73	115.88	52%	37	79.78	26%	32	46.94	23%
Spring	74	134.68	54%	36	98	26%	27	58.18	20%
ROI		0.93			1.03			0.89	

students who moved to a less intensive tier and remained there through the spring benchmark) had a mean ROI of 1.44. "Nonresponders" in Tier 3, the remaining 30 of 38 students, had an ROI of just 0.67 words per week. This is well below the overall average ROI for the third grade and insufficient to narrow the gap.

Similarly, although students placed in Tier 2 interventions had the highest average ROI of the three tiers, a full third of the students in Tier 2 interventions were not making adequate progress. Of the 36 students who were placed in Tier 2 interventions in the fall, 12 (33%) failed to achieve the target ROI. As a group these 12 students had an average growth of just under 0.5 words read correctly per week; fewer than 18 words a year! On the whole, the poorest readers were actually losing ground and were visible proof that implementation of the model needed tweaking if the goal was to have *all* students "catch up."

Closing the Achievement Gap

One interesting outcome of Project MP3 was a narrowing of the gap between Larue and the other two project schools. Figure 7.7 shows how the performance of Larue began to more closely resemble the other project schools over the 3 years since RTI had been in place. Although Larue's students had not, as a group, yet caught up with their neighboring buildings, they had made important strides in that direction.

Referrals to Special Education

At Larue, in 2008–2009, almost half (49%; *n* = 25) of the 51 third graders began the year requiring Tier 3 intensive intervention. The bulk of the remaining students required Tier 2 strategic intervention (29%; *n* = 15)

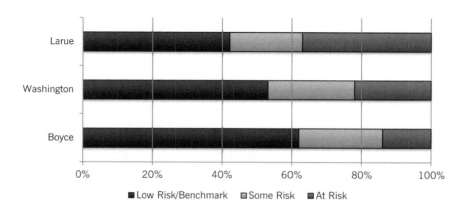

FIGURE 7.7. Distribution of DIBELS ORF scores at end of Year 3.

with only 22% (*n* = 11) reaching third-grade ORF benchmarks. By spring, the distribution of third graders had changed considerably, to 40% of students in Tier 3, 32% in Tier 2, and 28% in Tier 1. Achievement seemed to be "moving" in the right direction: fewer students at risk, more at low risk for reading failure. On the whole, Larue's third graders gained an average of 0.9 words per week across the school year—slightly below the one-word-per-week gain expected of "healthy" readers (Fuchs et al., 1993).

Among the 51 third graders in 2008–2009, 9 were students with IEP goals in reading. That constitutes a placement rate in special education of 17.6% of the third-grade cohort and does not count the additional two third graders with IEPs who did not have reading goals. ORF scores at the start of third grade for 7 of these 9 students with IEP reading goals placed them into Tier 3, intensive interventions, where they joined an additional 18 students who scored in the at-risk category but were not assigned to special education. The mean ORF rate for the special education students with reading IEP goals was 27 words correct per minute; their nondisabled low-performing peers read, on average, 36 words correct per minute. The fall benchmark goal for third graders was 77 words per minute (WPM). Over time, with the delivery of at least 30 minutes of daily small-group intensive intervention to supplement 60 minutes of third-grade core reading instruction, these rates increased by January to a mean of 43 WPM for students with IEPs and 53 WPM for students without IEPs, still far short of the 92 WPM cut score indicating benchmark performance. By spring, however, only 18 of the original 25 Tier 3 students remained in Tier 3. Two of the 7 students with IEPs had made sufficient progress to be placed in Tier 2 instead, as had 2 of the students without IEPs; 2 students without IEPs had moved to another school. On spring testing, the students with and without IEPs remaining in Tier 3 scored at about the same level, a mean of 60 words correct per minute and 64 words correct per minute, respectively. Three of the students without IEPs who remained in Tier 3 had been referred for special education evaluation during that third-grade year, and ultimately 2 were found eligible for services after the multidisciplinary evaluation was completed; none of the students already assigned to special education were designated as no longer eligible. That brought the placement rate for third graders from 11 of 51 (21.6%) to 13 of 49 (26.5%).

Two questions come to mind. First, in a traditional RTI model, wouldn't the poor rate of progress for all 14 Tier 3 students without IEPs who failed to move up a tier after 1 year of intensive intervention mean that all of these students (instead of just 2) should be found eligible for special education? Of course, that would have meant a placement rate of more than 50% of third graders [(11+14)/49], an unthinkable idea.

Second, what did being found eligible for placement in special education "purchase" for the students who had IEPs? The introduction of the MP3 RTI model in 2006 coincided with the settlement of the *Gaskin v.*

Pennsylvania Department of Education (2004) case, which called for increasing the amount of time all students with disabilities spent in general education classrooms. Special education resource rooms and self-contained classes at Larue were closed, and all students with disabilities attending Larue (i.e., students with speech–language impairments, learning disabilities, behavior disorders, and mild to moderate mental retardation) were returned to age-appropriate general education classrooms for most, if not all, of the school day. This meant that all students with IEPs were to receive core reading instruction on grade level in the general education classroom. The core reading block at Larue lasted approximately 60 minutes in grades 1 and 2 and 90 minutes in grades 3–5. At the start of the 2006–2007 school year, before intervention groups were established, the two elementary-level special education teachers were directed to "co-teach" during core reading instruction. In an effort to support each student on their caseload, the "primary-grades" special education teacher rotated among 10 classrooms— the four first-grade classrooms, the three second-grade classrooms, and the three third-grade classrooms—spending no more than 30 minutes in each classroom on any given day. This schedule allowed her to be present for at least some of core reading time in all classrooms at some point during the week. The "intermediate" special education teacher used the same model, dividing his time among six classrooms—the three fourth-grade classrooms and the three fifth-grade classrooms. Because of their staggered schedules and limited time, however, little "co-teaching" actually occurred (see Kloo & Zigmond, 2009). Instead, paraprofessionals were assigned to support individual students whose IEPs warranted more direct support (usually due to behavioral difficulties) during the grade-level core reading instructional time. This support typically entailed encouraging time on task, discouraging disruptive behaviors, and providing assistance as needed.

When reading intervention groups were formed in late fall 2006, the service delivery model was again altered to manage the large numbers of students with intensive intervention needs and the limited numbers of staff members available to provide the small-group intensive intervention required by the model. Special education teachers were reassigned to teach an intensive intervention group of the lowest achievers at each grade level (as long as this group had at least one student with a disability assigned to it, thus continuing to promote inclusive instruction). The schedule of intensive Tier 3 interventions kept each of the two special education teachers providing reading intervention to a group of students throughout each morning, thereby eliminating their time to co-teach and significantly reducing their time available to provide or support specially designed instruction to students with IEPs in math or other content subjects. For students with IEPs in reading, Tier 3 *was* their special education instruction, so in this RTI model, the value of being found eligible for special education services was questionable.

Summary

There can be no doubt that student academic achievement improved during the 3 years of MP3 implementation. The data chronicle a dramatic rise in the number of students reaching grade-level standards in reading and a decline in the number of students performing far below grade level. In analysis after analysis, outcomes reflected increased reading success in each of the three schools and at all grade levels 1–4.

Of course, it is important to put these improvements into perspective. Student achievement data from spring 2006 and additional data collected as school started in fall 2006 did not fit the standard RTI pyramid. In a theoretical RTI model, approximately 80% of students are achieving "benchmark" levels of proficiency on the DIBELS and need only Tier 1 instruction; 5% of students score in the at-risk range and are in need of intensive Tier 3 interventions. At the start of MP3 only 10% of Larue students, 31% of Washington students, and 24% of Boyce students scored at or above benchmark, while 67% of Larue students, 46% of Washington students, and 41% of Boyce students scored within the at-risk range and were in need of the intensive interventions typically associated with Tier 3 (see Figure 7.8). At all three schools, the RTI pyramid was essentially inverted. By the end of 3 years, the RTI pyramid began to reshape in all three schools (see Figure 7.8). At Larue 42% of students were achieving benchmark scores and only 37% were at risk. At Washington, 53% of students were achieving benchmark scores and 22% were at risk. In Boyce, 62% of students were achieving benchmark scores and 14% were at risk. These changes were phenomenal, but none of the schools achieved the percentages usually associated with a "healthy" school undertaking a tiered instruction–RTI model. Nevertheless, the district believed that its primary goals for RTI had been met.

CHANGES IN TEACHER AND INSTRUCTIONAL PRACTICE

In addition to monitoring student achievement during the implementation of MP3, we made a conscientious effort to collect systematic evaluation data on changes in teachers' thinking and behavior. We used formal and informal interviews, questionnaires and surveys, and classroom observations to evaluate the impact of MP3 on teachers in each of the three schools.

Measures of Teacher Outcomes

Numerous explorations of factors influencing successful applications of RTI methodology have reported on the significance of teachers' professional knowledge and pedagogical skills. Practices such as evidence-based

Distribution 1: RTI in Theory—Tier 1 (80%), Tier 2 (15%), Tier 3 (5%)

1%	1%	.5	.5	1%	1%	1%	1%	.5	.5	1%	1%
1%	1%	1%	1%	1%	1%	1%	1%	1%	1%		
1%	1%	1%	1%	1%	1%	1%	1%	1%	1%		
1%	1%	1%	1%	1%	1%	1%	1%	1%	1%		
1%	1%	1%	1%	1%	1%	1%	1%	1%	1%		
1%	1%	1%	1%	1%	1%	1%	1%	1%	1%		
1%	1%	1%	1%	1%	1%	1%	1%	1%	1%		
1%	1%	1%	1%	1%	1%	1%	1%	1%	1%		
1%	1%	1%	1%	1%	1%	1%	1%	1%	1%		
1%	1%	1%	1%	1%	1%	1%	1%	1%	1%		

School Population

Distribution 2a: Larue Prior to Implementation—Tier 1 (10%), Tier 2 (23%), Tier 3 (67%)

1%	1%	1%	1%	1%	1%	1%	1%	1%	1%		
1%	1%	1%	1%	1%	1%	1%	1%	1%	1%		
1%	1%	1%	1%	1%	1%	1%	1%	1%	1%		
1%	1%	1%	1%	1%	1%	1%	1%	1%	1%		
1%	1%	1%	1%	1%	1%	1%	1%	1%	1%		
1%	1%	1%	1%	1%	1%	1%	1%	1%	1%		
1%	.5	.5	1%	1%	1%	1%	1%	1%	.5	.5	1%
1%	1%	1%	1%	1%	1%	1%	1%	1%	1%		
1%	1%	1%	1%	1%	1%	1%	1%	1%	1%		
1%	1%	1%	1%	1%	1%	1%	1%	1%	1%		

School Population

Distribution 2b: Washington Prior to Implementation—Tier 1 (31%), Tier 2 (23%), Tier 3 (46%)

1%	1%	1%	1%	1%	1%	1%	1%	1%	1%		
1%	1%	1%	1%	1%	1%	1%	1%	1%	1%		
1%	1%	1%	1%	1%	1%	1%	1%	1%	1%		
1%	1%	1%	1%	1%	1%	1%	1%	1%	1%		
1%	1%	1%	1%	1%	1%	1%	1%	1%	1%		
1%	1%	1%	1%	1%	1%	1%	1%	1%	1%		
.5	.5	1%	1%	1%	1%	1%	1%	1%	1%	.5	.5
1%	1%	1%	1%	1%	1%	1%	1%	1%	1%		
1%	1%	1%	1%	1%	1%	1%	1%	1%	1%		
1%	1%	1%	1%	1%	1%	1%	1%	1%	1%		

School Population

FIGURE 7.8. Distribution of benchmark, some-risk, and at-risk students at the three target schools prior to MP3 implementation and 3 years later.

Distribution 2c: Boyce Prior to Implementation—Tier 1 (24%), Tier 2 (35%), Tier 3 (41%)

School Population

1%	1%	1%	1%	1%	1%	1%	1%	1%	1%
1%	1%	1%	1%	1%	1%	1%	1%	1%	1%
1%	1%	1%	1%	1%	1%	1%	1%	1%	1%
1%	1%	1%	1%	1%	1%	1%	1%	1%	1%
.5 .5	1%	1%	1%	1%	1%	1%	1%	1%	.5 .5
1%	1%	1%	1%	1%	1%	1%	1%	1%	1%
1%	1%	1%	1%	1%	1%	1%	1%	1%	1%
1%	1%	1%	1%	1%	1%	1%	1%	1%	1%
1%	1%	1%	1%	1%	1%	1%	1%	1%	1%
1%	1%	1%	1%	1%	1%	1%	1%	1%	1%

Distribution 3a: Larue End of Year 3 of Implementation—Tier 1 (42%), Tier 2 (21%), Tier 3 (37%)

School Population

1%	1%	1%	1%	1%	1%	1%	1%	1%	1%
1%	1%	1%	1%	1%	1%	1%	1%	1%	1%
1%	1%	1%	1%	1%	1%	1%	1%	1%	1%
1%	1%	1%	1%	1%	1%	1%	1%	1%	1%
1%	1%	1%	1%	1%	1%	1%	1%	1%	1%
1%	1%	1%	1%	1%	1%	1%	1%	1%	1%
1%	1%	1%	1%	1%	1%	1%	1%	1%	1%
1%	1%	1%	1%	1%	1%	1%	1%	1%	1%
1%	1%	1%	1%	1%	1%	1%	1%	1%	1%
1%	1%	1%	1%	1%	1%	1%	1%	1%	1%

Distribution 3b: Washington End of Year 3 of Implementation—Tier 1 (53%), Tier 2 (25%), Tier 3 (22%)

School Population

1%	1%	1%	1%	1%	1%	1%	1%	1%	1%
1%	1%	1%	1%	1%	1%	1%	1%	1%	1%
1%	1%	1%	1%	1%	1%	1%	1%	1%	1%
1%	1%	1%	1%	1%	1%	1%	1%	1%	1%
1%	1%	1%	.5 .5	1%	1%	.5 .5	1%	1%	1%
1%	1%	1%	1%	1%	1%	1%	1%	1%	1%
1%	1%	1%	1%	1%	1%	1%	1%	1%	1%
1%	1%	1%	1%	1%	1%	1%	1%	1%	1%
1%	1%	1%	1%	1%	1%	1%	1%	1%	1%
1%	1%	1%	1%	1%	1%	1%	1%	1%	1%

FIGURE 7.8. *(cont.)*

Distribution 3c: Boyce End of Year 3 of Implementation—Tier 1 (62%), Tier 2 (24%), Tier 3 (14%)

<table>
<tr><td rowspan="10" style="writing-mode:vertical-rl">School Population</td><td>1%</td><td>1%</td><td colspan="2">1%</td><td>1%</td><td>1%</td><td>1%</td><td colspan="2">1%</td><td>1%</td><td>1%</td><td>1%</td></tr>
<tr><td>1%</td><td>1%</td><td>.5</td><td>.5</td><td>1%</td><td>1%</td><td>1%</td><td>.5</td><td>.5</td><td>1%</td><td>1%</td><td>1%</td></tr>
<tr><td>1%</td><td>1%</td><td colspan="2">1%</td><td>1%</td><td>1%</td><td>1%</td><td colspan="2">1%</td><td>1%</td><td>1%</td><td>1%</td></tr>
<tr><td>1%</td><td>1%</td><td colspan="2">1%</td><td>1%</td><td>1%</td><td>1%</td><td colspan="2">1%</td><td>1%</td><td>1%</td><td>1%</td></tr>
<tr><td>1%</td><td>1%</td><td colspan="2">1%</td><td>1%</td><td>1%</td><td>1%</td><td colspan="2">1%</td><td>1%</td><td>1%</td><td>1%</td></tr>
<tr><td>1%</td><td>1%</td><td colspan="2">1%</td><td>1%</td><td>1%</td><td>1%</td><td colspan="2">1%</td><td>1%</td><td>1%</td><td>1%</td></tr>
<tr><td>1%</td><td>1%</td><td colspan="2">1%</td><td>1%</td><td>1%</td><td>1%</td><td colspan="2">1%</td><td>1%</td><td>1%</td><td>1%</td></tr>
<tr><td>1%</td><td>1%</td><td colspan="2">1%</td><td>1%</td><td>1%</td><td>1%</td><td colspan="2">1%</td><td>1%</td><td>1%</td><td>1%</td></tr>
<tr><td>1%</td><td>1%</td><td colspan="2">1%</td><td>1%</td><td>1%</td><td>1%</td><td colspan="2">1%</td><td>1%</td><td>1%</td><td>1%</td></tr>
<tr><td>1%</td><td>1%</td><td colspan="2">1%</td><td>1%</td><td>1%</td><td>1%</td><td colspan="2">1%</td><td>1%</td><td>1%</td><td>1%</td></tr>
</table>

KEY: �+ Students performing at high risk on DIBELS benchmark testing

▫ Students performing at some risk on DIBELS benchmark testing

☐ Students performing at or above benchmark on DIBELS benchmark testing

FIGURE 7.8. *(cont.).*

instruction and intervention in reading, math, and behavior; teaming and problem solving; and data-based decision making increase the likelihood of a successful RTI implementation for students and schools (Barnett et al., 1999; Fuchs, 2003; Gresham, 2004; Lentz, Allen, & Ehrhardt, 1996). Research also suggests that teacher efficacy is both an outcome and an influential variable in implementing best instructional practice. That is, as teacher efficacy increases, a school's capacity to effect positive student outcomes also increases (Guskey & Passaro, 1994). Teachers who possess a high level of efficacy better facilitate student performance, which may be associated with improved teaching practice and improved teacher self-efficacy beliefs overall (Bandura, 1997). In an exploration of the relationship between professional development, teacher efficacy, and RTI implementation, Nunn and Jantz (2008) highlighted substantive links between teacher beliefs and teacher practice with student outcomes.

In this implementation of and approach to RTI, three types of teacher change data were analyzed to capture changes in teacher behavior and instructional practices. These included interview data, focus group data, and instructional survey/observation data. Teacher interviews and observations of classroom reading instruction occurred at each target school during the spring prior to model implementation, in the spring after 1 year of implementation, then again after 2 years. Focus groups of teachers were convened after each year of implementation. The qualitative data gathered from these investigations helped us to capture teacher practice, as well as teacher feelings of self-efficacy. Both are powerful influences on student outcomes, school change, and innovation/initiative implementation (Bandura, 1994; Erdem & Demirel, 2007).

Teachers and Teaching before MP3

As we discussed in Chapters 5 and 6 of this volume, the teaching staffs at the three Alliance schools were not very sophisticated. In interviews with MP3 staff members before the implementation of the RTI model, teachers were quite candid about their limited knowledge or understanding of reading methodology, of instructional practices for struggling readers, or of PM and data-based decision making. Teachers reported feeling frustrated and ill equipped to meet the needs of struggling readers. They felt devalued by district administrators and colleagues from higher performing district schools because of their students' low achievement. They were overwhelmed by pressures to improve their students' performance on the state accountability assessment, the PSSA. Those teachers who did generate new ideas felt restricted in their ability to implement them in the face of districtwide curriculum constraints and mandates. Most had stopped attending available trainings or workshops because the new instructional strategies seemed to be in conflict with district ideologies. The Alliance School District teachers felt disconnected or professionally isolated from colleagues because there were no established, sanctioned joint planning or teaming opportunities.

The teachers at our three target buildings were also fearful. They had experienced years and years of negative evaluations by district administrators and the school board based on their students' low performance. They were embarrassed by their students' low performance and were angry about being blamed for their students' struggles with academic achievement. In building-based focus group meetings in the spring before the implementation of MP3, they were candid in expressing conflicting feelings of confusion, skepticism, negativity, and hopefulness.

Confusion

Teachers in the Alliance School District were receiving conflicting messages about best instructional practices from the director of curriculum and Title I teachers versus the MP3 staff and intermediate unit trainers. For years, they had been told that direct teaching of phonics or other discrete prerequisite reading skills inhibited their students' ability to fully engage with text on a language-rich, whole-word, meaning-based level. One third-grade teacher from Boyce described this feeling of confusion as being "like drafted soldiers in the Reading Wars . . . unsure of which side to fight for and terrified of becoming a casualty."

Skepticism

Teachers were also skeptical about investing their energies into a project introduced by "outsiders" to the district. Numerous initiatives had come and gone in the Alliance School District over recent years; none had had much impact on student performance or teacher practice. Teachers saw no reason to believe the results of the MP3 project would be any different. They were leery of Project MP3 staff and very uncomfortable with the prospect of direct, onsite daily consultation. They did not want to have "spies" observing instruction in their classrooms, criticizing their teaching, or reporting their failings to the principal or other district administrators.

Negativity

Many teachers openly resented the "extra work" the project entailed and were especially unconvinced that 1-minute-long oral reading assessments could provide *any* accurate or useful information about students' reading ability. They were certain that model implementation would take too much teacher time and use up too many school resources. They believed that including students with disabilities in core grade-level reading instruction was simply unrealistic because those students would disrupt other students' learning and require too much teacher attention. Many classroom teachers were nervous and upset that they would be expected to deliver Tier 1 core reading instruction *plus* various levels of intervention instruction to inclusive groups of regular education and special education students without specialized training in special education. And several of the teachers did not want to give up what they called "free periods" for common planning time or grade-level team meetings about student progress and reading instruction.

Hopefulness

Despite the somewhat negative tone of the initial focus groups, there were some teachers who looked forward to having sacrosanct collaborative planning time and opportunities for professional discussions with colleagues; such opportunities were currently extremely rare given current schedules and the day-to-day chaos of student behavior problems. Some teachers sincerely hoped that Project MP3 would help them reach their lowest performing students whom they now felt impotent to help.

Teachers and Teaching after Model Implementation

Even more impressive than the student-level growth observed as a result of implementation of the MP3 were the notable changes in instructional practice and teacher efficacy. Across the three years of the project, we witnessed a professional transformation of the Alliance School District. Classroom observation and instructional survey data showed dramatic changes in teachers' understanding and application of research-based reading practice. This is perhaps the most important outcome of the MP3 implementation in these low-performing schools. Although changes in student achievement are desired and sought, those changes affect one particular group of students at one point in time. Changes in the attitudes, thinking, perspectives, and approaches of the teaching staff members are what will sustain academic improvements into the future. For example, MP3 staff documented a steady increase in the explicit and systematic teaching of the National Reading Panel's (NRP) "5 Big Ideas" (National Institute of Child Health and Human Development [NICHD], 2000). Prior to model implementation, none of the teaching staff members reported feeling knowledgeable about the research-based instructional strategies recommended by the NRP to fully address phonemic awareness, alphabetic principle, ORF, vocabulary, and comprehension during reading instruction. Direct instruction of reading skills was rare. Teachers reported that the district was strongly committed to a "balanced literacy curriculum" in which instruction was centered on implementing guided reading (Fountas & Pinnell, 1991) in small groups of students using instructional-level books. Although district achievement data clearly indicated that this approach was not yielding good outcomes for many of the district's students, most teachers reported feeling restricted in, even prohibited from, teaching phonics or code-based strategies because, despite the data, whole-language ideologies were strongly supported by powerful district administrators and influential Title I teachers.

After 1 year of implementation, during which MP3 introduced an evidence-based core reading program to the district, we saw drastic positive changes in instructional practice. Eighty-five percent of the 36 first- through fourth-grade teachers across the three target schools reported doing both whole-group and small-group instruction on each of the "5 Big Ideas" more than 3 days per week during core reading time, compared with the 40% who reported addressing those skills before Project MP3. A total of 100% reported addressing these critical skills four to five times per week in small-group interventions, whereas only 60% had reported directly teaching these skills to students during guided-reading groups. School principals and MP3 staff used such terms as "deliberate," "explicit," and "focused" to describe the postimplementation instruction they observed in classrooms, compared with such words as "incidental" and "infrequent" that were used before implementation of RTI. Most dramatic was the increase in code-based reading instruction of phonemic and phonological skills and specific strategy instruction of comprehension and vocabulary skills. For example, 14 (38%) classroom teachers reported systematically teaching segmenting, decoding, and blending strategies for reading unknown words prior to receiving training in evidence-based reading instruction provided by MP3 staff. After participating in 1 year of ongoing, onsite professional development focused on reading instruction and RTI methodology, that number increased to 75%. By the end of Year 3, 89% of teachers responsible for Tier 1 core reading instruction reported explicitly teaching such skills to all of their students, along with providing supplemental small-group or individual support to the struggling readers in their classes. Furthermore, teachers, principals, and administrators had rated *data-based decision making to inform instructional changes based on assessment of students' reading skills* as "infrequent" prior to RTI implementation. Then, after the RTI model was well established at each site, teachers reported that *data-based decision making based on progress monitoring data* became a part of "daily" practice (i.e., 17% in Year 1; 23% in Year 2; 93% in Year 3).

Teachers also reported that their perceptions of self-efficacy improved as their facility with the model (tiered instruction with PM and regular data-based changes in groupings and interventions) improved.

Teacher interviews and focus group discussions confirmed substantive changes in Larue, Washington, and Boyce teachers. After 3 years of MP3 implementation, the teachers viewed themselves as burgeoning "reading experts" and "effective reading/language arts teachers." They were proud of their role in promoting student growth and success; they described themselves as "change agents," "motivators," "leaders," and "role models." Teachers reported feeling confident in their ability to make thoughtful, accurate instructional decisions based on multiple sources of student data. They felt supported by colleagues, principals, and administrators in their efforts to provide quality instruction and to implement new strategies. They no longer felt isolated, but instead were members of a collaborative team. And there appeared to be an increased passion for professional growth and learning; eight of the teachers decided to pursue advanced degrees in reading, guidance counseling, administration, or special education to build on what they had learned from collaboration and participation in Project MP3.

Teachers felt empowered, passionate, committed, and proud, as well as more knowledgeable and skilled as a result of MP3.

Empowerment

Instead of feeling that nothing they did had any positive effects, teachers now believed that their instruction positively influenced student growth. They were inspired and empowered by the increases in students' scores and improvements in students' self-esteem and motivation to read. Many felt more confident in their reading instructional skills and more knowledgeable about reading research and "best practice."

Passion

Many teachers reported having a renewed passion and energy for teaching after witnessing the positive impact their instruction had had on student achievement. One teacher from Larue said it best:

> "I feel like I'm finally really *teaching* kids to read! There's no better feeling on earth than the one I get when my students' eyes light up after learning a new word or improving on their last fluency score or successfully reading a book to a peer. I'm reminded each day why I went into teaching in the first place."

Commitment

Teachers felt better supported by principals, central administration personnel, and colleagues; this increased momentum for follow-through and sustainability. We saw an increased commitment to sustaining and continuing the model as teachers and administrators experienced, firsthand, concrete and significant changes in student performance and achievement overall. Joy reigned across the entire district when Larue Elementary made "adequate yearly progress" (AYP) on the statewide annual accountability assessment in 2009.

Pride

Teachers in all three target schools, but most remarkably at Larue, said they were proud to be teaching in Alliance School District. They were proud to have become professional role models for other teachers within the district, as well as for teachers in schools across the western part of the state, modeling intervention instruction, leading inservice trainings on RTI and PM, sharing experience and results at educational conferences, and so forth. And they were proud of students' accomplishments and of the positive school changes overall.

Knowledgeability

Teachers were quick to report that their understanding of reading instructional methods had improved and that they were now better "consumers of reading research" (i.e., more discerning when looking for workshops and conferences to attend, materials to purchase, etc.). They were better at developing instructional plans and evaluating progress of at-risk students and students already identified for special education. They appreciated the collaborations among reading intervention teachers (Title I), special educators, general education teachers, and literacy coaches that were nurtured during MP3. One teacher from Washington Elementary described it thus:

"The shared expertise and resources among all of us is terrific! You never feel like you are on your own. Someone is always there to help brainstorm, analyze, and evaluate. The next steps to helping a child improve are no longer mysteries you have to solve on your own."

CONCLUDING COMMENTS

"The Operation Was a Success . . ."

MP3 is a great success story. Alliance School District was transformed. When researchers met with district administrators and teachers in the spring of 2006, they faced a tough challenge. Larue, a low-performing school with a reputation for failure, struggled with high staff turnover and falling test scores. Three years later this school can boast of academic gains, including dramatic improvements in test scores and a staff dedicated to continuing that trend. Teachers, students, parents, and administrators are celebrating its successes. Results at Washington and Boyce (which joined the project in its second year) were equally positive, if less dramatic. The MP3 model of RTI, including tiered instruction, daily small-group reading interventions, PM, data-based instructional decision making, and optimism about the capabilities of both students and their teachers has been adopted districtwide. Plans are under way to implement RTI at the secondary level as well. Teachers are continuing to look for ways to strengthen instruction such that all children have an opportunity to become fluent readers. The central features of RTI—commitment to scientifically based core and supplemental instruction, the use of PM data to make instructional decisions, and the provision of targeted interventions in a multi-tiered structure—are no longer theoretical constructs in this district. The research-to-practice gulf has been bridged.

" . . . But the Patient Died"

But before we get carried away with self-congratulations, we are reminded that the model demonstration initiative was funded by the Office of Special Education Programs in the federal Department of Education and that, as special educators and special education researchers, our first responsibility is to the neediest learners. So, in the midst of the celebrating, we took a closer look at the performance of students who entered school with the most significant reading problems. How did they fare in the MP3 RTI model? Complete data were available for 17 students whose scores in the spring of 2006 on the DIBELS ORF measure placed them in the lowest quartile of first graders. At the time they were nearing the end of first grade and would become part of the first cohort to participate in Project MP3. By spring of 2009 they had completed fourth grade, having spent 3 full years in the model. Six are from Washington, one is from Boyce, and ten are from Larue. Five have IEPs. Each was placed in Tier 3 instruction in the fall of 2006. The mean fluency score for this group of first graders in the spring of 2006 was 5 words read correctly per minute.

Of these 17 Tier 3 beginning second-grade students, only four (24%) moved to a lower intensity intervention group before reaching the end of fourth grade (see Figure 7.9). Three moved to Tier 2, where they remained; one ultimately achieved benchmark. These four "responders" exited Tier 3 between the beginning of third grade and the end of fourth grade. None of these four were students with IEPs. For the 13 students who remained at the intensive level 3 years later, at the end of fourth grade, their average fluency score was only 58 words correct per minute on fourth-grade-level text, with spring 2009 ORF benchmark scores ranging from 31 to 89 words read correctly in 1 minute. The benchmark target score indicating on-grade-level reading fluency at the end of fourth grade is 118 words read correctly in 1 minute. And, of the original cohort of 17 students, only 3 scored in the proficient range on the fourth-grade PSSA reading test. These data are sobering. Yes, our MP3 model changed the failure trajectory for nearly 25% of the students in the lowest quartile of first grade. But, clearly, 90 minutes daily of grade-level core reading instruction plus an additional 45 minutes daily of small-group (three to six students) reading instruction was not enough to make a difference in the reading careers of the remaining 75%.

The MP3 model demonstration project in the Alliance School District showed that changes can be brought about by RTI, even if they are uneven and slow to emerge. Project MP3 demonstrated that, with persistence, dedication, and resources, an RTI model has the potential to effect change even in low-performing, poorly resourced schools. We join our colleagues in the district in celebrating the progress made at Larue, Washington, and Boyce

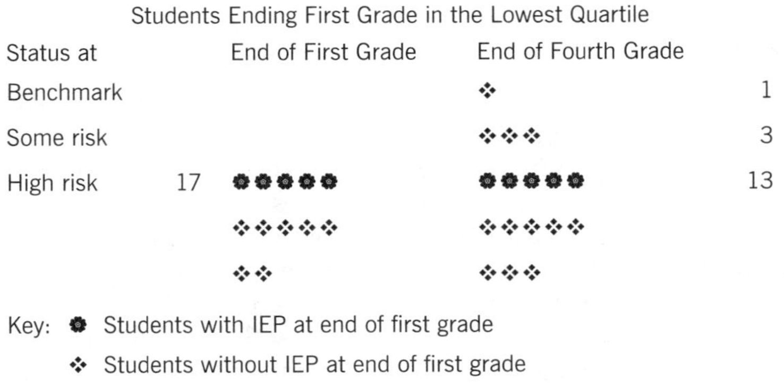

Students Ending First Grade in the Lowest Quartile			
Status at	End of First Grade	End of Fourth Grade	
Benchmark		❖	1
Some risk		❖ ❖ ❖	3
High risk	17 ● ● ● ● ●	● ● ● ● ●	13
	❖ ❖ ❖ ❖ ❖	❖ ❖ ❖ ❖ ❖	
	❖ ❖	❖ ❖ ❖	

Key: ● Students with IEP at end of first grade
     ❖ Students without IEP at end of first grade

FIGURE 7.9. DIBELS ORF performance of bottom quartile first graders ($n = 17$) before MP3 implementation and 3 years later.

Elementary schools. We have all learned a lot. It is one thing to espouse the virtues of RTI; it is quite another thing to figure out how to implement it successfully.

But even after 3 years, RTI in the Alliance School District is still a work in progress. Yes, we saw growth, but not enough, and not for everyone. Instruction at every tier needs to be strengthened. And attention must be paid to finding more effective interventions for a school's most especially vulnerable students. They deserved a more positive outcome from this investment.

REFERENCES

Bandura, A. (1994). Self-efficacy. In V. S. Ramachaudran (Ed.), *Encyclopedia of human behavior* (Vol. 4, pp. 71–81). New York: Academic Press.

Bandura, A. (1997). *Self-efficacy: The exercise of control.* New York: Freeman.

Barnett, D. W., Daly, E. J., III, Hampshire, E. M., Hines, N. R., Maples, K. A., Ostrom, J. K., et al. (1999). Meeting performance-based training demands: Accountability in an intervention-based practicum. *School Psychology Quarterly, 14*, 357–379.

Burns, M. K., & VanDerHeyden, A. M. (2006). Special series: Using response to intervention as a diagnostic tool for learning disabilities. *Assessment for Effective Intervention, 32*, 3–5.

Deno, S. (1985). Curriculum-based measurement: The emerging alternative. *Exceptional Children, 52*, 219–232.

Erdem, E., & Demirel, O. (2007). Teacher self-efficacy belief. *Social Behavior and Personality, 35*, 573–586.

Espin, C., Deno, S., Maruyama, G., & Cohen, C. (1989). *The Basic Academic Skills Samples (BASS): An instrument for the screening and identification of children at risk for failure in regular education classrooms.* Paper presented at the National Convention of the American Education Research Association, San Francisco.

Fountas, I. C., & Pinnell, G. S. (1991). *Guided reading: Good first teaching for all children.* Portsmouth, NH: Heinemann.

Fuchs, L. S. (2003). Assessing intervention responsiveness: Conceptual and technical issues. *Learning Disabilities Research and Practice, 18*, 172–186.

Fuchs, L. S., & Fuchs, D. (1992). Identifying a measure for monitoring student reading progress. *School Psychology Review, 21*, 45–59

Fuchs, L. S., & Fuchs, D. (2002). *What is scientifically based research on progress monitoring?* (Technical Report). Nashville, TN: Vanderbilt University.

Fuchs, L. S., Fuchs, D., Hamlett, C. L., Walz, L., & Germann, G. (1993). Formative evaluation of academic progress: How much growth can we expect? *School Psychology Review, 22*, 27–48.

Gaskin v. Pennsylvania Department of Education. (2004). Summary of principal provisions in the proposed settlement agreement. Retrieved September 7, 2010, from *www.portal.state.pa.us/portal/server.pt/community/gaskin_v_pennsylvania_department_of_education/7474.*

Good, R. H., III, & Kaminski, R. A. (Eds.). (2002). Dynamic Indicators of Basic Early Literacy Skills (6th ed.). Eugene, OR: Institute for the Development of Educational Achievement. Available at *http://dibels.uoregon.edu*.

Gresham, F. M. (2004). Current status and future directions of school-based behavioral interventions. *School Psychology Review, 33*, 326–343.

Guskey, T., & Passaro, P. (1994). Teacher efficacy: A study of construct dimensions. *Educational Research Journal, 31*, 627–643.

Hasbrouck, J., & Tindal, G. A. (2006). Oral reading fluency norms: A valuable assessment tool for reading teachers. *Reading Teacher, 59*, 636–644.

Hintze, J. M., & Silberglitt, B. (2005). A longitudinal examination of the diagnostic accuracy and predictive validity of R-CBM and high-stakes testing. *School Psychology Review, 34*(3), 372–386.

Kloo, A., & Zigmond, N. (2009). Response to intervention: A reality check. In T. E. Scruggs & M. A. Mastropieri (Eds.), *Policy and practice: Advances in learning and behavioral disabilities* (Vol. 22, pp. 67–107). Bingley, UK: Emerald.

Lentz, F. E., Jr., Allen, S. J., & Ehrhardt, K. E. (1996). The conceptual elements of strong interventions in school settings. *School Psychology Quarterly, 11*, 118–136.

Mead, R., Smith, R. M., & Swanlund, A. (2003, December). Technical analysis: 2003 Pennsylvania System of School Assessment, mathematics and reading. Available from the Pennsylvania Department of Education, *www.pde.state.pa.us*.

National Institute of Child Health and Human Development. (2000). *Report of the National Reading Panel. Teaching children to read: An evidence-based assessment of the scientific research literature on reading and its implications for reading instruction* (NIH Publication No. 00-4769). Washington, DC: U.S. Government Printing Office.

Nunn, G. D., & Jantz, P. B. (2008). Factors within response to intervention implementation training associated with teacher efficacy beliefs. *Education, 129*(4), 599–607.

Pennsylvania Department of Education. (2003, February). *Technical analysis: Pennsylvania system of school assessment, 2002 reading and mathematics PSSA*. Harrisburg, PA: Author.

Shapiro, E. S., Keller, M. A., Lutz, J. G., Santoro, L. E., & Hintze, J. M. (2006). Curriculum-based measures and performance on state assessment and standardized tests: Reading and math performance in Pennsylvania. *Journal of Psychoeducational Assessment, 24*, 19–35.

Shinn, M. R., & Shinn, M. M. (2002). Reading Maze—CBM. Eden Prairie, MN: Edformation. Available at *www.aimsweb.com*.

Wayman, M. M., Wallace, T., Wiley, H. I., Ticha, R., & Espin, C. A. (2007). Literature synthesis on curriculum-based measurement in reading. *Journal of Special Education, 41*(2), 85–120.

PART III

The Minnesota Demonstrating Progress Monitoring Project

Introduction to Part III

The Demonstrating Progress Monitoring for Early Identification, Account-ability, and Success (DPM) Project was a collaboration of the University of Minnesota and the Minneapolis Public Schools. Our project benefited from a long history of collaboration between these two institutions. The University of Minnesota, through the pioneering research efforts of Dr. Stanley Deno, has been a national leader in the use of curriculum-based measurement (CBM) for data-based decision making in education, and specifically in the problem-solving model, which is a forerunner of the response-to-intervention model (RTI). These efforts led to the establishment of the Research Institute for Progress Monitoring (RIPM), led by Dr. Teri Wallace and Dr. Christine Espin, which continued the research efforts on progress monitoring (PM) and the use of data for making valid and reliable decisions that inform instruction. The Minneapolis Public Schools (MPS), in its association with the University of Minnesota since the early 1980s, led by Dr. Doug Marston, Dr. Ann Casey, and Dr. Andrea Canter, has taken the lead as a school district in implementing CBM and using the problem-solving model as a framework to help students needing more intensive academic and behavioral interventions to meet standards. MPS has published several articles on how to translate the research of progress monitoring into practice in a large, urban school district level.

The DPM Project utilized the research on CBM, the problem-solving model, evidence-based research practices, and a district-developed Web-based student data warehouse to create an RTI model at three demonstration schools over a 3-year period. During this time University of Minnesota and MPS staff collaborated to build on the existing data-based decision-making structures to create an RTI approach to helping students struggling in the area of reading. The major components of the RTI model—universal screening, high-quality core instruction, target interventions for students not making benchmarks, frequent PM, grade-level data meetings for school staff, professional development on evidence-based practices, and monitoring of intervention integrity—were the essential elements of RTI implementation at the MPS demonstration sites.

The chapters in this section concentrate on RTI implementation at one of the demonstration schools, a K–5 school with 70% poverty, over 20% English language learner population, and over 60% students of color. In Chapter 8 we discuss the history of CBM and the problem-solving model in the MPS and why that was relevant to RTI implementation. In that chapter we also describe three critical components to successful implementation, including leadership, professional development, and support systems. In Chapter 9 we describe the process of translating research into practice at our model demonstration school. Each of the essential components of the RTI model is explained, and the views of school leadership are expressed. In Chapter 10 we describe the outcomes of RTI implementation at our model site. We include student data related to achievement (both formative and summative), behavior, attendance, engaged time, referrals to special education, and special education eligibility. We also include teacher data as it relates to implementation of progress monitoring, fidelity of targeted interventions, the completion of grade-level data review meetings, and staff attitudes toward the model. Our findings are generally positive, showing achievement gains, decreases in special education eligibility, and positive staff attitudes toward the model.

CHAPTER 8

The Context and Content of Implementation

Doug Marston
Ann Casey
Teri Wallace

The response-to-intervention (RTI) model has been described as a multi-layered framework for improving instruction for students at risk and preventing school failure (Fuchs & Fuchs, 2006). Successful implementation of this structure is dependent on three primary components: (1) valid and reliable measures that can be administered frequently and are sensitive to growth; (2) evidence-based interventions for students not meeting academic and behavioral standards, and (3) a coordinated system of screening, placement, and intervention implemented at the school level (Vaughn, Wanzek, Woodruff, & Linan-Thompson, 2007). The Minneapolis Public Schools (MPS) has a long history of implementing two of these essential features, and it is this experience that provides the current context for successful implementation of RTI in our district. The first element that has been evident in the district has been the use of valid, reliable measures sensitive to growth in the MPS, which can be traced to the early 1980s when the district began implementing curriculum-based measurement (CBM) procedures (Deno & Marston, 2007; Marston & Magnusson, 1985). The second element present in the district has been school-level coordinated data-based decision-making systems, which have been used in MPS since the 1990s when the problem-solving model was adopted to determine special education eligibility (Marston, Muyskens, Lau, & Canter, 2003). In the first part of this chapter we further describe the context of RTI in MPS by providing some of the details of our district's history with CBM and the problem-solving model. In the second part of this chapter, based on our years of experience with the RTI framework, we offer ideas on practices and procedures for effective implementation of RTI.

CONTEXT: HISTORY OF PROGRESS MONITORING AND THE PROBLEM-SOLVING MODEL IN THE MPS

Development and Implementation of CBM Procedures

The district's early utilization of CBM capitalized on research on student progress monitoring (PM) by Dr. Stanley Deno and his colleagues at the University of Minnesota (Deno, 1984; Deno, Marston, Shinn, & Tindal, 1983; Deno & Mirkin, 1977; Deno et al., 1980; Deno, Mirkin, & Chiang, 1982; Fuchs, Deno, & Mirkin, 1984; Marston, Mirkin, & Deno, 1984; Marston, Tindal, & Deno, 1984). In the early 1980s the Special Education Department of the MPS began using the CBM model for a range of purposes, including screening, eligibility, program planning, PM, and program evaluation (Marston, 1988; Marston, Fuchs, & Deno, 1986; Marston & Magnusson, 1985, 1988). The MPS district was one of the first school districts in the country to develop a set of CBM norms for the fall, winter, and spring in the areas of reading, spelling, math, and written expression for grades 1–6. An example of how CBM data can be useful for decision making is shown in Table 8.1, in which grade-level means for more than 8,400 students on words read correctly are reported. Just as important as the norms is the concept of growth from fall to spring, which can be used for judging student RTI. For example, students in second grade increased from an average of 51.3 words correct in the fall to 82.1 words correct

TABLE 8.1. Means and Standard Deviations for CBM of Reading in the Fall, Winter, and Spring

| Grade | Fall | | Winter | | Spring | |
	Mean	SD	Mean	SD	Mean	SD
1	18.9	36.0	51.7	49.8	71.3	38.4
2	51.3	41.2	72.8	43.9	82.1	38.7
3	87.7	40.1	106.9	40.6	114.6	38.4
4	105.5	42.5	114.6	40.7	118.3	42.8
5	117.7	40.2	129.2	42.6	134.4	40.1
6	115.2	39.4	120.2	37.4	131.3	39.1

Note. From Marston and Magnusson (1988). Copyright 1988 by the National Association of School Psychologists. Reprinted by permission.

in the spring. MPS staff also documented the differences between general education, Title I, and special education students, a finding that further informed both screening and eligibility practices (Marston & Magnusson, 1985; Shinn & Marston, 1985).

As the CBM model evolved, it soon expanded to the area of readiness, which included copying of letters and numbers, letter and sound identification, a word identification task, and a number naming probe. The district's screening and eligibility procedures for determining special education identification, which initially had a norm-referenced focus, also evolved. MPS staff developed a data-based decision-making system, known as the Six-Week Assessment Plan (SWAP), which was used for measuring student response to general education and was added to the eligibility process. During this 6-week assessment period, CBM procedures were used for PM and to determine whether general education interventions could be found that helped struggling students. "The purpose of SWAP is to collect data to determine if any specific intervention in a student's educational program allows him or her to make appropriate progress in a regular education curriculum. . . . The SWAP is carried out by the regular education teacher with support and monitoring from the special education staff" (Marston & Magnusson, 1988, p. 153). An example of the SWAP is shown in Figure 8.1, in which the progress of a fourth-grade student is monitored over a 6-week period while receiving Title I services. In this case study the student has responded to the general education intervention and does not require special education service.

PM and data-based decision making continued to be implemented in the district in the later 1980s and early 1990s in two initiatives: the Experimental Teaching Project (Casey, Deno, Marston, & Skiba, 1988) and the Formative Evaluation Demonstration Project (Marston, Deno, Kim, Diment, & Rogers, 1995; Yell, Deno, & Marston, 1992). In both projects teachers were trained to use CBM PM to judge the effectiveness of their reading interventions. In addition, district staff continued their development work on CBM procedures and documenting technical adequacy (Tindal & Marston, 1996). Later work in early literacy CBM procedures included the development of letter sound, onset phonemes, and phoneme segmentation probes (Marston et al., 2007).

As can be seen, the research of Stanley Deno on PM and its utility for helping teachers judge the effectiveness of their instructional programs has had a tremendous impact on our district. The significance of this research literature, which includes over 400 published articles, chapters, and books (Wayman, Wallace, Wiley, Ticha, & Espin, 2007), is underscored by the fact that two of Deno's articles are in the Top 10 of most cited articles in special education (McLeskey, 2007). The Fuchs and colleagues (1984) article, which demonstrated that teacher use of CBM PM can be used to improve student outcomes, has been identified as number 1 on the Top 50

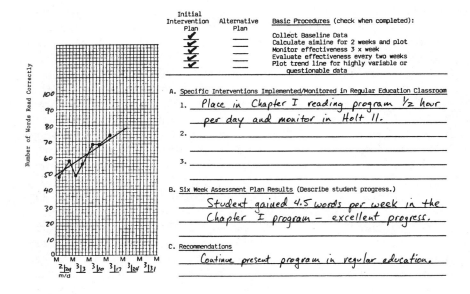

FIGURE 8.1. Six-week assessment plan for K–6 resource program. From Marston and Magnusson (1988). Copyright 1988 by the National Association of School Psychologists. Reprinted by permission.

most cited articles in the *American Educational Research Journal*. Our district's use of this research base and extensive experience with PM has created the context for RTI implementation in the MPS.

Development and Implementation of the Problem-Solving Model

A coordinated system for reviewing data and interventions at the school level has also been identified as necessary for successful RTI implementation (Vaughn et al., 2007). The use of CBM as a data-based decision-making system, as described in the previous section, continued to spread to general education in the early 1990s at the district's Hiawatha Elementary School (Self, Benning, Marston, & Magnusson, 1991) and created the roots for later implementation of the problem-solving model and RTI. At this model demonstration site, school staff developed a "collaborative teaching" model in which general education, Title I, and special education teachers reviewed the progress of all students at the school on a monthly basis and collaborated on providing academic interventions. Intensive, small-group reading instruction was provided to lower performing students, and reading progress was monitored and graphed on a weekly basis, as shown in Figure 8.2. Results from the Hiawatha Project, a forerunner of RTI, had a significant impact on the delivery of services to low-performing students by enhancing collaboration of all school staff, improving instructional planning, reducing the number of students qualifying for special education, and increasing the achievement of low-performing students.

The cooperative teaching project concepts soon evolved into the problem-solving model, which was implemented in the mid-1990s in the MPS as an alternative eligibility approach for special education (Marston, 2002). At that time the state had developed new criteria for learning disabilities (LD) and mildly mentally impaired students (MMI) that required the use of IQ tests. The MPS staff was concerned about the administration and interpretation of these tests with the district's many diverse learners. Building on the district's history of data-based decision making with CBM, the SWAP concept, and the findings from the cooperative teaching project at Hiawatha School, our district sought a waiver from these regulations and received permission to use the problem-solving model as an alternative eligibility approach. The primary essentials of the problem-solving model in MPS are to (1) define in detail the student's academic or behavior issues, (2) implement an intervention addressing the student's instructional needs, (3) collect frequent student data so that the effectiveness of the intervention can be evaluated, and (4) repeat these steps when data indicate a new intervention is necessary to better meet the student's needs (Marston et

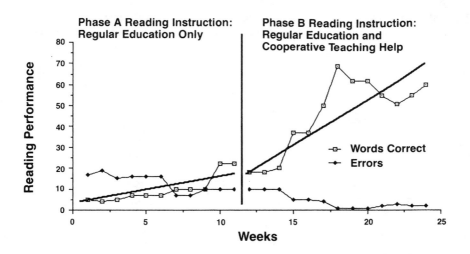

FIGURE 8.2. Weekly monitoring of students' reading progress. From Self, Benning, Marston, and Magnusson (1991). Copyright 1991 by the Council for Exceptional Children. Reprinted by permission.

al., 2003). This process is repeated at Stages 1, 2, and 3, as shown in the problem-solving model pyramid in Figure 8.3. Stage 1 is classroom intervention, and it is the responsibility of the general education classroom teacher to implement an intervention to help the low-performing student. If the student does not respond to this intervention, he or she advances to Stage 2 of PSM for the problem-solving team (PST) intervention. The PST includes grade-level general education teachers, special education teacher, Title I, specialists, school psychologists, and school social workers. The team identifies students who did not respond to Stage 1 interventions and selects more intensive interventions that can be implemented in general education. Student progress data is collected for Stage 2 interventions, and the PST reviews the results after 6–8 weeks of implementation. Students who have not responded to interventions at Stage 1 or Stage 2 move to Stage 3, special education evaluation. At this point a child-study team conducts a comprehensive assessment of the student, considering the intervention data from prior stages of PSM. Eligibility and service in special education is determined within 30 days of entry into Stage 3.

The problem-solving model was used in an effort to reduce disproportionate numbers of students of color referred and identified for special education as part of a district Office for Civil Rights (OCR) initiative. In this RTI effort, which required a more formal process for screening, MPS staff developed procedures for screening academic performance and behavior (Muyskens, Marston, & Reschly, 2007), documenting interventions, and measuring student progress (Marston, Lau, & Muyskens, 2007) to ensure that referrals to special education were based on instructional need. This system for reviewing student performance and analyzing student response to instruction resulted in creation of the data warehouse for the district

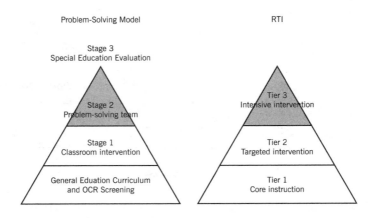

FIGURE 8.3. Comparison of MPS problem-solving model and RTI.

(Marston, Lau, & Muyskens, 2007), which is now used to evaluate disproportion on a school-by-school basis.

Despite differences in the labeling of the various components, the
Minneapolis problem-solving model described here is an RTI model. The
problem-solving model and the popular RTI pyramid are compared in Figure 8.3, showing multilayered instructional frameworks in which decisions
for serving students are data driven. Core instruction is identified in the
RTI pyramid as Tier 1, whereas in the problem-solving model the general
education curriculum and screening precedes Stage 1. The targeted interventions of Tier 2 of the RTI framework are equivalent to the interventions
of Stage 1 of the problem-solving model, and the intensive interventions of
Tier 3 in the RTI pyramid are similar to the more rigorous interventions
of Stage 2. In both the problem-solving model and RTI, student data are
collected frequently to determine whether the student is improving, and
in both models a team is convened to review interventions and look at
student data. Our prior experience with CBM and the existing problem-
solving model framework reviewed in this section provided the context for
implementing RTI at our demonstration school (funded by the Office of
Special Education Programs [OSEP]), described in the next two chapters.
For our project school, the problem-solving model was renamed RTI, and
the vocabulary associated with the pyramid was adopted, that is, Tiers 1,
2, and 3.

CONTENT: TOOLS OF IMPLEMENTATION FOR RTI

In this section we offer our suggestions from years of implementation experience with the RTI framework about what we see as some of the more
effective practices and procedures. We place significant emphasis on the
systems developed within the school or district that make certain needed
practices more likely to happen. We also discuss how student data should
drive all decision making in schools, including staff development. And,
finally, we address the need for a style of leadership that not only provides
vision and focus but also ensures that the systems and professional development supports are in place so that people can perform the job that is
expected so that more students are successful.

System Supports

RTI is a framework consisting of three parts: (1) measurement for universal
screening, PM, and instructional planning; (2) a tiered instructional delivery system; and (3) a problem-solving process that connects the data to the
instruction provided, requiring certain infrastructure supports. Thus one
of the most important systems to have in place is a measurement system.

All programs, priorities, initiatives, and professional development should be focused on what the data indicate the students need.

There are a variety of tools that can be used for universal screening, but the main criterion for selecting such tools should be predictive validity for high-stakes assessments. Thus we are looking for screening tools that provide us with a good indicator of whether a student is likely or not to be on track toward proficiency in the area measured. Screening tools, because they are used with all students, need to be quick and easy to use. Again, there are many assessments that provide a good indication of whether students are performing at the level expected and that are also useful for a variety of other purposes. Many of these tools, however, take more than an hour to administer to a student. For RTI we need a time-efficient tool for screening. Although not required, it is preferred that the screening measure and PM measure be the same system. If schools choose to use the same measure for screening and PM, their choices become more limited because very few measures have been validated for the purpose of determining whether a student's progress is moving toward the desired high-stakes outcome. The PM tools chart of the National Center on Response to Intervention (*www. rti4success.org*) provides a list of measurement systems that have been validated for this purpose.

Educators are sometimes confused by what constitutes a measure of progress. One thing to consider is whether the tool is a good measure of mastery of material that was taught or whether it is a measure of the general outcome you are assessing in your statewide high-stakes tests. For example, mastery monitoring of the number or kinds of errors a child makes in reading is a very good source of information for instructional planning but does not have strong predictive validity for overall reading achievement. This is good information to know when designing an intervention, but it doesn't indicate whether a student is on track to pass the third-grade state reading test. To date, one of the best and most efficient measures of reading achievement is oral reading proficiency or CBM (Deno, 2003). These are measures of the number of words read correctly in 1 minute that have good predictive validity with tests of reading comprehension—the desired outcome.

Once schools have made decisions about screening and PM tools, they will also need to discuss which additional assessments are needed to determine student skills and areas of need before we can match those skills with an appropriate intervention. There are both formal and informal measures that are quite useful for this purpose. To make good decisions, schools need multiple measures that help them identify and plan for students who need more support in the core areas of reading, math, and behavior.

In order to make data more usable, schools need an easy-to-use data management system. Data must be accessible if we expect teachers to use them to make core instruction more effective, as well as to design interventions for students. Although there are products schools can purchase for this purpose, some school districts have designed their own systems, such as the one mentioned previously for the MPS, described in more detail later in this chapter. But even without system data management support, individual schools can make use of spreadsheets that display all the data collected in the schools so that a teacher can see his or her entire class in one glance and compare students in the class on the various data collected. Useful tools of this type list all the students in a classroom with a column for each piece of data collected: district test scores, state accountability test results, attendance, office referrals, CBM screening data, and so forth. Finally, useful systems allow the user to sort on each column to array students from high to low scores and look for similarity and differences across different data sources. Data utilization must be an expectation for all staff in a functioning RTI system. If we want teachers to become data users, then we must provide easy ways for them to access, view, and analyze the data.

The next hurdle to overcome in data usage is finding time for teachers to work together to look at the data and make conclusions about what needs to happen next. Some of the questions that need to be addressed by teams are: Is the core instruction sufficient? Do we need to change it? What percentage of students is being successful with just core Tier 1 instruction? How many students need additional support? Are there clusters of students with the same instructional needs? School leaders can provide strong support by ensuring that there is time in the schedule for approximately monthly meeting times for grade-level teaching teams to meet specifically for this purpose. If the master calendar includes meeting times for the entire school year for each team, they are much more likely to happen. Expecting teachers to find this time themselves is unrealistic. There already are many demands on their time. For RTI to be effective, teachers need this kind of support to become skilled users of data to improve instruction.

A mistake some schools make when beginning RTI implementation is to jump right into developing interventions for Tiers 2 and 3. These interventions can be effective only if they rest on a strong foundation of core instruction in Tier 1. When large numbers of students are not being successful, it is an indication that we should focus more on the core, and not so much on the interventions. This is not necessarily an indictment of the curriculum and/or the instruction but rather a problem of matching the core instruction to the needs of the students. For example, if you have large numbers of students who are English language learners and you have a reading curriculum that isn't explicit about how to teach new vocabulary, then you may need to add to the core instruction so more students can increase their vocabularies and link to background knowledge. When the focus is on the core, all students can benefit from this additional emphasis.

Another very important system support is to ensure that the master schedule includes time for interventions—supplemental and intensive. More important is making every attempt to ensure that the intervention time does not conflict with the core instruction. If schools are serious about reducing gaps for students, then we cannot continue to take students out of their core instruction, making them miss important concepts, and expect that they will "catch up." Teachers already feel that there are not enough hours in the day to meet all the requirements for various content areas. Thus, to ensure that students who need targeted support receive it, the best thing a school leader can do is to include intervention time in the master schedule.

Time in general is an important concept in RTI. We have discussed the importance of ensuring that there is time in calendars for data meetings and time in the master schedule for supplemental and intensive intervention support. But perhaps most important is ensuring that school professionals make the best use of the time available during the core instruction. A focus on increasing academic engaged time is often a good place to begin (Brophy & Good, 1986) and can be as important as the content being taught. In an RTI framework, we want teachers to collaborate with one another to ensure that every student has the opportunity to learn the core content. This often requires an emphasis on differentiated instruction within the core curriculum. If we are serious about all students learning the "big ideas" of the core lessons, then it will behoove us to find new and different ways to make this happen.

Professional Development

RTI requires the entire system to respond to student performance data by making decisions about the amount and kind of instruction students might need. Thus student data should drive the type of professional development that educators receive. Staff development programs have evolved over the years from one-shot topical seminars with no follow-up to in-depth exploration and knowledge development in a particular topic over time. However, in many cases the choice of what to study is often left up to the educator. In an RTI system, educator choice is still important, but it is confined to areas in which the data indicate students need more support. The presumption is that whatever students need to learn more about, educators also need to learn more about, as well as different ways to teach the topic.

Professional learning communities (PLCs) can be well integrated with this approach. In fact, PLCs and RTI fit together quite well. RTI is the framework for student improvement, and PLCs are the mechanism for changes that are needed in professional practices so that more students are successful in school (Buffum, Mattos, & Weber, 2009). Because RTI requires a shift in the fundamental assumptions we have about learning, PLCs are the ideal tool for educators to learn together new ways of thinking and teaching. Successful schools have added PLCs to their master calendars, in which teachers meet in groups on a regular basis with a focus on a particular topic they will learn together. In our demonstration school example that follows, the PLCs originally began with exploring the five topic areas of the National Reading Panel. Teachers read articles, committed to trying strategies, and reported back to their peers about the successes and challenges, as well as learned from each other.

Another topic that has professional development implications is fidelity of implementation of the interventions designed to meet student needs. We certainly do not want to move students to more restrictive services based on a poor response that was related to poor implementation. Thus intervention fidelity is critically important. There are several issues to be considered. First is matching the student's needs with an appropriate intervention. If a student has decoding problems, then the intervention should be focused on improving decoding skills, not some other aspect of reading. Although this seems straightforward, it is unfortunate that some schools have developed rigid systems in which just one intervention approach is available for all students at a particular grade level. This approach might meet many students' needs but is unlikely to be well matched for every student who is struggling at that grade level. Thus instructional match is a prerequisite for fidelity of implementation.

Once we have a well-matched intervention, then we need to ensure that the intervention is delivered to the student in the manner that it was designed, based on the research that is known about this intervention. Interventions have varying degrees of complexity. The more complex it is, the more support an educator will need in providing the intervention with integrity to the original design. Professional development then consists of learning the intervention itself and also the process of giving and receiving feedback about how well the intervention is being provided. Fidelity checks are one of the most important aspects in ensuring that students get the kind of instruction they need to be successful. Our experience in trying various methods of determining fidelity of implementation has been to use either (1) a checklist of important components that either indicate that element was present or not present or (2) a three-item rubric of "present," "partially present," "not present."

Leadership

We have already addressed a few things that school leaders can do to support the implementation of RTI. A master schedule that includes time for tiered instruction is a given in an RTI system. Let's examine an example in which every teacher has at least 90 minutes for core literacy instruction and a 60-minute math block. This schedule can be easily modified to meet the needs of schools. However, the schedule includes additional blocks of time to allow making these periods longer or shorter as needed. If necessary, a school could also add an additional intervention period for students who might need extra support in both literacy and math. These intervention periods become time periods in which students who do not need extra support can receive instruction that enhances or extends their learning in a particular topic. Some schools use this time period differently, give the time period a clever name, and provide all students extra support regardless of whether they are above, below, or at benchmark. What is important to note about this schedule is that the intervention period comes at a different time for each grade level. This allows the efficient use of precious human resources for intervention delivery. Finally, this schedule (Figure 8.4) also emphasizes that intervention (Tiers 2 and 3 or special education), as much as possible, should be provided in addition to the core instruction. If we are serious about bridging gaps for students, we need to ensure that students have strong core instruction with additional support in those skills in which they struggle.

Special education service for students with disabilities is governed by the IEP and may require more minutes of service than the block of time provided in a schedule such as this one. It is challenging to find time for these services that does not interfere with important core instruction. Compromise will be important when making these difficult decisions about when a child should receive special education service and the decisions should be made collaboratively by the IEP team. However, if at all possible, all students should be present when the "big idea" of the lesson is being presented. For many students a better time to receive special education service would be during a portion of the class in which students were practicing a skill or working independently. In this scenario, locations of the service do not have bearing. There are justifiable reasons for having a variety of service delivery models within the general education classroom, as well as pull-out models. The important issue is ensuring that students with disabilities have access to the core curriculum and also have an opportunity to receive additional special education service that is designed to meet the learner's unique needs.

The most important aspect of school leadership may be the messages that are given to staff members. In some schools, the teachers will tell you that they have 30 or more initiatives occurring in their schools, whereas in other schools, teachers will say that they have one goal of improved student outcomes. In the second type of school, the leader has given the message that student improvement is everyone's job. These leaders find a way to fit various district initiatives into their RTI framework so that they become strategies to achieve this goal.

It is impossible for teachers to embrace what are often perceived as multiple efforts that are focused on the same or similar issues. Instead, strong school leaders ensure that such efforts are presented as linked and a part of the one major goal. They make explicit connections for staff members to show how efforts build on each other to accomplish the main goal.

Time	Kinder.	1st gr.	2nd gr.	3rd gr.	4th gr.	5th gr.
8:00	Reading	Specialist	Science	Intervention	Reading	Social Studies
8:15	Reading	Specialist	Science	Intervention	Reading	Social Studies
8:30	Reading	Reading	Intervention	Math		Social Studies
8:45	Reading	Reading	Intervention	Math		Social Studies
9:00	Reading	Reading	Reading	Math		Science
9:15	Reading	Reading	Reading	Math		Science
9:30	Math	Reading		Reading	Specialist	Science
9:45	Math	Reading		Reading	Specialist	Science
10:00	Math	Intervention			Specialist	Specialist
10:15	Math	Intervention			Social Studies	Specialist
10:30	Math	Intervention	Specialist		Social Studies	Reading
10:45	Math	Intervention	Specialist		Social Studies	Reading
11:00	Specialist	Science		Social Studies	Math	
11:15	Specialist	Science		Social Studies	Math	
11:30	Lunch	Lunch	Lunch	Specialist	Math	
11:45	Lunch	Lunch	Lunch	Specialist	Math	
12:00	Intervention	Read-Aloud	Science	Lunch	Lunch	Lunch
12:15	Intervention	Math	Science	Lunch	Lunch	Lunch
12:30	Read-Aloud	Math	Science	Intervention		Math
12:45	Social Studies	Math		Intervention		Math
1:00	Social Studies	Math			Intervention	Math
1:15	Social Studies	Math		Science	Intervention	Math
1:30	Social Studies	Math		Science	Intervention	Math
1:45	Science	Math	Math	Science		Math
2:00	Science	Social Studies	Math	Science	Science	Intervention
2:15	Science	Social Studies	Math	Science	Science	Intervention

FIGURE 8.4. Example of a master schedule for RTI implementation.

Finally, they ensure that professional development that is needed is also all linked to the primary goal.

Let's take an example. An elementary school may be focusing on guided reading instruction in the core as a mechanism for increasing student reading achievement. This school might also have an alternative teacher compensation plan in place, a large after-school program, and initiatives focused on student engagement and behavior. Rather than presenting these to staff as four areas of focus for the year, quality leaders present these in such a way that they all relate to the school's goal of student improvement. The after-school program, then, is no longer a hodgepodge of activities for students but includes specialized instruction in areas of need for students who are struggling and builds on what students are learning during the school day. The schoolwide behavior plan becomes a way to set the stage for high-quality instruction, and the alternative compensation plan becomes a means of providing monetary reinforcement to staff members who work to improve their instructional skills in the school's area of needs.

RTI provides the needed framework in which schools can find their focus. In too many schools, principals are faced with implementing a district agenda with overwhelming numbers of components. Those who are managers rather than leaders dutifully tell their staff members that they must add another initiative to their overflowing plates. But instructional leaders will advocate for those initiatives that will help their school achieve its goals and question those that do not. Instructional leaders will ensure that staff members understand how all their work is linked and that it leads directly to the goal of improved student outcomes.

Fidelity Checks of Interventions

Gresham, MacMillan, Beebe-Frankenberger, and Bocian (2002) emphasize the importance of the integrity of instructional treatments delivered in intervention research. This concept is not limited to researchers but extends to the day-to-day instruction of all students. Treatment integrity is often included as a basic principle of model implementation and is suggested in IDEA legislation (Johnson, Mellard, Fuchs, & McKnight, 2006; Vaughn et al., 2007). Sanetti and Kratochwill (2009) identify four important components for treatment fidelity: content, quality, quantity, and process. When treatment fidelity addresses content, the focus is on the intervention steps that are implemented. Quality examines how well the interventions are applied, and quantity centers on variables such as duration of intervention, frequency of intervention, and dosage. How the intervention was implemented is addressed when treatment fidelity examines process.

As part of our evolution from the problem-solving model to RTI, we have developed two fidelity checklists that can be used by school leaders to ensure that the Tier 2 and Tier 3 assessments and interventions possess integrity. First, in the fall of each year, teachers completed a Teacher CBM Survey (Wallace, 2006) in which they reported whether they felt prepared to use and the degree to which they implemented CBM to inform their instruction. The areas of the survey (see Figure 8.5) in which teachers rated their use of CBM included preparing, administering, scoring, charting data, and utilizing scores. In the survey the preparation key is a 3-point rubric: (0) Not At All Prepared, (1) Somewhat Prepared, and (2)

	How prepared do you feel for this task?			How often do you implement this task?			
Preparing for CBM							
• Preparing materials (stopwatch, pen, copies of probes)	0	1	2	0	1	2	3
• Preparing specific CBM probes	0	1	2	0	1	2	3
Administering CBM							
• Administering CBM probes	0	1	2	0	1	2	3
• Training others to administer CBM probes	0	1	2	0	1	2	3
• Conducting reliability checks when others are administering probes	0	1	2	0	1	2	3
Scoring CBM							
• Scoring oral reading/fluency probe	0	1	2	0	1	2	3
• Computing score for oral reading/fluency probe	0	1	2	0	1	2	3
• If others are involved, checking for reliability of scoring	0	1	2	0	1	2	3
Charting CBM Data							
• Setting up the CBM chart	0	1	2	0	1	2	3
• Charting baseline data	0	1	2	0	1	2	3
• Establishing a performance goal	0	1	2	0	1	2	3
• Charting an aim line	0	1	2	0	1	2	3
• Charting scores	0	1	2	0	1	2	3
• Charting intervention	0	1	2	0	1	2	3
Utilizing CBM Scores							
• Interpreting charted data	0	1	2	0	1	2	3
• Changing interventions based on data	0	1	2	0	1	2	3
• Participating in the development of IEP goals using CBM	0	1	2	0	1	2	3
• Utilizing CBM data for progress monitoring	0	1	2	0	1	2	3
• Using CBM data for presenting student performance at parent conferences, problem-solving meetings, and IEP meetings	0	1	2	0	1	2	3
• Using OCR website to view student CBM data—three times a year	0	1	2	0	1	2	3
• Using OCR website to view student CBM data—frequently	0	1	2	0	1	2	3

FIGURE 8.5. CBM teacher survey.

Well Prepared. The implementation key is 4-point rubric (0) Never, (1) Rarely, (2) Sometimes, (3) Often. In addition, the teachers are observed on the reliability of their administration of CBM procedures. Second, staff members observed Tier 2 and Tier 3 intervention strategies twice during the year, including repeated reading, duet reading, Soar to Success, and direct instruction. Fidelity checklists were developed specifically for each of the reading interventions, either by the authors of the curriculum itself or by RTI staff. Figure 8.6 is an example of a fidelity checklist that was used for Tier 2 small-group tutoring sessions provided by the Minnesota Reading Corps. This checklist, which was developed by project staff for our demonstration project, shows 2 of the 10 instructional components rated for fidelity: letter–sound correspondence and phoneme blending. The 4-point scale that was used for each item includes: (1) Implemented, (2) Partially Implemented, (3) Not Implemented, and (NA) Not Applicable During Observation.

Component	Scale				Comments
1. *Letter–Sound Correspondence*	1	2	3	NA	
a. Teacher has five letter cards with three known and two unknown letters	1	2	3	NA	
b. Teacher explains task to student	1	2	3	NA	
c. Teacher models task with two letter cards	1	2	3	NA	
d. Teacher initiates practice by repeating task directions	1	2	3	NA	
e. Teacher corrects errors immediately	1	2	3	NA	
f. Teacher uses appropriate hand signals	1	2	3	NA	
g. Teacher maintains brisk pace of presentation	1	2	3	NA	
	1	2	3	NA	
2. *Phoneme Blending*	1	2	3	NA	
a. Teacher has a list of words for blending	1	2	3	NA	
b. Teacher explains task to student	1	2	3	NA	
c. Teacher models task with two words	1	2	3	NA	
d. Teacher initiates practice by repeating task directions	1	2	3	NA	
e. Teacher corrects errors immediately	1	2	3	NA	
f. Teacher uses appropriate hand signals	1	2	3	NA	
g. Teacher maintains brisk pace of presentation	1	2	3	NA	

FIGURE 8.6. Fidelity of implementation example.

Fidelity Checks for RTI implementation

An implementation tool developed by our staff was a protocol for monitoring the degree to which the RTI framework was evident in the school. We chose to concentrate on an important element of the RTI framework, the team data meeting. It is in this meeting that school staff members meet on a frequent basis throughout the school year to review student progress data, discuss the instructional groups for Tier 2 and Tier 3 interventions, and move students to new groups if necessary. In these meetings the components of the RTI framework are on display. Just as it is essential to ensure that instructional interventions are implemented with fidelity, it is critical that these teams conform to standards. For our implementation schools, Marston and Lau (2008) developed an integrity checklist for data teams that can be used by school leaders to evaluate the degree to which the teams are carrying out the principles of the RTI framework. The key questions asked about the performance of the data team were: Did the team review student data? Were the instructional groupings based on student data? Did the team have time to discuss the instructional activities carried out in each Tier 2 and 3 intervention? Was there a discussion about moving students into different groups when indicated by data? and Did the teams meet frequently? There were 11 items on the integrity checklist, and the observer used a 5-point rubric to rate the quality of the implementation. The 11 items included agenda, meeting length, review of at-risk students, review of instructional methods, graphing, reviewing graphs, benchmarks, reviewing other data, team input, moving students between groups, and adjusting the instructional methods used at Tiers 2 and 3. A copy of this checklist is provided in Chapter 9. Also in Chapter 10, we share data on how well an RTI school implements these concepts.

Tools for Data Analysis

As part of the district's problem-solving model and Office for Civil Rights initiatives, our staff developed a Web-based student data system that is used for RTI (Marston, Lau, & Muyskens, 2007). For every student in our district, the OCR website has a complete history of student attendance, suspensions, program service, behavior screening, district and state reading and math assessments, and CBM fall, winter, and spring benchmark results. We document math, reading, and behavior interventions and goals at Stage 2 and 3 of the problem-solving model or Tiers 2 and 3 for RTI. In addition, teachers document parent input and individual learning plans, graph weekly data, and link to reading, math, and behavior intervention ideas and training videos. The website also provides detailed reports on the state No Child Left Behind (NCLB) reading and math tests, strand analyses for these tests, and "report writer" features for customizing reports.

It has "drill down" and "dashboard" capabilities extending from district-level analysis to school-, grade-, classroom-, and student-level analyses and sorting capabilities that provide teachers with a tool for determining which students are in the red, yellow, or green zones. It also gives school staff a summary of special education student IEPs and test accommodations. Figure 8.7 is an example of a summary organizer that includes student achievement, attendance, and suspension data. The data can be reported by classroom or grade level. An important feature of this data tool is the ability to sort all students on the organizer from low to high on any selected variable. The summary organizer also features color coding of student performance as red, yellow, or green.

The ability to determine whether students fall into the red, yellow, or green zones is based on an analysis of CBM scores predicting perfor-

Name	Grade	GPA	Read MAP Scale	Read MAP %tile	Math MAP Scale	Math MAP %tile	Fall Behavior Total	% Attend	Abs. Exc*	Abs. UnExc*	# Susp.*	CBM FALL
	02		155	■	158	■	17.0	96.7	1		1	■
	02		153	■	169	16	12.0	98.3	0		1	■
	02		158	3	169	16	22.0	95.0	2		1	■
	02		153	■	168	14	34.0	91.7	5	0		■
	02		146	■	150	■	21.0	96.7	2	0		■
	02		149	■	163	■	24.0	93.3	3	1		■
	02		148	■	171	23	19.0	90.0	6	0		■
	02		166	17	179	63	16.0	86.7	6	3		■
	02		150	■	164	■	12.0	95.0	3	0		■
	02		146	■	158	■	23.0	89.2	2	5		■
	02		162	9	172	26	12.0	89.2	7	0		23
	02		174	37	185	■	17.0	98.3	1	0		25
	02		165	15	181	60	21.0	100.0	0	0		29
	02		166	17	185	73	12.0	100.0	0	0		36
	02		181	56	178	49	12.0	98.3	1	0		37
	02		166	17	167	11	15.0	100.0	0	0		37
	02		177	45	178	49	12.0	100.0	0	0		40
	02		171	29	177	45	15.0	90.0	3	3		47
	02		169	24	176	41	22.0	98.3	1	0		49
	02		195	87	191	86	18.0	88.3	7	0		54
	02		161	8	175	38	15.0	100.0	0	0		59
	02		185	66	170	18	20.0	98.3	1	1		79
	02		179	50	175	38	13.0	98.3	1	0		80
	02		199	93	191	86	12.0	100.0	0	0		80
	02		195	87	184	70	14.0	91.7	5	0		94

FIGURE 8.7. Summary organizer that displays academic and social/behavioral data for students in a second-grade classroom.

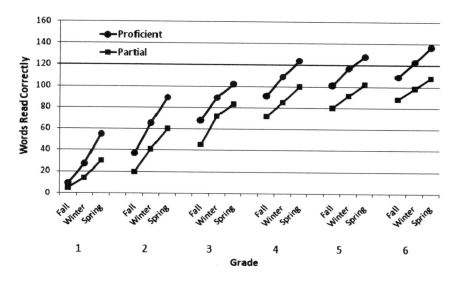

FIGURE 8.8. CBM benchmarks correlated to scoring "proficient" and "partially proficient" on the Minnesota Comprehensive Assessment (MCA) of reading.

mance on the state NCLB tests of accountability, or, for our district, the Minnesota Comprehensive Assessments (MCA). Figure 8.8 displays fall, winter, and spring CBM benchmarks that predict "proficient" or "partially proficient" on the MCAs. This information can be utilized within the RTI model for screening performance and determining which students are in need of Tier 1, 2, and 3 interventions.

Another tool for implementation of RTI is the weekly graph, shown in Figure 8.9. Students in Tiers 2 and 3 are monitored on a weekly basis, and the data are entered into the OCR website. Teachers enter the number of words read correctly and the number of errors, and they have the option of describing the intervention in a text box. When creating the student graph, the teacher sets a year-end goal, and a goal line is generated on the chart, which assists the teacher in evaluating student progress and determining whether the student is responding to the intervention.

SUCCESSES AND CHALLENGES OF RTI IMPLEMENTATION

Implementing an RTI process in MPS has resulted in several successes, including positive parent attitude toward the model, stability in the numbers of students identified with mild disabilities, and a decrease in disproportion

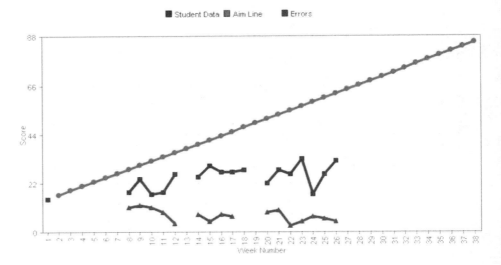

FIGURE 8.9. Example of weekly graph available on district student data website.

at schools implementing the model (Marston et al., 2003). With respect to the latter point, the number of African American students identified for special education dropped from roughly 68% to 55% after implementation. Moreover, the percentage of students declared eligible for special education after receiving a Tier 3 intervention averaged only 27% (Marston, Reschly, Lau, Muyskens, & Canter, 2007). In another study, investigators found higher quality general education interventions at problem-solving model schools, earlier delivery of special education services, and positive attitudes toward the model exhibited by staff (Reschly & Starkweather, 1997). A review of four large-scale implementations of RTI models that included MPS reported positive outcomes (Burns, Appleton, & Stehouwer, 2005).

Lau and colleagues (2006) studied implementation and reported favorable attitudes toward the model and its impact on the roles of school staff. These researchers identified the principal as a key person who functioned as the building "change agent." In this role the principal plans for the collection of screening and PM data in the school, finds the resources for extra interventions, plans professional development supporting these activities, and creates a master schedule that allows for implementation of the model. The special education teacher becomes a collaborator with general education teachers and focuses on student RTI as part of the eligibility process. For school psychologists, the role of "tester" has changed and now includes more direct interaction with students and parents, consultation with teachers, and a leadership role in school implementation.

Despite positive outcomes, there are challenges to implementing an RTI model, two of which are addressed in our recent RTI implementation. First, with our original version of RTI, the initial interventions provided to individual students not meeting benchmarks varied from classroom to classroom within schools and were not delivered in the standard protocol approach described by Vaughn and colleagues (2007). These differences from teacher to teacher can lead to variability in using evidence-based practices. Our recent implementation of RTI, as described in the next chapter, provides an opportunity and a recommendation for building leaders to select and use standard researched interventions across classrooms for students needing interventions.

A second challenge was that, currently, teachers were on their own when determining initial instructional interventions for a student, and only after the student continued to show no progress was the PST consulted. An improvement on this approach would be to have grade-level teams of teachers convene earlier and meet more frequently throughout the academic year for the purpose of viewing student performance.

In this chapter we described the MPS experience with PM and utilizing an RTI framework based on the problem-solving model. We then provided suggestions, based on the context of our experience, as to how schools and districts can improve their RTI implementation. Without question, schools need comprehensive professional development, system supports, and strong leadership. Chapter 9 illustrates how one school blended the "old" with the "new" to create a more effective RTI model.

REFERENCES

Brophy, J., & Good, T. L. (1986). Teacher behavior and student achievement. In M. Wittrock (Ed.), *Handbook of research on teaching* (pp. 328–375). New York: Macmillan.

Buffum, A., Mattos, M., & Weber, C. (2009). *Pyramid response to intervention: RTI, professional learning communities, and how to respond when kids don't learn.* Bloomington, IN: Solution Tree Press.

Burns, M. K., Appleton, J. J., & Stehouwer, J. D. (2005). Meta-analytic review of responsiveness-to-intervention research: Examining field-based and research-implemented models. *Journal of Psychoeducational Assessment, 23,* 381–394.

Casey, A., Deno, S., Marston, D., & Skiba, R. (1988). Experimental teaching: Changing teacher beliefs about effective instructional practices. *Teacher Education and Special Education, 11*(3), 123–132.

Deno, S., Mirkin, P., Chiang, B., Kuehnle, K., Lowry, L., Marston, D., et al. (1980). Current status of research on the development of a formative evaluation system for learning disability programs. In W. C. Cruickshank (Ed.), *The best of ACLD* (pp. 125–147). Syracuse, NY: Syracuse University Press.

Deno, S. L. (1985). Curriculum-based measurement: The emerging alternative. *Exceptional Children, 52*(3), 219–232.

Deno, S. L. (2003). Developments in curriculum-based measurement. *Journal of Special Education, 37,* 184–192.

Deno, S. L., & Marston, D. (2007). Curriculum-based measurement of oral reading: An indicator of growth in fluency. In S. J. Samuels & A. E. Farstrup (Eds.), *What research has to say about reading instruction* (pp. 179–203). Newark, DE: International Reading Association.

Deno, S. L., Marston, D., Shinn, M., & Tindal, G. (1983). Oral reading fluency: A simple datum for scaling reading disability. *Topics in Learning and Learning Disability, 2,* 53–59.

Deno, S. L., & Mirkin, P. (1977). *Data-based program modification.* Reston, VA: Council for Exceptional Children.

Deno, S. L., Mirkin, P., & Chiang, B. (1982). Identifying valid measures of reading. *Exceptional Children, 49*(1), 36–45.

Fuchs, D., & Fuchs, L. S. (2006). Introduction to response to intervention: What, why, and how valid is it? *Reading Research Quarterly, 41*(1), 93–99.

Fuchs, L. S., Deno, S. L., & Mirkin, P. (1984). The effects of frequent curriculum-based measurement and evaluation on pedagogy, student achievement, and student awareness of learning. *American Education Research Journal, 21*(2), 449–460.

Gresham, F. M., MacMillan, D. L., Beebe-Frankenberger, M. E., & Bocian, K. M (2000). Treatment integrity in learning disabilities intervention research: Do we really know how treatments are implemented? *Learning Disabilities Research and Practice, 15,* 198–205.

Johnson, E., Mellard, D. F., Fuchs, D., & McKnight, M. A. (2006). *Responsiveness to intervention (RTI): How to do it.* Lawrence, KS: National Research Center on Learning Disabilities.

Lau, M., Sieler, J., Muyskens, P., Canter, A., Vankeuren, B., & Marston, D. (2006). Perspectives on the use of the problem-solving model from the viewpoint of a school psychologist, administrator, and teacher from a large Midwest urban school district. *Psychology in the Schools, 43*(1), 117–127.

Marston, D. (1988). The effectiveness of special education: A time-series analysis of reading performance in regular and special education. *Journal of Special Education, 21*(4), 13–26.

Marston, D. (2002). A functional and intervention-based assessment approach to establishing discrepancy for students with learning disabilities. In R. Bradley, L. Danielson, & D. P. Hallahan (Eds.), *Identification of learning disabilities: Research to practice* (pp. 437–447). Mahwah, NJ: Erlbaum.

Marston, D., Deno, S. L., Kim, D., Diment, K., & Rogers, D. (1995). Comparison of reading intervention approaches for students with mild disabilities. *Exceptional Children, 62*(1), 20–37.

Marston, D., Fuchs, L., & Deno, S. L. (1986). Measuring pupil progress: A comparison of standardized achievement tests and curriculum-related measures. *Diagnostique, 11*(2), 77–90.

Marston, D., & Lau, M. (2008). *Data review meeting integrity checklist.* Unpublished manuscript.

Marston, D., Lau, M., & Muyskens, P. (2007). Implementation of the problem solving model in Minneapolis Public Schools. In S. R. Jimerson, M. K. Burns, & A. M. VanDerHeyden (Eds.), *Handbook of response to intervention: The science and practice of assessment and intervention* (pp. 279–287). New York: Springer.

Marston, D., & Magnusson, D. (1985). Implementation of curriculum-based measurement in special and regular education settings. *Exceptional Children, 52*(3), 266–276.

Marston, D., & Magnusson, D. (1988). Curriculum-based measurement: District-level implementation. In J. Graden, J. Zins, & M. Curtis (Eds.), *Alternative educational delivery systems: Enhancing options for all students* (pp. 137–172). Kent, OH: National Association for School Psychologists.

Marston, D., Mirkin, P. K., & Deno, S. L. (1984). Curriculum-based measurement of academic skills: An alternative to traditional screening, referral, and identification of learning disabled students. *Journal of Special Education, 18,* 109–118.

Marston, D., Muyskens, P., Lau, M., & Canter, A. (2003). Problem-solving model for decision making with high-incidence disabilities: The Minneapolis experience. *Learning Disabilities Research and Practice, 18*(3), 187–200.

Marston, D., Pickart, M., Reschly, A., Muyskens, P., Heistad, D., & Tindal, G. (2007). Early literacy measures for improving student reading achievement: Translating research into practice. *Exceptionality, 15*(2), 97–118.

Marston, D., Reschly, A., Lau, M., Muyskens, P., & Canter, A. (2007). Historical perspectives and current trends in problem solving: The Minneapolis story. In D. Haager, J. Klinger, & S. Vaughn (Eds.), *Evidence-based practices for response to intervention* (pp. 265–286). Baltimore: Brookes.

Marston, D., Tindal, G., & Deno, S. L. (1984). Eligibility for learning disability services: A direct and repeated-measurement approach. *Exceptional Children, 50,* 554–556.

McLeskey, J. (Ed.). (2007). *Reflections on inclusion: Classic articles that shaped our thinking.* Arlington, VA: Council for Exceptional Children.

Muyskens, P., Marston, D., & Reschly, A. L. (2007). The use of response to intervention practices for behavior: An examination of the validity of a screening instrument. *California School Psychologist, 12,* 31–45.

Reschly, D., & Starkweather, A. (1997). *Evaluation of an alternative special education assessment and classification program in the Minneapolis Public Schools.* Ames: Iowa State University.

Sanetti, L. M., & Kratochwill, T. R. (2009). Toward developing a science of treatment integrity: Introduction to the special series. *School Psychology Review, 38*(4), 445–459.

Self, H., Benning, A., Marston, D., & Magnusson, D. (1991). Cooperative Teaching Project: A model for students at risk. *Exceptional Children, 58*(1), 26–34.

Shinn, M., & Marston, D. (1985). Assessing mildly handicapped, low achieving, and regular education students: A curriculum-based approach. *Remedial and Special Education, 6*(2), 31–45.

Tindal, G., & Marston, D. (1996). Technical adequacy of alternative reading measures as performance assessments. *Exceptionality, 6*(4), 201–230.

Vaughn, S., Wanzek, J., Woodruff, A., & Linan-Thompson, S. (2007). Prevention and early identification of students with reading disabilities. In D. Haager, J. Klinger, & S. Vaughn (Eds.), *Evidence-based reading practices for response to intervention* (pp. 11–27). Baltimore: Brookes.

Wallace, T. (2006). *Teacher CBM survey*. Minneapolis: University of Minnesota.

Wayman, M., Wallace, T., Wiley, H., Ticha, R., & Espin, C. (2007). Literature synthesis on curriculum-based measurement in reading. *Journal of Special Education, 41*(2), 85–120.

Yell, M. L., Deno, S. L., & Marston, D. B. (1992). Barriers to implementing curriculum-based measurement. *Diagnostique, 18*(1), 99–112.

CHAPTER 9

The Process of Implementation

Doug Marston
Teri Wallace
Jane Thompson
Matthew Lau
Paul Muyskens

Mosteller (1981) noted in his keynote address to the American Psychological Association that, despite knowing the treatment for the disease scurvy, which killed countless sailors, it took the British Navy over 250 years to implement the cure and the British mercantile marine another 60 years. Although this is an extreme example of the difficulty of translating research into practice, the notion that implementing educational research in school settings is challenging is well documented (Constas & Sternberg, 2006). Not surprisingly, implementing the response-to-intervention (RTI) model at the school level and translating these concepts into practical and effective practices will be challenging. In this chapter we describe how one school in a large, urban district with high poverty and a diverse student population used the existing research on data-based decision making to create an RTI framework.

Our implementation site was selected as one of the three schools to participate in the Demonstration of Progress Monitoring project, an Office of Special Education–funded demonstration grant that was a collaboration of the University of Minnesota and the Minneapolis Public Schools (MPS). The major focus of the project was to build on prior experience with curriculum-based measurement (CBM) (Marston & Magnusson, 1985), progress monitoring (PM), and the problem-solving model to implement an RTI model (Deno, 2005; Marston, Muyskens, Lau, & Canter, 2003). We adopted the familiar RTI pyramid, shown in Figure 9.1, and began the implementation of a multilayered framework with Tiers 1, 2, and 3 interventions (Fuchs & Fuchs, 2006; Vaughn, Wanzek, Woodruff, & Linan-Thompson, 2007). The data-based decision-making system driving the RTI framework was based on the district-developed CBM screening and PM procedures (Minneapolis Public Schools, 2002).

The MPS has an enrollment of about 38,000 students and is quite diverse, with more than 80 languages represented in the 2008–2009 school year. A breakdown of the ethnic groups shows the largest group is African American students at 39.6%, followed by white American students at 29.8%, Hispanic American students at 17.1%, Asian American students at 9.0%, and American Indian students at 4.5%. The percentage of students living in poverty is 65.6%, and 23.2% of the students are English language learners (ELLs). Special education students make up 15.9%. The demonstration school, which is located in north Minneapolis, is a K–5 school with a population of 372 students and is representative of the district, with 77% of the students living in poverty and 20% are ELLs. The ethnic composition of the school is 43% African American, 25% white American, 16% Hispanic American, 10% Asian American, and 5% American Indian. Special education students make up 8% of the school enrollment. The staff is composed of a principal, one social worker, 16 classroom teachers, four

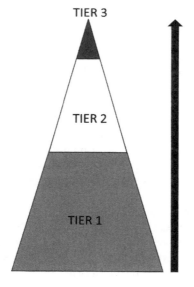

FIGURE 9.1. Major components of the RTI model.

specialists, two ESL teachers, two special education teachers, three associate educators, three educational assistants, and a school psychologist. The
average length of teaching experience at the school is 18.3 years.

CHARACTERISTICS OF SUCCESSFUL RTI IMPLEMENTATION

Marston, Casey, and Wallace (Chapter 8, this volume) identified three
important characteristics associated with successful RTI implementation:
leadership, professional development, and system supports. The extent to
which these traits were evident during implementation of RTI at the school
is examined, with links to the literature base that supports the importance
of each of these in the development of an RTI model.

Leadership

Strong leadership is vital in constructing the framework for success in
urban classrooms (Corbett, Wilson, & Williams, 2002). Shepherd (2006)
examined the role of principals in developing effective RTI teams and
concluded that the leadership provided by the building administrator was
essential. Leadership was demonstrated by: (1) showing a commitment to
participation and support of the teams, (2) ensuring that the teams had an
interdisciplinary membership and met on a frequent basis, (3) modeling collaboration in the meeting process, (4) linking the RTI teams to professional
development and the school improvement process, and (5) collaborating
with other administrators to implement district and state policies related to
RTI development. In describing the role of the principal in RTI implementation, Butler (2009) identified necessary leadership skills, including selecting effective interventions, using data, articulating to staff how RTI would
work at the school, arranging professional development, and participating
in student data meetings.

Building on 31 years of experience in the district, 22 as a social worker
and 9 as a school administrator, the principal at our demonstration school
provided that type of leadership. She described herself as an advocate for
children with a strong commitment to creating a professional environment
for her school and data-based decision making. The project staff noted
she had excellent communication with the staff. She welcomed ideas and
input, was in classrooms on a regular basis, and had an extensive knowledge of research-based interventions. As pointed out in Chapter 8 in this
volume, the messages given to staff by the principal were key to successful implementation. At our demonstration site the principal was consistent
with many of the ideals described by McCoun (2006), Butler (2009), and
Shepherd (2006) by delivering strong messages about meeting the needs of

all students, providing the best possible instructional methods by highly trained teaching staff, using data to improve the decisions about the students served in the school, and providing the collaborative environment in which staff members claim ownership of implementation.

Professional Development

Butler (2009) noted that professional development can be a challenge in RTI implementation and described a need for staff to learn about effective interventions and how to implement problem solving and to provide coaching. One of the five important factors contributing to successful implementation identified by Shepherd (2006) was professional development. At successful schools the development of a data-based culture was a natural link to determining needs for professional development. "These principals recognized the need to appropriate human and fiscal resources in a professional development model that brought general and special educators together to build their capacity to serve all students" (Shepherd, 2006, p. 36). As a result, professional development activities focused on learning new strategies for improving achievement and behavior for all students.

The literacy team (composed of the Title I lead teacher, the RTI coordinator, and the principal) met monthly to discuss professional development needs and schoolwide data and to plan future activities for improving student performance. Professional development activities at the demonstration site played a major role in the school. All teachers, including specialists, participate in weekly study groups, which alternate between reading and math. The guiding framework in the area of reading has been influenced by the school's participation in Reading First and uses the National Reading Panel as a guide for topics in the study groups. The groups have focused on the five essential skills of reading: phonemic awareness, phonics, fluency, vocabulary, and comprehension. Teachers discuss current research and implementation. The study groups include mentor teachers to demonstrate teaching and coaching. The study group leaders rotated between staff members weekly.

According to the principal, the study groups are an example of job-embedded staff development, which means that every week, every teacher participates in meetings in which they study research, talk about how to implement these concepts in the classroom, and look at student data. The study groups formed at the implementation site to support the RTI implementation are consistent with the literature on professional learning communities (PLC). Dufour (2005) described the core principles of the PLC as (1) making sure that students are learning, (2) developing a culture of collaboration at the school, and (3) concentrating on student results. In job-embedded staff development at the school, coaches model lessons in the classroom, observe teachers, and provide mentoring that helps teachers look at how they teach and what they believe about teaching. In part due to this professional development model, the principal believes there has been a paradigm shift in which teachers have moved from standing and lecturing to creating learning situations in which students are more engaged and are learning.

Because staff had prior experience with Reading First, most teachers had the skills to administer and score CBM procedures. However, at the beginning of the project, "refresher" training was provided to all staff on CBM screening, PM, and using district technology to analyze student data. The principal observed each classroom weekly, if not more. She provided informal feedback related to assessment and instructional practices on a frequent basis.

System Supports

McCoun (2006) states that RTI models "involve new methods of evaluation and intervention; development of base-line assessment data, setting and planning goals, treatment integrity, and student progress monitoring" (p. 63). Developing and maintaining a data-based decision-making culture was identified by Shepherd (2006) as an important step toward effectively implementing RTI. Both of these observations point to the measurement system as an important factor supporting implementation of the RTI model. As described in Chapter 8, this volume, MPS has a long history of using CBM procedures (Marston & Magnusson, 1985). District staff has developed oral reading passages by selecting stories from the district basal reading series, Houghton Mifflin Reading Series (2000), and created a standard set of procedures and materials for screening and monitoring student progress (MPS, 2002). For grade levels 1–6, approximately 30 passages per level have been created and are available to staff. Based on the procedures outlined in the online district manual, district staff provide training on the administration, scoring, and data entry for the measures.

When the CBM procedures were first used in the district, data collection and graphing were completed with paper-and-pencil materials. Using percentile rank tables developed by district staff, schools were able to interpret screening data to determine how discrepant the student was in comparison with district norms. Recent analyses by district staff, as described in Chapter 8, link CBM screening data to the important No Child Left Behind (NCLB) accountability tests. With the help of the district's electronic student data system, the screening data are entered into the district Office for Civil Rights (OCR) website and summarized by classroom or grade level and color-coded for interpretation. Student screening scores that predict that the student is at or above grade-level benchmarks are coded in green. However, students whose CBM performance predicts only partial proficiency on the Minnesota Comprehensive Assessment (MCA) reading test are coded in yellow. Finally, students performing significantly low on the CBM measures are predicted to not be proficient and are coded in red. To further support teacher interpretation of the data, the OCR website can sort student data from low to high, which facilitates data analysis for the school staff.

Originally, CBM PM data points were plotted by hand on graph paper, and aim lines and trend lines were drawn by the teacher. Again, with the help of technology, a Web-based data collection and graphing system is available that automatically graphs data, generates aim lines, and supports the decision-making process for students (Marston, Lau, & Muyskens, 2007). Input from the staff served to refine the district's graphing system. District staff is available to support staff for training and to provide technical assistance when needed.

The OCR website also serves as a student data warehouse that provides staff with other relevant sources of information related to academics and behavior. At student data review meetings the team can review student current and past attendance rates, behavior screening scores, suspension data, and other district achievement measures. For each student a complete history of all reading and math achievement scores from state and local assessments is available. Historical data from the Northwest Achievement Levels Test (Northwest Evaluation Association, 2003), the district's standardized achievement measure, is charted for each student and compared with benchmarks established by the district's research and evaluation department. In addition, the state's assessment for NCLB, the MCA, is provided in the student data warehouse. Teachers have access to all current and prior MCA test scores, which include scaled scores and an indicator of the student's level of proficiency. At the classroom level the summary organizer is used to report student performance on achievement, attendance, and behavior indicators, which can also be sorted from low to high.

The planning process for the implementation of RTI is another system support component that is critical to the successful use of the model. At our implementation school, the building principal and leadership staff began the planning in the spring of the academic year before beginning RTI. The leadership team first built a timeline for the RTI activities for the school year. This school calendar is shown in Figure 9.2. Initial professional development activities related to interventions and PM were scheduled for the first week in August. Fall, winter, and spring screenings were scheduled for September, January, and May. Student data meetings were scheduled monthly, while professional development study groups, as described earlier in the chapter, met on a weekly basis.

Strongly advocated by the principal, the staff's desire to create a school schedule that met student instructional needs helped make data-based decision making and targeted interventions a reality. Reading and math interventions were given highest priority and not shortchanged because of typi-

August
  Training on PM
  Tiers 2 and 3 intervention training

September
  Schoolwide screening: Fall
  Formation of groups for Tiers 2 and 3
  Begin PM
  Study groups

October
  PM
  Student data meetings
  Study groups

November
  PM
  Student data meetings
  Study groups

December
  PM
  Student data meetings

January
  Schoolwide screening: Winter
  PM
  Student data meetings
  Study groups

February
  PM
  Student data meetings
  Study groups

March
  PM
  Student data meetings
  Study groups

April
  PM
  MCA testing

May
  Schoolwide screening: Spring
  PM
  Student data meetings
  Study groups

FIGURE 9.2. Time line for implementing training, screening, data meetings, PM, and study groups for the school year.

cal issues that often occur with the traditional school schedule (Marston, Casey, & Wallace, Chapter 8, this volume). All students had an uninterrupted 2-hour literacy block. The first hour was for whole-class instruction, and the second hour focused on differentiated instruction, which included Tier 2 and Tier 3 interventions. The school schedule provided reading group time in which group sizes were decreased, students had access to intervention and supplemental materials, and teachers had monthly PM meetings to discuss data and "next steps." All teachers in the building had 55-minute common preps. The principal delivered a strong expectation that scheduled data review meetings were not to be canceled or skipped by staff—RTI implementation had top priority in the building.

MAJOR COMPONENTS OF RTI

There are several important components in implementing the RTI three-tiered continuum support framework shown in Figure 9.1. First, universal screening of all students needs to be established and completed on a routine basis. Second, all students receive core instruction at Tier 1 that is provided with high fidelity. Third, targeted interventions to be used at Tiers 2 and 3 for students performing below standards need to be selected. Fourth, based on screening data and other sources of information, students are placed in the intervention groups. Fifth, all students in Tiers 2 and 3 interventions are monitored for progress and the data are graphed. Sixth, grade-level teams of school staff meet on a regular basis during the school year to review student progress and make adjustments to student interventions when indicated. Seventh, the fidelity of targeted interventions and model implementation are checked for fidelity. Over a 3-year period staff implemented these seven components.

Screening: Summary Organizer

Universal screening occurred three times each academic year, in fall, winter, and spring. The primary measure used for grades 1–4 was words read correctly. In kindergarten the measures included letter sounds, phoneme segmentation, and onset phoneme identification. In addition, the district's standardized reading achievement test, the Northwest Achievement Levels Test (NALT), was used at grades 3 and 4 to supplement the screening information. Behavior screening information, collected in late September, was also used as part of the universal screening process (Muyskens, Marston, & Reschly, 2007). The building leadership assembled a screening team that collected all school data. The team consisted of a project facilitator, a Title I teacher, a special education teacher, and two building educational assistants. Fall screening data were collected in the first week of September so that instructional groups could be formed immediately. The principal emphasized that she did not want any lost instructional time. The screening teams, with up to five members, would collect data for one classroom at a time and were often able to finish a class of 25 students within an hour. Typically, the schoolwide screening was completed within 2 days.

Screening data were entered into the district website, and students were rank-ordered within class and grade level. District CBM benchmarks, as presented in Chapter 8 (this volume), were used by the school leadership team to assign the tier of instruction for each student. Students at or above the benchmarks for proficiency on the MCA were coded green on the OCR website summary organizer and assigned to Tier 1 instruction, as shown in Figure 9.3. These students received 60 minutes of core instruction and a second 60 minutes of literacy instruction that extended core instruction. Students whose screening scores placed them below the "proficiency" benchmark but above the "partial" proficiency benchmark are coded yellow. These students received the 60 minutes of core instruction in a whole-group setting and a Tier 2 small-group intervention. Students who scored

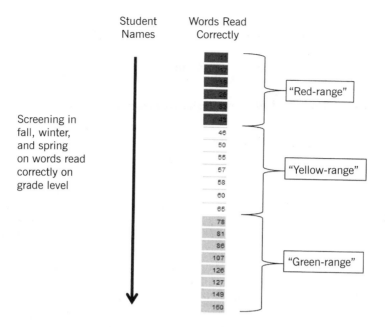

FIGURE 9.3. Example of classroom results for universal screening and color coding of students as "green," "yellow," or "red."

below the "partial" proficiency benchmark were coded red and assigned to the most intensive interventions at Tier 3.

Ensuring That Core Instruction at Tier 1 Is Implemented with Fidelity

The core reading curriculum at the implementation school is the Houghton Mifflin (2002) reading series, which is central to the 2-hour literacy block scheduled for each student. In the first 60 minutes of the literacy instruction block, all students receive whole-group instruction using the Houghton Mifflin materials in three areas: reading comprehension, word work, and writing and language. In the area of reading comprehension, the types of activities used by the teacher were: teacher read-alouds, preparing to read, wrapping up, rereading, comprehension skill instruction, story structure, information and study skills, rereading for fluency, spiral review, and launching the theme. In the area of word work, teachers focused on spelling, pretests and posttests, vowel sounds, decoding longer words, base words, endings, and vocabulary expansion. The third area addressed during core instruction was writing and language and included: daily language practice, grammar instruction, writing, journal writing, news articles, and listening and speaking activities. As stated earlier, the building principal observed classrooms at least once every 2 weeks, and in some cases weekly, and provided teachers with feedback on their instruction.

Identifying Targeted Interventions for Tiers 2 and 3

In the second 60 minutes of the 2-hour literacy block, the Tier 2 and Tier 3 small-group interventions are provided. As part of the planning process, the leadership team selected small-group interventions for students not making benchmarks. Based on available research and the school's experience with Reading First consultants, the team selected Reading Mastery from SRA/McGraw-Hill (2003), Corrective Reading, also from SRA/McGraw-Hill (1999), Early Success from Houghton Mifflin (1997), Soar to Success from Houghton Mifflin (1999), Read Naturally (Ihnot, 1991), and Early Intervention in Reading (EIR; Taylor, 2008) for Tiers 2 and 3 interventions. An outline of the grade levels and the tiers of interventions used at the implementation school is presented in Table 9.1. These interventions were implemented by the school staff during the second hour of the 120-minute literacy block and provided instruction related to the five major components of the National Reading Panel: phonemic awareness (Reading Mastery, Cor-

TABLE 9.1. Core Reading Instruction and Targeted Interventions Provided at Each Grade Level

Grade	Tier 1: Core (green)	Tier 2 (yellow)	Tier 3 (red)
K	Houghton-Mifflin; Core Materials Leveled Library	PALS Program	Reading Mastery Phonemic Awareness
1	Houghton-Mifflin Leveled Library Collins Writing	EIR Leveled Library Read Naturally Reading Mastery	EIR Reading Mastery
2	Houghton-Mifflin Core Materials Leveled Library	Leveled Library Read Naturally Reading Mastery	EIR Reading Mastery
3	Houghton-Mifflin Core Materials Leveled Library	Houghton-Mifflin Core Materials Leveled Library	Reading Mastery
4	Houghton-Mifflin Core Materials Leveled Library	Houghton-Mifflin Core Materials Leveled Library Soar to Success	Corrective Reading

rective Reading, Early Success, EIR), phonics (Reading Mastery, Corrective Reading, Early Success, EIR), fluency (Read Naturally, Corrective Reading, Reading Mastery, EIR, Early Success), vocabulary (Early Success, Soar to Success, EIR), and comprehension (Early Success, Soar to Success, EIR).

Creating Instructional Groups

The results of the fall universal screening with CBM measures led to the creation of the instructional groups. Based on the CBM benchmarks that predict proficiency on the MCA in reading, criteria were established for the fall, winter, and spring and are presented in Table 9.2. To demonstrate how the screening data are used, we outline an example using the third-grade data from the fall of Year 1. Based on the benchmarks similar to the criteria presented in Table 9.2, students reading above the proficiency benchmark in the fall receive Tier 1 instruction only. These students are on track to be proficient on the state MCA reading test and are not placed in a Tier 2 or Tier 3 small group. In the first year of implementation, 32 out of 58 students met this condition and were placed in a group that focused on vocabulary, comprehension, and writing activities. Twenty students performed at the level that predicted partial proficiency. These students received a Tier 2 intervention that was delivered in small groups for approximately 60 minutes. In this case the intervention was Reading Mastery II, supplemented with vocabulary and comprehension activities. For those students who were not on track to proficiency, the most intensive intervention at Tier 3

TABLE 9.2. Guidelines for Establishing Intervention Tier Based on Words Read Correctly on CBM Probes

Grade		Fall	Winter	Spring
1	Tier 1	Above 8	Above 26	Above 54
	Tier 2	5 to 8	14 to 26	30 to 54
	Tier 3	Below 5	Below 14	Below 30
2	Tier 1	Above 37	Above 61	Above 83
	Tier 2	23 to 37	44 to 61	62 to 83
	Tier 3	Below 23	Below 44	Below 62
3	Tier 1	Above 56	Above 82	Above 95
	Tier 2	37 to 56	68 to 82	81 to 95
	Tier 3	Below 37	Below 68	Below 81
4	Tier 1	Above 77	Above 99	Above 115
	Tier 2	62 to 77	81 to 99	94 to 115
	Tier 3	Below 62	Below 81	Below 94

was provided. For these six students there was one small group in which the teacher used Reading Mastery I for the primary intervention, supplemented with vocabulary work. The size of Tier 2 groups typically ranged from 7 to 10 students, whereas Tier 3 groups ranged from about 4 to 7 students.

Progress Monitoring

Students receiving Tier 2 and Tier 3 small-group instruction were monitored for progress on a weekly basis. During the third year of RTI implementation, the students in Tier 2 were monitored every other week. Screening data are collected by a cadre of teachers in the fall, winter, and spring, but all teaching staff are expected to collect PM data for some students. The procedures from the district's Performance Assessment for the Problem-Solving Model were used for student PM in reading and early literacy. The manual, which was created prior to the demonstration project, includes an introduction to using CBM, procedures for administration, scoring rules, reading and early literacy probes, and normative tables and figures that were used in the project. The manual, which was developed in the mid-1990s by district staff, has been very popular with special and regular education staff and is currently available online on the district's local website.

Students are monitored on grade-level passages unless their performance falls below CBM placement criteria, in which case students are monitored on passages one grade level lower. The graphs are set up on the OCR website, in which the teacher enters the initial baseline data and sets a weekly goal. The weekly goal is used to create an aim line for the remainder of the year. For example, a student with a baseline of 20 words read correctly and a weekly goal of 2 words per week would have an accelerating line on his or her graph with a target of 80 words at the end of 30 weeks. An example of an aim line is shown in Figure 9.4. The student reads one passage per week, except for short weeks affected by a holiday, teacher conventions, parent conferences, and so forth. Throughout the year staff members continue to enter the data in the OCR website from which graphs are generated and can be printed or viewed on LCD projectors at data meetings.

After 3 weeks of PM data collection, teachers plot the moving median when viewing student graphs. The moving median is the middle score of the last 3 data points collected for PM. The general guideline for when to adjust the student's intervention is 4 consecutive data points below the aim line. Examples of student PM graphs are shown in Figures 9.4 and 9.5. In Figure 9.4 the plotted moving medians are above the aim line, a clear demonstration of a student responding to the Tier 2 interventions. In Figure 9.5, however, the moving medians for the student are consistently below

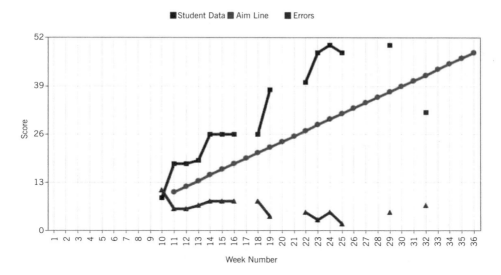

FIGURE 9.4. Sample PM graph of student showing student above aim line and responding to instruction.

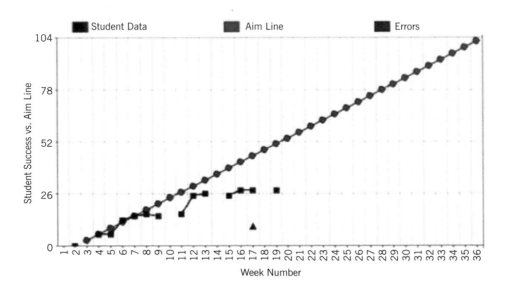

FIGURE 9.5. Sample PM graph of student showing student below aim line and not responding to instruction.

the aim line. They indicate that the student is not responding to instruction and that an instructional change is necessary.

Grade-Level Team Meetings and Reacting to the Data

Student progress meetings for each grade level were set for each month of the academic year with the purpose of reviewing student data to inform instructional decisions about the student. At the implementation school, the data review meeting was structured to address screening, tiered interventions, and PM. Each meeting was typically followed by a 4-week period of core instruction (Tier 1) and targeted interventions (Tiers 2 and 3). Participants in the data review meeting included a meeting facilitator, classroom teachers, administrators such as the principal, and support staff such as associate educators, educational assistants, an ESL teacher, a Title I teacher, a special education teacher, a social worker, and a school psychologist. The principal, classroom teachers, and support staff, such as the educational assistants, were the core members of this meeting at the site.

Based on the RTI framework, the purpose of the data review meeting is to address these critical components: (1) reviewing PM data and/or graphs for all students; (2) determining adequacy of progress based on objective data related to benchmarks and slope; (3) discussing general and specific instructional strategies and/or programs for targeted interventions; and (4) recommending movement of students based on their PM data between tiered interventions. To ensure that *all* students benefit from the RTI process, it is important that academic progress and appropriate instructional strategies and interventions are discussed for all students, including those who have average or above-average skills. All meeting participants are expected to provide input at the meeting.

At the building, the meeting facilitator provided a structured agenda, maintained the general flow of the meeting, and assisted staff to adhere to the primary purpose of the meeting. The typical agenda included a review of screening data, placement of students in intervention groups, a discussion of the interventions used and the potential need for professional development in areas of concern, a review of student progress data, and a decision about moving students between groups. A list of all students within each grade level was organized by intervention groups based on the three-tiered model was provided to the meeting participants. Copies of the graphs were printed for the monthly student data meetings, or the graphs were viewed with an LCD projector. Discussion of student academic progress would typically begin with the students who received significantly below-average or below-passing scores based on the district assessments or state accountability tests. Specific academic and other relevant data, such as PM graphs and attendance and behavioral records, retrieved from the district's "data warehouse" could be projected on the screen to facilitate an in-depth discussion addressing the following questions:

1. Has the student been placed in an appropriate instruction/intervention group?
2. How did the student respond to the instruction/intervention?
3. Was the academic goal set for this student appropriate?
4. Was modification or alternative instruction needed for this student?
5. Did this student need to move to a different instruction/intervention group within the current tier or to another tier?

The discussion regarding matching needs of students with instruction continued for the rest of the students including those who had average or above-average academic skills. Each meeting lasted 90–120 minutes.

To ensure process integrity, a checklist was developed to monitor the extent to which the identified critical components were addressed during the data review meeting (Marston & Lau, 2008). With this checklist, observers rate each of the critical components on a 5-point Likert scale, from 5 (full implementation) to 1 (no implementation). In addition, the "not applicable" category is an option. Qualitative data can be submitted as part of the comment section for each item. The final version is an 11-item checklist focusing on the data review process, shown in Figure 9.6.

The principal stated that she needed to be part of these meetings so that she could be informed about what was happening with individual students and aggregately across the school. In addition, her participation was important because professional discussions of the teachers informed her ability to improve professional development in the building. The meetings helped her identify (1) the knowledge base of the teachers, (2) where professional development needed to be added, and (3) where support for teachers and students was necessary to more effectively implement RTI and improve the overall achievement of students.

Fidelity of Interventions

Although the principal made frequent visits to classrooms and observed small groups, a formal system of analyzing the fidelity of the interventions did not exist. Project staff contributed to the implementation school by either creating or locating existing fidelity checklists for the Tiers 2 and 3 interventions. For Reading Mastery, Corrective Reading, Read Naturally, and EIR, checklists were already available and were used by school or project staff to observe instruction. For Early Success and Soar to Success, checklists were created by staff to be used for the evaluation of treatment integrity. Observations were conducted twice a year, and teachers were provided feedback about implementation.

School: _____ Date: _____ Observer: _____

Team members who attended the meeting (check all that apply):

☐ Building facilitator   ☐ Principal   ☐ Social worker
☐ General education teacher   ☐ Special education teacher   ☐ Title I
☐ ESL teacher   ☐ School psychologist   ☐ Other: _____

Comments: _____
_____
_____

Please select one of the six ratings for each of the following statements:

5 = Full implementation   4 = Partial to full implementation 3 = Partial implementation
2 = Some implementation   1 = No   0 = N/A

1. Agenda was presented and expectations were announced.	
Comments:	
2. The meeting was 90 minutes in length.	
Comments:	
3. Students in red and yellow zones were reviewed.	
Comments:	
4. Teachers described instructional methods and materials for targeted interventions.	
Comments:	

(cont.)

FIGURE 9.6. Data review meeting integrity checklist (Marston & Lau, 2008).

5. Graphing data were completed (title/comments correct, no missing data, appropriate aim line, appropriate levels).	
Comments:	
6. Individual student graphs were reviewed (slope and level).	
Comments:	
7. Benchmark data were reviewed.	
Comments:	
8. Other data (comprehension, expression, behavior, attendance, etc.) were reviewed.	
Comments:	
9. Team input (full member participation).	
Comments:	
10. Decision related to criterion (stay or move to another tier).	
Comments:	
11. Adjustment to targeted intervention.	
Comments:	

FIGURE 9.6. *(cont.)*

SUMMARY AND DISCUSSION

In this chapter we have described how the implementation site used existing research on PM (Marston & Magnusson, 1985), problem solving (Deno, 2005), and RTI (Fuchs & Fuchs, 2006; Vaughn et al., 2007) to implement a framework for improving the achievement of all students at the school. Given the complexity of applying evidence-based methods in school settings (Constas & Sternberg, 2006), the school addressed the "translating research into practice" challenge of implementing RTI at the school level with success. Core instruction is implemented with fidelity across grade levels, and professional development is designed to contribute to teacher expertise in its implementation. Screening in the fall, winter, and spring is embedded in school practices and has a high priority on the school calendar. High priority is also placed on the Tier 2 and Tier 3 interventions, and the principal ensures that adequate funding is available to implement these small groups for students not making standards. Student data meetings are scheduled monthly and are the focal point of efforts to accelerate achievement. Contributing factors to the success in these areas can be directly attributed to strong leadership, embedded professional development through professional learning communities, and system supports, particularly in the area of technology for data-based decision making.

Project staff used the RTI Readiness and Implementation: Self-Assessment Tool created by the Pennsylvania Department of Education (2007) to evaluate RTI implementation. This tool describes 10 indicators of readiness and implementation, which include: standards-aligned curriculum and research-based instruction, universal screening, shared ownership, data-based decision making, tiered intervention and service delivery, parent engagement, behavior, eligibility determination, leadership, and professional development activities. Based on observations of professional development, data meetings, and observations of interventions, project staff found the school to rate "high" on all 10 indicators of readiness and implementation of RTI concepts.

However, implementation is not a foregone conclusion for any school attempting the adoption of the RTI model. Many challenges confront these schools. Foremost are the need for a leader who understands the nature of the framework and to have a staff that is ready and willing to undertake this venture. The planning of leadership, and no doubt prior experience with Reading First, prepared staff to implement the major components of the RTI model. Our project staff noticed that there was little turnover at the implementation site, which some teachers attributed to the excellent staff development that was available and opportunities for professional growth. According to the principal, "The stability in turn contributes to a positive climate, a shared work ethic, and a shared vision of what can be accomplished for students."

A second challenge to implementation is often the resistance that occurs when any new initiative is attempted at the school level. Hall, George, and Rutherford (1977) addressed this issue and concluded that educators progress through a series of stages when faced with innovation. Typically, individuals are concerned with how the innovation affects them directly. However, as the innovation continues, the concerns of staff progress to ways in which the innovation can positively influence the school, the district, and others. At the implementation school, staff had a very positive attitude about the RTI model and its effects on student achievement. Some of these perceptions can be attributed to the principal, who believed that making the project a schoolwide initiative with shared ownership, and not a project with a narrow focus, would increase the probability of success.

To meet the challenges of implementing RTI, the principal observed that, first, you need a belief system that every student can learn and deserves appropriate instruction at his or her skill level; without that belief system, it is hard to move forward. Second, a school needs informed teachers— teachers who understand reading research, understand instructional practices, and are willing to be uncomfortable as they learn a new way of doing things. Third, the principal needs to foster communication and teaming; "otherwise, you have pockets of things happening."

A recent quality review report (Cambridge Education, 2009) by an independent evaluation team concluded, "School leaders make very good use of a wide range of data in identifying what the school does well and where it needs to improve." Furthermore, the report stated, "The best teaching is exceptionally well-planned so that it fully engages students and ensures that they make rapid progress. The school has also ensured that the curriculum is broad and stimulating and so has a positive impact on students' academic and personal development" (2009, p. 4).

The principal observed that staff "buy-in" was very high. Furthermore, there is evidence of a sense of mutual dependency and high expectations among the staff. Because of the implementation, the school has predictable and productive systems in place that assess and monitor student achievement, has embedded staff development that addresses the quality of instruction, and many other benefits, including the following.

1. Instructional time engages students more because staff plans have improved and is more focused on what needs to be taught and how. The students are more engaged.
2. Behavior referrals and time off task have decreased.
3. Teachers have become more collegial, with more discussion in the staff lounge about instructional issues.
4. The staff is excited about learning as adults.
5. Special education referrals are lower because the quality of instruc-

tion has improved in Tier 1 and evidence-based strategies are used in Tiers 2 and 3.

Finally, the principal stated, "One thing I've noticed for teachers, and especially mid-career teachers—they found the joy in teaching again." One teacher remarked, " I thought I was an 'OK" teacher and having been through the whole process of learning more about instruction, understand the developmental aspects of reading, knowing what to do because I have good assessment data—"I feel like a great teacher." And the principal noted, "That is great for a principal to hear."

These qualitative observations by the building principal and project staff point to important benefits associated with the process of RTI model implementation, which includes attention to high-quality core instruction, implementing evidence-based interventions with fidelity, monitoring student progress on a frequent basis, and meeting in PLCs to review student results and share ideas on instruction. In the next chapter we move from a study of process to reviewing outcomes as measured by the quantitative data collected on RTI implementation at this demonstration site. In that chapter we review student achievement data, attendance, behavior, engaged time, teacher use of data, data-based decision making at the team level, and staff attitudes.

REFERENCES

Butler, L. (2009). A step-by-step guide to response to intervention. *Principal, 89*(1), 46–48, 50, 52.

Cambridge Education. (2009). *Quality review report.* Cambridge, UK: Author.

Constas, M. A., & Sternberg, R. J. (2006). *Translating theory and research into educational practice: Developments in content domains, large-scale reform, and intellectual capacity.* Mahwah, NJ: Erlbaum.

Corbett, D., Wilson, B., & Williams, B. (2002). *Effort and excellence in urban classrooms.* New York: Teachers College Press.

Deno, S. L. (2005). Problem-solving assessment. In R. Brown-Chidsey (Ed.), *Assessment for intervention: A problem-solving approach* (pp. 10–40). New York: Guilford Press.

Dufour, R. (2005). What is a professional learning community? In R. Dufour, R. Eaker, & R. Dufour (Eds.), *On common ground: The power of professional learning communities* (pp. 31–43). Bloomington, IN: Solution Tree.

Fuchs, D., & Fuchs, L. S. (2006). Introduction to response to intervention: What, why, and how valid is it? *Reading Research Quarterly, 41*(1), 93–99.

Hall, G. E., George, A. A., & Rutherford, W. L. (1977). *Measuring stages of concern about the innovation: A manual for use of the SoC questionnaire.* Austin: University of Texas, Research and Development Center for Teacher Education.

Ihnot, C. (1991). *Read naturally.* St. Paul, MN: Read Naturally.

Marston, D., & Lau, M. (2008). *Data review meeting checklist.* Unpublished manuscript.

Marston, D., Lau, M., & Muyskens, P. (2007). Implementation of the problem solving model in the Minneapolis Public Schools. In S. R. Jimerson, M. K. Burns, & A. M. VanDerHeyden (Eds.), *Handbook of response to intervention: The science and practice of assessment and intervention* (pp. 279–287). New York: Springer.

Marston, D., & Magnusson, D. (1985). Implementation of curriculum-based measurement in special and regular education settings. *Exceptional Children, 52*(3), 266–276.

Marston, D., Muyskens, P., Lau, M., & Canter, A. (2003). Problem-solving model for decision making with high-incidence disabilities: The Minneapolis experience. *Learning Disabilities Research and Practice, 18*(3), 187–200.

McCoun, B. (2006). Case in point: RTI as a general education initiative and the new role for educational support teams. *Journal of Special Education Leadership, 19*(2), 62–63.

Minneapolis Public Schools. (2002). *Performance assessment of reading in the problem solving model.* Minneapolis, MN: Author.

Mosteller, F. (1981). Innovation and evaluation. *Science, 211,* 881–886.

Muyskens, P., Marston, D., & Reschly, A. L. (2007). The use of response to intervention practices for behavior: An examination of the validity of a screening instrument. *California School Psychologist, 12,* 31–45.

Northwest Evaluation Association. (2003). *Technical manual for the NWEA measures of academic progress and achievement level tests.* Portland, OR: Author.

Pennsylvania Department of Education. (2007). *Response to intervention readiness and implementation: Self-assessment tool.* Harrisburg: Pennsylvania Department of Education.

Shepherd, K. G. (2006). Supporting all students: The role of school principals in expanding general education capacity using response-to-intervention teams. *Journal of Special Education Leadership, 19*(2), 30–38.

Taylor, B. (2008). *Early intervention in reading program.* Blaine, MN: EIR Professional Development Program.

Vaughn, S., Wanzek, J., Woodruff, A., & Linan-Thompson, S. (2007). Prevention and early identification of students with reading disabilities. In D. Haager, J. Klinger, & S. Vaughn (Eds.), *Evidence-based reading practices for response to intervention* (pp. 11–27). Baltimore: Brookes.

CHAPTER 10

Evaluation of Implementation

Teri Wallace
Doug Marston
Renáta Tichá
Matthew Lau
Paul Muyskens

In this chapter the outcomes associated with response-to-intervention (RTI) implementation over 3 years are described. The analyses are both quantitative and qualitative and divided into student and teacher outcomes. The results shared include student measures such as changes in curriculum-based measurement (CBM; used as a universal screening measure), changes in standardized test and state accountability data, movement between and within tiers of instruction, special education eligibility, data related to attendance and behavior, and the proportion of time students are engaged in academic behaviors. Results related to teacher instructional activities, use of progress monitoring (PM), fidelity of interventions, quality of teacher meetings, and teacher attitudes toward the RTI model are also provided. The following set of questions frame the process of evaluating student outcomes associated with the implementation of the model:

- Within the RTI framework, what is the typical performance and growth rate of students at the implementation school on the universal screening measure (CBM) each fall and spring across 3 years?
- Within the RTI framework, what is the typical performance and growth rate of students at the implementation school on the universal screening measure (CBM) each fall and spring across the three RTI tiers?

- What is the impact of RTI on attendance and behavior?
- What is the impact of RTI on academic engaged time?
- How much student movement exists between and within tiers of the RTI model during the academic year?
- What is the impact of RTI on special education eligibility?
- What is the impact of RTI on the No Child Left Behind (NCLB) accountability tests (Minnesota's MCA-II tests)?

The following questions examine the impact of the implementation of the model on teachers:

- How has the implementation of RTI affected teacher use of PM procedures?
- What is the fidelity of the interventions implemented at Tiers 2 and 3 of the RTI model?
- What is the fidelity of the RTI data review meetings?
- What are the teacher attitudes toward the primary components of the RTI model?

DESCRIPTION OF THE STUDENTS IN THE IMPLEMENTATION SCHOOL

Students in grades 1–4 participated in this study over the period of 3 years. In Year 1, a total of 238 students participated in the study. Table 10.1 provides demographic information regarding the students involved in the implementation. The initial achievement levels for participating students at the implementation school in the fall averaged across 3 years are documented in Table 10.2 for students in grades 1–4 on the reading-aloud CBM and in grades 3 and 4 also on the Northwest Achievement Levels Test (NALT; Northwest Evaluation Association, 2003). CBM—as a measure of oral reading fluency—can be used as a standardized screening tool of academic progress in reading (Deno, 1985; Wayman, Wallace, Wiley, Tichá, & Espin, 2007). The median score of the three 1-minute samples is used as an indicator of the student's reading performance. Initially, the average score of words read correctly for the first graders was 17.8, for the second graders was 47.3, for the third graders was 66.7, and for the fourth graders was 87.5. A review of national norms on CBM shows that these means ranged from the 31st percentile to the 35th percentile (Muyskens & Marston, 2008), suggesting that the students initially performed below the grade level of their peers around the country.

The NALT in reading (Northwest Evaluation Association, 2003) is a norm-referenced standardized test designed to measure the performance of different student reference groups and to assess the effectiveness of instruc-

TABLE 10.1. Student Demographics: Years 1, 2, and 3

	Year 1		Year 2		Year 3	
	n	%	*n*	%	*n*	%
Grade						
1	66	27.7	61	23.8	69	25.6
2	55	23.1	76	29.7	66	24.4
3	62	26.1	56	21.9	78	28.9
4	55	23.1	63	24.6	57	21.1
Gender						
Male	122	51.3	132	51.6	133	49.3
Female	116	48.7	124	48.4	137	50.7
Ethnicity						
American Indian	9	3.8	15	5.9	13	4.8
African American	99	41.6	120	46.9	129	47.8
Asian	26	10.9	24	9.4	29	10.7
Hispanic	44	18.5	45	17.6	43	15.9
White	60	25.2	52	20.3	56	20.7
ELL						
ELL	52	21.8	56	21.9	57	21.1
Non-ELL	186	78.2	200	78.1	213	78.9
Special education						
Yes	19	8.0	24	9.4	24	8.9
No	219	92.0	232	90.6	246	91.1
Total	238	100	256	100	270	100
SES						
Receiving free/ reduced-price lunch	185	79.7	179	71.9	172	65.9
Not receiving	47	20.3	70	28.1	89	34.1
Total	232	100	249	100	261	100

Note. ELL, English language learner; SES, socioeconomic status.

TABLE 10.2. Descriptive Statistics for Initial Achievement (Fall) Averaged across 3 Years

	CBM words read correct			NALT correct		
Grade	Mean	*SD*	*N*	Mean	*SD*	*N*
1	17.75	19.79	169	—	—	—
2	47.26	30.39	151	—	—	—
3	66.67	31.42	151	186.35	15.38	169
4	87.47	28.86	127	193.91	14.65	149

tion. The NALT reading test questions are multiple choice and focus on word meaning, literal comprehension, interpretive comprehension, and evaluative comprehension. On the NALT, as shown in Table 10.2, the third-grade mean was 186.4, and the fourth-grade mean scaled score was 193.9. In this study, the NALT has a correlation ratio of .77 with CBM at grade 3 ($N = 56$) and .72 at grade 4 ($N = 48$), showing a moderate to strong correlation (Wayman et al., 2007).

IMPACT ON STUDENT LEARNING

The next section provides information about the impact that RTI implementation had on student learning and other key indicators. The section is organized using the implementation evaluation questions. The section reviews each question related specifically to student learning outcomes.

• *Within the RTI framework, what is the typical performance and growth rate of students at the implementation school on the universal screening measure (CBM) each fall and spring across 3 years of implementation?* The CBM reading-aloud measure (words read correctly) was used as one of the measures to assess student performance and progress. Three times a year—during universal screening—students individually read from three passages at their grade level. The median oral reading scores (the number of words read correctly for 1 minute for each student) were used for analysis. Only those students who had both fall and spring CBM scores within each year were included in the analysis. The means, standard deviations, and average growth on the CBM reading measure are presented in Table 10.3 for all three years of the project. The data indicate that on average students in first and second grades read 45 words more, students in third grade 38 words more, and students in fourth grade 26 words more in the spring than in the fall. This average growth rate, based on a 35-week period, can be translated into an improvement of 1.3 words per week in first and second grades, 1.1 words per week in third grade, and 0.8 words per week in fourth grade. These growth rates are quite similar to the average growth rates for students proficient on the state NCLB reading test (see Figure 8.8 in Chapter 8, this volume). The average weekly growth for first graders is 1.2 words per week; for second grade it is 1.4 words per week; for third grade, 1.0 word per week; and for fourth grade, 0.9 word per week.

• *Within the RTI framework, what is the typical performance and growth rate of students at the implementation school on the universal screening measure (CBM) each fall and spring across the three RTI tiers of implementation?* Given the RTI practice of intervening with students who do not meet grade-level benchmarks, we studied the typical performance

TABLE 10.3. Descriptive Statistics Including Average Gain of Student Performance on CBM for Fall and Spring for All 3 Years

Grade	Year	Fall		Spring		Mean growth	n
		Mean	SD	Mean	SD		
1	1	16.94	20.17	65.15	35.70	48.21	62
	2	14.91	18.78	58.09	35.21	43.18	46
	3	21.41	20.43	63.74	33.24	42.33	61
2	1	41.98	28.88	85.37	38.43	43.39	43
	2	49.18	30.05	94.15	35.65	44.97	60
	3	50.63	32.24	96.60	33.91	45.97	48
3	1	65.33	30.77	105.45	34.03	40.12	51
	2	63.32	31.20	99.10	34.38	35.78	41
	3	71.36	32.28	110.31	35.49	38.95	59
4	1	81.70	27.65	113.59	33.49	31.89	46
	2	93.76	30.97	113.93	31.04	20.17	45
	3	86.94	27.96	114.00	30.06	27.06	36

of students at each tier of intervention during the project. The means, standard deviations, mean difference scores, and sample sizes for each grade are shown in Table 10.4. As one might expect, there is a clear pattern of decrease in scores with the increase in the intensity of the tier that holds true for all grade levels. At all four grade levels, the average student receiving only Tier 1 reading instruction is well above the district CBM benchmarks described in Chapter 8 in this volume. However, the average fall CBM scores for students who receive Tier 2 or Tier 3 instruction are below these benchmarks. For example, the first-grade students in Tier 2 or Tier 3 average only 9.0 and 4.1 words correct in the fall, whereas the average was 31.3 for Tier 1. At fourth grade students in Tier 2 and Tier 3 had means of 73.6 and 52.6 words correct in the fall, whereas Tier 1 students averaged 102.6. As one would expect based on the RTI pyramid, at all four grades the number of students in each tier dropped as the intensity of the intervention increased.

Table 10.5 shows mean scores on the NALT assessment in reading for students in third and fourth grades in the different tiers across the 3 years of the study. The mean scores on both assessments and in both grades indicate that the more intense the level of instruction (higher tier) is, the lower the mean score is. According to Northwest Evaluation Association (NWEA; 2008) norms, the average scaled scores of the third-grade students receiving only Tier 1 instruction in the fall is roughly equivalent to those of midyear third-grade students. The average third-grade students who also received

TABLE 10.4. Descriptive Statistics Including Average Gain of Student Performance on CBM for Fall and Spring Averaged across 3 Years for Tiers 1, 2, and 3

Grade	Tier	Fall		Spring		Mean growth	n
		Mean	SD	Mean	SD		
1	1	31.34	22.75	90.03	26.57	58.69	75
	2	9.04	5.28	52.83	15.42	43.79	58
	3	4.09	1.70	19.07	11.68	14.98	33
2	1	66.70	27.56	116.33	25.31	49.63	80
	2	34.33	13.04	83.01	18.92	48.68	40
	3	13.44	7.19	42.18	13.15	28.74	30
3	1	85.84	66.72	124.93	22.53	39.09	83
	2	50.37	12.28	92.62	12.50	42.25	40
	3	19.54	8.03	58.70	29.72	39.16	25
4	1	102.64	21.25	128.75	23.19	26.11	73
	2	73.58	25.72	101.83	22.85	28.25	33
	3	52.61	24.67	73.02	29.62	20.41	18

Tier 2 interventions perform at the equivalent of midyear of second grade, and the average third-grade students receiving Tier 3 interventions show beginning-of-first-grade performance. In fourth grade the Tier 1 NALT score is approximately at midyear of fourth grade; students receiving Tier 2 interventions score at the middle of second grade; and students receiving Tier 3 interventions score at the end of first grade. These results appear to validate the process of using CBM reading scores to assign students to instructional tiered groups.

TABLE 10.5. Descriptive Statistics for NALT Reading Averaged across 3 Years for Tiers 1, 2, and 3

Grade	Tier	Mean	SD	Minimum	Maximum	n
3	1	196.09	10.47	174.67	219.67	84
	2	188.89	6.04	178.00	197.67	43
	3	163.03	8.70	153.67	177.67	24
4	1	203.10	6.58	189.33	216.33	74
	2	187.37	11.21	165.67	201.67	37
	3	173.28	14.80	153.00	195.67	20

Note. Scale scores are reported.

Noted earlier, one of the key components of RTI is monitoring the progress of students in each tier of instruction to assess whether they are responding to instruction at successful rates. CBM (Deno, 1985) is a formative assessment system with a long history of research (Wayman et al., 2007) that has been effectively used to monitor student progress in reading. In addition to reviewing the level of performance, we examined student growth in reading within tiers at each grade level. Table 10.4 and Figure 10.1 illustrate the amount of growth for each tier within each grade. The greatest variability in growth scores is evident at grade 1, in which students receiving only Tier 1 instruction improved 58.7 words, whereas students receiving Tier 2 interventions gained an average of 43.8 words and students receiving Tier 3 interventions gained only 15.0 words. However, at grade 3 it is apparent that the slope of growth was approximately the same for all three tiers (39.1, 42.3, and 39.2). With the exception of grade 3, the growth rates of students receiving Tier 3 interventions were typically lower than those of students receiving Tier 1 instruction only and those of students receiving Tier 2 interventions. It is also important that growth of Tier 2 students was similar to that of Tier 1 students, and in some cases greater, an indicator that these interventions were effective in accelerating reading growth of students whose initial levels of performance were below benchmarks.

These data for grades 1–3 are consistent with the growth data reported by Deno, Fuchs, Marston, & Shinn (2001). When the fall-to-spring gains are converted to average weekly growth scores, the slopes for Tier 1 stu-

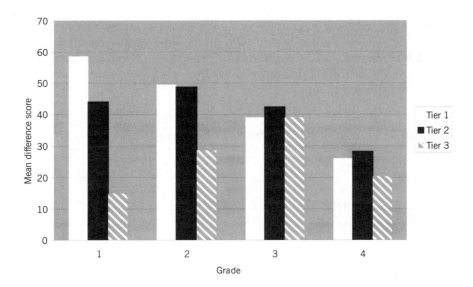

FIGURE 10.1. CBM average gain scores by tier and grade.

dents at grades 1–3 ranged from 1.1 to 1.7 words per week, and for Tier 2 they ranged from 1.2 to 1.4. Deno and colleagues report that the average slopes for general education students at grades 1–3 ranged from 1.2 to 1.8. Average weekly growth data for the Tier 3 students at the implementation school in grades 1–4 ranged from 0.4 to 1.1 words per week. These results were also similar to the data presented in Deno and colleagues, in which special education students had average slopes of 0.6 to 0.8 words per week for grades 1–4.

In addition to the differences in reading growth rates between tiers within each grade, one can observe distinct trends across grades for each tier. For example, Figure 10.1 illustrates a gradual decrease in reading growth rate in Tier 1 from grade to grade, with the greatest improvement in CBM reading scores within grade 1 (58.7 words read correctly in 1 minute) and the smallest in grade 4 (26.1 words read correctly in 1 minute). In contrast, in Tier 3 the trend of growth across grades is upward (15.0, 28.7, and 39.2 words read correctly in 1 minute, respectively), with the exception of grade four (20.4 words read correctly in 1 minute). Regardless of which tier students are placed in, the rate of growth from fall to spring is the least in grade 4. The trend of greater growth rates in earlier grades is also similar to the findings of Deno and colleagues (2001).

• *What is the impact of RTI on attendance and behavior?* Measures of behavior and attendance of the students during the 3-year project are reported in Table 10.6. The attendance indicator is the percentage of days present at school. The average attendance overall was 94.9%, with percentages for grades ranging from 94.6 to 95.4%. The proportion of students who average 95% or higher in attendance is used as a key indicator in the district's annual quality performance index (QPI). During the 3 years of RTI implementation, these proportions were 62% in Year 1, 65% in Year 2, and 66% in Year 3 at the school. The percentages for Years 2 and 3 were above the average for district elementary schools in 2008–2009, which was 62%.

TABLE 10.6. Descriptive Statistics of Attendance, Suspension, and Behavior Averaged across 3 Years

Grade	Mean attendance %	Suspensions per 100 students	BSC score Mean	SD
1	94.59	2.79	17.40	5.95
2	94.61	5.36	15.10	7.90
3	95.35	5.63	12.43	6.22
4	95.21	6.67	17.27	7.56
Total	94.91	4.98	15.73	7.89

In addition to attendance, two indicators of behavior are used: suspensions and ratings on the Office for Civil Rights (OCR) Behavior Screener Checklist (BSC; Muyskens, Marston, & Reschly, 2007). Suspensions are reported as the average number of suspensions that occur for every 100 students.

The BSC is a 12-item questionnaire on which teachers use a 5-point rubric to rate how well students perform on classroom management, externalizing, and socialization behaviors. A rating of "1" represents no problem, and a "5" represents significant behavior issues. Overall total scores range from 12 to 60. The average number of suspensions per 100 students was 5 and ranged from 2.8 to 6.7 per 100 students. Not surprisingly, suspensions were most prevalent at grade 4 and lowest at grade 1.

On the BSC, on which higher ratings are indicative of more behavior issues, the average ratings were similar across grade levels, with an overall mean of 15.7. The overall average for the district for the same 3-year period was 18.0. It is difficult to draw conclusions about the patterns of attendance and behavioral data given the small sample involved in the study. However, the attendance and behavior data suggest that the implementation school evidenced slightly better attendance and behavior when compared with district averages.

- *What is the impact of RTI on academic engaged time?* In Years 1 and 2 of the overall study, a small group of students was observed using the Ecobehavioral Assessment Systems Software (EBASS; Greenwood, Carta, Kamps, Terry, & Delquadri, 1994). The EBASS is a computerized time-sampling observation system used to examine student and teacher behaviors in the classroom. For students, three major categories of response were coded: task management, competing responses, and engaged academic time. In this case, the focus was on academic engagement of the students. A total group of 60 students was randomly selected from all implementation school students receiving Tier 1 and Tier 2 reading interventions at the end of Year 1, including 30 students at grade 1 and 30 more students at grade 2. These students were observed once with the EBASS in Tier 1 instruction and once again while in a Tier 2 intervention group. During the second year of the examination of academic engagement, the same students were observed when in grades 2 and 3. Due to student mobility, 28 students were observed during Tier 1 and 27 students were observed during Tier 2 instruction. The data reported in this chapter are the proportions of time students were observed being engaged in one of five academic response behaviors: writing, task participation, reading aloud, reading silently, and academic talk.

Descriptive results in Table 10.7 indicate that in Year 1, the total percentage of time students spent academically engaged was higher in Tier 2 instruction (46%) than in Tier 1 instruction (29%). In Year 2, engaged academic time increased for both Tier 1 and 2 reading instruction (52% in Tier 1 and 56% in Tier 2). Looking in more detail at the types of academic

TABLE 10.7. EBASS: Student Academic Responses Variables: Year 1 and 2

	Tier 1 mean %		Tier 2 mean %	
	Year 1	Year 2	Year 1	Year 2
Academic response: Writing	6.03	19.19	12.37	11.17
Academic response: Task participation	1.75	9.85	2.54	7.95
Academic response: Read aloud	2.39	5.61	12.37	12.88
Academic response: Read silently	15.39	13.36	14.44	19.57
Academic response: Academic talk	3.34	3.59	3.98	3.89
Academic response: Total	28.90	51.60	45.70	55.46
Academic response: Missing	0.00	0.50	0.15	0.71

responses, it is worth noting that for both tiers, the prevalent academic response was reading silently (15% in Tier 1 and 14% in Tier 2). In Year 2, however, writing took the largest proportion of academic response time in Tier 1 (19%), while reading silently remained the most prevalent academic response in Tier 2 (20%). Task participation across time increased for students in both tiers. In addition, reading aloud occupied more than twice the amount of instruction time in Tier 2 than in Tier 1, although time spent reading aloud increased in Tier 1 over time.

How are differences in Tier 1 and Tier 2 instruction explained? For the most part, Tier 1 instruction is delivered in a whole-class situation, which means higher teacher–student ratios and may include more task management activities at the expense of instructional activities. However, it should be emphasized that the academic response rate improved from 29% in Year 1 to 52% in Year 2, which is quite remarkable and approaches that found in Tier 2 during Year 2. Since Tier 2 instruction occurs in smaller groups and with increased intensity using specific interventions, one would expect a higher rate of engagement based on the setting. Improvement from Year 1 to Year 2 was found here as well. Increased academic engagement leads to application of the evidence-based interventions, which leads to continued growth and improvement.

O'Sullivan, Ysseldyke, Christenson, and Thurlow (1990) provide comparison data for 47 students with mild disabilities and 30 typically developing students in grades 2–4 using the same observational instrument, EBASS, to describe reading instruction in regular and special education settings. Students in the O'Sullivan and colleagues study were observed for the duration of 1 day, except for breaks, but the data reported in the article are based on observations during reading instruction only, which is comparable to our study. O'Sullivan and colleagues reported academic response time for typically developing students at 40%. Academic response time for students with mild disabilities in a regular classroom was 30%, whereas in special education it was 56%. Thus the 40% academic response rate reported by O'Sullivan and colleagues falls between the academic response rates in Year 1 and 2 for Tier 1 but below the academic response rate for both years in Tier 2 in the current study. In addition, the academic response time in the study by O'Sullivan and colleagues of 56% for students with mild disabilities in a special education setting is identical to the academic response rate observed in the current study in Tier 2, Year 2, which is what we might expect given the similar settings.

• *How much student movement exists between tiers of the RTI model during the academic year?* In the Minneapolis Public School District, the RTI pyramid is composed of Tier 1 instruction, as well as Tier 2 and Tier 3 interventions that are selected by data review team members for students based on screening and PM data. One assumption of the RTI model is that students would experience some tier movement as specific interventions are provided in an effort to meet learning needs with the intent of increasing performance and growth. For example, Vaughn (2003) reported that about 76% of the students receiving Tier 2 reading interventions exited because of improvement; however, the remaining 24% needed more intensive instruction. During Year 1, the data teams changed the tier of instruction for 86 students during the academic year. Based on PM data, 41 of the 273 students (15%) did not respond to instruction and required more intensive assistance (moving from Tier 1 to Tier 2, Tier 2 to Tier 3, or Tier 3 to special education). Forty-five students (16.5%) needed less intensive assistance and moved down a tier (either Tier 3 to Tier 2 or from Tier 2 to Tier 1). In all, 31.5% of the students during Year 1 changed their level of service in the RTI model. In Year 2 a decrease in movement of students was observed. Only 17 of 283 students needed more intensive help (6%), whereas 25 students moved down a tier. A total of 42 students, or 14.8%, changed tiers during Year 2. The movement of students between tiers in Year 3 was similar to Year 2. In Year 3, 43 of the 281 students (15.4%) changed at least one level. Thirty-one students (11.1%) did not respond to the intervention and were identified by the data review team as needing more assistance. Twelve students (4.3%) were judged to improve, needed less intensive help, and moved down a tier. Overall, during the 3-year implementation, the movement of students was approximately twice as high in Year 1 (31.5%) than in Year 2 (14.8%) and Year 3 (15.4%).

One explanation for the reduction in tier movement in the last 2 years of implementation may be a change in project facilitators from Year 1 to Years 2 and 3. An examination of adherence to data decision rules for making instructional changes over the course of RTI implementation might provide insight. It is also plausible that the reduction in movement during Years 2 and 3 is due to the successful implementation of the RTI model, as teachers and other school staff increase their knowledge and skills in this regard. For instance, teachers and staff were more skillful over time in matching instruction with the needs of the students. In addition, the overall RTI system became better understood and utilized, including the use of data in making instructional decisions. Given the limitations of observing student tier movement at only one site, generalizations cannot be made without replication at other schools implementing RTI.

• *What is the impact of RTI on special education eligibility?* One of the major assumptions of RTI is that utilization of research-based interventions and PM of student performance can potentially reduce the number of students going through special education evaluation by ensuring that students get what they need early on. The impact of model implementation on special education eligibility at the school was examined over a 3-year period for students with mild disabilities. A declining trend in the number of students found eligible was apparent. Specifically, during Year 1 of implementation, six students were identified as eligible for special education, which represents 2.1% of the school population. Three of the students were ELL students. In Year 2 of RTI implementation, the number of students identified as eligible for special education decreased to three students, which is 1% of student enrollment. In Year 3 of implementation, three students, or 1% of the K–4 student population, were eligible for special education. The district average for special education eligibility for students with mild disabilities was 1.4%, indicating that the school had reduced its eligibility numbers.

One theory supporting this reduction is that student needs are being met earlier through the tiered system of instruction and intervention, and therefore these students do not require special education evaluation. Tilly (2003) reported that use of an RTI approach to serving students in kindergarten through third grade reduced special education placement by 19, to 39%. O'Connor, Fulmer, and Harty (2003) compared a traditional school with an RTI school in which Tier 2 and 3 reading interventions were available and found that only 8% of the students were later placed in special education compared with 15% for the control group. In both of these studies, as with the implementation school, evidence-based reading interventions were implemented with students not meeting screening criteria, and the students ultimately did not respond to the tiered interventions. These data indicate that RTI implemented with fidelity may be an effective approach to prevention.

• *What is the impact of RTI on the NCLB accountability tests?* The Minnesota Comprehensive Assessment (MCA-II) is a criterion-referenced standardized state achievement test used to evaluate achievement and academic progress on state academic standards. The MCA-II is administered to all Minnesota students in grades 3–8 and grade 10 (Minnesota Department of Education, 2007). The test is administered in the spring of each year, when students answer questions to demonstrate their skills in vocabulary, comprehension, and literature. Standard scores are used to evaluate student performance.

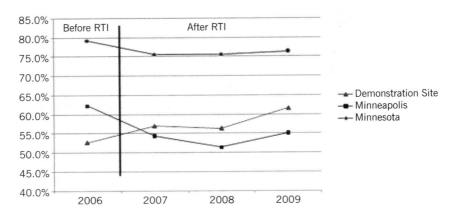

FIGURE 10.2. MCA scores of implementation school (grades 3 and 4).

The results of 4 years of MCA testing at grades 3–5 are presented in Figure 10.2. Year 2005–2006 represents the year before RTI implementation. In that year, 52.7% of students in grades 3 and 4 at the implementation school were proficient on the MCA reading test, whereas within the district 62.2% of grade 3 and 4 students were proficient. After Year 1 of implementation, the school's performance improved to 57% proficient, whereas the district declined to 54.4%. During Years 2 and 3, the proficiency rate continued to climb, to 56.4% and 61.6% proficiency, respectively, at the school, whereas the district had 51.4% and 55.1% proficiency rates, respectively. Figure 10.2 also shows that the school reduced the gap when compared with state proficiency rates. Before RTI implementation, the gap between the implementation school and the state was 26.5%. By Year 3, the gap had been reduced to 15.4%. It is important to note that the demographic data for the state of Minnesota are significantly different from those of the school. For example, in Minnesota 33% of students live in poverty, compared with 77% who live in poverty in the implementation school, a fact that makes the results even more significant.

IMPACT ON TEACHER ACTIONS AND PERCEPTIONS

Although impact on student learning is the most important outcome of RTI, it is interesting and informative to review the impact that RTI implementation and the accompanying professional development had on the teachers' actions and perceptions. With the launch and implementation of RTI in the schools, numerous articles and chapters have been written on the impact of RTI on student achievement. In contrast, empirical literature on the impact of RTI on teacher practices and attitudes is limited. In their article on building the capacity of teachers to implement RTI with struggling students, Richards, Pavri, Golez, Canges, and Murphy (2007) focus on the need for ongoing professional development for teachers at the school, as well as the district level, within the RTI context. Specifically, Richards and colleagues point out the need for continuous training in PM, in data use for making instructional decisions, and in implementing evidence-based intervention. In this section we examine teacher use of PM procedures, the fidelity of implementation of Tier 2 and 3 interventions, the fidelity of the student data meetings, and the attitude of the teachers toward the major components of the RTI model.

• *How has the implementation of RTI affected teacher use of PM procedures?* At the beginning of each year of the study, teachers completed a survey assessing their preparedness to use—as well as their actual implementation of—CBM data. The Teacher CBM Survey was developed specifically for this study by Wallace (2006). The total numbers of teachers who completed the survey in Years 1, 2, and 3, respectively, were 14, 10, and 11. Given that the primary objective of the project was to demonstrate the impact of a schoolwide RTI model with PM as one of the key components, one of the important purposes of this teacher survey was to identify professional development needs and to determine whether teachers were using CBM in their teaching.

Table 10.8 indicates how prepared teachers felt to use CBM scores. There was an increase from 93 to 100% in the number of teachers feeling well prepared to use CBM data from Year 1 to Years 2 and 3. In addition, data in Table 10.8 show how often teachers utilized CBM data across the 3 years of the study. There was an increase in the proportion of teachers using CBM data *often*, from 46% in Year 1 to 57% in Year 3. The proportion of teachers who *never* used CBM data decreased from 8% in Year 1 to 3% in Year 3. A key concern in the assessment literature is that data are collected and then never used in instructional decision making (Roehrig,

TABLE 10.8. Teacher CBM Survey: Utilizing CBM Scores

Year	Preparedness	%	Implementation	%
1	Not at all prepared	6.60	Never	8.10
	Prepared	93.40	Sometimes	45.90
			Often	45.90
2	Not at all prepared	0.00	Never	0.00
	Prepared	100.00	Sometimes	57.70
			Often	42.20
3	Not at all prepared	0.00	Never	3.20
	Prepared	100.00	Sometimes	38.10
			Often	57.20

Duggar, Moats, Glover, & Mincey, 2008; Yell, Deno, & Marston, 1992). It is important to see teachers both feel prepared to use and actually use the CBM data in their teaching.

• *What is the fidelity of the interventions implemented at Tiers 2 and 3 of the RTI model?* In Year 3 of the project, when the routine of tiered reading interventions was established at the school, the fidelity with which the interventions were implemented was evaluated. For those interventions that had their own evaluation checklist already in place, we used the data generated by that fidelity instrument. For the remaining interventions, project staff created new fidelity checklists based on the main components of particular interventions. Chapter 9 (this volume) provides an example of a checklist used for this purpose. The percentage of the elements observed during instruction was used as a fidelity indicator. The observers were school or project staff members familiar with a particular intervention. Instruction at Tiers 2 and 3 was observed. Four different instructional strategies were observed across 10 small groups: repeated reading, duet reading, direct instruction, and Soar to Success. Each intervention group was observed twice, once in the winter and again in the spring. To increase the number of observations per intervention for analysis, results are reported here aggregated across time. Duet reading with two observations had the highest fidelity ratio of 100%, followed by repeated reading with the greatest number of observations (10) and a fidelity ratio of 99%, then Soar to Success with two observations and a fidelity ratio of 94%, and finally direct instruction, observed six times with a fidelity ratio of 81%. In the case of repeated reading, which had the greatest number of observations (10), we were able to calculate fidelity for each grade level observed. The fidelity ratio at first grade was 100%, second grade 98%, third grade 100%.

This particular evaluation of intervention fidelity has been referred to in the limited literature on this subject as "interventionist adherence" and was conducted by direct observations (Hagermoser Sanetti, Chafouleas, Christ, & Gritter, 2009). Hagermoser Sanetti and colleagues (2009) call for a multimethod and multiformat approach to intervention fidelity within RTI in future research and practice. Even though in this project only one method was used to assess intervention fidelity, the obtained results can serve as an indicator of fidelity for individual interventions and, to a lesser extent, for individual grades, in this particular school. The number of fidelity observations per intervention did not allow us to analyze fidelity of intervention for Tiers 2 and 3 separately. It is the task of future projects and studies of intervention fidelity to assess this important component of RTI across multiple sites and in greater detail.

The most important goal is to attain high fidelity of intervention implementation by individual teachers. Their ability to accurately implement an intervention has an impact on student achievement and results. Fidelity must be assessed through observations, and, when it is lacking, immediate coaching must follow.

• *What is the fidelity of the RTI data review meetings?* Ensuring that instruction and interventions are implemented with fidelity is essential to the RTI model. However, it is equally important to confirm that data review meetings are occurring with integrity. Decisions about students are made during these important meetings, which must be done in an appropriate manner with the required data and information.

Within the RTI framework, one essential component is a systematic review of student progress to make instructional decisions. This is accomplished in a data review meeting. During a data review meeting, classroom teachers, typically within a grade level, along with other staff members, engage in a comprehensive discussion regarding instructional methods, academic progress, and instructional needs of the students.

As described in Chapter 9, this volume, an integrity checklist was developed to monitor the extent to which the identified critical components were addressed during the data review meeting (Marston & Lau, 2008). A staff person observed the meeting, using the checklist to rate each of the critical components on a 5-point Likert scale, from 5 (full implementation) to 1 (no implementation). The observer also provided qualitative data as part of the comment section for each item, as needed. In all, an 11-item checklist was used to evaluate the fidelity of the data review process (a copy is provided in Figure 9.6 in Chapter 9, this volume).

During Year 3 of implementation, 19 data review meetings were rated at the implementation school by one observer. The 11-item checklist could have a total score of 55. The average rating for the 19 meetings was 50.79 with a standard deviation of 2.94. These results suggest that staff at the implementation school had effectively implemented the critical components of the data review meeting. Specifically, staff at the school had done an excellent job ensuring that performance of all students at risk of low achievement were discussed, students' progress monitoring graphs were reviewed, additional data and information were used to determine the needs of the students, and full team participation was evident.

• *What are the teachers' attitudes toward the primary components of the RTI model?* A total of 21 staff members at the implementation school were asked to complete an "end of project" survey on the RTI implementation project developed by Marston and Lau (2009). The primary purpose of this survey was to evaluate the effectiveness of the RTI process and to seek specific feedback on the process for future research and usability improvement. The years of school experience for these staff members ranged from 2 to 35 years, with a mean of 18.3 years ($SD = 7.4$). Thirteen of the teachers were general education classroom teachers, one an ESL teacher, one a special education teacher, three reading interventionists, two associate educators, and one an educational assistant. Teachers responded that they had experience with CBM, with a mean of 10.7 years ($SD = 7.6$). Nine teachers participated in the RTI implementation project for 3 years, five teachers for 2 years, and six teachers for 1 year. Teachers were asked to review 13 items in four major categories related to implementation: screening, targeted interventions and small groups, PM, and data review meetings. For each item the staff member was asked to use a 5-point rubric ranging from Strongly Disagree (1) to Strongly Agree (5).

Overall, the implementation school staff was in agreement with the 13 items related to the implementation of RTI. The average ratings for the items were all between 4.0 (Agree) and 5.0 (Strongly Agree). The ratings ranged from 4.1 ("Weekly progress monitoring should be implemented for all students who fall into the 'Does not meet Standards' category on state and district assessment measures") to 4.7 ("Data review team meetings allow teachers to collaborate and discuss intervention strategies in order to develop a better plan for the instructional needs of their students"). Of the four clusters, the highest average rating was for the data review meetings cluster, with a mean of 4.6. The mean for targeted interventions was 4.6; for screening, 4.4; and for PM, 4.3. In sum, staff members at the implementation school had found that the CBM process and data had helped their instructional decision-making process and that the student database was a useful tool that provided them with academic and behavioral data for instructional decisions. Moreover, they reported that the RTI process was beneficial to all students, including those with average and high academic skills. In terms of the PM process, staff agreed that it yielded informative data regarding how students responded to the instruction. Finally, staff members also reported that data review meetings allowed them to engage in high levels of discussion, collaboration, and sharing on instruction-related activities. The survey items and their descriptive statistics are listed in Table 10.9.

On the same questionnaire, these staff members were asked to comment on the "challenges to implementing progress monitoring and RTI" and "benefits of progress monitoring and RTI." The benefits identified by the participants could be clustered into four areas: data, instruction, grouping, and collaboration. Listed here are some of the teachers' comments related to each cluster:

Data

- It helped very much to know where the students are in reading.
- I look forward to the progress monitoring meeting to see how my students are progressing in reading.
- Gives the data you need to support grouping.

Instruction

- Interventions are provided for students not making progress.
- Student needs are being met quickly.
- Helps eliminate students falling through the cracks.
- Research-based interventions very helpful.

TABLE 10.9. End-of-Year Survey Results

Survey items	M	SD
Screening	4.44	0.62
• Screening all students in reading in the fall, winter, and spring improves instructional programming for students.	4.52	0.68
• In the screening process, data gained from the CBM procedures and district benchmarks contributes to the instructional decision-making process.	4.38	0.50
• The OCR website is a useful tool that allows teachers to access student academic and behavioral data for instructional decisions.	4.43	0.68
Targeted interventions and small groups	4.59	0.56
• The progress monitoring–RTI project promotes differential instruction for students with various academic performance through core curriculum and small-group interventions, which benefits low-performing students.	4.62	0.59
• The progress monitoring–RTI project promotes differential instruction for students with various academic performance through core curriculum and small-group interventions, which benefits average-performing students.	4.62	0.50
• The progress monitoring–RTI project promotes differential instruction for students with various academic performance through core curriculum and small-group interventions, which benefits high-performing students.	4.52	0.60
Progress monitoring	4.29	0.75
• Progress monitoring with CBM provides informative feedback in a time-efficient manner on how the student is responding to our instruction.	4.33	0.73
• Weekly progress monitoring should be implemented for all students who fall into the "Does not meet standards" category on state and district assessment measures.	4.14	0.85
• Progress monitoring data provide teachers information regarding student placement in various intervention groups to supplement the core curriculum.	4.38	0.67
Data review meeting	4.60	0.65
• Data review team meetings allow teachers to collaborate and discuss intervention strategies in order to develop a better plan for the instructional needs of their students.	4.71	0.46
• Data review meetings should be held monthly.	4.40	0.83
• RTI and the data review meetings give teachers time to have meaningful discussions about research-based interventions.	4.62	0.59
• RTI and the data review meetings improve collaboration among school staff.	4.67	0.66
Grand total	4.49	0.66

Grouping
- Helps all of us with grouping.
- Groups based on data.
- Leveled groups for students at their reading level.

Collaboration
- It really helps each teacher become familiar with one another's students.
- Great for all of us to get together to talk and discuss where the students are.
- Nice way to monitor student progress and discuss as a group.

Challenges include time, scheduling of meetings, and need for further instructional diagnostic information. It was also noted that it would be helpful to have cross-grade-level team meetings at the beginning and end of the year to facilitate getting to know students and to help with transition at the end of year.

SUMMARY

The RTI model holds promise as a systemic approach schools can use to address the instructional needs of all students. As described earlier, the key components of the model include (1) universal screening of all students; (2) selecting research-based interventions to be used at Tiers 2 and 3; (3) monitoring the progress of these students; (4) reviewing the response to the interventions at monthly grade-level team meetings; (5) ensuring the fidelity of interventions and model implementation; and (6) providing professional development to improve model implementation. Support was found for the continued implementation of RTI, including these key components, as indicated in the following summary.

Using CBM benchmarks correlated with the state NCLB tests enabled school staff to efficiently assign students to instructional groups at Tiers 1, 2, and 3 based on universal screening of all students. CBM clearly differentiated students in those groups. Typically, the average number of words read correctly changed by 30–40 words for each tier. The achievement levels of students served in Tiers 1, 2, and 3 are considerably different. Placement in these tiers is also validated by the reading achievement test—the NALT—used by the district. Based on our reported results, the Tier 1 students at the implementation school are about ½ year ahead of grade-level peers, the Tier 2 students are about ½ to 1 year behind, and Tier 3 students are more than 1 year behind their peers. These data support the use of CBM for universal screening to set instructional groups.

We also asked about the type of gains made by students in the RTI implementation school. The average weekly gains at each grade level were similar to the average weekly gains associated with our CBM benchmarks for fall, winter, and spring. However, there was variability among the tiers, most noticeably for Tier 3 at three of four grade levels. Despite the use of intensive research-based interventions at this level, significant gains were not made. The lack of progress made by these students suggests that more intensive instruction (perhaps in the form of special education services) may be necessary. However, consideration should be given to the reliability and validity of the CBM measures used with students who require Tier 3 interventions to ensure the appropriateness of the measures.

The intent of the tiered RTI model is to provide more intensive small-group interventions in Tier 2, in addition to the core curriculum provided in Tier 1, to enhance student performance and achievement. Academic engaged time has been established as an important predictor of student achievement (Brophy & Good, 1986). Therefore, we used the Ecobehavioral Assessment Systems Software (EBASS) in the first 2 years of implementation to measure academic engaged time and found that students were more engaged during Tier 2 than they were during Tier 1 instruction. During Year 2 of implementation, student engagement was similar in both Tier 1 and Tier 2—both at higher levels than reported in other literature. Academic engagement, as measured by EBASS, improved from Year 1 to Year 2 for both Tier 1 and Tier 2 instruction. Not surprisingly, academic engaged time during the Tier 2 interventions was greater than the engaged time during Tier 1 instruction, which is typically whole-class instruction and has a higher staff-to-student ratio. The component of increasingly intensive tiers of intervention is supported by these findings.

Within the RTI model, when students need additional support or when they respond to the intervention and meet benchmarks, a change in intervention is suggested. The amount of movement between tiers that one might expect is yet unclear in the RTI literature. However, the implementation school's data indicate that student movement between and within tiers was at twice the level during Year 1 than during Years 2 and 3. We speculate that when an RTI system is first implemented utilizing new interventions and using data teams to make decisions about tiers and interventions based on PM data, movement is likely and confounded, perhaps, with the new system and development of staff. However, as the teams learned the interventions, the assessments, and the process for making decisions, a reduction in movement occurred. This could imply that the instructional decisions made in Years 2 and 3 were based more on student data than on other factors that staff face during a significant systemic change.

Measuring fidelity of intervention within an RTI model is crucial to being able to distinguish between instruction that is ineffective for a student and instruction that is not implemented according to protocol. The fidelity of treatment analysis from Year 3 suggests, with the exception of one group, that interventions were implemented with fidelity. Where fidelity fell below 80%, additional professional development and follow-up coaching were provided. Based on the limited results generated in evaluating the RTI model in the Minneapolis Public School District, more research needs to be conducted in examining the fidelity of interventions related to number of observations needed, who conducts observations, and the criteria for establishing fidelity.

Another vital component of an RTI model is a data review meeting. In order for such a meeting to be effective, a way to evaluate the fidelity of implementation has to be in place so that such a meeting does not stray from the agenda of reviewing student progress. The examination of the integrity of the monthly data meetings showed a high degree of implementation of the RTI components at the implementation school. The results of 19 data review meeting observations indicate 92% fidelity. This level of fidelity ensures that the meetings are fulfilling their intended purpose and confirms the importance of this RTI component.

As a conclusion to the RTI model demonstration project, staff asked teachers to evaluate the importance of RTI components. Teacher attitudes toward the concepts of RTI were supportive, positive, and aligned well with evaluation results. With respect to screening, implementation school staff agreed that CBM procedures and benchmarks improved instructional planning. On the topic of targeted interventions for small groups, the staff endorsed the RTI model as effective in differentiating instruction for low-, middle-, and high-performing students. Staff viewed the PM aspect of RTI as essential for informing instruction and aiding the placement of students in appropriate groups. Finally, the staff strongly agreed that data review meetings increased collaboration and discussion of instructional issues and should be held monthly.

In closing, looking at the data collected by this project has reiterated all the complexities of bringing research to practice in the schools. Certainly the strong leadership at the school increased the probability of successful translation of research to implementation. The attitudes and perceptions of the building leaders and teaching staff are positive and supportive of the RTI model. In addition, the implementation school is viewed in the district as a leader in RTI implementation. The quantitative indicators provided in this chapter also suggest positive results, but these must be tempered by some limitations of our evaluation methodology. Although the low numbers of students reflected in these results make generalization difficult, the data generated by this project and the new measures it employed raises several interesting research questions, provides insight into the relationship between personnel and practice, and points toward future models for RTI implementation.

As work continues, some questions remain that can guide future research, whether through a model demonstration and evaluation approach or through specific research. Either way, the following are important questions to be addressed in the field.

1. How much and what type of professional development is needed to equip a teacher to implement an RTI model effectively?
2. What does is cost to implement RTI in terms of staff, coaching, professional development, and so forth?
3. Will the positive effects on student achievement last over time?
4. How much—what dosage of—intervention is needed to have true impact on student learning?
5. Are the benchmarks for success the same for ELL students as they are for the general population of students? If not, what impact does that have on the RTI model?
6. Are new CBM measures needed to monitor the progress of students needing Tier 3 interventions?
7. How should fidelity be measured? Are different approaches important for different reasons?
8. What impact does the effective implementation of an RTI model have on the rates of special education eligibility? Are the effects long lasting?

Uncovering the answers to these and other questions will ensure that RTI models become technically stronger and will provide needed information to assist schools in preparing for implementation. Although our efforts provided positive results regarding the impact RTI can have on student outcomes, there is more to do, and we look forward to those next steps.

REFERENCES

Brophy, J., & Good, T. L. (1986). Teacher behavior and student achievement. In M. Wittrock (Ed.), *Handbook of research on teaching* (pp. 328–275). New York: Macmillan.

Deno, S. L. (1985). Curriculum-based measurement: The emerging alternative. *Exceptional Children, 52*, 219–232.

Deno, S. L., Fuchs, L. S., Marston, D., & Shinn, J. (2001). Using curriculum-based measurement to establish growth standards for students with disabilities. *School Psychology Review, 30*(4), 507–524.

Greenwood, C. R., Carta, J. J., Kamps, D., Terry, B., & Delquadri, J. (1994). Development and validation of standard classroom observation systems for school practitioners: Ecobehavioral Assessment Systems Software (EBASS). *Exceptional Children, 61*(2), 197–210.

Hagermoser Sanetti, L. M., Chafouleas, S. M., Christ, T. J., & Gritter, K. L. (2009). Extending use of direct behavior rating beyond student assessment. *Assessment for Effective Intervention, 34*(4), 25–28.

Marston, D., & Lau, M. (2008). *Student data meeting fidelity checklist*. Minneapolis, MN: Minneapolis Public Schools.

Marston, D., & Lau, M. (2009). *End of Project Survey*. Minneapolis, MN: Minneapolis Public Schools.

Minnesota Department of Education. (2007). *The Minnesota Assessment Technical Manual*. Roseville, MN: Author.

Muyskens, P., & Marston, D. (2008). *Curriculum-based measurement linking between Minneapolis Public Schools passages and national norms*. Unpublished manuscript, Minneapolis Public Schools, Minneapolis, MN.

Muyskens, P., Marston, D., & Reschly, A. L. (2007). The use of response to intervention practices for behavior: An examination of the validity of a screening instrument. *California School Psychologist, 12*, 31–45.

Northwest Evaluation Association. (2003). *Technical Manual for the NWEA Measures of Academic Progress and Achievement Level Tests*. Portland, OR: Author.

Northwest Evaluation Association. (2008). Normative data. Retrieved from *www.nwea.org/sites/www.nwea.org/files/support_articles/Normative%20 Data%20Sheet_v2.pdf*.

O'Connor, R. E., Fulmer, D., & Harty, K. (2003, December). *Tiers of intervention in kindergarten through third grade*. Paper presented at the National Research Center on Learning Disabilities Responsiveness-to-Intervention Symposium, Kansas City, MO.

O'Sullivan, P. J., Ysseldyke, J. E., Christenson, S. L., & Thurlow, M. L. (1990). Mildly handicapped elementary students' opportunity to learn during reading instruction in mainstream and special education settings. *Reading Research Quarterly, 25*(2), 131–146.

Richards, C., Pavri, S., Golez, F., Canges, R., & Murphy, J. (2007). Response to intervention: Building the capacity of teachers to serve students with learning difficulties. *Issues in Teacher Education, 16*(2), 55–63.

Roehrig, A. D., Duggar, S. W., Moats, L., Glover, M., & Mincey, B. (2008). When teachers work to use progress monitoring data to inform literacy instruction. *Remedial and Special Education, 29*(6), 364–382.

Tilly, W. D. (2003, December). *How many tiers are needed for successful prevention and early intervention?: Heartland Area Education Agency's evolution from four to three tiers*. Paper presented at the National Research Center on Learning Disabilities Responsiveness-to-Intervention Symposium, Kansas City, MO.

Vaughn, S. (2003, December). *How many tiers are needed for response to intervention to achieve acceptable prevention outcomes?* Paper presented at the National Research Center on Learning Disabilities Responsiveness-to-Intervention Symposium, Kansas City, MO.

Wallace, T. (2006). *Teacher CBM Survey*. Minneapolis, MN: University of Minnesota.

Wayman, M., Wallace, T., Wiley, H. I., Tichá, R., & Espin, C. A. (2007). Literature synthesis on curriculum-based measurement in reading. *Journal of Special Education, 41*, 85–120.

Yell, M. L., Deno, S. L., & Marston, D. B. (1992). Barriers to implementing curriculum-based measurement. *Assessment for Effective Intervention, 18*(1), 99–112.

PART IV

The University of Oregon–Eugene School District 4J RTI Model

Introduction to Part IV

In the University of Oregon–Eugene School District 4J collaboration to develop a system for both response to intervention (RTI) and progress monitoring (PM), we focus on three big ideas. The first is the process of change, in which we address both the theoretical underpinnings and the local district applications. The second highlights the need for technically adequate measures so that change over time can be captured accurately. The third big idea addresses the construct of RTI and both delineates essential features and describes a pilot study.

In Chapter 11, we were propelled by a need to systemically address achievement, particularly the gap faced by students of color and those with disabilities, as well as English language learners (ELL). We took both a bottom-up and a top-down approach. A district-leveraged coaching system was implemented in which the early implementers (grant-funded school teams) were supported in adopting key components of RTI and PM. We also describe the unique features of the district, which in many ways can be described as a district of schools rather than a school district, a prominent feature of the district that needed to be addressed from the outset, with both a strong district central office and a collaborative relationship with the University of Oregon. We describe the district, provide a chronology of the change process, and highlight the procedures that we implemented. By the close of this project, the district had fully adopted a comprehensive system for integrating general and special education through an *instructional intervention/progress monitoring* (IIPM) *model* that has allowed the project to become a program with a firm hold across the entire district.

In Chapter 12, on measurement development, we extend the original guiding principles of curriculum-based measurement (CBM) to include more recent analytic models typically used with large-scale assessments. We introduce the Rasch model that was used to place items and students on the same scale. This model is useful because it allows alternate forms to be developed with more precision and accuracy. We also describe how we attempted to ensure that the measures developed were grade appropriate. With alternate forms strategically developed to provide comparable data over time (both across and within grades), we then focus on the use of the outcomes to make decisions, emphasizing both screening/benchmarking and PM. For the former decisions, made from screens, the issue is resource allocation and prevention of false negatives (failing to identify students at risk); for the latter decisions, made from PM measures, the focus is on instructional evaluation. We end by noting the need for further validation research to take place in an iterative fashion.

In Chapter 13, on implementation of RTI, we unpack the construct into six components that reflect our RTI/IIPM model. We describe a rubric with operational definitions and illustrations of each component: (1) Tier 1 instruction (comprehensive reading/math program), (2) universal screening, (3) Tier 2 and Tier 3 differentiated and targeted instructional interventions, (4) PM, (5) evidence-based decision making, and (6) organizational supports. To document these six components, we describe a pilot study in which we reviewed archival records and school IIPM documents and directly observed classrooms, interviewed teachers, and collected physical artifacts from the classroom (e.g., lesson plans and data displays). We conclude with the recommendation for future research to be done so that the field can either adopt from others or create their own. Most important, we recommend that fidelity of implementation be explicitly addressed rather than assumed.

CHAPTER 11

The Context and Process of Implementation

Yvonne Curtis
Larry Sullivan
Julie Alonzo
Gerald Tindal

In this chapter, we describe the process for adopting a reform initiative, our instructional intervention/progress monitoring (IIPM) model. Our description includes the context of the schools (students and teachers); the history of previous district initiatives, including efforts to integrate general and special education services; and concurrent work on professional development. Our model is the result of a collaboration between researchers at the University of Oregon and practitioners at Eugene School District 4J (hereafter referred to as 4J, as the district is known locally).

FACILITATING EFFECTIVE CHANGE
WITHIN A SCHOOL DISTRICT

We incorporated four basic insights from the work of Fullan (1992) as we developed and adopted our response-to-intervention (RTI) model: (1) active initiation and participation; (2) pressure and support; (3) focused and well-documented changes in behavior and beliefs; and (4) establishment of ownership of the model among district educators.

Active Initiation and Participation

Fullan's (1992) study of school reform suggests that an effective strategy is to start with a small, clearly focused leadership team to provide the impetus needed to begin the change process. In our model, we began with four key leaders: two from the district (one representing general education, the other special education) and two from the university. Working closely together, this group of four mapped out a multiyear strategy for building capacity, first within schools with an expressed interest in taking part in the project and then within the district as a whole. In our work, we were committed to "active initiation, starting small and thinking big, bias for action, and learning by doing" (Fullan, 1992, p. 25).

To that end, we worked directly with teachers, using data from their own classes to illustrate the need to do things differently and to build their capacity for and ownership of change. We started with volunteers—teachers ready and eager to make changes in their practices. Shoemaker (1993), in her study of the implementation of an educational innovation in 4J, found many teachers unwilling to embrace the change in practice because they simply did not "get it." District teachers she studied explained that they had difficulty envisioning how the educational innovation would work, logistically, in their own classrooms. Using Shoemaker's findings to guide our work, we structured our project to avoid some of the pitfalls that had limited teachers' successful adoption of earlier innovations.

Through the use of coaches, by beginning with volunteers, and by purposefully limiting involvement to the classrooms of just a few teachers at each school in the first 2 years, we helped teachers in our participating district "get it"—we made the practice concrete. Our volunteers, who were eager to help create a structure for successful RTI implementation in the district, were able to provide others with clarity about the innovation, as well as the results of its effectiveness, when we were ready to expand beyond their classrooms to the rest of the teachers at their school sites (in Year 3) and at additional schools (in Years 3 and 4).

Pressure and Support

"Pressure without support," according to Fullan, "leads to resistance and alienation; support without pressure leads to drift or waste of resources" (1992, p. 25). Pressure and support occur in contexts in which there is interaction among implementers, their peers, and other technical and administrative leaders. We built this concept into our model in two ways: through school-based partners responsible for facilitating monthly meetings at their school sites and through "combined lead team" meetings scheduled every month, during which the lead team members from each school shared their insights and collaborated to problem-solve with each other, as well as with the university researchers and district administrators.

Changes in Behaviors and Beliefs

Dealing effectively with an innovation means changing behaviors (new skills, activities, practices) and changing beliefs (new understandings, commitments); therefore, understanding the implementation means understanding how the process of change unfolds in relation to these two factors. In many cases, changes in behavior precede rather than follow changes in belief, and it is not uncommon for behaviors to get worse before they get better as people grapple with use of the innovation (Fullan, 1985). Because implementation involves new behaviors and beliefs, a critical factor for success is staff development in support of the specific innovations (Huberman & Miles, 1984). In examining the change process from a teacher development perspective, Fullan (1985) suggests that what is ultimately important is the capacity of teachers to manage change by finding meaning among an array of innovative possibilities and by becoming adept at knowing when to seek change aggressively.

Ownership

One of the most challenging components of lasting school improvement is providing ways in which school personnel can develop a feeling of ownership of the change. Support, understanding, and skill use do not constitute ownership of an innovation. Ownership is a process involving increasing clarity, skill, and commitment. In most successful change projects, ownership develops gradually. It is weakest at the beginning, greater in the middle, and strongest at the end. "In effect, successful improvement can be best thought of as a process of *mobilization* and *positive contagion*" (Fullan, 1992, p. 26). To help mobilize participating teachers as change agents within their schools and the district as a whole, we actively sought opportunities for them to develop their effectiveness as teachers and then to share the positive results of their new approach to instruction with others. Development and use of a Web-based progress monitoring (PM) assessment system (*easyCBM*) with the capacity to track students' instructional histories and evaluate the effectiveness of different curricular and instructional approaches provided teachers with a critical mechanism by which to share with others their evidence-based learning.

A SYSTEMIC FOCUS ON IMPROVING ACHIEVEMENT

If schools are to transform themselves, efforts must be directed at the classroom level to enhance the impact that a teacher can have on student achievement. Studies conducted by William Sanders and his colleagues (Sanders & Horn, 1994; Wright, Horn, & Sanders, 1997) are most revealing in determining the achievement of students who spend a year with a highly effective teacher as opposed to a less effective teacher. They report that, on average, "the most effective teachers produced gains of 53 percentage points in student achievement over one year, whereas the least effective teachers produced achievement gains of about 14 percentage points over one year" (in Marzano, 2003, p. 72). In our model, school-based teams made up of teachers from different grade levels, a school psychologist, a special education teacher, and the principal engaged in regular and systematic discussions of student learning and strategized about how best to meet students' educational needs. This focus on student achievement and collegial coaching was an integral part of our model's success.

As a component of continuous school improvement efforts, Showers and Joyce (1996) studied the effects of coaching. They reported that "teachers who had a coaching relationship—that is, who shared aspects of teaching, planned together, and pooled their experiences—practice[d] new skills and strategies more frequently and applied them more appropriately than did their counterparts who worked alone to expand their repertoires" (Showers & Joyce, 1996, p. 14). The Annenberg Institute for School Reform works with school districts to help them consider or support coaching in the belief that coaching can lead to systemic change, which in turn creates lasting improvements in the classroom. In *Instructional coaching: Professional development strategies that improve instruction* (Annenberg Institute for School Reform, 2004), staff authors, citing the work of Poglinco and colleagues at the University of Pennsylvania (2003), noted that evidence of increased learning as a direct result of coaching is not yet well established. However, a growing body of research suggests that coaching is a promising element of effective professional development when it incorporates collaborative, reflective practice, embedded professional learning to promote positive cultural change, use of data analysis to inform practice, reciprocal accountability, and collective, interconnected leadership across a school system.

CONTEXT OF THE 4J DISTRICT

Educational innovation—both the process by which it is implemented and the effectiveness of that process—is affected by the context in which the innovation is undertaken. To understand the RTI model developed by the University of Oregon model demonstration center, it is important to describe the context in which we worked. In the creation of the RTI model in 4J, this context includes the types of students who attend the district schools, the types of schools in operation within the district, and the history of previous and related initiatives.

Demographics

Eugene School District 4J, with approximately 18,000 students, is the fifth largest school district in Oregon. The district's open enrollment and school choice policies allow students to attend any school in which space is available. At the elementary school level, 18 neighborhood schools and 9 alternative schools operate within the district. Each neighborhood school reflects the uniqueness of its students, staff, and community. In contrast, each alternative school reflects a particular educational vision or theme held by parents and staff, emphasizing instructional programs, such as language and culture immersion, fine and performing arts, nongraded classrooms, and family involvement. At the secondary school level (grades 6–12), the district hosts eight neighborhood middle schools, one alternative technology-focused middle school, three language-immersion middle schools, four regional high schools, three high school completion programs, and four international high school programs (where students focus on foreign languages, history, and culture). In addition, the district has three public charter schools.

The district includes approximately 22% minority students, with a racial and ethnic mix of 3% African American; 8% Hispanic; 6% Asian/Pacific Islander, American Indian, or Native Alaskan; 5% multiethnic; 73% white; and 5% unspecified. The operating cost per student is $6,543, with an average daily attendance of 94.4%. In 2003–2004, the dropout rate was 2.5%, creating a 4-year dropout rate of 3.9%. In the early years of the 21st century, more than half of the district's graduating seniors went on to postsecondary education.

Like many districts in the past few years, the Eugene community has suffered the effects of a downturn in the national economy; in particular, this has come about because of the prolonged decline of the wood products and computer technology industries in the Pacific Northwest. Although in many of the district's schools the socioeconomic status (SES) of most students is considered middle- or upper-middle class, in November 2005, more than 5,500 students (31%) were living below the federal poverty index, as measured by participation in the free/reduced-price meal program. Nine of the district's elementary schools and three of the alternative schools were designated as Title I schools, which means they were eligible for federal aid for schools that serve low-SES families. Of these, five schools were designated as Title I schoolwide projects, meaning that at least 50% of their students come from families living in poverty. In six of the alternative schools, the student population was predominantly white and from a higher SES background than students in other schools in the district.

In 2006, the year the joint project between Eugene School District 4J and the University of Oregon received funding for this initiative,[1] there continued to be distinct differences in student demographics at the differ-

---

[1] A federal grant awarded to the University of Oregon from the Office of Special Education Programs, U.S. Department of Education: *Model Demonstration Centers on Progress Monitoring* (PR/Award No. H326M050003, funded from January 2006 to December 2008).

ent schools, in large part due to school choice and a lottery system used to enroll students in alternative schools. Inequalities related to schools' capacity to address *all* students' educational needs affected student performance and contributed to a significant achievement gap between students from different racial and ethnic groups, students with and without identified disabilities, students with different socioeconomic status, and students with different levels of English language proficiency.

Innovation and Creativity with Previous Initiatives

In the late 1980s, Eugene School District 4J had become known throughout Oregon as a leader in school reform and student achievement. District schools had moved significantly toward integrated curriculum, and site-based decision making was embraced throughout the district. By the 1990s, each school had become accustomed to making its own decisions about staffing, school budget allocations, curriculum and instruction, and course offerings. The district's schools did not look to the central office for guidance. Because the choice in curriculum and instruction was made at the building and classroom levels, instruction varied across the district, although student achievement overall was high. There was neither a shared understanding nor any expectation that teachers would use a common curriculum or teach to state standards. In short, rather than acting as a unified school district, Eugene School District 4J operated as a district of schools.

For many years, district staff had negative views about required standardized testing in academic areas. Administrators and teachers believed that testing was an infringement on professional educators' area of expertise and creativity; they regarded any time devoted to standardized testing as taking away from valuable instructional time. From 1999 to 2000, a district reading kit was developed in conjunction with Behavioral Research and Teaching (BRT) at the University of Oregon. These standards-based reading assessments initially were designed to identify K–3 students at risk of reading failure and were later expanded to include other grades. By the 2005–2006 school year, the assessments included at least three measures from kindergarten through ninth grade administered in fall and spring, and they covered math as well as reading. Implementation and districtwide use of the reading kit assessments helped reduce many staff members' generalized resistance to standardized testing and paved the way for most staff members to accept the state's mandate to assess all students at specific grade levels in selected academic subjects. These district tests, in both reading and math, were used to predict student performance on end-of-year state tests, helping educators anticipate whether students would exceed, meet, or fail to meet state standards so they could provide additional assistance to those students who were unlikely to pass the state test.

In addition to these tests, the district's Title I coordinator recommended implementing the Dynamic Indicators of Basic Early Literacy Skills (DIBELS) benchmark and progress monitoring assessments for Title I schools in the 2004–2005 school year. By the fall of 2006, all 12 Title I schools had begun administering DIBELS. Nevertheless, lingering concern existed among building staff and administrators that adding DIBELS assessments to district and state assessments was overwhelming.

General Education and Special Education

As in many schools (Avramidis & Norwich, 2002; Scruggs & Mastropieri, 1996) in the 1980s and 1990s, teachers across the district believed that students with disabilities were best served and should receive services in resource rooms or other special education programs. Many teachers, of both general and special education, did not take ownership of *all* students. At that time, special education services were a combination of traditional "pullout" classrooms and special programs. Special education teachers often had neither access to nor responsibility for teaching the general education core curriculum or integrating special education services and general education instruction. However, building-based and early initiatives to reform special education services in the Eugene School District from 2003 to 2007 helped establish a foundation for change in the structure and services for all students, including initial efforts to integrate students with disabilities into the general education environment. The district also supported the development of innovative programs for students on the autism spectrum and targeted additional funding to reduce special education student–teacher ratios in the district.

Professional development was severely restricted due to the combination of a loss of state revenue (years 1999–2004) and a 1990 Oregon initiative (i.e., Ballot Measure 5) that placed limits on voters' ability to pass a local levy to support schools. The initiative had an immediate and drastic effect on the district's capacity to provide professional development and content support for teachers. District leadership reduced central office staff and academic content support specialists to ensure that cuts were kept as far from affecting classrooms as possible. The district attempted to continue professional development and to partner with local universities. However, it was unable to provide important professional development and academic content supports for classroom teachers and school staff.

THE DISTRICT'S STORY OF CHANGE: 2005–2010

A number of district initiatives and activities came together to create a readiness for dramatic and systematic change in Eugene School District 4J.

This confluence of events had a profound effect on the development and successful adoption of the RTI model described in this chapter.

1. The Eugene School District 4J board of directors established a goal to increase achievement of *all* students and close the achievement gap. The board also committed to providing equal opportunities for *all* students to succeed and to gain the supports needed to find success in school.

2. Throughout a 5-year period (2004–2009), the district collaborated closely with the Office for Civil Rights (OCR) as it developed and submitted changes to special education policies, procedures, and practices related to the prereferral, referral, evaluation, placement, and provision of services to special education and English language learner (ELL) students. In 2009, the district entered into a settlement agreement with the OCR (Case No. 100354). In response to this OCR settlement and as a component of the district's RTI model, a Special Education Comprehensive Evaluation for Culturally and Linguistically Diverse (CLD) Students was developed.

3. Three administrators were hired from outside the district: a director of student achievement, a director of educational support services, and a curriculum coordinator for high school services.

4. The district and the University of Oregon were awarded a U.S. Department of Education Office of Special Education Programs (OSEP) Model Demonstration Grant. The director of student achievement, Yvonne Curtis, and the director of educational services, Larry Sullivan, joined Gerald Tindal and Julie Alonzo from the University of Oregon as the lead team for the grant. The online PM system *easyCBM* was developed by the University of Oregon as a component of the model demonstration grant.

5. An instructional leadership team was formed to provide leadership and guidance to school administrators and staff in raising achievement for all students in District 4J.

6. The Access to General Education committee was formed to provide direction to general and special education teachers, classified staff, and administrators as they made decisions regarding options for integrating special education students.

7. District guidelines for a new language arts adoption were developed for grades K–12. A district language arts committee recommended—and subsequently the district adopted—two comprehensive reading program (CRP) curricula at the elementary level for the 2007–2008 school year. In a related decision, elementary literacy coaches were hired to support the implementation of the CRP curricula.

8. A tiered (RTI) IIPM model was developed and implemented to support the new reading and language arts curricula as a component of the

OSEP model demonstration grant and OCR settlement. The IIPM prerefer-ral and referral process replaced the traditional special education-focused student support team/intervention assistance team (SST/IAT) procedures.

9. The district adopted a special education comprehensive evalu-ation model for specific learning disabilities that incorporated a pattern of strengths and weaknesses assessment methodology to provide a frame-work for organizing, reviewing, and making decisions based on assessment data.

Each of these initiatives or activities was significant on its own, but together they propelled the district toward a dramatic shift in teaching, assessment, and student learning. For ease in understanding the story of change in the Eugene School District, the following narrative is divided into school years, beginning with 2005–2006.

2005–2006 School Year

From the 1980s through 2004, senior administrative leadership in the dis-trict was "homegrown," with director-level administrators working their way up through the ranks. The district culture was stable; there was a sense of security among the 4J staff. There also was a sense of pride in the way the district conducted its business (i.e., there were the ways other districts worked, and then there was "the 4J way").

In 2005, three administrators were hired from outside the district: the director of student achievement, the director of educational support ser-vices, and a curriculum coordinator/director of high school services. These administrators were given the goal of improving the academic performance of *all* students by closing the achievement gap and restructuring special education services. It was clear to the administrative leadership that this goal could only be accomplished by integrating general education and spe-cial education.

The superintendent reorganized the central office, changing admin-istrators' responsibilities and the instructional leadership in the district and creating an instructional leadership team (ILT). The superintendent directed the ILT "to provide leadership and guidance to school adminis-trators and staff in order to improve achievement for all students in Dis-trict 4J." Membership of the ILT included instructional directors, resource principals (i.e., principal representatives from elementary, middle, and high school), educators who were serving on the superintendent's staff, coordi-nators of federal title programs and secondary curricula, and the director of educational support services.[2]

---

[2]In 2009–2010, the assistant superintendent added three important members to the ILT: coordinators of research and evaluation, instructional technology, and equity.

It would be difficult to overemphasize the importance of including the director of educational support services as a member of the ILT. Prior to the 2005–2006 school year, the director of instruction and the director of educational support services had functioned independently. Special education staff and general education staff were on parallel tracks. There were no *shared understandings* about instruction and learning or responsibilities for student achievement between the two groups.

To reach the goal of improving education for all students and eliminating the achievement gap, the ILT identified six objectives to guide their work together: (1) create a culture of belief that all students can learn and meet high standards, (2) prioritize standards at every grade level, (3) identify benchmarks for measuring student success, (4) ensure that all students receive and engage in a rigorous curriculum, (5) hold schools accountable for providing high-quality instruction and improving student achievement, and (6) give support and assistance for high-quality instruction. Among the nine priority projects identified by the ILT to attain their objectives, five are particularly significant for framing developments in the district through 2010 aimed at closing the achievement gap.

1. The district's attention to literacy was expanded and refined by emphasizing district reading assessments, prioritizing standards for language arts, beginning to work on adopting language arts materials and programs, integrating school literacy goals with school improvement plans, and training teachers on effective reading and writing instruction.

2. A focus on mathematics was initiated districtwide that included completing and implementing District 4J math assessments, prioritizing standards for math, employing a math task force to determine best practices and programs to improve student achievement in math, and training teachers on effective math instruction, especially for teaching algebraic relationships and concepts.

3. Special and general education services were integrated in the process, improving the effectiveness of SSTs through training on interventions and best practices. Teams of principals and teachers representing both special and general education were involved in staff development on best practices, policy requirements, and assessments.

4. High school reform was addressed by developing a task force that would outline work to be done in the high schools over the next 5 years so that all students would graduate from high school ready for college. In addition, graduation requirements were reviewed to establish standards for measuring student performance in grades 9–12.

5. During the 2005–2006 school year, educational support services (ESS) reviewed special education services, revised the policies and proce-

dures manual, and began working intensively with the OCR to improve services provided for culturally and linguistically diverse (CLD) students, including the prereferral and referral processes, special education evaluation, eligibility, and IEP development procedures, in compliance with the OCR.

In January of 2006, the Eugene School District and the University of Oregon were awarded a model demonstration grant from OSEP. The model demonstration grant approach was fundamentally different from previous OSEP grants in requiring grantees to answer the "how" question and not just describe or deliver the "what" of expected outcomes. The grant gave the district and university the opportunity to plan, develop, and implement a tiered intervention model using curriculum-based assessment for PM of student achievement. Furthermore, by making process as well as outcomes transparent, the district was able to address important development and implementation issues at different stages of the process. An essential component of the process for developing and implementing an instructional intervention and PM model was the work completed by four teams, each with a different focus. The teams were:

District/University Lead Team

Two faculty members from the University of Oregon, Gerald Tindal and Julie Alonzo, and two district directors, Yvonne Curtis, Director for Student Achievement, and Larry Sullivan, Director of Educational Support Services, led the model demonstration grant. The district took the lead in the work with grant schools and district teams, and the university took the lead in developing the benchmark and PM assessments (*easyCBM*) and providing ongoing professional development and program support for grant school teams.

Special Education Team

Representative members of the district's school psychologists and special education consultants (teachers), a positive behavior support consultant, and the ESS director reviewed the research and best practices in special education prereferral/referral procedures, comprehensive evaluations, and RTI models. The team initially formulated a prereferral/referral process that included a review of instruction in the core curriculum, tiered instructional interventions, PM data, and the special education comprehensive evaluation, as outlined with the general evaluation requirements of the Individual with Disabilities Education Improvement Act (IDEIA; 2004). Their initial work in this area, in conjunction with the grant school teams' efforts to design and implement a tier-intervention and PM system at each participating school, led to the development of the district's RTI methodology. The district methodology for RTI was operationalized into an IIPM model. There were three reasons that the district decided to refer to the model as IIPM rather than RTI: (1) the focus was on general education instruction, tiered differentiated and targeted instruction, and PM; (2) there was confusion and controversy in the state regarding RTI models and special education evaluation and eligibility procedures; and (3) the district wanted to use terminology familiar to and understood by *all* teachers rather than terms that had limited exposure beyond special education.

Grant-Funded School Teams

These teams were composed of seven members: the school principal, a special education teacher, a school psychologist, and four classroom teachers from grades K–4. The grant-funded school team focused on key staff at each participating school, providing professional development and building common understanding across sites and allowing each school to design and implement an IIPM model, often with many stops and starts.

District Team

The director for student achievement assembled a group that initially included lead teachers from the grant school teams and Title I schools. The group was expanded to include a Reading First consultant, a school psychologist from a grant-funded school team, and two special education administrators. The district team was created to address broad issues, for example, defining instructional strategies and interventions and curriculum alignment.

Project Development: District's IIPM Model

The first step in project development was the identification of potential school sites. District members of the lead team met with elementary principals to share the guidelines, expectations, and supports offered to a participating grant site. Principals were then asked to share this information with their staff. Ensuring that essential members of the grant-funded school teams (e.g., general education teachers and the special education teacher, school psychologist, and principal) were committed to the project was important. Initially, four schools volunteered to become grant schools. However, after the first meeting, one school withdrew because it could not obtain a commitment from all members of the team. The three remaining schools included:

- Gilham Elementary School, with approximately 500 students; this non–Title I school had participated in developing and piloting the district reading assessment and then used both it and DIBELS benchmark assessments. The school had been collecting and analyzing the DIBELS PM measures to make instructional decisions prior to becoming a grant school.

- Meadowlark Elementary, a small (approximately 240 students) neighborhood school with Title I services. The teachers at Meadowlark had administered the DIBELS benchmark assessments and the district reading assessment, but not the DIBELS PM measures.

- Buena Vista Spanish Immersion School, a small (approximately 250 students) school of choice in which students received instruction entirely in Spanish for their first 2 years, then switched to a combination of English and Spanish beginning in grade 3. The teachers at Buena Vista had administered the district reading assessment but did not have a history of using student assessment data to guide instructional decision making.

The district and university lead team reviewed the guidelines of the model demonstration grant with the three grant school teams. However, rather than moving to adopt an established RTI model, the district's approach was to demonstrate at the building level the development and implementation of a tiered instructional intervention and PM model. The lead team gave the grant school teams the latitude to design the model and make it work within the context of their building. This flexibility in "how the process could go" demonstration approach fit the culture of innovation and creativity in the district. The building-level process and input ultimately led to the development of the district's IIPM model.

The lead team met monthly with representatives from the grant school teams (i.e., lead teacher, principal, school psychologist, and grade-level teachers). The grant school teams reported on the evolving processes for developing and implementing a tiered instructional intervention and PM model in their buildings. As the teams shared their successes, they also learned from the specific obstacles encountered at the other school sites and collaborated on solutions to overcome these problems.

In spring 2006, the district/university lead team, in conjunction with the ILT and grant school teams, further delineated and expanded the goals to include:

1. supporting and implementing a core language arts curriculum in K–8;
2. developing a tiered instructional intervention model incorporating instruction in the core curriculum with both differentiated and targeted interventions;

3. piloting and implementing benchmark and PM assessments for K–8 in reading and mathematics;
4. developing and implementing a new prereferral/referral process (RTInst) as an alternative to the traditional SST process that had traditionally been a special education–focused prereferral/referral process;
5. developing and implementing a special education comprehensive evaluation model that utilizes both RTI and patterns of strengths and weaknesses (PSW) methodologies. This model was an alternative to current practices in evaluation and eligibility determination for students with specific learning disabilities (SLD); and
6. improving academic results for students with disabilities by ensuring that they can access and are taught the core curriculum, receive appropriate instructional interventions, and are monitored for progress. In addition, the district was to use PM assessments to develop and monitor IEP goals and annual student achievement.

The district was allocated grant funds to distribute to each grant school to support the development and implementation of the model so teams could meet monthly to review PM data and discuss instructional interventions. Individual schools participating in the project decided whether they would release teachers with substitutes for these data meetings or pay teachers to work beyond their contractual hours. The school team leads (school psychologist and lead teacher) were given an additional stipend to collect and organize student data and facilitate team meetings. Grant schools were given funds to pay an instructional assistant to administer *easyCBM* assessments and then enter PM data into the *easyCBM* site. The decision to fund a part-time PM data collector at each site was controversial. Although the teams understood from the beginning that the funds were available only while the model was being developed, throughout the project school-based educators expressed frustration with the challenge of creating and transforming practices when no additional funds would be available for assistance with administering PM assessments.

In addition to the teachers from the grant school teams, the lead team asked elementary teachers across the district to volunteer to administer the *easyCBM* reading measures in their classrooms to provide local norms for the newly developed assessments. With incentives, enough teachers volunteered to provide approximately 250 students at each grade level, K–4, to pilot and norm measures.

To help build additional capacity within the district, the University of Oregon and the Eugene Foundation, a community-based nonprofit organization, provided funds to support leadership training for both principals and teachers. This leadership was critical at each stage of the work.

2006–2007 School Year

It took 3 months, starting in the fall of 2006, for the district's elementary and middle school principals to reach consensus and commit to lead the work necessary for their schools to have a successful language arts adoption and implementation process. After the principals came to consensus, the director for student achievement met with a group of language arts teachers to review research, prioritize state standards, review language arts programs on the state adoption list, and recommend two CRPs for elementary and two language arts curricula for the middle school level.

In September 2006, the following guidelines for the elementary and middle school language arts adoption were approved, with every elementary school expected to:

1. adopt one of the two comprehensive language arts programs approved by the school board for adoption;
2. adopt one comprehensive program for language arts instruction that best met the needs of all students at the school, including special education students, ELLs, and students identified as talented and gifted (TAG);
3. accept support from the district office, including ongoing professional development and funds for purchasing materials;
4. ensure that every teacher implemented the school's adopted comprehensive program as designed by the program designers, using the core program and the interventions and supplements as appropriate for best meeting the needs of individual students;
5. ensure that all students received language arts instruction in their school's adopted comprehensive program from 2007–2008 through 2012–2013;
6. ensure that every teacher taught to the district prioritized English language arts standards using instructional practices found to be effective through sound research; and
7. use a building team (i.e., an administrator with SST, IEP, PM, or TAG team) to determine when an individual student needed intervention outside or beyond the core program.

Every middle school was also given the preceding guidelines plus an additional one: to develop a schoolwide literacy plan to ensure the development of literacy skills for all students specific to each content class and provide intensive support for students reading below grade level.

Instructional leaders—with the unanimous backing of the district's board of directors—supported the efforts to balance the long-standing practice of site-based decision making with the district leadership's guidance regarding adopted curriculum and instruction in schools. To say the least, with this dramatic shift, many teachers and staff members experienced a significant culture shock. Requiring adoption of one of only two CRP curricula was an important step in changing the culture of the district while respecting the innovation and creativity that characterized both the district and its individual schools.

The grant-funded school teams started the 2006–2007 school year, intending to implement the components of the grant. One of the first stumbling blocks encountered by these teams was identifying and/or developing differentiated or targeted instructional interventions. The teachers were working without a core reading curriculum; the language arts adoption was a year away. By the end of September, the grant-funded school teams were asking the lead team, "What are the reading interventions?" In response to the question, the director for student achievement assembled the district team. The team struggled in the first meeting with how to respond to the concerns about instructional interventions. During the second meeting, the team realized that because the buildings were not teaching a core curriculum, and because instruction (and materials) could vary from classroom to classroom, they could not identify appropriate instructional interventions (e.g., vocabulary, word fluency, or other elements of reading proficiency). The lead team decided to refocus the district's efforts toward supporting the development of an instructional intervention model and decision rules for the model. For the remainder of the fall and early spring 2007, the grant-funded school teams began to incorporate the prereferral/referral process created by the special education team to design and to implement a tiered intervention and PM model in their buildings. At the same time, district staff and grant-funded school team members identified critical elements that a comprehensive reading program must have to support the implementation of our model. These elements included: (1) materials to support differentiation of instruction within the core program; (2) assessments for screening, diagnostic, and outcome evaluation; and (3) research-based strategies that support student acquisition of reading skills based on the National Reading Panel's "big five."

Throughout the 2006–2007 school year, the school grant teams administered the *easyCBM* PM measures and met for 4–6 hours each month to discuss the school's grade-level and individual-student data. The grant-funded school teams gave feedback to the lead team about the *easyCBM* measures (e.g., individual items, grade-level standards alignment, administration of the measures, and data displays on the website). This feedback was used to guide revisions of the assessment system.

In May 2007, the district adopted two CRPs for the elementary level. Each elementary school was to choose one of the two programs. These programs (curricula) had both strengths and weaknesses when compared with each other and with the district's adoption criteria, but both incorporated a tiered-instructional approach. The publishers of the two programs provided professional development for all of the schools, explaining how to use the materials in a three-tiered model. The district and the Eugene Education Association agreed to fund 2 days of professional development on the newly adopted curricula for every elementary teacher and language arts teacher (grades 6–8) prior to the start of the 2007–2008 school year.

The district—for the first time—provided special education teachers with CRPs and intervention materials (K–5). The special education teachers were included in the professional development activities and received ongoing supports for their implementation needs. However, the most important change for special education teachers was the decision to use the CRP for all students, leaving the core only when curriculum modifications for a student required supplemental interventions. This change supported the district's commitment to ensure that students with disabilities had access to and received instruction in the general education curriculum.

At the end of the 2006–2007 school year, the lead team made a decision to support the work of the existing grant schools in the 2007–2008 school year rather than add more schools. The decision was based on the need to focus district efforts on implementing the two new comprehensive reading and language arts programs, providing ongoing professional development for teachers, continuing to use the *easyCBM* PM measures, and refining the district's IIPM model.

2007–2008 School Year

In August 2007, the lead team assembled the grant-funded school teams to review the model demonstration grant goals, guidelines, and expected outcomes. The grant-funded school teams were given 2 workdays to:

1. review the current reading/language arts instruction in their buildings;
2. formalize the team component process (i.e., meeting times, agenda, data facilitation, intervention planning, and PM administration);
3. schedule team meetings to review model and processes;
4. review tiered instructional intervention models; and
5. begin to design an alternative prereferral/referral process that incorporated tiered-instructional interventions and PM and, most important, was embedded in general education.

To provide ongoing support for the implementation of the new CRPs and language arts curricula in the 2007–2008 school year, the district decided to fund a literacy coach model for 2 years. The district allocated 4.5 full-time equivalent (FTE) for literacy coaches: 3.5 FTE was used for literacy coaches to assist at the elementary schools, and each middle school received 0.2 FTE for literacy coaches.

Toward the end of the full first year of the grant (2006–2007) and continuing through 2007–2008, the lead team's meetings with the school grant teams proved to be very useful. In fact, the grant-funded school teams requested continued meetings with the other teams and the lead team. The sharing of implementation issues and successes led the whole group to focus on problem solving, duplicating what was working, and rethinking some of the important implementation components (i.e., a tiered model with decision rules, PM [easyCBM measures], and identifying instructional interventions linked to specific skill deficits in reading).

Once the CRPs arrived in schools in the fall of 2007, the grant-funded school team at Gilham Elementary School reviewed the curriculum materials to determine alignment with the easyCBM PM measures. Teachers across the district started the year struggling to determine how many students to monitor and were concerned with the alignment of measures with instruction. There was also concern regarding how to use the assessment information. The grant-funded school team developed a grid to describe the different assessments available to teachers in the district (see Figure 11.1).

In addition, the grant-funded school team focused on developing instructional strategies rather than relying on published intervention curricula or other materials and distributed a table of reading intervention curricula to which teachers in the district would have access (see Figure 11.2).

In the spring of 2008, the staff development specialists reviewed the instructional intervention/PM practices that the grant-funded school teams had been developing and implementing in their buildings. Based on that information, the staff development specialists designed documents and forms to begin the process of building a common framework for the district model. Chief among these documents are a Student Profile Form, used to guide teachers through the IIPM process (see Appendix 11.1), a Student Progress Monitoring Summary Log (see Figure 11.3), and a rubric to help school staff self-identify their phase of IIPM model implementation (see Appendix 11.2). The staff development specialists also identified professional development needs at each of the grant-funded school teams' buildings and began work on developing professional development modules based on these identified needs that would be used later (in 2008–2010) for all schools.

In the spring of 2008, the district formed the Access to General Education (ATGE) committee made up of district general and special education administrators (District Office K–12) and leaders from the teachers' union and the classified employees' union, representing nonteaching employees in the district. The ATGE committee worked to provide direction to general education and special education teachers, classified staff members, and

(text resumes on page 293)

	Frequency	Skills Assessed	Grades Available	Group vs 1:1	Time Allocation
Screener					
District Reading Kit (easyCBM)	3x yearly	PA, P, F, V, C	K–5	both	(Test week)
DIBELS Benchmark	3x yearly	PA, P, F, V, C	K–5	1 to 1	5–10 min per student
OAKS	up to 3x yearly	V, C	3rd–5th	group	varies 45 min+
	Frequency	**Skills Assessed**	**Grades Available**	**Group vs 1:1**	**Time Allocation**
Diagnostic Assessments					
Treasures Diagnostic (IRI)	3–4 weeks	PA, P, F, C	K–3 (4–5)	1 to 1	varies
Triumphs Phonics	Pre/post	P	K–3 (4–5)	1 to 1	varies
Treasures Placement Test	Pre/post	P, V, C	K–5		varies
*Treasures Running Records	3–4 weeks	P,F,V,C	K–5	1 to 1	varies
*DIBELS	Pre/post	PA, P. F. V, C	K–5	1 to 1	varies
*easyCBM	Pre/post	PA, P. F. V, C	K–5	both	varies
*Basic Reading Inventory (BRI)	Pre/post			1 to 1	varies
	Frequency	**Skills Assessed**	**Grades Available**	**Group vs 1:1**	**Time Allocation**
Progress Monitoring					
easyCBM	2–4x mo	PA, P, F, V, C	K–5	both	1 min & up
DIBELS	2–4x mo	PA, P, F, V, C	K–5	1 to 1	1 min & up
Treasures Fluency Assessments	2–4x mo	P, F,C	K–5	1 to 1	1 min
*Treasures Benchmark Assessments	3x per year	Varies	K–5	group	30–45 min
*Treasures Unit Assessment	5 weeks	Varies	K–5	group	1 hour
*OSAS Format Unit/Benchmark Assessments	5 weeks/3x per year	Varies	K–5	group	1 hour
*Treasures Weekly Assessments	TBD	varies by grade level	K–5	group	30 wkly
*Triumphs Weekly Assessments	TBD	varies by grade level	K–5	group	30–45 min wkly

FIGURE 11.1. Different assessments available to teachers in the district. *This assessment can be used as a screener or diagnostic assessment depending on how the data are analyzed (Eugene 4J School District, October 2008). *Note.* DIBELS, Dynamic Indicator of Basic Literacy Skills; OAKS, Oregon Assessment of Knowledge and Skills; OSAS, Oregon Statewide Assessment System; PA, phonemic awareness; P, phonics; F, fluency; V, vocabulary; C, comprehension.

Intervention Program	Supplemental or Comprehensive	Focus Skill Areas (PA, P, F, V, C)	Grades	Time	Suggested Group Size	Cost	Other
Corrective Reading (A, B1, B2, C) Comprehension and Decoding	Comprehensive or Supplemental	If both used-(PA), P, F, V, C	3rd and up	30–45 min	small group		
Earobics	Comprehensive or Supplemental	PA, P, (F, V, C)	K–3	30 min +	1:1		Technology based
Horizons	Comprehensive or Supplemental	PA, P, F, (V, C)	1–3rd+	45 min	small group		
Edmark Reading Program—specifically for students with cognitive impairments	Supplemental	sight words (vocabulary)	K–3rd+	20–30 min	1 to 1		sight word focus, paper or computer based
Fluency First	Supplemental	F	K–3rd	10–30 min	small group, 1 to 1		
Phonics for Reading (levels 1, 2, and 3)	Supplemental	P, (F, V, C)	1st–3rd+	30–45 min	small group		
Read Naturally	Supplemental	F	(1) 2nd–up	30 min +	1:1, small group		paper or computer based
Rewards Intermediate	Supplemental	P (F, V)	4th–5th		small or whole group		
Rewards (Secondary)	Supplemental	P (F, V)	6th–up		small or whole group		
Scott Foresman Early Reading Intervention (ERI or Optimize)	Supplemental	PA, P, F (V)	K–1	30 min +	small group		

Intervention Program	Supplemental or Comprehensive	Focus Skill Areas (PA, P, F, V, C)	Grades	Time	Suggested Group Size	Cost	Other
Six Minute Solution	Supplemental	F	2nd–up				
Soar to Success (intermediate)	Supplemental	F, C (P, V)	3rd–up	45 min	small group		
Soar to Success (primary)	Comprehensive or Supplemental	PA, P, F, V, C	K–2	45 min	small group		
Triumphs	Comprehensive or Supplemental	PA, P, F, V, C	K–up	45 min	small group		
Read 180	Comprehensive or Supplemental	P, F, V, C	4th–up				
Reading Mastery Classic 1	Supplemental	PA, P, F, (V, C)	K–1	45 min	small group		
Reading Mastery Classic 2	Supplemental	P, F, (V, C)	1st–2nd	45 min	small group		
Reading Mastery Classic FC	Supplemental	PA, P, F, (V, C)	1st–2nd	45 min	small group		
Read Well K	Supplemental	PA, P, V, C	K	30–45 min	small group		
Read Well	Supplemental	PA, P, F, (V), C	1st	30–45 min	small group		

FIGURE 11.2. Reading intervention curricula guide. Information for this table came from Oregon Reading First, the Florida Center for Reading Research, and local staff development specialists. *Note.* PA, phonemic awareness; P, phonics; F, fluency; V, vocabulary; C, comprehension.

Grade	Last Name	First Name	Teacher	Area of Concern	Date Parent Notice Sent	Tier Start Date	Tier 3 Start Date	Exit Date (note Tier 2 or 3)	Data Review Date and Decision	Data Review Date and Decision	Data Review Date and Decision

FIGURE 11.3. Student progress monitoring summary log.

administrators as they made decisions regarding services for special education students. The committee developed three core principles to guide educational practices throughout the district:

1. All students must have access to the general education curriculum.
2. Districtwide, a continuum of services must be provided for students receiving special education services; special education students are served in the least restrictive environment (LRE).
3. Throughout the district, approximately 70% of the students receiving special education services must be in general education classrooms/environments at least 80% of the time.

The ATGE committee continued to meet throughout the spring of 2008 to work on clarifying the district's approach to these issues. It was critical that this committee create a shared understanding across administrative, instructional, and classified staff about the concepts and context surrounding access to the general education curriculum. It quickly became obvious that the district needed to undergo a fundamental change in beliefs and practices related to special education students' participation in the general education environment and instruction in the core curricula. The ATGE committee developed a three-phase work plan that was to begin in the spring of 2008 and continue through spring 2010.

Phase 1 (November 2007–June 2008)

In this phase it was important for all members of the ATGE steering committee to understand the core principles. The ATGE committee presented the core principles to a representative group from all schools in the district (i.e., the principal, a special education teacher, and a general education teacher from each school). The groups worked with the ATGE committee to present to the full staff at each school. Additional presentations were made to the board of directors and key groups in the district's central office.

Phase 2 (August 2008–June 2009)

Support was provided for implementation of the core principles and removal of any barriers at the building level. Core principles were integrated with other key district initiatives, such as the CRP, language arts adoption, and IIPM model implementation.

Phase 3 (August 2009–June 2010)

In the final phase, efforts were made to increase understanding of ATGE principles across the district by: (1) reviewing ATGE principles with key building teams (IIPM and positive behavioral support teams and site councils); (2) collecting achievement and discipline/behavior data; and (3) developing a survey to identify promising ATGE practices in buildings.

Other Important Components

The ATGE committee and the district made a commitment to a systematic, thoughtful, and long-term process that was inclusive of all and allowed for dialogue in every building to create a shared understanding and change beliefs and practices. The shared understanding of the three core ATGE principles ensured that all students, including special education and CLD students, would have access to and participate in the general education curriculum. Operating schools and classrooms following these core principles would guarantee special education and CLD students the opportunity to learn and receive instruction in the general education environment using the CRP in conjunction with special education services and the English language development (ELD) program, as needed.

The district's implementation of the ATGE principles, the CRP adoption districtwide and buildingwide, and the IIPM model converged to change the landscape of teaching and learning across the district. Important to all the change initiatives and activities was the inclusion of and leadership from both the teachers' and classified employees' unions. The work of the ATGE committee began a critical conversation about changing the role of special education teachers.

Throughout the 2007–2008 school year, the special education team, the grant-funded school teams, the instructional leadership team, and the OCR collaborated to develop the district's IIPM model and IIPM prereferral/referral process. The district's IIPM model and IIPM prereferral/referral process incorporated an instructional intervention and PM framework derived from RTI methodology (see Appendix 11.3). The IIPM model was designed to provide a formal, structured approach to the provision of high-quality instruction and intervention matched to students' needs. The approach required frequent PM to assess student academic performance and learning rates and to use those data to guide instruction; therefore, the approach was conceptualized in the district's IIPM model as a response-to-instruction (RTInst) methodology. The IIPM prereferral/referral process provided extensive information necessary for nondiscriminatory and fair assessments of all students, including CLD students. The IIPM prereferral/referral process incorporated RTInst methodology to effectively address early identification of and instructional intervention for academic difficulties within the general education environment. The district's IIPM model and IIPM prereferral/referral processes included procedures and guidance for instructional interventions, PM, Tier 1–3 frameworks, and decision rules. We have presented in Appendix 11.3 an explanation of the IIPM model Tiers 1–3 describing the model for reading. A similar process with variation for instructional time was also utilized for students receiving instruction in mathematics. Finally, the district also committed resources and IIPM model guidelines for CLD students (see Appendix 11.4).

2008–2009 School Year

The school year started with the grant-funded school teams continuing and refining their work in developing a model that "works" in their building. The teams were faced with changing building schedules in order to reorganize and find time to provide instructional interventions and integrate special education services. The monthly team meetings continued but were challenged by the addition of more teachers in each building and the need for additional meetings to review intervention data. At the same time, the district asked the grant-funded school teams to incorporate and implement "what works" at the building level with the district's IIPM model.

As the school year continued, the grant schools used buildingwide professional development days to review and learn more about *easyCBM*, as well as the diagnostic assessments in the CRPs. The staff development specialists produced a data team notebook to assist school teams. A recurring theme that emerged during the 2008–2009 school year was how to implement and identify resources for Tier II (instructional differentiation) and Tier III (targeted instructional interventions). The grant schools, as well as other district small schools that did not receive additional Title I and district resources, found it difficult to find sufficient time or to efficiently utilize limited staffing to fully implement the IIPM model.

In the third year of the grant, two more elementary schools were added. Holt Elementary School was a large Title I school that had been administering both the district reading assessment and the DIBELS assessments. The teachers were aware of the three-tier model and anticipated the district's implementation of the IIPM model. The school had effective principal and teacher leadership and staff support. Edgewood Elementary School, a small non–Title I school, also joined the grant. Edgewood had effective leadership and staff, had used DIBELS for benchmarking and PM, and had made initial efforts to use data to inform instruction. Both of these new grant-funded school teams recognized the value of sharing in the work of developing and implementing the district's IIPM model.

Beginning in the fall, all district elementary schools were required to send an instructional team, including specialists, school psychologists, and the building principal, to attend three half-day trainings on the district's IIPM model and the IIPM prereferral/referral process. Two sessions were devoted to reviewing the district's IIPM model: (1) the process used to develop the IIPM model, (2) components of the IIPM model, and (3) guidelines and expectations for implementation at each building and across the district. The third session provided an overview of the district's new IIPM prereferral/referral process and comprehensive evaluation for CLD students and the revised special education comprehensive evaluation model. More in-depth trainings on the IIPM model and special education/CLD comprehensive evaluations were provided for special education and ELL teachers and itinerant groups (e.g., school psychologists, speech/language specialists, and special education consultants). The staff development specialists scheduled ongoing school-based professional development and supports for the spring of 2009.

Implementation of the IIPM model, in conjunction with the district's adoption of two comprehensive reading programs at the elementary level, was an important step toward a systemic approach to instructional improvements and the integration of special education services. Support at all levels—superintendent and school board, administration, teachers, and classified staff—was necessary for the district to establish expectations and direction systemwide. At the end of the 2008–2009 school year, all elementary schools had started the implementation of the IIPM model in their buildings—some at different levels, but all were ready for full implementation in the fall of 2009.

The district's efforts focused on developing and implementing new special education procedures that addressed inadequacies in the evaluation, placement, and provision of services to students with disabilities. A core perspective was promulgated that this outcome could only be accomplished within the context of a systemic and integrated approach to change. The model demonstration grant helped develop a prereferral/referral process that utilizes a tiered model for instructional intervention and PM. The special education comprehensive evaluation included two components and incorporated evaluation procedures with accompanying assessment methodologies for both an IIPM prereferral/referral process and a special education comprehensive evaluation. This latter component included both evaluation planning and completion of a special education comprehensive evaluation that included a PSW assessment methodology and an interpretation of evaluation data. The district developed the PSW methodology to provide an organizing framework. The PSW methodology integrated and evaluated multiple sources of data to establish a convergent pattern (convergent validity principle) indicating correspondence between measures of the same construct (e.g., an SLD, memory, etc.).

2009–2010 School Year–Postgrant Activities

As grant funding ended, we have had the opportunity to explore the degree to which our model has become part of the district's accepted practice, moving from optional innovation to expected performance. Much of the sustainability of the IIPM model can be attributed to what Elias, Zins,

Graczyk, and Weissberg (2003) refer to as embracing an action-research perspective and ensuring that professionals at the school are prepared with the skills needed to scale up the reform efforts. Although we did not specifically refer to our data-focused team-based approach as action research, one could argue that the IIPM model is, in effect, a school-based collaborative action research project (Sagor, 1992) with the goal of improving teaching and student achievement.

The school year started without funding from the model demonstration grant. In addition, the district made significant budget cuts early in the year. District leadership, however, was committed to fully implementing the IIPM model at the elementary school level. Each elementary school had begun planning IIPM model implementation in spring 2009. The district provided IIPM guidelines earlier in the trainings, but, as in the grant schools, building personnel were challenged to integrate the model within the unique context of each school. The work of the grant schools over the previous 3 years had laid the foundation for implementation across the district. Each school's readiness for implementation, however, was determined by instructional and resource capacity, level of understanding of the IIPM model guidelines, and the strength of instructional leadership.

An important transformation of beliefs and practices occurred within the elementary schools as teachers and administrators grappled with understanding and implementing the IIPM model. The grant schools had demonstrated how this model could work in different schools, but essential to the change in teaching was the concurrent transformation of teacher and leadership beliefs about students and instruction. The district's focus on equity, ATGE principles, and support for the implementation of the IIPM model had built both a foundation and a framework for that transformation. The elementary schools across the district had made an important change and were eager to implement the IIPM model, but they asked the district for help.

The district supported the implementation of the IIPM model across all elementary schools and the PM component at the middle schools by prioritizing its efforts in three areas: (1) increasing the number of staff development specialists, (2) providing targeted professional development across the district, and (3) expanding benchmark and PM measures in reading and mathematics (K–8). The district strategically utilized American Recovery and Reinvestment Act funds (Title I and IDEA) and district professional development funds and realigned other resources, including administrators and staff, to support these focus areas.

The number of staff development specialists at the elementary level was increased to 4, an additional 3.2 FTE specialists were allocated for building-based staff development at the middle schools, and 2 special education staff development specialists were assigned. As the implementation needs varied in elementary schools depending on the stage or phase of the building's implementation of the IIPM model, the elementary staff development specialists responded by providing differentiated support to teachers and grade-level teams. The staff development specialists had previously provided training on the IIPM model and, at the start of the school year, shifted their supports to helping schools implement components of the IIPM model. The following components of the model were addressed: (1) utilizing benchmark and PM assessments, (2) setting up and structuring data teams, (3) expanding knowledge and use of the CRPs, (4) facilitating identification of differentiated and targeted instructional intervention strategies in reading and mathematics, and (5) clarifying roles of general and special education, Title I, and ELL teachers.

At the middle school level, the staff development specialists were phasing in the implementation of the IIPM model through the PM component. The *easyCBM* benchmark and PM assessments in reading and mathematics were administered in all middle schools in the fall of 2009. Until then, the use of either state or district assessments had varied across the middle school buildings. The middle school staff development specialists worked with teachers and building teams to understand and use the data to inform instruction and guide intervention services at the building level. At the same time, the high school staff development specialists began to narrowly focus their efforts on supporting intervention programs and integrating general and special education services.

A plan was created in the spring of 2009 that prioritized the professional development activities throughout the district for the entire school year. The plan identified two district values or lenses through which all proposed professional development activities were viewed: equity and access to general education. The plan further provided a narrow framework for organizing the professional development activities. This framework listed three priority areas for professional development: IIPM model, mathematics/algebra, and instructional technology. All proposed professional development activities in 2009–2010 were aligned with the values and framework of the district's plan. The district's professional development decisions and funding allocations continued to support the scaling up and implementation of the IIPM model as a high priority.

The decision to expand the *easyCBM* benchmark and PM assessments in reading and mathematics (K–8) was an important step in fully implementing the IIPM model. The IIPM model and *easyCBM* development had been initially embedded in the district's implementation of the new comprehensive reading programs (K–5). The IIPM model's guidelines provided elementary schools with a framework for tiered instructional intervention and PM in reading that could also be used for mathematics. At the middle school level, the use of *easyCBM* benchmark assessments in reading and mathematics provided teachers and building teams with accurate and applicable data for monitoring student achievement across grade levels and developing appropriate instructional interventions.

CONCLUSION: THE DISTRICT'S STORY OF CHANGE

The model demonstration grant afforded the district and the University of Oregon an incredible opportunity to help shape the future of the Eugene School District 4J. In the current challenges to the district—increasing student performance and reforming special education services—and in the context of diminished resources, there has been a transformation in the teaching, values, beliefs, and culture of the district. First steps in any change process are sometimes leaps, but by building on a culture of innovation and creativity, the district has taken a long and thoughtful leap forward.

Taking a conceptual–empirical approach to RTI demands that new research be conducted to understand the innovation. Just as we would not expect teachers to continue implementing poor instructional practices in the presence of countervailing data, we should expect no less from systems implementation of RTI without empirical support. In this concluding section, we present the next steps for a program of research that could guide the empirical basis for change.

The formal application of the term RTI is most readily visible in the recent legislation of Individuals with Disabilities Education Improvement Act of 2004 (IDEIA) (Yell, Shriner, & Katsiyannis, 2006). "RTI has been broadly described as a process in which students are provided quality instruction, their progress is monitored, those who do not respond appropriately are provided additional instruction and their progress is monitored, and those who continue to not respond appropriately are considered for special education services" (Bradley, Danielson, & Doolittle, 2006, p. 486).

In the RTI research, major concerns have been expressed about the elimination of the discrepancy formula (ability minus achievement), appropriate definitions of learning disabilities (Kavale, 2005; Kavale & Forness, 2000), legislative requirements and authoritative recommendations (Reschley, Hosp, & Schmied, 2003), and, finally, reflections on practical implications for teachers and school psychologists (Vaughn & Fuchs, 2003). A key focus in this literature has been the merits (and criticisms) of the use of various definitions and the potential unintended consequences that might arise from adoption of (or the failure to adopt) an RTI model. Much of the literature on RTI has come from the field of school psychology.

Missing from this literature, however, is the organizational and leadership literature for developing RTI in practice. Although clear policies are important, they need to be considered a means to an end and be concurrently enacted in practice with teachers as active participants in professional development. Although a number of models for professional development are available, we relied on a coaching model, primarily because of the empowerment it provided seasoned teachers. We also added technical training on measurement and data use because of its primary presence in RTI models.

The measurement component of RTI had been part of a program of research in the late 1970s and 1980s at the Institute for Research on Learning Disabilities (IRLD) at the University of Minnesota. In this research, which resulted in the development and validation of CBM, the focus was on monitoring student progress using measures that tapped skills relevant for classroom success. This literature was published in a series of technical reports that eventually appeared in a number of peer-reviewed journals throughout the 1980s and 1990s. A special edited issue of *Journal of Special Education* described the technical features in writing, reading, and mathematics CBM (Wallace, Espin, McMaster, Deno, & Foegen, 2007).

We relied on this rich empirical basis for further development of our progress measures (easyCBM); however, we provided a theoretical basis for measurement development and extended the classical test theory (CTT) for item development to include item response theory (IRT). (This is more thoroughly discussed in Chapter 12 of this volume.) As a consequence, we were able to (1) more explicitly develop alternate forms that were equivalent and (2) better understand how our measures functioned concurrently at both the person and item levels. In addition, we added systems implementation as a focus of our measurement. Although the early research was justified in its reliance on teacher-created tests and measures, it has become increasingly important to have technically adequate measures, given the centrality of RTI in making critical decisions (about the need for and outcomes from specialized instruction).

Increasingly, literature on RTI has begun to address models for practice. For example, Deno (2005) presents a problem-solving model in which five steps are identified: (1) problem identification, (2) problem definition, (3) design of intervention plans, (4) implementation of interventions, and (5) problem solution. For Chard (2004), the focus is on professional development with system data and person knowledge considered in framing "the complex context in which professional development is situated" (p. 178). Gersten, Vaughn, Deschler, and Schiller (1997) consider sustainability in proposing a model for using research-based practices, attending to reality principles, scope, technical issues, conceptual underpinnings, social networks, and linkages between teaching and learning (also see Johnson, Hays, Center, & Daley, 2004, for a similar model that focuses on sustainability).

However, little recent research has addressed the components of RTI: the process for adoption, use of frequent measures, decision rules for placements, or integration of the various components within a system. Indeed, RTI has typically been bundled with these components. Yet, for a successful launch at the district level, they need to be carefully tendered. We described how a district organized these various components to ensure that personnel worked in sync, change was phased in, and attention turned to increasingly finer and more specific issues, from adopting a core curriculum to specifying instructional supports in a tiered fashion and with professional development teams.

This process, time-consuming and intensive as it was, has resulted in dramatic changes in district policy and classroom practice. Our decision to focus on developing the capacity within the district to serve as leaders and change agents rather than depending on the university for guidance may have required slightly more time initially, but we believe it will result in more sustainable change.

In Chapter 12, we describe one of the university's primary contributions to the sustainability of the model both within the Eugene School District 4J and other districts across the country, an online assessment system developed specifically to support RTI initiatives. In Chapter 13, we share the outcomes of our model demonstration project that we feel will be most relevant to others engaged in this work.

REFERENCES

Annenberg Institute for School Reform. (2004). Instructional coaching: Professional development strategies that improve instruction. Providence, RI: Brown University. Available at *www.annenberginstitute.org/publications/tlpubs.html.*

Avramidis, E., & Norwich, B. (2002). Teachers' attitudes towards integration/inclusion: A review of the literature. *European Journal of Special Needs Education, 17,* 129–147.

Bradley, R., Danielson, L., & Doolittle, J. (2006). Response to intervention. *Journal of Learning Disabilities, 38*(6), 485–486.

Chard, D. (2004). Toward a science of professional development in early reading instruction. *Exceptionality, 12,* 175–191.

Deno, S. L. (2005). Problem-solving assessment. In R. Brown-Chidsey (Ed.), *Assessment for intervention: A problem solving approach* (pp. 10–39). New York: Guilford Press.

Elias, M. J., Zins, J. E., Graczyk, P. A., & Weissberg, R. P. (2003). Implementation sustainability and scaling up of social-emotional and academic innovations in public schools. *School Psychology Review, 32,* 303–319.

Fullan, M. (1985). Change process and strategies at the local level. *Elementary School Journal, 84*(3), 391–420.

Fullan, M. (1992). *Successful school improvement.* Buckingham, UK: Open University Press.

Gersten, R., Vaughn, S., Deschler, D., & Schiller, E. (1997). What we know about using research findings: Implication for improving special education practice. *Journal of Learning Disabilities, 30,* 466–476.

Huberman, A. M., & Miles, M. B. (1984). *Innovation up close: How school improvement works.* New York: Plenum Press.

Individuals with Disabilities Education Improvement Act, 20 U.S. C. 1415(k) (2004).

Johnson, K., Hays, C., Center, H., & Daley, C. (2004). Building capacity and sustainable prevention innovations: A sustainability planning model. *Evaluation and Program Planning, 27,* 135–149.

Kavale, K. (2005). Identifying specific learning disability: Is responsiveness to intervention the answer? *Journal of Learning Disabilities, 28*, 553–562.

Kavale, K., & Forness, S. R. (2000). What definitions of learning disability say and don't say: A critical analysis. *Journal of Learning Disabilities, 33*, 239–256.

Knight, J. (2000, April). *Another damn thing we've got to do: Teacher perceptions of professional development.* Paper presented at the meeting of the American Educational Research Association, New Orleans, LA.

Marzano, R. J. (2003). *What works in schools: Translating research into action.* Alexandria, VA: Association for Supervision and Curriculum Development.

Poglinco, S., Bach, A., Hovde, K., Rosenblum, S., Saunders, M., & Supovitz, J. (2003). The heart of the matter; the coaching model in America's choice schools. Philadelphia: Consortium for Policy Research in Education, University of Pennsylvania. Available at *www.cpre.org/images/stories/cpre_pdfs/AC-06.pdf.*

Reschley, D., Hosp, J. L., & Schmied, C. (2003). *And miles to go . . . State SLD requirements and authoritative recommendations.* Unpublished manuscript, Vanderbilt University.

Sagor, R. (1992). *How to conduct collaborative action research.* Alexandria, VA: Association for Supervision and Curriculum Development.

Sanders, W. L., & Horn, S. P. (1994). The Tennessee value-added assessment system (TVAAS): Mixed-model methodology in educational assessment. *Journal of Personnel Evaluation in Education, 8*, 299–311.

Scruggs, T. E., & Mastropieri, M. A. (1996). Teacher perceptions of mainstreaming/inclusion, 1958–1995: A research synthesis. *Exceptional Children, 63*, 59–74.

Shoemaker, B. J. (1993). *An evaluation study of the implementation of an integrated curriculum model in selected elementary schools in Eugene, Oregon.* Eugene: University of Oregon.

Showers, B., & Joyce, B. (1996). The evolution of peer coaching. *Educational Leadership, 53*(6), 12–16.

Vaughn, S., & Fuchs, L. (2003). Redefining learning disabilities as an inadequate response to instruction: The promise and the potential problems. *Learning Disabilities: Research and Practice, 18*, 137–146.

Wallace, T., Espin, C., McMaster, K., Deno, S. L., & Foegen, A. (2007). CBM progress monitoring within a standards based system: Introduction to the special series. *Journal of Special Education, 41*, 66–139.

Wright, S. P., Horn, S. P., & Sanders, W. L. (1997). Teacher and classroom context effects on student achievement: Implications for teacher evaluation. *Journal of Personnel Evaluation in Education, 11*, 57–67.

Yell, M. L., Shriner, J. G., & Katsiyannis, A. (2006). Individuals with Disabilities Education Improvement Act of 2004 and IDEA regulations of 2006: Implications for educators, administrators, and teacher trainers. *Focus on Exceptional Children, 39*(1), 1–24.

APPENDIX 11.1. Student Profile Form Developed by Eugene School District 4J

Name _____ Grade _____ Teacher _____

Area(s) of concern: Reading____ Math____ Writing____ Behavior____ Social Skills____

Other_____

Services- IEP > Reading, Writing, Math, Behavior, Social Skills, Speech, Language/
ELL/504 **(Circle those that apply)**

Tier I-	60 min daily, Heterogeneous group, core curriculum
Tier II **Start date:** **End date:**	30 min daily with progress monitoring *See easyCBM graph for details (frequency, time, group size, skill focus, materials, etc.)* ____ pre/reteach, ____ leveled readers, ____ Intervention Program that comes with the core
Tier III **Start date:** **End date:**	60 min weekly, *See easyCBM graph for details (frequency, time, group size, skill focus, materials, etc.)*

Data Team Review (6 weeks)	**Data Team Review (12 weeks)**	**Data Team Review (18 weeks)**
Date:	Date:	Date:
Reflection on data:	Reflection on data:	Reflection on data:
Next steps/decision & who implements:	Next steps/decision & who implements:	Next steps/decision & who implements:
1. Who:	1. Who:	1. Who:

Date Parent Notified of Intervention/Progress Monitoring: _____

Who made the contact: _____

Intervention Profile to be reviewed with progress monitoring data and graphs (attach)

*See page 2 of form for additional data on accommodations and modifications

(cont.)

Progress Monitoring Materials and Skill Area
(Minimum every 2 weeks for 6 weeks/ 3 data points)

____easyCBM
    ____Letter Naming ____Sounds ____Word Reading
    ____Segmenting ____Fluency ____Comprehension

____DIBELS
    ____Initial Sound ____Letter Naming ____Segmenting
    ____Nonsense Words ____Fluency ____Retelling

Person responsible for progress monitoring: _____

Possible Accommodations and Modifications

Environment

____Preferential seating   ____Change in classroom

____Seating away from distractions   ____Change in schedule

____Work with volunteer   ____Tools or cues on desk

____Assign peer buddy   ____Visual schedule

____Other _____

Organizational

____Time limits for assignments   ____Limit materials at desk

____Additional time   ____Color code materials

____Highlighting main facts   ____A.M. check-in

____Personal schedule   ____Mini schedule by subject

____Other _____

Motivation

____Sending home daily/weekly progress report   ____Goal setting

____Immediate reinforcement for correct responses   ____Conferencing with student

____Charts and graphs of student progress   ____Individual point system

____Other _____

Presentation

____Give instruction orally and visually   ____Increase active participation

____Taping texts/books so student can listen   ____Provide visual prompts

____Give immediate feedback to student   ____Frequent review of key concepts

____Small-group instruction   ____Conferencing with student

____Reteach materials/vocabulary

____Other _____

(cont.)

Curriculum

___Special materials   ___Manipulatives

___Provide study guide   ___Graphic organizers

___Extra drill and practice   ___Reduce quantity of work

___Provide materials at student's level   ___Break tasks into small chunks

___Other _____

APPENDIX 11.2. IIMP Model Implementation, Description of Phases

	Phase 1 (Beginning Implementation)	Phase 2 (Midway Implementation)	Phase 3 (Full Implementation)
Core Instruction			
Materials Core and supporting materials	Using core materials for all students (Tiers 1 and 2) at least some of the time. *Except when determined not appropriate by IEP team	Using core materials with almost all students (Tiers 1 and 2) most of the time. Supplemental materials used, but not always linked to the core. *Except when determined not appropriate by IEP team	Using only core materials with almost all students (Tiers 1 and 2) all the time*. Supplemental materials used only after exhausting core materials and matched to student need using diagnostic assessment. *Except when determined not appropriate by IEP team
Schedule 90 min reading block including Tiers 1 and 2 instruction	At least 60 min protected reading block (1st–5th grade) includes Tiers 1 and 2 level instruction	60 min reading block, some grade levels at 90 min block, all include Tiers 1 and 2 level instruction. (Schedule that allows for Tier 3 targeted instruction.)	Protected 90 min reading block that includes Tiers 1 and 2 level instruction (1st– 5th) 30–45 minute-kindergarten. (Schedule that allows for tier 3 targeted instruction outside core time.)
Differentiation (Tier 2) Designated time, part of core, differentiated to meet needs	Begin to use leveled readers during this time period in the classroom, whole group instruction	Smaller groups, grade/class level grouping, use of core materials, all students receive Tier 2.	Tier 2 reading includes differentiation of materials and instruction to meet various levels of learners across grades and schools, all students receive this tier and it is part of the 90–120 min block
Who Participates? All (gen/sp ed) students have access to the gen ed core curriculum, in gen ed setting as much as possible	All gen ed, some sp ed students. *Except when determined not appropriate by IEP team	All gen ed, most LC	All students (gen ed, most LC) participate in the core curriculum and in the gen ed setting and RLC students do for at least a portion of their reading time as appropriate for their skill level.

(cont.)

Core Instruction	Phase 1 (Beginning Implementation)	Phase 2 (Midway Implementation)	Phase 3 (Full Implementation)
Professional Development What is happening? What is needed?	Training in core, What is it?/ Why use it?, differentiated instruction	Teaching all of the Big 5 components, fine tuning teaching strategies, teacher observation opportunities	PO on using the core and still meeting various student needs (differentiation), how to provide intervention to meet the needs of the students, promote academic success and access in the core
Staff Roles Gen Ed, Sp Ed, Title 1, etc.	Limited to no sharing of students, but all using core curriculum or curriculum that supports the core	Some sharing of students across various service providers, all supporting the core and student needs	Lines of services are grayed with the focus being meeting all kids' needs, but still meeting regulations and requirements.

Intervention	Phase 1 (Beginning Implementation)	Phase 2 (Midway Implementation)	Phase 3 (Full Implementation)
Schedule Tier 2 within core reading time, Tier 3 at least 60 min weekly	30 min differentiation within the core reading time	Also, some additional targeted instruction at some grade levels	Tier 2 differentiation and at least 60 min weekly targeted instruction available to all as needed
Assessments Screener for all 2–3× yearly, PM for below 20th %ile at least every 2 wks, diagnostic to guide instruction	2× yearly screener, core program diagnostics to help identify skills missing, progress monitoring 2× mo	3 × yrly screener, diagnostics as needed for any of big 5 areas, PM below 20th %ile	All of phase 2, correctly matching type of assessments to the purpose, using information to guide instruction and match interventions
Materials/Strategies Focus first on supporting the core, then supplement to go more intense on targeted skills	Use of core materials for instruction and varying curriculum to address student needs	Using core and inst. intervention strategies across tiers and supplemental material only for Tier 3	Focus first on supporting the core with inst. Strategies and differentiation, then supplement to go more intense on targeted skills in Tier 3
Who Provides? Gen ed. Title I, Sp ed, IAs, other	Gen ed Tiers 1 and 2, some service provider support for 3	Gen ed Tiers 1 and 2, some service provider support for 3 and consult for 2	Gen Ed and Sp Ed across tiers, Title I Tiers 2 and 3 (Bldg staffed to help with 3) highest trained matched with the lowest skilled students

(cont.)

Intervention	Phase 1 (Beginning Implementation)	Phase 2 (Midway Implementation)	Phase 3 (Full Implementation)
Time/Frequency of Service Tier 2- (Within core) time?, Freq?, Tier 3- 60 min weekly above core time	Tier 2, at least 30 min daily; Tier 3, only with Title I or some Sp Ed students	Tier 2, 30 min daily; Tier 3, 60 min wkly for some grades/students	Tier 1 and 2 = 90 min reading block daily(60/30 or 45/45), Tier 3= 60 min weekly minimum outside the core block
Group Size Tier 2, Tier 3 smaller groups allow higher intensity, more response opportunities, etc.	Whole group Tiers 1 and 2 with differentiation in instruction; Tier 3, small group Title I or sp ed	Tier 1, whole group; Tier 2, wkly rotating small groups within whole group; Tier 3, up to 50% of whole class size	Tier 1, heterogeneous group; Tier 2, may be heterogeneous and/or homogeneous groups, include some small(er) groups; Tier 3, small group on targeted skill area
Intervention Grid (curriculum/strategies) What happens at various grade levels across Tiers 2 and 3 depending on identified need?	Tier 2, leveled readers; Tier 3, only with Title I or sp ed support or only based on curriculum intervention	Some grade levels have a fluid continuum, but not all are connected to the core	Fluid full continuum of services based on student need and response to intervention provided, all connected to supporting the core
Professional Development What is happening? What is needed?	Intervention versus accommodations, IIPM model, locating resources in bldg, district, etc.	Correct diagnosis, matching interventions to needs, instructional intervention strategies	Stays current with research-based instructional strategies and programs, effective practices, matching interventions to needs
Progress Monitoring	Phase 1 (Beginning Implementation)	Phase 2 (Midway Implementation)	Phase 3 (Full Implementation)
Benchmark/Screeners What and how often?	District testers 2× yearly (easyCBM Benchmark)	District testers 2× yearly (easyCBM Benchmark) bldg-winter benchmarking	Bldg- benchmarks 3× yearly, reviewed by whole staff
Diagnostic/Placement All 5 areas? What measures?	Identify assessments available within the core and their purpose	Understand and use error analysis	Menu of diagnostics in all 5 areas and teacher skill to choose, use, and interpret data and match to intervention

(cont.)

Progress Monitoring	Phase 1 (Beginning Implementation)	Phase 2 (Midway Implementation)	Phase 3 (Full Implementation)
Progress Monitoring What measures? How often? Who does it?	DIBELS Or easyCBM, conducted by volunteers, practicum students, staff 2× month with students below 20th %ile	2× monthly, 1 by teacher, 1× district/bldg staff	2× mo, district staffing support/student achievement coordinator
Data Review Meetings (grade level, bldg level) When? Who? Process?	SST model with progress monitoring data	SST model with progress monitoring data and intervention documentation	IIPM team review conducted by classroom teachers with support staff (grade/primary/intermediate) bldg wide 3× yrly, grade level every 6 wks
Student Intervention Profile Students below 20th %ile, includes PM, review interventions and progress	Identify students at and below the 20th %ile and set up progress monitoring	Also identify area of need and introduce appropriate intervention and make sure PM matches skill area and level	Completed on all students below 20th %ile, progress reviewed/updated and intervention/instruction adjusted, form goes with student when moves to next grade
Assessment Grid Note what is available and purpose	Identify assessments within the core and their purpose	Also identify what other assessments are in the building and their purpose	Match assessment to information desired, have common assessment agreements by grade level and across grade levels, use info gained
Intervention Grid Note what is in place for Tiers 2 and 3 for specific needs, grade levels	Identify intervention within the core and supplemental curriculum	Identifying strategies as well as curriculum for intervention, differentiation strategies and targeted inst. interventions	Not letting curriculum drive the intervention, kid needs and data guide intervention, ongoing development of staff "tool box," targeted versus comprehensive
Professional Development What is happening? What is needed?	easyCBM training	Understanding of various assessments and the use and application of data received from them	Using and applying data-based instructional decisions to provide interventions, make instructional decisions and meet student needs

Note. RLC, regional learning center.

APPENDIX 11.3. IIPM Model, IIPM Prereferral/Referral Process and Special Education Comprehensive Evaluation: Guidelines and Resources for Eugene School District 4J (2009)

Tier 1
Comprehensive Core Reading Instruction

Instruction:
- All students access the general education curriculum.
- Instruction in the comprehensive core curriculum focusing on the five essential components of reading.

Implementation Responsibility:
- The general education teacher (specified students may receive instruction from other support staff).

Assessment:
- All students assessed a minimum of 2x a year using the district reading assessment. In addition, other measures such as easyCBM and DIBELS may be used.

Decision Rule:
- If a student scores below the 20th percentile on assessments, the IIPM team may recommend Tier 2 instructional differentiation with progress monitoring for a minimum 6-week period.
- The IIPM team may recommend that a student be moved directly to Tier 3 targeted intervention with progress monitoring for a 12-week period.
- **For culturally and linguistically diverse students (CLD) review the District's CLD: Guidelines and Resources document.**

Tier 2
Comprehensive Core Reading Instructional Differentiation
(with Progress Monitoring)

Instruction:
- All students access the general education curriculum.
- All students receive instruction in the Tier 2 comprehensive core reading and the five essential components of reading with differentiation.
- Tier 2 instruction is more differentiated and skill focused than in Tier 1 and allows the teacher to address the instructional, learning, and cultural/linguistic needs of individuals and/or groups of students (on, below, language support, or challenge level) in the core curriculum.

Implementation Responsibility:
- The general education teacher, with collaborative support from Title I, reading specialist, facilitating teacher, and/or special education teacher.

(cont.)

Progress Monitoring:
- Students recommended from Tier 1 for progress monitoring receive a minimum of 6 weeks of differentiated instruction with three progress monitoring data points in Tier 2 instructional differentiation.
- School teams or programs may decide to progress monitor students at or above the 20th percentile.
- Written parent notification for progress monitoring is required in Tiers 2 and 3.

Decision Rule:
- A student may be recommended by the IIPM team for Tier 3 targeted instructional intervention:
  1. After receiving a minimum of 6 weeks of Tier 2 comprehensive core reading instruction with differentiation and progress monitoring
  2. After collection of three data points
  3. If measured achievement falls below the projected aim line or produces a flat progress trend
- The IIPM team may discontinue or extend Tier 2 progress monitoring if interventions are successful based on progress monitoring and RTInst methodology data.

Tier 3
Targeted Instructional Interventions
(with Progress Monitoring)

Instruction:
- All students access the general education curriculum.
- All students receive instruction in the Tier 2 comprehensive core reading and the five essential components of reading with differentiation.
- Students receiving Tier 3 targeted instructional interventions will have an additional 60 minutes per week of small-group targeted instruction that is matched to the student's academic, learning, and cultural/linguistic needs over a 6-week period.

Implementation Responsibility:
- Interventions may be provided by the general education teacher, Title I, reading specialist, ELD curriculum teacher, facilitating teacher, and/or special education teacher depending on the instructional and staffing resources available at each building.

Progress Monitoring:
- Students will be progress monitored a minimum of every 2 weeks using *easyCBM* or DIBELS measures.
- Written parent notification is required for progress monitoring in Tiers 2 and 3 as part of the IIPM model and the IIPM prereferral/referral process.

(cont.)

Decision Rule:
- The IIPM Team will review and analyze the 6–12 weeks of Tier 2 and Tier 3 targeted interventions progress monitoring data, as well as other assessments or background information, i.e., classroom performance, exclusionary factors, and other/CLD information.
- The IIPM Team may:
  ○ discontinue Tier 3 targeted instructional interventions if the student's data suggests interventions have been effective.
  ○ determine the need for additional data and extend the Tier 3 intervention for 6 weeks.
  ○ if the student is not making progress, i.e., continues to perform at a level below the academic aim line or measurements of progress produce a flat trend line and the IIPM team suspects the student may have a disability, refer the student for a Spec Ed comprehensive evaluation
- If the student is referred for a Spec Ed comprehensive evaluation, Tier 3 interventions will be reviewed (evaluation planning meeting) and continued through the evaluation period with progress monitoring weekly.

• **Refer to the IIPM Guidelines and Resources document for further details for Tier III**
•• **For specific information regarding the prereferral/referral process and special education comprehensive evaluation process, please see the IIPM Guidelines and Resources document.**

APPENDIX 11.4. IIPM Model, IIPM Prereferral/Referral Process, and Special Education Comprehensive Evaluation for Culturally and Linguistically Diverse (CLD) Students: Guidelines and Resources for Eugene School District 4J (2009)

Student: _____ Grade: _____ School: _____

Contact Person: _____

<table>
<tr>
<td colspan="2" align="center">Tier 1
Comprehensive Core Reading Instruction/Instruction in the ELD Curriculum</td>
</tr>
<tr>
<td>Step 1</td>
<td>

_____ Review District Reading Assessment (or CBM measures) scores for all students.

_____ Identify students with scores below the 20th percentile.

_____ Consider recommending students for Tier 2 differentiated instruction with progress monitoring.

_____ Determine if the student is a CLD or CLD/English Language Learner. (Check program page on ESIS to determine if the student is in the ELD program, on monitoring status, or has been reclassified as FEP).

*If student is determined to be a CLD or CLD/ELL:

_____ Review guiding CLD questions with IIPM Team (questions at end of this form) and

_____ Follow appropriate column below for next steps.
</td>
</tr>
<tr>
<td></td>
<td>

☐ **CLD/FEP year exited: _____**   ☐ **CLD/ELL in ELD Program**
</td>
</tr>
<tr>
<td>Step 2</td>
<td>

<table>
<tr>
<td valign="top">

For CLD/FEP/ELL students not on monitoring status and only receiving instruction in the general education curriculum:

_____ Gather information about the student's language proficiency in the native language (L1) and English (L2), if applicable;

_____ Review information about the student's language proficiency in the native language (L1) and English (L2); and
</td>
<td valign="top">

ELL students receiving Tier 1 instruction in the ELD curriculum

_____ Confirm the student has received instruction in the ELD curriculum for at least 18 weeks (a minimum of 90 minutes per week);

_____ Review student performance on the ELD curriculum (chapter tests or other CBM measures);

_____ Determine if the student is not making progress in the ELD curriculum;
</td>
</tr>
</table>
</td>
</tr>
</table>

(cont.)

_____ Complete designated portions of the CLD Student Summary form.	_____ Gather information about the student's language proficiency in the native language (L1) and English (L2); and
	_____ Complete designated portions of the CLD Student Summary form.

Prior to the start of Tier 2 comprehensive core reading instructional differentiation (with progress monitoring)

_____ Initiate (start) the Student Profile Form for each student; and

_____ Send parent notification for progress monitoring in Tier 2 and/or Tier 3

*Consult with the CLD/Sp Ed team if any questions in the above process or information
**ELL students are monitored for 2 years after exiting from the ELD program for academic success.

<table>
<tr><td colspan="3" align="center">Tier 2
Comprehensive Core/ELD Reading Instructional Differentiation
(with Progress Monitoring)</td></tr>
<tr><td></td><td>☐ CLD/FEP year exited: _____</td><td>☐ CLD/ELL in ELD Program</td></tr>
<tr>
<td></td>
<td>Comprehensive Core Reading Instructional Differentiation with Progress Monitoring
Differentiated instruction with progress monitoring. Instructional methodology is based on the cultural, linguistic, and learning needs of the student.</td>
<td>ELD Curriculum Instructional Differentiation with Progress Monitoring
Instruction is more differentiated and skill focused using the ELD curriculum and additional supplemental materials.</td>
</tr>
<tr>
<td>Step 1</td>
<td>_____ Provide appropriate instructional differentiation for the referred student for at least 6 weeks;

_____ Assess each student using progress monitoring measures a minimum of every 2 weeks;

_____ Document three progress monitoring data points;

_____ Review student progress after 6 weeks of instructional differentiation and progress monitoring; and

_____ Complete designated portions of the CLD Student Summary form.</td>
<td>_____ Provide appropriate instructional differentiation for referred students in the ELD curricula for at least 12 weeks;

_____ Assess each student using progress monitoring measures a minimum of every 2 weeks;

_____ Document six progress monitoring data points;

_____ Review student progress after 12 weeks of instructional differentiation and progress monitoring; and

_____ Complete designated portions of the CLD Student Summary form.</td>
</tr>
</table>

(cont.)

APPENDIX 11.4. *(cont.)*

Step 2	Determine the next step (Decision Rules):	Determine the next step (decision rules):
	_____ Continue (extend) Tier 2 comprehensive core reading instruction with differentiation and progress monitoring if progress monitoring data indicate the student is making adequate progress;	_____ Continue (extend) Tier 2 ELD curriculum with differentiation and progress monitoring if progress monitoring data indicate the student is making adequate progress;
	_____ Discontinue Tier 2 comprehensive core reading instruction with differentiation and progress monitoring, if progress monitoring data indicate the instructional differentiation is successful; or	_____ Discontinue Tier 2 ELD curriculum with differentiation and progress monitoring if progress monitoring data indicate the instructional differentiation is successful; or
	_____ Move to Tier 3 targeted instructional interventions with progress monitoring if the student is not making adequate progress.	_____ Move to Tier 3 targeted instruction intervention with progress monitoring if the student is not making adequate -progress.
	*Suggested additional data and information for consideration during the decision process; writing samples, below-grade-level CBM, BICs, and CALP	***Targeted intervention is in the ELD program, but additional intervention may include an academic area focus in general education**

*Consult with the CLD/Sp Ed team if any questions in the above process or information

	Tier 3 Targeted Instructional Interventions with Progress Monitoring	
	☐ **CLD/FEP year exited:** _____	☐ **CLD/ELL in ELD Program**
	Targeted Instructional Interventions with Progress Monitoring *Targeted, direct and explicit instructional interventions with progress monitoring. Instructional methodology is based on the cultural, linguistic, and learning needs of the student.*	**Targeted Instructional Intervention in the ELD Curriculum with Progress Monitoring** *Instruction is more direct, explicit and skill focused using the ELD curriculum and additional supplemental materials.*
Step 1	For CLD/FEP monitor/postmonitor students receiving Tier 3: _____ Provide a minimum of 60 minutes per week of targeted instructional interventions in a small group for at least 6 weeks;	For ELL/CLD students in ELD program receiving Tier 3: _____ Provide a minimum of **30** minutes per week of targeted instructional interventions in a small group for at least 6 weeks;

(cont.)

	_____ Assess each student using progress monitoring measures a minimum of every 2 weeks;	_____ Assess each student using progress monitoring measures a minimum of every 2 weeks;
	_____ Document three progress monitoring data points;	_____ Document three progress monitoring data points;
	_____ Review student progress after 6 weeks of targeted instructional intervention and progress monitoring;	_____ Review student progress after 6 weeks of targeted instructional interventions and progress monitoring;
	_____ Complete designated portions of the CLD Student Summary form.	_____ Complete designated portions of the CLD Student Summary form.
	_____ Apply decision rules;	_____ Apply decision rules;
	_____ Obtain written parent consent to collect additional information; and	_____ Obtain written parent consent to collect additional information; and
	_____ Arrange for interpreter or translation services, if needed.	_____ Arrange interpreter or translation services, if needed.
Step 2	Collect additional information:	Collect additional information:
	_____ Conduct an interview with the parent;	_____ Conduct an interview with the parent;
	_____ Conduct a comprehensive review of student's academic records;	_____ Conduct a comprehensive review of student academic records;
	_____ Gather information about language dominance and the student's motivation to learn English or to speak in his/her native language;	_____ Gather information about language dominance and the student's motivation to learn English or to speak in his/her native language;
	_____ Gather information about the student's language proficiency in the native language (L1) and English (L2);	_____ Gather information about the student's proficiency in the native language (L1) and English (L2);
	_____ Review services, accommodations, and instructional interventions implemented in the classroom; and	_____ Review services, accommodations, and instructional interventions implemented in the classroom; and
	_____ Consult with district CLD/Sp Ed team prior to applying decision rules to review information and process.	_____ Consult with district CLD/Sp Ed team prior to applying decision rules to review information and process.

(cont.)

Step 3	Determine the next step:	Determine the next step:
	_____ Continue (extend) targeted instructional interventions with progress monitoring, if progress monitoring data indicate the student is making adequate progress;	_____ Continue (extend) targeted instructional interventions with progress monitoring if progress monitoring data indicate the student is making adequate progress;
	_____ Discontinue targeted instructional interventions with progress monitoring, if progress monitoring data indicate the targeted instructional intervention is successful;	_____ Discontinue targeted instructional interventions with progress monitoring if progress monitoring data indicate the targeted instructional intervention is successful;
	_____ Consider any apparent exclusionary factors and/or factors that must be further explored; or	_____ Consider any apparent exclusionary factors and/or factors that must be further explored; or
	_____ If the student is not making adequate progress and the IIPM Team suspects the student has a disability, the team will refer the student for a CLD/Sp Ed comprehensive evaluation;	_____ If the student is not making adequate progress and the IIPM team suspects the student has a disability, the team will refer the student for an CLD/Sp Ed comprehensive evaluation;
	_____ Develop a working hypothesis to guide the IEP evaluation planning; and	_____ Develop a working hypothesis to guide the IEP evaluation planning; and
	_____ Review and continue the Tier 3 targeted instructional interventions throughout the evaluation period with progress monitoring weekly.	_____ Review and continue the Tier 3 targeted instructional interventions throughout the evaluation period with progress monitoring weekly.
	*Suggested additional data and information for consideration during the decision process; writing samples, below-grade-level CBM, BICs, and CALP	

* **Prior** to deciding to refer a student for a CLD/Sp Ed comprehensive evaluation, consult with the district CLD/Sp Ed team

Note. ELL, English language learner; ELD, English language development; FEP, fluent English proficient.

CHAPTER 12

The Measurement System Behind the RTI Model

Julie Alonzo
Gerald Tindal

We began developing a district response-to-intervention (RTI) system with the following two premises: (1) RTI is a general education initiative with implications for identifying and providing services to students with special needs and for the improvement of instructional effectiveness for all students, and (2) technically adequate assessments are essential. In this chapter, we describe the development and use of assessments as universal screeners and measures of progress, with sufficient alternate forms to allow for frequent monitoring of student learning.

Because we were not satisfied with the measures of progress available for use at the time our model demonstration center was initially funded, we began our work by developing state-of-the-art progress monitoring (PM) measures that covered the range of skills required for developing literacy (from early phonological awareness through phonics, fluency, and—finally—reading comprehension itself), as well as the technological infrastructure for an online curriculum-based measurement (CBM) assessment system that would facilitate the RTI process. This online system (*easyCBM. com*) has proven to be an integral part of our success.

When our work began, our partner district had been using a twice-yearly screening assessment in reading for 8 years. This screener was administered to all students, K–9, in the fall and spring. The district expectation was that teachers would use the information from these screening assessments to make decisions about instructional emphases and groupings, but there was little, if any, oversight on how—or even whether—the data were used. Because we had collaborated with the district in developing these screeners, we were quite familiar with their structure and intent. We used this information, along with research on key skills in the area of literacy, as we developed newer, state-of-the-art PM measures.

Our goal was to create measures that would on the surface resemble as closely as possible the screening measures with which the district was already familiar, yet would offer distinct improvements in terms of their technical adequacy. To achieve this goal, we decided to use item response theory rather than classical test theory as we developed the measures. We begin this chapter with a brief summary of the research on reading CBMs that directly influenced our measurement development, then discuss the psychometrics we used in developing CBMs. Finally, we describe the design principles we used in developing our Web-based system, principles that inform not only what information the system presents but also how it is presented.

RESEARCH SUPPORTING CBM

CBM is probably the most empirically based system for monitoring progress in reading skill development. Since 1982, considerable research and development has been conducted on CBM. CBM has been described by Deno (2003) as having the following characteristics: It is composed of repeated measurement on a single task with alternate forms; it uses empirically selected tasks; it is technically adequate with sufficient reliability; and it is economical and efficient, which means that it requires little time, can generate multiple forms easily, is not very expensive, and is easy to use.

Tindal (1998) has presented a review of the early research in this area, noting that the measurement system has been used to assess students with disabilities, to write individualized education plans (IEPs), and to evaluate student progress. The CBM model developed by Deno and University of Minnesota associates (Deno, 1985; Marston, Mirkin, & Deno, 1984) and implemented in applied settings (Marston & Magnusson, 1988) is a proven, replicable model that improves services for children with disabilities. Measurement focuses on basic skills and provides teachers with important information to formatively evaluate and modify instructional programs.

CBM is a system of measurement tools designed to be critical indicators of general proficiency in reading, writing, spelling, and math, allowing both special and regular education teachers to change their instruction by measuring student progress, charting results, and administering interventions before students fail (Espin, Busch, Shin, & Kruschwitz, 2001). Traditionally, CBMs have been most popular at the elementary school level, where they have been used to predict performance on state-mandated large-scale tests. CBMs are versatile for use in screening, diagnosing, and PM (Fiala & Sheridan, 2003).

As screening tools, CBMs are administered at grade level, and student performance is used to identify students who score substantially lower than average and to determine appropriate placement. When used districtwide, local norms can facilitate identification of benchmarks for flagging students at risk. In some areas, national norms are available. For example, Hasbrouck and Tindal (2005) report on a nationally representative group of students in grades 1–8, presenting percentile rank data in the fall, winter, and spring on oral reading fluency (ORF) measures. In mathematics, researchers at the University of Oregon began developing grade-level norms (K–8) based on a geographically stratified sample of students from four regions of the country in 2010.

CBMs also can be used as a diagnostic tool for assessing patterns in student strengths and weaknesses. For example, CBMs can identify a student's or a group of students' difficulty in applying specific skills (e.g., letter names or sounds, phonemic segmentation, word reading skills, etc.), and the teacher can use this information to help guide instruction by reviewing incorrect items. Concurrently, the results of this measure can be used to determine the strengths of a teacher's instruction by identifying skills that a student or group of students have mastered.

Administering multiple CBMs throughout the academic year can allow educators to monitor growth in student performance over time. Using CBMs for this purpose has been shown to improve teachers' instruction and student performance (Foegen, Espin, Allinder, & Markell, 2001). Indeed, CBMs are recommended by the U.S. Department of Education for teachers to assess student progress toward making adequate yearly progress (Fuchs, 2002). To reliably depict growth, however, CBMs must provide reliable and valid information similar to that required of formal, standardized tests (Deno, Fuchs, Lynn, Marston, & Shin, 2001).

Each CBM is an alternative form that is predictive of performance desired on a summative criterion (e.g., a standardized test) (Fuchs, 2004). Research demonstrates that CBM produces accurate, meaningful information about students' academic levels and growth. CBM is sensitive to student improvement; when teachers use CBM to inform their instructional decisions, students achieve better (Fuchs, 2002). The CBM score "represents an individual's global level of competence in the domain," which can then be used by educators to "identify discrepancies in performance levels between individuals and peer groups, which helps inform decisions" about instructional interventions and accommodations (Deno et al., 2001, p. 507). Although mastery measurement can demonstrate individual skill proficiency, it assumes that the curriculum standards are equally represented on the criterion measure, which may or may not be the case.

CBM measures individual progress on the curriculum domain measured on an end-of-the-year test. The alternate form reliability of CBM allows educators to monitor their students' progress toward skill attainment subsequently measured on the criterion test. When the criterion measure is a statewide test, a major challenge is aligning the constructs from it with the skills measured on the CBM (Fuchs, 2004). This alignment is done either by "identifying a task that correlate[s] robustly with the various component skills constituting the academic domain" or by "systematic sampling of the skills constituting the annual curriculum to ensure that each weekly CBM represents the curriculum equivalently" (Fuchs, 2004, p. 2). In the development of our CBM measures, we followed the first approach, selecting tasks with strong correlations to the outcome goal: the end-of-year state assessment of reading.

ASSESSING READING: OUR PERSPECTIVE

Reading is a somewhat fluid construct, shifting over time from a focus on discrete skills necessary for working with language in both written and spoken forms to those more complex combinations of skills associated with decoding and finally to comprehension—a construct in which all previously learned literacy skills are called on for understanding. Reading assessment typically follows this general progression as well (National Institute of Child Health and Human Development [NICHD], 2000). Assessments of emerging literacy skills evaluate student mastery of the alphabetic principle. These measures focus on students' ability to correctly identify and/or produce letters and the sounds associated with them. They reflect students' ability to manipulate individual phonemes (sound units) within words—when, for example, students are asked to identify the sounds that begin or end a word, blend a list of phonemes into a word, or segment a word into its corresponding phonemes (Ritchey & Speece, 2006).

The relationships between these constructs in English are well documented in the research literature. In early readers, ability to identify letter names and the sounds that letters make predicts phonemic awareness. Phonemic awareness predicts fluency (NICHD, 2000). ORF, which measures a combination of students' sight vocabulary and their ability to decode novel words rapidly and accurately in increasingly longer phrases, is consistently identified in the literature as one of the best predictors of student reading comprehension in the early grades (Graves, Plasencia-Peinando, Deno, & Johnson, 2005; Hasbrouck & Tindal, 2005). Eventually, however, the information provided by measures of ORF becomes limited as students grow older and become fluent (Yovanoff, Duesbery, Alonzo, & Tindal, 2005). Readers attain a fluency threshold that enables them to attend to comprehension rather than decoding (Ehri, 1991, 2005). Once this threshold has been reached, fluency is no longer sensitive to increases in reading comprehension. At this point, one must turn to measures designed to assess comprehension more directly.

USING MODERN PSYCHOMETRICS TO ADVANCE CBM DEVELOPMENT

Early work related to CBM, led by Deno and Mirkin at the University of Minnesota (see Deno, Mirkin, Chiang, & Lowry, 1977), was instrumental in promoting the use of short, easily administered assessments to provide educators with information about student skill development useful for instructional planning. In the three decades since, such *progress monitoring probes*, as they have come to be called, have increased in popularity, and they are now a regular part of many schools' educational programs (Alonzo, Ketterlin-Geller, & Tindal, 2007). However, CBMs—even those widely used across the United States—often lack the psychometric properties expected of modern, technically adequate measures. Although the precision of instrument development has advanced tremendously in the past 30 years, with the advent of more sophisticated statistical techniques for analyzing tests on an item-by-item basis rather than relying exclusively on comparisons of means and standard deviations to evaluate comparability of alternate forms, the world of CBMs has not generally kept pace with these statistical advances.

A key feature of measures designed for PM is that alternate forms must be as equivalent as possible to allow meaningful interpretation of student performance data across time. Without such cross-form equivalence, changes in scores from one testing session to the next are difficult to attribute to changes in student skill or knowledge. Improvements in student scores may, in fact, be an artifact of successive measurement forms being easier than the first one administered. The increasing availability of more sophisticated data analysis techniques (such as the Rasch modeling used in the development of the *easyCBM* measures) have made it possible to increase the precision with which we develop and evaluate the quality of assessment tools.

For effective PM, it is important to have sufficient and comparable measures to sample student performance frequently. The system created in our Progress Monitoring Center includes multiple alternate forms of each measure and at each grade level. These forms are comparable in difficulty and sensitive to showing growth in a discrete skill area over short periods of time.

These two equally important needs also informed all phases of our measurement development: the construction of the technical specifications for each of the measures, the design of studies used to gather data on item and test functioning, and, finally, the analytical approaches used to interpret the results of the pilot studies and subsequent revision of the measures. In all phases, we sought approaches that would provide us with enough information to evaluate (1) *comparability of the different forms* of each measure to allow meaningful interpretation of growth over time and (2) *sensitivity of the individual measures* to detect small differences in student performance.

STATISTICAL ANALYSIS

We analyzed data from the pilot testing of all our measures (with the exception of passage reading fluency) with a one-parameter logistic Rasch analysis using the software *Winsteps3.61.1* (Linacre, 2006). Rasch analyses differ from approaches using classical statistics in that they consider patterns of responses across individuals, using this information to provide a level of specificity in results unattainable with approaches based on classical statistics used in the development of most CBMs. In a complex iterative process, a Rasch analysis concurrently estimates the difficulty of individual test items and the ability level of each individual test taker. The results one obtains from this analysis, relevant to our discussion here, include an estimation of the difficulty (referred to as the "measure" of each item), the standard error of measure associated with each item's estimated difficulty, and the degree to which each item "fits" the measurement model (referred to as the "mean square outfit" of each item). In addition, a Rasch analysis can provide information about the average estimated ability of students who selected each of the possible answer choices, in the case of multiple-choice questions. All of this information must be considered when evaluating the technical adequacy of a measure, as described next.

Considering Each Item's Estimated Difficulty

Rasch analyses, which examine each item's reliability, provide a more precise treatment of reliability than classical statistics, which examine the issue only at a more global test level. The most reliable estimation of a test taker's ability can be gained from tests composed of items that represent the fullest range of difficulty possible for the population with which the test is intended to be used. Thus, in evaluating the technical adequacy of the *easyCBM* measures, we looked for items representing a range of difficulties. In Rasch analyses, this information is gleaned from examining each item's difficulty, which is referred to as the item's *measure*. Easy items will have measures represented with negative numbers; difficult items will have measures represented with positive numbers. A measure of zero indicates an item that a person of average ability would be expected to have a 50%

chance of getting correct. Thus, we sought a full range of measures on every *easyCBM* test.

Examining the Standard Error of Measure

Rasch analyses provide information about the standard error of measure associated with the estimation of each item's measure. In general, the smaller the standard error of measure, the more reliable the estimation. We sought standard errors of measure of .20 or less on all items on our tests.

Using the Mean Square Outfit to Evaluate Goodness of Fit

An additional piece of information used to evaluate technical adequacy in a Rasch model is the mean square outfit associated with each item. Values in the range of 0.50 to 1.50 are considered *acceptable fit*. Mean square outfits falling outside this acceptable range indicate the need for further evaluation of item functioning. In general, items with a mean square outfit less than 0.50 are considered less worrisome than items with mean square outfits higher than 1.50. In the case of multiple-choice questions, distractor analysis provides useful information to further evaluate the technical adequacy of each item.

Analyzing Distractor Selection Information

A distractor analysis provides information on the average estimated ability of test takers who selected a particular distractor (multiple-choice item) on a test. In evaluating the technical adequacy of an assessment instrument, one hopes to see that the correct answer is selected by test takers with the highest average estimated ability and the remaining distractors are selected by test takers with lower estimated abilities. In addition, every distractor in a well-constructed measure will be selected by at least some test takers.

Use of item response theory analysis as an integral part of the item development process is one of the key distinguishing features of the measures available on *easyCBM*. Item response theory analysis enabled us to control the variability in difficulty of the different forms of the measures, as well as to strategically locate easier items near the start of our test forms, with the forms incrementing up in difficulty as students progress. This instrumentation design increases the reliability of student scores on fluency-based measures in much the same way that a computer-adapted test does: by providing students with items close to their ability levels. Whereas computer-adapted tests use item response theory–based estimates of each item's difficulty to select items from an item bank that are appropriately "difficult" for each student, the forms on the *easyCBM* system are designed to increment up in difficulty, so that students with lower ability in a particular skill area will "time out" before they get to the more challenging items that will be beyond them, whereas those who have a great deal of ability will move quickly through the easy items and encounter more challenging items, more appropriate for their particular skill level, before the timed test has been completed.

MEASURES COMPOSING
OUR COMPLETE ASSESSMENT SYSTEM

Based on previous empirical studies of early literacy assessment, we decided to develop two measures of alphabetic principle (letter names and letter sounds), one measure of phonological awareness (phoneme segmenting), two measures of fluency (word-reading fluency and passage-reading fluency), and one measure of comprehension (multiple-choice reading comprehension). Table 12.1 presents the grade levels at which each measure type is available. Technical reports describing the development and piloting of these measures can be found on the *easyCBM* website (Alonzo, Liu, & Tindal, 2007; Alonzo & Tindal, 2007a, 2007b), but a brief description of each of the measures is included here.

Letter Names

The letter names measure (Alonzo & Tindal, 2007a) tests students' ability to name the letters of the English alphabet, both in their lowercase and capitalized forms. In this individually administered measure, students are

TABLE 12.1. The easyCBM Progress Monitoring Assessments

Grade	Assessment					
	Phoneme segmenting	Letter names	Letter sounds	Word-reading fluency	Passage-reading fluency	Multiple-choice reading comprehension
K	X	X	X	X		
1	X	X	X	X	X	
2				X	X	X
3				X	X	X
4–8					X	X
Recommended number of weeks between test administrations	2	2	2	2–3	2–3	3–4

Note. Each X = 20 alternate forms.

shown a series of letters organized in a chart on one side of a single sheet of paper and given 60 seconds to name as many letters as they can. A trained assessor, reading a standardized set of instructions, then follows along as the student names the letters, indicating on a test protocol each letter the student reads incorrectly and prompting the student to go on if any hesitation occurs at a letter for more than 3 seconds. Student self-corrections are counted as correct responses. At the end of 60 seconds, the assessor marks the last letter named and calculates the total number of letters read correctly to arrive at the student's score. A total of 120 letter names correct is possible.

Letter Sounds

This measure is identical to the letter names test except that, rather than naming the letters on the test form, the student produces the sound associated with each letter (Alonzo & Tindal, 2007a). Again, the measure is individually administered for a period of 60 seconds. The trained assessor follows along on a test protocol while the student produces the sound associated with each letter or combination of letters on the test itself. The score, reflecting total number of letter sounds correctly produced in 1 minute, is recorded once the student has completed the test. A total of 120 sounds correct is possible.

Phoneme Segmenting

Unlike the previous two measures, the phoneme segmenting measure (Alonzo & Tindal, 2007a) is administered entirely orally. The assessor reads from standardized written directions printed on a test protocol and then administers the measure to the student by reading individual words. The assessor demonstrates three examples of how to segment a word into its constituent phonemes, then the assessor delivers the first word and starts the timing. The assessor says a word aloud, and the student articulates the individual phonemes that compose the word. Students receive 1 point for every phoneme they segment correctly. At the end of 60 seconds, assessors add the number of correct phonemes to arrive at a final score. A range of 108 to 114 phonemes correct is possible on the various forms of this measure.

Word Reading

In the word-reading measure (Alonzo & Tindal, 2007b), students are shown a page with words written in five columns. The words are from grade-level word lists and represent a range of difficulty, with the words getting successively more challenging. The items are a combination of sight words and decodable words and include terms used in science, social studies, and everyday use. Assessors read the standardized written directions, indicating that students should start at the top of the page and read across the rows (assessors are instructed to demonstrate by running a finger across the row of words, then down to the next row). If a student pauses for longer than 3 seconds, the assessor supplies the word, counts the response as incorrect, and prompts the student to move on to the next word on the list. At the end of 60 seconds, assessors mark the last word read on their copy of the test protocol, count the number of words read correctly to that point, and write the student's score (total words read correctly). A total score typically ranges from 10 to 130 words read correctly, depending on the grade level and proficiency of the student.

Passage-Reading Fluency

The passage-reading fluency measure (Alonzo & Tindal, 2007b) is a standard ORF measure. It consists of a narrative passage typed on a single page. In the lower grades, the passages are approximately 250 words long, and in grades 5 and above they are approximately 350 words in length. As in the other measures already described, an assessor reads the directions from a set of standardized written instructions and marks incorrect responses on a test protocol while the student is reading. Assessors are directed to supply the correct word and count the response as incorrect any time a student pauses longer than 3 seconds. Student self-corrections are counted as correct responses. At the end of 1 minute, assessors mark the last word read and then count the total words read correctly per minute, which represents the student's score. Scores typically range from 10 to 250, depending on the grade level and proficiency of the student.

Grade-level appropriateness of the passages was calculated using the Flesch–Kincaid Readability Formula on Microsoft Word, which calculates readability based on the mean number of letters per word and the mean number of words per sentence. Passages were written to produce readability scores ranging within 2 months of the middle of the school year. For instance, fourth-grade passages ranged from 4.4 to 4.6 on the Flesch–Kincaid Readability Scale. This readability index was used in creating successive paragraphs, so that the readability of the entire passage, as well as each individual paragraph, falls within the same middle-of-the-year range. As part of our measurement development process, we piloted all the passage-reading-fluency measures at each grade with a group of approximately 80 grade-level students to check for comparability across forms. We increased the difficulty of any forms that were initially easier (on which students in the pilot sample scored, on average, more than 10 words per minute more than they scored on the other passage-reading-fluency measures) by substituting words from the passage with more difficult words from our item bank of individual words with specific estimates of grade-level difficulty based on our prior item response theory analysis. Forms that were initially more challenging than the norm were made easier using the same methodology, by substituting easy words for more challenging ones from our item bank of individual words. All passages were written using easily decodable short names for characters and set in a context with which most students should have some familiarity.

Multiple-Choice Reading Comprehension

Unlike other reading CBM systems, *easyCBM* includes comprehension measures, beginning with grade 2 and extending to the end of middle school in grade 8. The passages were written to be accessible and interesting to young readers and feature children their age as the main characters in settings with which the majority of children in the United States would be familiar. These untimed measures comprise original works of narrative fiction (700 words long in grade 2; 1,500 words long in grades 3–8), followed by multiple-choice questions sampling literal, inferential, and evaluative comprehension. The second-grade tests each contain 7 questions measuring students' literal comprehension and 5 questions measuring their inferential comprehension. At other grade levels, the 20 questions are divided into 7 literal, 7 inferential, and 6 evaluative. Each item consists of a question stem and three plausible answer choices: the correct response and one near and one far distractor. The comprehension measures are taken online and can be either individually or group-administered. Figure 12.1 presents a screen shot of the comprehension interface on the *easyCBM* system. Students receive 1 point for every correct response, for a total possible score of 12 in grade 2 and 20 in grades 3–8.

We analyzed the technical adequacy of the reading comprehension measures with a one-parameter logistic Rasch model using Winsteps 3.61.1 (Linacre, 2006). In this analysis, tests are functioning appropriately when all items on them represent a range of difficulties and have a mean square outfit within the acceptable range of 0.5–1.5. Distractor analysis also is used to ensure that all items are correctly keyed and that distractors appropriately differentiate between students of different estimated abilities. In all cases, for the reading comprehension measures on easyCBM, students with the highest estimated ability selected the correct answer most often, and at least one student selected either of the two incorrect options. For a more detailed presentation of these findings, readers are encouraged to refer to the technical report (Alonzo, Liu, & Tindal, 2007).

The comprehension measures on *easyCBM* represent the most challenging of the reading measures available on our system. They are intended to be used with students who are already reading at or above grade-level fluency standards. Students who are not yet fluent readers would be more

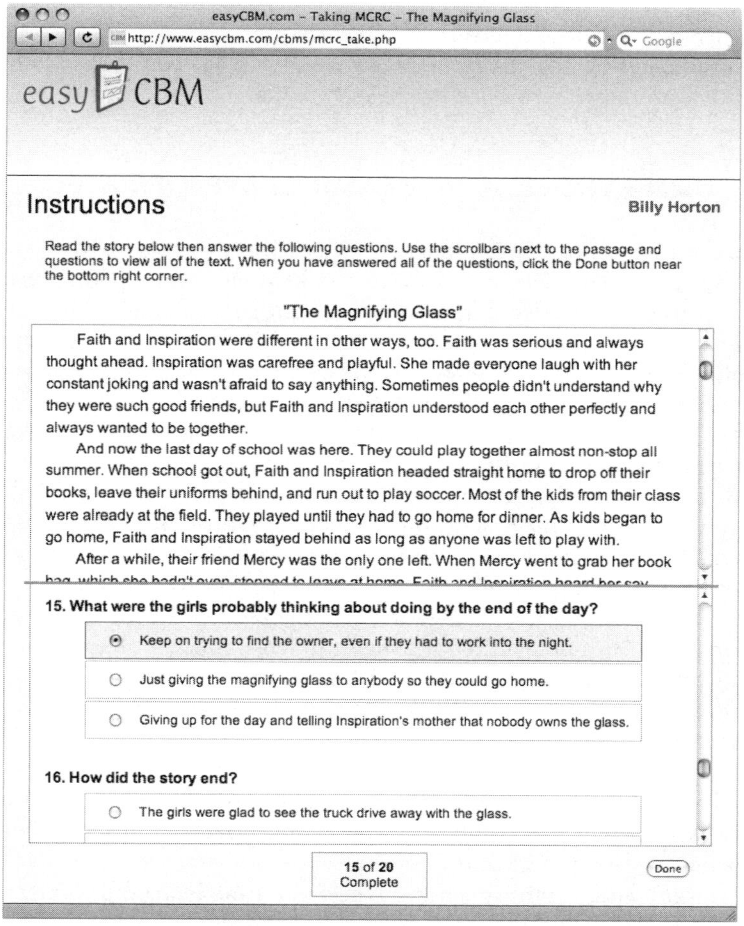

FIGURE 12.1. Screen shot of the reading comprehension interface on the *easyCBM* system. Copyright by *easyCBM*. Reprinted by permission.

appropriately assessed using the passage-reading fluency measures. In designing the measures, we tried to balance the desire for challenging material with the need to ensure that students could finish the tests within a single class period. Because we wanted to go beyond literal comprehension (which is simple to assess with very short passages), we needed to make the stories long and complex enough to allow for the deeper thinking involved in inferential and evaluative comprehension. Shorter passages, although appealing to many teachers, would not allow for the depth of questions we needed to include for the measures to be useful with students working on higher order comprehension skills. Because of their length, however, we recommend limiting the frequency with which the comprehension measures are administered to once every 3–4 weeks.

USING THE *easyCBM* MEASURES APPROPRIATELY

The *easyCBM* assessments are built on a scale of progressive difficulty, with each grade level becoming more challenging and each measure type within a grade level also "stair-stepping" up in difficulty. For example, with a third-grade student, teachers have the following tests to select from: multiple-choice reading comprehension (which provides information about that student's skill in literal, inferential, and evaluative comprehension), passage-reading fluency (which provides information about the student's ability to read aloud connected narrative text with accuracy), and word-reading fluency (which provides information about the student's ability to read a combination of sight and decodable words in isolation). Teachers might begin by administering the on-grade-level measures of passage-reading fluency and multiple-choice comprehension to that student. Once the scores are in the system, they look at the student's graph. If the score falls above the 50th percentile line, they can feel confident that this particular skill area is not the issue. If the student's score falls between the 10th and 50th percentile, they might decide that this particular skill is an area of weakness and select that measure to use for PM.

If the student's score falls below the 10th percentile, then teachers know that (1) there may be reason to suspect an even earlier skill deficit (in this case, maybe the student has never mastered phonics, so the letter sounds or word-reading fluency measure would be the most appropriate to use for monitoring progress while at the same time instructing the student in phonics); (2) if the subsequent test of letter sounds (available on the K and Grade 1 tabs on *easyCBM*) indicates that the student is at or above the 50th percentile in that skill area, then the issue is probably not one of basic phonics but is, instead, indicative of a need for additional fluency-building work but at an earlier grade level (to firmly establish sight words). If the student scored well below the 10th percentile on the third-grade word-fluency measure, teachers would probably want to drop two grades (to first grade). Hopefully, teachers would then get a score that would fall between the 10th and 50th percentile lines; this is the range at which the measures on *easyCBM* are most sensitive to growth and most appropriate to use. If the student's score is right at or just below the 10th percentile on the third-grade measure, teachers can bump him or her down to the second grade instead.

The goal is twofold: to determine what underlying skill deficit might be leading to the student's lack of proficiency and to identify the appropriate measure to use to monitor the student's improving skill as he or she receives targeted intervention and instruction aimed at addressing skill deficits in particular broad skill areas (alphabetic principle, phonics, fluency, comprehension). In all cases, teachers need to get the student up to the most challenging grade-level tests they can, as quickly as they can. Each student's trajectory is likely to be slightly different; it will depend on his or her level of initial skill and underlying skill deficits; the intensity of intervention provided to him or her; his or her ability to benefit from that particular intervention (as well as motivation to improve); his or her attendance (a student must be present to benefit from instruction), and so forth. For a third grader who needs to go all the way back to intensive instruction in phonics (letter sounds), it is unlikely that teachers will be able to make up all the ground they need in order to get her or him to grade-level comprehension by the end of the year, but teachers can certainly make good progress toward that goal, with the intention of continuing to make progress in grade 4 and thereafter. Letter sounds/basic phonics is a skill area in which teachers should be able to see dramatic improvement with intensive intervention in a matter of weeks for older students (again, though, this assumes intensive and appropriate instructional intervention to ensure that the student gains the skills he or she missed). Ideally, teachers should see an older student (grade 2 and above) move from the 10th percentile to the 50th on the letter sounds measure in a month's time or less.

Building fluency takes longer, but average growth is about four to six words per week. However, for students who are far behind their peers *and* who are receiving instructional interventions specifically targeting fluency building (repeated readings; choral readings; reading aloud to younger children, parents, mentors, etc.), teachers should see the rate of growth exceed six words per week (otherwise, the student is not catching up, but merely maintaining the existing gap).

Ideally, teachers might select an out-of-grade-level fluency measure for students whose scores indicate this need but bump the student to the next grade level up as soon as he or she hits the 50th percentile mark. If teachers start a sixth grader on the second-grade passage-reading fluency measure, then after 4–6 weeks of intensive fluency-building work (designed to reinforce phonics for unfamiliar words and to move additional words into the student's sight vocabulary through repeated exposure), they should be ready to move to third-grade passage-reading fluency, a month or 6 weeks later, then to fourth grade, and so on. Once students are reading fluently at grade level (50th percentile mark on grade-level passage-reading fluency measures), they probably have sufficient fluency skill to be able to start focusing more on comprehension. Until they are at that threshold, it is likely that too much "brain power" is being used to decode unfamiliar words and hold them in working memory to allow them to attend to the bigger picture of actual comprehension, except at the most literal level. Once students are able to read more fluently, they are able to focus on making meaning from the words in the text, and instruction can move to inferential and evaluative, as well as literal, comprehension.

A lack of growth could have several causes. Each of the different forms of each measure is designed to be of equivalent difficulty, so teachers would expect to see growth from one test administration to the next if students are, indeed, making growth. That said, each measure has an optimal range of ability that it is designed to measure. If teachers are administering these measures to enough students, they should be able to see a pretty nice distribution approximating a normal curve on the most recent measure. If the scores are clustered either toward the left (the tests are too hard for the students) or toward the right (the tests are too easy for the students; there is no room for them to show growth), then teachers should probably consider using a different measure. For instance, if teachers are looking at third-grade students and the word-reading fluency tests are too easy, they should move to the passage-reading fluency measures. If the passage-reading fluency measures are too easy, teachers can move to the comprehension measures. The comprehension measures are designed to be the most challenging of all the measures at each grade level. So, if teachers are specifically not seeing any substantial growth on those measures, it is important to keep in mind that an increase of 1 or 2 points would actually be pretty significant on that particular test.

It is also important to remember that there is a certain amount of unreliability associated with every score (whether it be correct number of words per minute on a word-reading or passage-reading test or number of correct answers on a multiple-choice comprehension test). Students have bad days and good days; students may be more interested in one passage being read or another. Some test-to-test fluctuation in scores is to be expected. But failure to see growth over a longer period of time is something for a teacher to be concerned about and may require that he or she closely examine the instruction or curriculum the students are focusing on. If students have not been receiving instruction in a particular skill area, then they cannot be expected to show improvement on measures of that skill. In the case of the word- and passage-reading fluency measures, classroom instruction and curricula that emphasize increasing students' ORF skills should result in increased scores on these measures. If instruction has focused on building understanding of literary devices or elements of literature, a growth in fluency would not be expected.

One of the most powerful features of the *easyCBM* system is its capacity to give teachers an opportunity to track progress quickly and make adjustments to the curriculum or instruction accordingly rather than waiting for the state assessment yearly score (which arrives too late to be very helpful). If teachers fail to see much progress across three or more times of measurement, they are directed to use that information to help guide a discussion about instruction.

AN ONLINE ASSESSMENT SYSTEM

The measures themselves, however, represent only part of the measurement model in our system. An equally important component is a computer-based online system created specifically to support an RTI framework and implementation. Working closely with our school partners, we sought to ensure that the computer interface was as intuitive as possible, as well as efficient and accurate. In creating the website, we used the following design principles.

- Include essential information only; extraneous information is distracting and clutters the interface.
- Whenever possible, reduce the number of clicks it takes for students or teachers to access the screens they need to use.
- Streamline the computer code to decrease load on networks, which is especially important for schools having slower connection speeds or less advanced technology.
- Seek teachers' feedback at all stages of design, development, and refinement to ensure that the site meets their needs.
- Use software safeguards to protect the integrity of student data.
- Provide a student interface for the measures students take directly on the computer and incorporate the principles of universal design for assessment (Thompson, Johnstone, & Thurlow, 2002), ensuring accessibility for the widest possible array of users.

In addition to carefully considering issues related to website navigation, we also addressed data use through the design of the graphs that teachers use in making decisions. Graphs were designed to facilitate discussion at data-team meetings. The group reports screen starts with a histogram that show the heterogeneity of student groups; if student skills are too divergent, teachers may want to consider dividing the group and targeting specific skill deficits of smaller groups of students. Below the histogram display, teachers see a table in which specific test items are split into two groups: those most students answered correctly ("top easiest" items) and those most students answered incorrectly ("top hardest" items) (see Figure 12.2). For the comprehension measures, this item analysis provides information on how students performed with literal, inferential, or evaluative comprehension questions. These tables allow teachers to see at a glance which specific skills can be ignored or need to be reinforced with further and more intensive instruction.

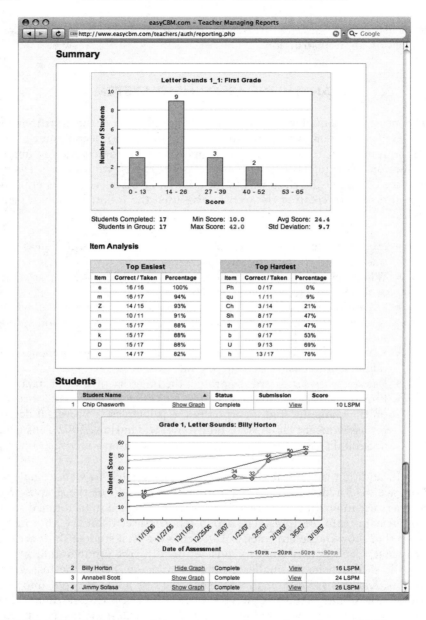

FIGURE 12.2. Screen shot of the groups graph page from the *easyCBM* system. Copyright by *easyCBM*. Reprinted by permission.

Teachers can easily compare the effectiveness of particular interventions for students in an instructional group by selecting the "view all graphs" option on the group reports page. By comparing the level, slope, and variability of students' scores before and after an intervention, teachers can determine which interventions are working for which students in the group. This information can help them target individual students' needs more effectively because they can see which students are failing to respond to an intervention. If, for example, four of the five students in an intervention group show marked improvement in the measured skill, but the fifth student does not, the teacher can draw two reasonable conclusions: (1) the intervention appears to be having a positive effect for some students and (2) for one student in particular, the specific intervention alone does not appear to be sufficient.

The interventions interface allows teachers to document the specific content, duration, and frequency of interventions being provided to students (see Figure 12.3). Because it is an open-ended field, teachers can include detailed information such as who is providing the intervention, what materials they are using, what reinforcement parents have been asked to provide, and so forth. This information becomes part of the student's educational history and is retained in the system so that teachers to whom the student is assigned in the future can look back and see what did—and did not—produce results for a particular student.

An additional feature of *easyCBM* that increases its utility and accessibility—and thus its scalability—is the online training for test administration and scoring. In this section of our website, we provide teachers with instructions for reliable administration and scoring of the assessments, as well as videotaped examples of the assessments being administered to students. After

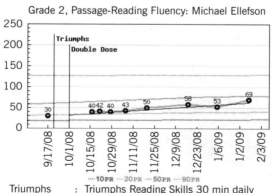

FIGURE 12.3. Individual student progress graph, showing intervention lines and progress over time.

they have completed a series of lessons on how to administer and score each type of assessment, educators can test their proficiency on a series of online test administration performance assessments. Teachers have the opportunity to practice with the assessments until they achieve proficiency by scoring at least 90% on the administration and scoring of each individual measure type. Figure 12.4 presents a screen shot of one of these training modules.

TECHNICAL ADEQUACY OF THE *easyCBM* MEASURES

Although the assessments on the *easyCBM* system are relatively new, a growing body of research exists documenting their reliability and providing evidence of their validity for use as benchmark screeners and measures of progress. Tindal, Nese, and Alonzo (2009a) used hierarchical linear model-

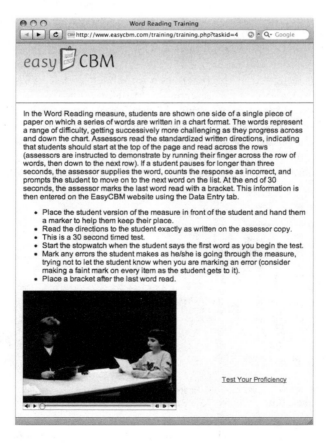

FIGURE 12.4. Screen shot of one of the *easyCBM* test administration and scoring training modules. Copyright by *easyCBM*. Reprinted by permission.

ing (HLM) to examine growth on passage-reading fluency measures related to student characteristics and multiple regression (Tindal, Nese, & Alonzo, 2009b) to examine the relationship between student characteristics, performance on easyCBM reading measures, and student performance on the statewide test of reading. Tindal, Alonzo, and Anderson (2009) report on the development of local reading norms for the fall, winter, and spring benchmark screener assessments, K–8. Alonzo and Tindal (2009) present the results of a study to examine the test–retest and alternate form reliability of the *easyCBM* PM measures. Additional studies involving nationally representative samples are in progress.

CONCLUSION

Although *easyCBM* had its birth as part of our model demonstration project, its impact has far exceeded use by our local district partner in the grant. As of January 12, 2010, the *easyCBM* assessment system had a total of 38,729 registered teacher accounts, with 320,610 unique students having taken 1,157,076 tests (see Figure 12.5). Of the measures available, the multiple-choice reading comprehension tests have been used most widely, followed by the passage-reading fluency measures. It is worth noting that we have not engaged in a plan to market *easyCBM*; it has spread through word of mouth, from one educator to another and via Internet searches. As the number of *easyCBM* users continues to grow, we receive suggestions from teachers and administrators across the country for enhancements they would like to see included.

We have made several significant expansions to the system since our model demonstration project ended. Based on requests from the field, we developed a district version that includes specific benchmark screener assessments, in addition to the PM measures available on the teacher version, as well as different levels of access to facilitate the meaningful sharing of student data while complying with the Family Educational Rights and Privacy Act (FERPA) regulations. In addition, we expanded the assessments offered on *easyCBM* to include K–8 math measures, aligned with the National Council of Teachers of Mathematics' (NCTM) focal point standards. With an average of over 100 new teachers signing up for accounts each day, we anticipate that the impact of *easyCBM* will continue to grow.

As RTI becomes more widely adopted, educators will continue to seek reliable, research-based tools that will facilitate its implementation. With its carefully constructed, sophisticated approach to measurement development and validation and its focused attention to the principles of universal design to help make the system accessible to a wide range of users, we anticipate that *easyCBM* will continue to grow in popularity. The online platform and structure of the database behind the assessment system are both designed to support continued expansion.

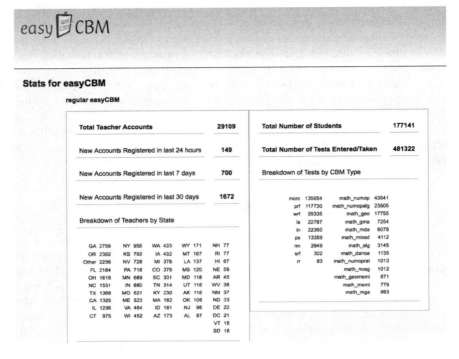

FIGURE 12.5. Statistics on use of the teacher version of *easyCBM* as of January 12, 2010. Copyright by *easyCBM*. Reprinted by permission.

As our district partners explained in Chapter 11 of this volume, having the right tools easily accessible is a critical component in successful RTI implementation. We developed the *easyCBM* assessment system with this in mind and anticipate that other districts adopting RTI will find the system a valuable tool. Of course, although they are very important, assessments are not the only requirement for successful RTI implementation. In Chapter 13, we discuss outcomes of our model demonstration project, with an emphasis on a rubric developed to evaluate how fully RTI has been implemented in a school and initial findings of student-level outcomes.

REFERENCES

Alonzo, J., Ketterlin-Geller, L. R., & Tindal, G. (2007). Curriculum based measurement in reading and math: Providing rigorous outcomes to support learning. In L. Florian (Ed.), *Handbook of special education* (pp. 307–318). Thousand Oaks, CA: Sage.

Alonzo, J., Liu, K., & Tindal, G. (2007). *Examining the technical adequacy of reading comprehension measures in a progress monitoring assessment system* (Technical Report No. 41). Eugene, OR: Behavioral Research and Teaching.

Alonzo, J., & Tindal, G. (2007a). *Examining the technical adequacy of early literacy measures in a progress monitoring assessment system: Letter names, letter sounds, and phoneme segmenting* (Technical Report No. 39). Eugene, OR: Behavioral Research and Teaching.

Alonzo, J., & Tindal, G. (2007b). *Examining the technical adequacy of word reading and passage reading fluency measures in a progress monitoring assessment system* (Technical Report No. 40). Eugene, OR: Behavioral Research and Teaching.

Alonzo, J., & Tindal, G. (2009). *Alternate form and test–retest reliability of easy-CBM reading measures* (Technical Report No. 0906). Eugene, OR: University of Oregon, Behavioral Research and Teaching.

Deno, S. L. (1985). Curriculum-based measurement: The emerging alternative. *Exceptional Children, 52*, 219–232.

Deno, S. L. (2003). Curriculum-based measures: Development and perspectives. *Assessment for Effective Intervention, 28*(3 & 4), 3–12.

Deno, S. L., Fuchs, L. S., Lynn, S., Marston, D., & Shin, J. (2001). Using curriculum-based measurements to establish growth standards for students with learning disabilities. *School Psychology Review, 30*(4), 507–524.

Deno, S. L., Mirkin, P. K., Chiang, B., & Lowry, L. (1980). *Relationships among simple measures of reading and performance on standardized achievement tests* (Research Report No. 20). Minneapolis: Institute for Research on Learning Disabilities, University of Minnesota.

Ehri, L. C. (1991). Development of the ability to read words. In R. Barr, M. L. Kamil, P. B. Mosenthal, & P. D. Pearson (Eds.), *Handbook of reading research* (Vol. 2, pp. 383–417). New York: Longman.

Ehri, L. C. (2005). Learning to read words: Theory, findings, and issues. *Scientific Studies of Reading, 9*, 167–188.

Espin, C. A., Busch, T. W., Shin, J., & Kruschwitz, R. (2001). Curriculum-based measurement in the content areas: Validity of vocabulary matching as an indicator of performance in social studies. *Learning Disabilities Research and Practice, 16*(3), 142–150.

Fiala, C. L., & Sheridan, S. M. (2003). Parent involvement and reading: Using curriculum-based measurement to assess the effects of paired reading. *Psychology in the Schools, 40*(8), 613–626.

Foegen, A., Espin, C. A., Allinder, R. M., & Markell, M. A. (2001). Translating research into practice: Pre-service teachers' beliefs about curriculum-based measurement. *Journal of Special Education, 34*(4), 226–236.

Fuchs, L. (2002). Strategies for making adequate yearly progress [Slide show]. Retrieved March 3, 2005, from the U.S. Department of Education website, *www.ed.gov/admins/lead/account/aypstr/edlite-slide001.html*.

Fuchs, L. S. (2004). The past, present, and future of curriculum-based research. *School Psychology Review, 33*(2). Retrieved July 7, 2005, from Academic Search Premier database.

Graves, A. W., Plasencia-Peinando, J., Deno, S. L., & Johnson, J. R. (2005). Formatively evaluating the reading progress of first-grade English learners in multiple-language classrooms. *Remedial and Special Education, 26,* 215–225.

Hasbrouck, J., & Tindal, G. (2005). *Oral reading fluency: 90 years of measurement* (Tech. Rep. No. 33). Eugene: University of Oregon, College of Education, Behavioral Research and Teaching.

Linacre, J. M. (2006). Winsteps3.61.1 [Computer software]. Chicago: Author. Available at *www.winsteps.com.*

Marston, D., & Magnusson, D. (1988). Curriculum-based measurement: District-level implementation. In J. Garden, J. Zins, & M. Curtis (Eds.), *Alternative educational delivery systems: Enhancing options for all students* (pp. 137–172). Kent, OH: National Association of School Psychologists.

Marston, D., Mirkin, P. K., & Deno, S. L. (1984). Curriculum-based measurement: An alternative to traditional screening, referral, and identification. *Journal of Special Education, 18,* 109–118.

National Institute of Child Health and Human Development. (2000). Report of the National Reading Panel: Teaching children to read: An evidence-based assessment of the scientific research literature on reading and its implications for reading instruction: Reports of the subgroups. (NIH Publication No. 00-4754). Washington, DC: U.S. Government Printing Office. Available at *www.nichd.nih.gov/publications/nrp/smallbook.cfm.*

Ritchey, K. D., & Speece, D. L. (2006). From letter names to word reading: The nascent role of sublexical fluency. *Contemporary Educational Psychology, 31,* 301–327.

Thompson, S. J., Johnstone, C. J., & Thurlow, M. L. (2002). *Universal design applied to large-scale assessments* (Synthesis Report No. 44). Minneapolis: University of Minnesota, National Center on Educational Outcomes.

Tindal, G. (1998). Assessment in learning disabilities. In J. Torgesen & B. Wong (Eds.). *Perspectives in learning disabilities* (pp. 146–152). San Diego, CA: Academic Press.

Tindal, G., Alonzo, J., & Anderson, D. (2009). *Local normative data on easyCBM reading and mathematics: Fall 2009* (Technical Report No. 0918). Eugene: University of Oregon, Behavioral Research and Teaching.

Tindal, G., Nese, J., & Alonzo, J. (2009a). *Hierarchical linear modeling of passage reading fluency growth as a function of student characteristics* (Technical Report No. 0922). Eugene: University of Oregon, Behavioral Research and Teaching.

Tindal, G., Nese, J., & Alonzo, J. (2009b). *Criterion-related evidence using easy-CBM reading measures and student demographics to predict state test performance in grades 3–8* (Technical Report No. 0910). Eugene: University of Oregon, Behavioral Research and Teaching.

Yovanoff, P., Duesbery, L., Alonzo, J., & Tindal, G. (2005). Grade-level invariance of a theoretical causal structure predicting reading comprehension with vocabulary and oral reading fluency. *Educational Measurement: Issues and Practice, 24,* 4–12.

CHAPTER 13

Implementation and Outcomes

Kimy Liu
Julie Alonzo
Gerald Tindal

Our model demonstration project resulted in several key outcomes. Some, such as the creation of the *easyCBM* online assessment system, are fairly easy to document. Others, such as the cultural shift that is transforming the Eugene School District 4J, are more subtle, requiring mechanisms to capture the ways in which response to intervention (RTI) has changed practice at the schools that have adopted it. We decided to focus on systems-level outcomes for the first few years. Our primary objective was to develop the infrastructure and common understandings necessary for change to be adopted deeply. Key educational leaders (general and special education teachers, school psychologists, building and district administrators) were provided with opportunities to become recognized as change agents not only at their individual schools but also in the district as a whole and as leaders in the state's RTI movement. And we created an online assessment and intervention system (*easyCBM*) to ensure that student data are available for teachers, parents, and other decision makers in the district. These, then, are the key outcomes of our project: *easyCBM*, the forms and structures that enable district and school educators to share a common understanding of RTI, and teacher leaders within the district with the capacity to serve as coaches to other educators adopting RTI.

Two additional outcomes—a rubric designed to assess the degree to which a school has successfully implemented the most critical components of the RTI approach and evidence of improved student learning—are worth noting. Creating and piloting the implementation rubric involved more than a year of work. The result, a rubric grounded in the literature with evidence of its reliability and validity for use in elementary schools adopting RTI, is described in detail in this chapter and is provided in its entirety as an appendix. Because our approach was to look at systemic change, student outcomes at the system level are still a number of years away. The full impact of the district's adoption of RTI cannot adequately be assessed until a sufficient number of teachers and schools have implemented the approach with integrity. However, the students of early adopters (those teachers with whom we worked throughout the model demonstration project) do provide some evidence of the impact on student learning. We present data from a case study of five of these students in the second half of this chapter.

THE RTI IMPLEMENTATION RUBRIC

As schools begin to adopt RTI, they need a means by which to evaluate the adoption. Systems-level changes require evaluation tools that give a broad and deep perspective on the innovation being implemented. A number of rubrics have been developed across states, one of which has been referenced in the first two parts of this volume (Project MP3, discussed in Chapters 2–7). As part of our work, we decided to develop a rubric to evaluate the degree to which schools had implemented RTI and then validate the instrument for use in elementary schools. Two features set our rubric apart from others. First, we focused on grounding each component of the rubric in the research literature, and, second, we evaluated the technical adequacy of the instrument through a focused study of its use. The information gleaned from use of this rubric can inform instructional and professional development planning, as well as resource allocation and goal setting.

The Six Essential Components of the RTI Model

The six components included in our RTI implementation rubric are distilled from the relevant research literature of RTI, with an emphasis on elements of RTI implementation that influence students' learning outcomes. Although different conceptualizations of RTI are present in the literature, these six components appear across multiple models and capture the most important components of RTI in practice. These components include: (1) effective Tier 1 instruction (Burns & Ysseldyke, 2005; Denton, Vaughn, & Fletcher, 2003; Fuchs, Mock, Morgan, & Young, 2003; Marston et al., 2007), (2) universal screening (Foorman & Ciancio, 2005; Fuchs, 2003; Jenkins, 2003; VanDerHeyden, Witt, & Naguin, 2003), (3) effective Tier 2 and Tier 3 interventions (Fuchs, 1995; Fuchs & Fuchs, 1998; Harn, Kame'enui, & Simmons, 2007), (4) progress monitoring (Burns & Ysseldyke, 2005;

Christ & Hintze, 2007; Gresham et al., 2005), (5) evidence-based decision making (Bollman, Silberglitt, & Gibbons, 2007; Callender, 2007; Marston et al., 2007; Tilly, 2003), and (6) organizational support (Justice, 2006; Lau et al., 2006).

Effective Tier 1 Instruction

In our RTI implementation rubric, Tier 1 instruction was defined as the comprehensive core reading instruction provided to all students in general education classes (Burns & Ysseldyke, 2005; Denton et al., 2003; Fuchs et al., 2003; Graden, Stoller, & Poth, 2007; Marston et al., 2007; McMaster & Wagner, 2007) for a sufficient amount of time to meet grade-level instructional goals (Harn et al., 2007; Justice, 2006). Teachers should teach all "5 Big Ideas" specified in the National Reading Panel Report (Institute of Child Health and Human Development [NICHD], 2000; Foorman & Torgesen, 2001; O'Connor, Harty, & Fulmer, 2005; Snow, Burns, & Griffin, 1998) or relevant ones to specific grade levels (Good, Simmons, & Kame'enui, 2001; Marston, 2005), using evidence-based strategies (NICHD, 2000). Because the quality of Tier 1 instruction affects the first step in identifying students at risk of developing reading problems (Speece, Case, & Molloy, 2003), the RTI assessment rubric includes criteria to evaluate the Tier 1 instruction in terms of content, duration, use of time, student time on task, and teacher satisfaction.

Multiple studies (e.g., Bollman et al., 2007; Callender, 2007; Foorman & Moats, 2004; O'Connor et al., 2005; Peterson, Prasse, & Shinn, 2007; Pikulski, 1998; Treptow, 2006; Vaughn, Linan-Thompson, & Hickman, 2003) recommend that schools allot at minimum 90 minutes each day for reading, writing, and language arts. This 90-minute block is designed to ensure that sufficient time is reserved to teach and develop reading. Because this duration of instruction devoted to reading is so prevalent in the research literature, we used the minimum of 90 minutes as an additional indicator of instructional quality in Tier 1 instruction.

In addition to the amount of time allotted to Tier 1 reading instruction, the use of instructional time, as well as teacher behaviors, is indicative of the quality of instruction provided. Allington (2002) reports that exemplary elementary school teachers spend at least 50% of instructional time throughout the school day on reading and writing. They teach reading using various materials, including curricula from other content areas (such as math and science). These effective teachers are often engaged in active teaching, using explicit explanation and direct instruction, and modeling useful comprehension strategies employed by proficient readers. Moreover, there is a growing body of literature (Edmonds & Briggs, 2003; Foorman & Moats, 2004; Foorman & Schatschneider, 2003; Graves, Gersten, & Hagger, 2004; Hagger, Gersten, Baker, & Graves, 2003; Kim, Briggs, &

Vaughn, 2003) on classroom observation that links the use of instructional time to effective teaching behaviors. These studies provide evidence that effective use of instructional time increases the percentage of time students are engaged in active reading.

Academic learning time is the portion of instructional time in which students are actively engaged in learning. Gambrell, Wilson, and Gantt (1981) reported that, on average, good readers maintained higher engagement rate (as indicated by percent of time on task) than poor readers during reading instruction. In this rubric, in the context of reading instruction, "on task" is defined as students sitting in their seats properly, eyes looking either at teachers or at the instructional materials attentively, and focusing on assigned reading or writing activities.

Teachers' perception of the curriculum can influence their use and delivery of that curriculum, as well as the quality of instruction. Similarly, students' beliefs about their ability and their perception of the curriculum also influence their buy-in for the curricular programs, thereby influencing the quality of learning (Blumenfeld et al., 1991). With this in mind, a criterion to solicit teachers' understanding of RTI implementation and students' opinions of their instructional experience was included.

Universal Screening

The purposes of universal screening are threefold: to determine the quality of general education (Tier 1) instruction, to identify students who are at risk for long-term difficulties in learning to read, and to cluster students to form homogenous intervention groups for targeted and focused differentiated instruction (Foorman & Ciancio, 2005; Kamps & Greenwood, 2003). Practitioners use universal screening to determine whether the instructional quality in general education classes is sufficient to bring most students to grade-level benchmarks and what progress rate can be reasonably expected of individual students (Foorman & Ciancio, 2005; Fuchs, 2003; Jenkins, 2003; VanDerHeyden et al., 2003). Although RTI is designed to identify students who are at risk of failing to meet grade-level performance benchmarks, researchers appear to be in agreement that a low score on a screening measure should not be considered sufficient to qualify students for differentiated interventions. If a significant number of students in class all scored below the cut score on the screening measure, then improving Tier 1 instruction should take priority over providing students with additional interventions (Fuchs et al., 2003; Speece et al., 2003).

In addition to technical adequacy, the implementation of universal screening is judged by frequency of test administration and data presentation, targeted students, and uses of the screening data. To avoid selection bias, the screening measures must be administered to all students. To make the presentation of the screening assessment data user-friendlier, the data must be arranged in a way that facilitates the identification of low-performing students and the creation of homogenous intervention groups.

Effective Tier 2 and Tier 3 Interventions

Consistently across the different studies reviewed, Tier 2 and Tier 3 interventions were considered appropriate for students identified as at risk of developing reading difficulty or who did not respond to Tier 1 instruction, as indicated by the fact that their levels and rates of progress were both lower than those of their peers (Fuchs, 1995; Fuchs & Fuchs, 1998; Harn et al., 2007). In a well-functioning school, it would be expected that approximately 15% of the student population would need Tier 2 interventions and that only 5% of students would need Tier 3 interventions (Simmons, Kame'enui, Beck, Brewer, & Fien, 2003). To accelerate these students' learning, teachers must change the learning conditions to intensify instruction (Denton, Fletcher, Anthony, & Francis, 2006; Fuchs et al., 2003; Kovaleski, 2003; Marston, 2005; Torgesen et al., 2001). One way to help struggling readers accelerate their learning is to provide purposeful and strategic intervention (Foorman & Torgesen, 2001; Torgesen et al., 2001; Vellutino et al., 1996; Vellutino, Scanlon, & Tanzman, 1998), using research-based supplemental programs for Tier 2 students and research-based intervention programs for Tier 3 students (Coyne, Kame'enui, Simmons, & Harn, 2004). Another way to meet these students' needs is to modify or reteach the selected sections of the research-based core curriculum with these students.

Tier 2 and Tier 3 interventions differ from Tier 1 instruction in their targeted population, purpose, instructional emphases, frequency, duration, and intensity of instruction (Harn et al., 2007; Marston, 2005; O'Connor et al., 2005; Tilly, 2003). Tier 2 and Tier 3 interventions are provided to students who cannot meet grade-level benchmark with Tier 1 instruction alone (Dickson & Bursuck, 1998; Kamps & Greenwood, 2003; McMaster, Fuchs, Fuchs, & Compton, 2005; Vaughn, Wanzek, Linan-Thompson, & Murray, 2007). The intervention programs at Tier 2 and Tier 3 are supplementary to the core curriculum (Simmons et al., 2003). The purpose of Tier 2 and Tier 3 interventions is to remediate specific areas of skill deficits; therefore, they are targeted, purposeful, and focused on only one to three of the five critical aspects of reading as specified by the report of the National Reading Panel (Foorman & Ciancio, 2005; O'Connor et al., 2005; VanDerHeyden & Jimerson, 2005; Vaughn et al., 2003).

To accelerate at-risk students' learning and to prevent future performance deficits, teachers provide these low-performing students with scaffolding and immediate feedback during additional practice on essential skills (e.g., alphabetic principle and decoding) so that students can achieve mastery in basic reading skills (Foorman & Moats, 2004; O'Connor,

2000; Torgesen et al., 2001; Torgesen, Rashotte, Alexander, Alexander, & MacPhee, 2003; Vellutino et al., 1996). To increase students' engagement rate and the intensity of instruction, these interventions should be delivered in small-group settings (Bollman et al., 2007; Foorman & Ciancio, 2005; Kamps & Greenwood, 2003).

Evidence of effective Tier 2 and Tier 3 interventions can be obtained by a combination of observing Tier 2 and Tier 3 interventions, attending school-based meetings (to observe how decisions are made in configuring Tier 2 and Tier 3 intervention groups), reviewing school schedules and chosen intervention program materials, and conducting teacher and student interviews.

Progress Monitoring

In the literature reviewed, progress monitoring (PM) is defined as the regular collection of students' responses to a chosen assessment. The purpose of PM is to document students' incremental change on the targeted early literacy skills (Good, Gruba, & Kaminski, 2002) and to gather evidence on whether students have responded to additional instructional supports provided within an RTI approach (Burns & Ysseldyke, 2005; Christ & Hintze, 2007; Gresham et al., 2005).

In the RTI assessment rubric, the implementation of PM is judged by the technical adequacy of the measures, the quality of data collection, and the presentation of data (Good et al., 2002). Without evidence of technical adequacy, the use of PM measures might not be justifiable. If the tests are not administered and scored according to standardized protocols and the data are not gathered systematically and regularly, the inferences made from the data being gathered might be invalid. Likewise, if the data are presented in such a way that teachers cannot easily differentiate students who make good progress from students who do not, the utility of the test would be in question.

Evidence-Based Decision Making

Evidence-based decision making is the logic and rationale behind RTI (Reschly, Coolong-Chaffin, Christenson, & Gutkin, 2007). By practicing evidence-based decision making, teachers and administrators use scientific inquiry and empirical evidence to guide the decision-making process in the design and delivery of instructional service (Stoner & Green, 1992). This approach is best illustrated in the problem-solving model within the RTI framework (Bollman et al., 2007; Callender, 2007; Graden et al., 2007; Marston et al., 2007; Tilly, 2003; VanDerHeyden et al., 2003). Good, Simmons, Kame'enui, and Chard (2003) advocate that the evidence-based decision-making process and outcomes should not only be reliable and valid but also manualized, meaning that other qualified educators review-ing the same set of data, using the same decision rules, would arrive at the same conclusion. For evidence-based decision making to be manualized, all instructional support team members (i.e., general and special education teachers, administrators, etc.) should be knowledgeable about the assess-ments, the curriculum, and the instructional delivery. More important, all team members should have a thorough understanding of the decision rules and how to use the data to modify instruction.

Organizational Support

The effectiveness of RTI is influenced by both the coherence of instructional support across different tiers of interventions and the dynamic feedback between instruction and assessment. Organizational support is instrumen-tal in attaining these goals. Organizational support can be found through examples of strong leadership that organizes administrative support (Jus-tice, 2006; Lau et al., 2006) and provides targeted and meaningful pro-fessional development for teachers (Batsche et al., 2005). Administrators with strong instructional leadership secure the necessary funding, time, and human resources to accomplish these tasks (Fuchs & Fuchs, 2006). In addition, they set clear standards or expectations for professional train-ing and program implementation, as well as helping teachers prioritize the activities pertinent to the design and implementation of RTI (Justice, 2006; Lau et al., 2006; Marston et al., 2007).

According to Hiebert (1999) and Friend (2000), opportunities for teachers to learn new teaching methods aimed at enhancing students' learning should be sustained by collegial support and ongoing collegial collaboration. These learning opportunities are often anchored by shared visions and explicit goals that are related to students' cognitive processes, curricula, and pedagogy (Friend, 2000; Garet, Porter, Desimone, Birman, & Kwang, 2001). Professional collaboration appears to facilitate use of col-lective knowledge and skills. Teachers benefit from observing other teach-ers and reflecting on the reasons for their effectiveness.

In contrast, insufficient professional training often leads to ineffec-tive teaching and weak support from teachers. General education teach-ers often have not received adequate preservice training on how to dif-ferentiate instruction and use data to inform instruction (Lyon, Fletcher, & Barnes, 2002). To avoid the problems associated with poor training, leadership must include professional development opportunities, including coaching and time to collaborate with colleagues (Callender, 2007). In RTI reading interventions, teachers need professional training on how to imple-ment research-based reading instruction and PM effectively. Within an RTI approach, professional collaboration and administrative support were reported as being important in designing and implementing research-based reading instruction and PM (Grimes & Kurns, 2003; Kamps & Greenwood, 2003; Kovaleski, 2003; Marston, 2005).

THE RTI IMPLEMENTATION RUBRIC IN PRACTICE: RESULTS OF THE FIELD TESTING

After the implementation rubric was developed (during Year 2 of our model demonstration project), it was field tested in the two schools partnering with us in Year 3 (see Table 13.1 for school demographics, Table 13.2 for teacher demographics, and Table 13.3 for student demographics). Using the rubric, the RTI implementation in School 1 was judged as fully implemented across all six components by both independent raters and participating teachers. School 1 had all the essential components of RTI in place. At School 2, there was slightly less agreement, with one rater agreeing with participating teachers that RTI was partially implemented in five of the six components and fully implemented in the sixth and a second rater indicating that two components, PM and universal screening, were fully implemented. It appeared that staff at School 2 were still developing consensus about what was meant by evidence-based decision making and were still solidifying buy-in among staff. Teachers in School 2 needed more ongoing technical support in interpreting assessment data and using the data to modify instruction. But all sources of data indicated that School 1 was in a more advanced stage of RTI implementation than School 2.

TABLE 13.1. School Characteristics

	School 1	School 2
School structure	K–5; three classes per grade	K–5; two classes per grade for grades K–3 and four for grades 4/5 combined classes
Enrollment	500+	< 300
Special programs (e.g., Title I, ELL programs)	Non–Title I school No ELL programs Regional Learning Center on campus	Non–Title I school No ELL programs Regional Learning Center on campus
Other instructional supports	Reading specialist, student achievement coordinators	Reading specialist
Prior experience in PM before adopting RTI model	Yes; they used DIBELS for screening and PM	No prior experience in PM

Note. Data from MDP-RTI study: school profiles.

TABLE 13.2. Teacher Characteristics

	School 1				School 2	
	Teacher 1	Teacher 2	Teacher 3	Teacher J	Teacher 4	Teacher 5
Primary assignment	General education	General education	Special education	Instructional Assistant	General education	Special education
Highest level of education	BA	MA	MA	BA	MA	MA
Teaching certification	Yes, general education	Yes, general education	Yes, general education	Certified as instructional assistant	Yes, general education	Yes, special education
Years of experience in teaching	6	10	1	8	26	29
Years of teaching students with disabilities	3	10	1	8	26	29
Instructional role(s) in RTI	Tiers 1 and 2	Tiers 1 and 2	Tier 2	Tiers 2 and 3	Tiers 1 and 2	Tiers 2 and 3

Note. Date from MDP-RTI study: Teacher survey.

TABLE 13.3. Student Characteristics

	School 1			School 2	
Student	Carl	Diane	Eric	Albert	Becky
Grade	2	2	2	2	2
Gen. ed. teacher	Teacher 1	Teacher 1	Teacher 2	Teacher 4	Teacher 4
Race	White	Unknown	White	White	White
Primary language	English	English	English	English	English
Have IEP?	No	No	No	No	No
Have been retained in grade	No	No	No	No	No
Screening score, CWPM (percentile)	8 (1st–10th)	24 (11–20th)	29 (11–20th)	10 (1st–10th)	17 (11–20th)
Recommended to receive Tier 3 interventions	Yes	Yes	Yes	Yes	Yes

Note. Data from MDP-RTI study: student characteristic surveys; district assessment data; teacher interviews. Grade 2 general education teachers nominated the three lowest students in their classes who fit the selection criteria: (1) scoring at or below 20th percentile in the district's fall reading assessment and (2) being recommended for Tier 3 interventions. When three students' parents from a class all gave consent, two with the lowest scores were chosen. In Teacher 2's class, only one student's parents gave consent.

Table 13.4 lists examples of evidence gathered to rate the different components of RTI implementation. These examples are provided as a guide to others using the rubric. In addition to classroom observation data and analyses of school artifacts such as the master schedule, we used interviews with teachers to gather information about how well RTI was being implemented at each site. Table 13.5 lists the initial interview questions used, categorizing each by the component of the RTI implementation rubric it was intended to assess. After observations of a few students from each teacher's class, follow-up interview questions probed specifically the profiles of individual students and the teacher's decision making related to them (see Table 13.6).

TABLE 13.4. Examples of Evidence Categorized by Types

Types of evidence	Examples
Archival Records	• Students' Student Support Team (SST) Plan or IEPs (if applicable). • Students' scores on the PM measures. • Students' district reading assessment scores.
Documents	• Agenda or minutes of professional development meetings. • Agenda or minutes of district-based/school-based RTI meetings. • Agenda or minutes of school-based grade-level meetings. • Students' progress reports retrieved from the *easyCBM* website that pertain to students' PM scores, progress measures used, as well as interventions that were implemented.
Direct observation	• Classroom observations: Identify the programs being used in class. • Classroom observations: Use E-COVE to document the number of minutes teachers spend teaching the "5 Big Ideas" as specified in NRP 2000. • Classroom observation: Evaluate the effectiveness of instruction using the Classroom Observation Checklist (Gersten, Baker, Haager, & Graves, 2005). • Classroom observations: Describe the mood of the class, evidence of effectiveness of instruction in the field notes. • School-based meeting: Describe how teachers interpret data and use data to inform decision making in the field notes.
Interviews	• Two interviews for each participating educator, one prior to the classroom observation, the other after the classroom observation.
Physical artifacts	• School's master schedules. • Students' *easyCBM* scored protocols. • Students' other work products, if appropriate.

TABLE 13.5. Organization of the Initial Interview Questions and Six Critical Components

	US	T1	T2/3	PM	ED	OS
How do you determine which students receive additional intervention?	X				X	
Tell me about the curriculum you use. How do you know it is a research-based curriculum?		X				X
Tell me about your routine in teaching reading on a typical day.		X	X			
What are your instructional emphases in reading?		X	X			
What kind of instructional supports do the students with most intensive needs receive?			X			
How do you provide instructional support for students who have severe reading skill deficits?			X			
Describe the three-tiered intervention in your school.		X	X			
How do you monitor students' learning outcomes? Tell me about the tool(s) you use.				X		
How do you know if the intervention was effective?					X	
What professional training do you receive for this curricular program?						X
What do you know about RTI? How did you learn about RTI?						X
Describe the instructional support you receive from your principal and other teachers in the school.						X

Note. US, universal screening; T1, Tier 1 instruction; T2/3, Tier 2 and Tier 3 interventions; PM, progress monitoring; ED, evidence-based decision making; OS, organizational support.

TABLE 13.6. Organization of the Second Interview Questions and Six Critical Components

	US	T1	T2/3	PM	ED	OS
How do you determine Student X needs additional intervention?	X				X	
What kinds of skill deficits does student have? How does the chosen curriculum address Student X's educational need?		X				X
What were your instructional emphases for Student X?		X	X			
What instructional support does Student X receive?		X	X			
How do you provide Student X additional instructional support?			X			
How does Student X move through the RTI system?		X	X			
How do you determine if Student X makes progress?				X	X	
How does the RTI team determine what support Student X needs?					X	
How do professional training and collaboration with your colleagues help you implement reading programs under RTI?						X
How do professional training and collaboration influence the quality of instruction you provide for Student X?						X
How would you grade the support you receive from your principal and your colleagues?						X

Note. US, universal screening; T1, Tier 1 instruction; T2/3, Tier 2 and Tier 3 interventions; PM, progress monitoring; ED, evidence-based decision making; OS, organizational support.

STUDENT PERFORMANCE DATA

During the field testing of the RTI implementation rubric, we conducted a case study of five second-grade students who had been identified as needing support beyond Tier 1 instruction. Over the course of 8 weeks, the students were observed in their classrooms during Tier 1 reading instruction and Tier 2 and 3 interventions, and all staff who instructed the literacy development of these students were interviewed to gather additional information about the instruction the students had received in the weeks prior to the classroom observations. In addition, we gathered information about the students' reading skill and rate of progress.

The five students, drawn from three different teachers' classrooms at two schools, were selected by their teachers for participation in the case study because they fit the selection criteria and had received parental permission to participate: all had scored below the 20th percentile on the fall screening assessments and had been recommended for Tier 3 interventions. None of the students had been retained a grade in school, nor did any of them have an individualized education plan (IEP) at the time of the case study (although one was subsequently qualified for special education services). All five students had grown up speaking English in their homes, and all five were identified as Caucasian. Three of the five were male. Table 13.3 provides demographic information for the five students.

Based on their scores on the fall screener assessment, all five students were identified as being at risk for reading failure. Carl[1] and Albert scored only 8 and 10 correct words per minute (CWPM) on the fall passage-reading fluency measure, respectively, putting them below the 10th percentile for second-grade students in the fall. Becky scored 17 CWPM in the fall, and Diane and Eric scored 24 and 29 CWPM, respectively. These scores placed them in between the 11th and 20th percentiles for second-grade students in the fall. On this measure, a score of 57 CWPM would have placed the students in the 50th percentile, so all five were performing significantly below expected levels (see Tables 13.7 and 13.8 for additional fall performance measures).

As is recommended in the RTI literature, students' instruction varied, as teachers focused on different aspects of literacy during whole-class Tier 1 instruction (see Table 13.9) and small group Tier 2 and 3 interventions (see Table 13.10). Instruction for all five students focused on addressing skill deficits, although the specific instructional foci varied by student. During Tier 2 and 3 interventions, Becky's and Albert's teachers focused primarily on phonics and fluency, whereas more of Eric's Tier 2 interventions focused on phonemic awareness and vocabulary. Carl's and Diane's Tier 2 interventions focused on fluency, whereas their Tier 3 interventions

---

[1]All names are pseudonyms to protect confidentiality.

TABLE 13.7. Targeted Students' Fall Screening Data: School 1

	DIBELS[a] CWPM (%ile)			easyCBM[b] CWPM (range of %ile ranking)			Composite percentile ranking
Students	NWF[c]	ORF[d]	Composite risk status	WRF[e]	PSF[f]	MCRC[g]	
Carl	30 (8)	6 (4)	Intensive; needs substantial intervention	8 (1–10)	10 (1–10)	—	9
Diane	32 (11)	16 (13)	Intensive; needs substantial intervention	20 (11–20)	24 (11–20)	7	25
Eric	41 (21)	28 (26)	Strategic, additional intervention	28	29 (11–20)	6	26

Note. Data from teacher interviews, school schedule, School 1 DIBELS grade 2 fall benchmark report, School 1 *easyCBM* grade 2 fall benchmark report, *easyCBM* PM scores interpretation guidelines.
[a]DIBELS fall benchmark was administered September 4–10.
[b]*easyCBM* fall benchmark was administered September 22–26.
[c]Nonsense-word fluency. Goal: 50 letter sounds per minute.
[d]Oral-reading fluency. Goal: 44 CWPM.
[e]Word-reading fluency. Grade 2 fall: 10%ile = 12 cwpm, 20%ile = 20 cwpm, 50%ile = 40 cwpm, 75%ile = 62 cwpm, 90%ile = 80 cwpm.
[f]Passage-reading fluency. Grade 2 fall: 10%ile = 18 cwpm, 20%ile = 30 cwpm, 50%ile = 57 cwpm, 75%ile = 84 cwpm, 90%ile = 127 cwpm.
[g]Multiple-choice reading comprehension. Grade 2 fall: 10%ile = 3, 20%ile = 5, 50%ile = 8, 75%ile = 9, 90%ile = 11. Total possible score = 12.

TABLE 13.8. Targeted Students' Fall Screening Data: School 2

	easyCBM CWPM (range of %ile ranking)[a]			Composite percentile ranking
Students	WRF[a]	PSF[b]	MCRC[d]	
Albert	14 (11–20)	10 (1–10)	1	6
Becky	8 (1–10)	17 (1–10)	4	11

Note. Data from teacher interviews, school schedule, School 2 *easyCBM* grade 2 fall benchmark report, *easyCBM* PM scores interpretation guidelines.
[a]Red = 1–10 percentiles; yellow = 11–20 percentiles.
[b]Word-reading fluency. Grade 2 fall: 10%ile = 12 CWPM, 20%ile = 20 CWPM, 50%ile = 40 CWPM, 75%ile = 62 CWPM, 90%ile = 80 CWPM.
[c]Passage-reading fluency. Grade 2 fall: 10%ile = 18 CWPM, 20%ile = 30 CWPM, 50%ile = 57 CWPM, 75%ile = 84 CWPM, 90%ile = 127 CWPM.
[d]Multiple-choice reading comprehension. Grade 2 fall: 10%ile = 3, 20%ile = 5, 50%ile = 8, 75%ile = 9, 90%ile = 11. Total possible score = 12.

TABLE 13.9. Tier 1 Instruction: Instructional Minutes Spent on Activities during Case Study Week

	School 1		School 2
	Carl and Diane	Eric	Albert and Becky
Teacher-led activities focusing on:			
Phonemic awareness	0	9	0
Phonics	31	50	0
Fluency	23	42	0
Vocabulary	47	35	0
Comprehension	63	33	0
Student-led activities			
Read-aloud[a]	49	31	12
Silent reading[b]	8	63	17
Independent seatwork[c]	36	26	0
Total time on academic activities	257	289	29
Total time on other activities, such as transitions, discipline, or housekeeping	150	119	109
Total time spent on Tier 1 Instruction	407	408	138
% of time spent on academic activities	63	71	21
% of time students appeared on task	80+	80+	50–80
Average scores of Classroom Observation Checklist[d] (range of scores)	42 (40–44)	41 (39–43)	N/A

Note. Data from classroom observation.
[a]Students read list of words or connected text with minimal teacher scaffolding.
[b]Students read the assigned passages or books of their choice quietly. Teacher sometimes asked vocabulary and comprehension questions afterward.
[c]The worksheets were directly related to phonics, vocabulary, or comprehension.
[d]In effective classes, teachers scored at or above 39 when summed across all 24 items.

TABLE 13.10. Tier 2 and Tier 3 Interventions: Instructional Minutes Spent on Activities during Case Study Week

| | School 1 | | | | School 2 | |
| | Carl and Diane | | Eric | | Albert and Becky | |
	Tier 2	Tier 3	Tier 2	Tier 3	Tier 2	Tier 3
Teacher-led activities focusing on:						
Phonemic awareness	0	0	29	0	0	3
Phonics	1	12	9	11	12	124
Fluency	54	11	12	12	11	123
Vocabulary	18	9	34	5	9	10
Comprehension	5	3	9	12	3	13
Student-led activities						
Read-aloud	7	0	15	0	0	27
Silent reading	11	0	6	0	0	37
Independent seatwork	8	0	12	0	0	0
Total time on academic activities	109[a]	35	125	40	35	227
Total time on nonacademic activities	25	2	29	5	10	40
Total time for reading instruction	134[a]	38	154	45	45	267
% of time spent on academic activities	81	92	81	89	78	85
% of time students appeared on task	90+	90+	90+	90+	64	90+
Average scores of Classroom Observation Checklist (range)	40 (38–42)	42 (41–43)	44 (42–46)	42 (41–44)	37 (32–41)	43 (42–44)

Note. Data from classroom observation.
[a]Four-day week.

touched almost equally on phonics, fluency, and vocabulary. Based on students' performance on the fall screener, as well as additional data such as attendance, performance on PM assessments, and instructional intervention/progress monitoring (IIPM) team recommendations, case study students either continued to receive the same level of instructional support or had their instructional support adjusted in an attempt to better meet their needs (see Table 13.11) as the year progressed.

Figures 13.1, 13.2, and 13.3 (pp. 360–361) show the PM data for the five students, with the straight diagonal lines indicating aim lines (expected progress) and the more jagged lines indicating actual observed progress. The figures provided a way for teachers to examine the relative positions between the trend line and aim line as students progressed toward the year-end goal. Of these five students, Albert, from School 2, and Eric, from School 1, were both on track in terms of their progress (see Figure 13.1). Both Diane's and Becky's progress was approaching the aim line, with an upward trend, whereas Carl's progress was below the aim line with little discernable progress. In all, two of the five case study students were on track, two of them had made some progress, and only one student was not making good progress.

Although these results (with four of the five students making better-than-anticipated progress toward catching up to their grade-level peers) might suggest the effectiveness of the RTI approach for improving the learning outcomes of at-risk students, significant limitations related to sample size, potential selection bias, and the short duration of the case study demand caution in drawing any conclusions based on these data. We offer the cases as an initial look at how impact on student learning might be assessed in hope that others will find the information useful.

Batsche and colleagues (2005) and Fuchs and colleagues (2003) suggest that implementing RTI can improve academic outcomes for all students. Although the case studies provide some indication that implementation of RTI might be beneficial to students' progress, the data are insufficient to draw any real conclusions. Between September and January, there is an expected growth rate of 1.4 words per week on the second-grade passage-reading fluency measures on *easyCBM* for students performing at the 50th percentile (Alonzo, Tindal, Ulmer, & Glasgow, 2006). On average, students in the case study exceeded this growth rate. The one student (Carl) who failed to make significant progress toward his instructional goal during the 8 weeks in which data were collected showed a nine-word improvement, a rate of 1.3 words per week, which is slightly less than the expected rate of growth. In other words, although Carl was improving, his rate of improvement was insufficient to close the gap between his achievement and that of grade-level peers.

(text resumes on page 360)

TABLE 13.11. Documentation of Evidence-Based Decision Making

	School 1			School 2	
	Carl	Diane	Eric	Albert	Becky
Data used: *easyCBM* PM data					
Three data points since last data meeting	X	X	X	X	X
Description of progress	Flatline; below aim line	Upward trend; below aim line	Upward trend; on track	Upward trend; below aim line	No trend detected; below aim line
Teacher input					
Attendance	Good	Absence and tardiness	Good	Some absence	Good
Classroom performance	Good; with attending issues	Good	Good; with attending issues	Good; close monitoring is needed	Good; close monitoring is needed
Additional assessments	10/29: Test for eligibility	No	No	No	No

Others (specified)	No	Troubled home life	No	This is his seventh school	Mom resisted the idea of testing
Decision-making process					
Follow decision rules	X	X	X	No explicit decision rules	No explicit decision rules
Decisions made by a multidisciplinary team	X	X	X	Decisions made by two general education teachers	Decisions made by two general education teachers
Decisions made					
Change of current interventions	No	No	Yes; move from Group 2 to Group 3 in Tier 2 interventions	No	No
Refer to receive special education	Pending the results of the evaluation	No	No	No	No

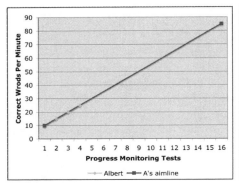
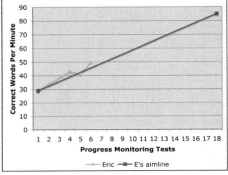

FIGURE 13.1. Progress of two "on-track" students, case study students Albert (School 2) and Eric (School 1).

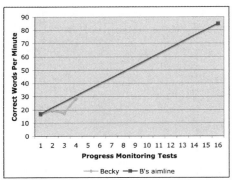
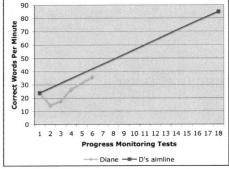

FIGURE 13.2. Progress of two "approaching" students, case study students Becky (School 2) and Diane (School 1).

Findings from the case study suggested that both partial and full implementation of RTI might lead to improved student learning outcomes, although caution is warranted given the small sample size and the lack of a control group. The RTI approach at School 1 was considered fully implemented across all six components of the rubric based on all sources of data. Two of the three case study students at School 1 demonstrated above-average growth rate, with the remaining student demonstrating slightly less than the expected rate of growth. The average rate of growth on the passage-reading fluency measures of the three students at School 1 was 2.2 words per week. When the data for the sole nonresponding student were removed, the average rate of progress of the two remaining students was

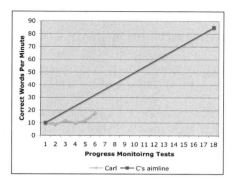

FIGURE 13.3. Progress of a nonresponder, case study student Carl (School 1). The trajectory of Carl's progress was rather flat in comparison with his expected progress. He appeared not to be responding to the provided instruction and interventions.

2.7 CWPM per week, almost double the expected growth rate for students in grade 2 *who are already performing at the 50th percentile*. It is worth noting that the accelerated learning demonstrated by all five case study students is a marked improvement over learning gains typically made by students who begin the year far below grade-level peers, as did all five of the students in our case study.

In contrast, School 2 had lower levels of RTI implementation based on the RTI implementation rubric yet had an average rate of progress of 2.25 CWPM per week across the two students. Again, this rate of growth substantially exceeds the expected growth rate for students in this grade level, 1.4 words per minute. Given the short duration of the study, this finding is promising for the RTI approach in general. However, as in all case studies, the small sample size prevents generalizing beyond the immediate cases. Perhaps a larger sample would reveal more conclusive differences; however, it is equally plausible that the level of RTI implementation is less important to student outcomes than the adoption of the RTI approach in general. Additional research is needed in this area.

CONCLUSION

Fullan (2001) writes that lasting school reform cannot take place without a clear focus on changing the culture of the schools in which that reform is to be enacted, along with substantial support from school leaders. The Oregon model demonstration project suggests that these factors are also important in successful implementation of the RTI model in elementary schools. In addition, however, the RTI model requires several key resources: appropriate screening and PM measures, an efficient system by which to make those measures available to educators, effective curriculum and intervention materials, and the flexibility to change student, teacher, and instructional assistant schedules to take advantage of the limited resources available to students in need.

With these factors in place, the findings suggest that the RTI approach can be implemented at elementary schools. Moreover, where it is implemented with fidelity, we have seen preliminary data to indicate that this approach can improve student achievement, as well as enhance the collegiality among school employees. None of our data support Huberman's (1993) assertion that U.S. educators, being independent artisans, would rebel against policies that would force more collaboration and conformity. Rather, our findings support Nias's (1989) and Talbert and McLaughlin's (2002) belief that collaboration actually improves educators' artisanship.

In fact, one of the strengths of the RTI approach often mentioned by the school district partners, both teachers and administrators, centered on the way in which the RTI approach fostered increased collaboration and a stronger feeling of community at their schools. It would be interesting to investigate whether this same interpretation would be shared by teachers at the secondary level—all of the teachers in our model demonstration project were elementary educators. As the district expands the model into the middle and high school levels in the coming years, it is likely to need substantive changes.

Differences in school context related to scheduling, content specialization of instruction and staff, less established assessments for screening and monitoring the progress of older students in reading, and a dearth of evidence-based interventions designed for use with secondary students present significant challenges. Moving RTI into secondary settings is likely to require a reconceptualization rather than merely an extension of approaches successful at the elementary level. Additional research is needed in this area.

The University of Oregon and Eugene School District 4J model demonstration project resulted in positive outcomes at the district, school, classroom, and individual teacher levels. These outcomes, however, were not achieved without a great deal of effort on the part of all participants. Teachers struggled at first with flexible scheduling, the expectation that they would use data to inform all their discussions about students, and the use of the online assessment system. District administrators fielded concerns from parents about their children's test performance and from union representatives about the amount of time teachers would be expected to devote to collecting assessment data, meeting with their colleagues, and logging information about interventions they were trying. Special education teachers and school psychologists at times struggled with the ways in which their roles were altered by the adoption of RTI. Despite these challenges, however, the story remains one of success.

Whereas before, teachers had depended on their impression of student need and learning progress to guide their instructional decision making, they now had a variety of evidence-based assessments, K–8, at their fingertips. The technology of *easyCBM* now facilitated record keeping and the sharing of information about curriculum and instruction that have proven to be successful with individual students and—perhaps even more important—about those that did not positively affect student learning. Access to this historical information provides teachers with the opportunity to continue successful initiatives and avoid repeating unsuccessful ones as students progress from grade to grade. The district now has a tool by which to rate the degree to which a particular school has implemented RTI, a rubric that can help guide school leaders in their planning, as well as provide district administrators with data to assist in orchestrating professional development opportunities. Although we are still a few years away from being able to document widely the effect on student learning outcomes, initial evidence from our case study, as well as from teacher focus groups over the years, suggests that as the schools adopt the RTI approach, general education teachers assume more responsibility for trying to meet the individual learning needs of their students (rather than referring them to special education teachers when they first notice them lagging behind their peers), and their focus on instructional effectiveness increases. In the final analysis, this may well be the most important outcome of our model demonstration project: increased teacher efficacy and commitment to making a difference in their students' lives.

REFERENCES

Allington, R. (2002). The six Ts of effective elementary literacy instruction. *Phi Delta Kappan, 83*(10).

Alonzo, J., Tindal, G., Ulmer, K., & Glasgow, A. (2006). *easyCBM online progress monitoring assessment system.* Eugene: University of Oregon, Behavioral Research and Teaching.

Batsche, G. M., Elliott, J., Graden, J., Grimes, J., Kovaleski, J. F., Prasse, D., et al. (2005). *Response to intervention: Policy considerations and implementation.* Alexandria, VA: National Association of State Directors of Special Education.

Blumenfeld, P. C., Soloway, E., Marx, R. W., Krajcik, J. S., Guzdial, M., & Palincsar, A. (1991). Motivating project-based learning: Sustaining the doing, supporting the learning. *Educational Psychologist, 26*(3/4), 369–398.

Bollman, K. A., Silberglitt, B., & Gibbons, K. A. (2007). The St. Croix River Education District Model: Incorporating system-level organization and a multitiered problem solving process for intervention delivery. In S. R. Jimerson,

M. K. Burns, & A. M. VanDerHeyden (Eds.), *The handbook of response to intervention: The science and practice of assessment and intervention* (pp. 319–330). New York: Springer.

Burns, M. K., & Ysseldyke, J. E. (2005). Comparison of existing response to intervention models to identify and answer implementation questions. *California School Psychologist, 10,* 9–20.

Callender, W. A. (2007). The Idaho result-based model: Implementing response to intervention statewide. In S. R. Jimerson, M. K. Burns, & A. M. VanDerHeyden (Eds.), *Handbook of response to intervention: The science and practice of assessment and intervention* (pp. 331–342). New York: Springer.

Christ, T. J., & Hintze, J. M. (2007). Psychometric consideration when evaluating response to intervention. In S. R. Jimerson, M. K. Burns, & A. VanDerHeyden (Eds.), *Handbook of response to intervention* (pp. 93–105). New York: Springer.

Coyne, M. D., Kame'enui, E. J., Simmons, D. C., & Harn, B. A. (2004). Beginning reading intervention as inoculation or insulin: First-grade reading performance of strong responders to kindergarten intervention. *Journal of Learning Disabilities, 37*(2), 90–104.

Denton, C. A., Fletcher, J. M., Anthony, J. L., & Francis, D. J. (2006). An evaluation of intensive intervention for students with persistent reading difficulties. *Journal of Learning Disabilities, 39,* 447–466.

Denton, C. A., Vaughn, S., & Fletcher, J. M. (2003). Bringing research-based practice in reading intervention to scale. *Learning Disabilities Research and Practice, 18*(3), 201–211.

Dickson, S. V., & Bursuck, W. D. (1998). Implementing a model for preventing reading failure: A report from the field. *Learning Disabilities Research and Practice, 14,* 191–195.

Edmonds, M., & Briggs, K. L. (2003). The instructional content emphasis instrument. In S. Vaughn & K. L. Briggs (Eds.), *Reading in the classroom* (pp. 31–52). Baltimore: Brookes.

Foorman, B. R., & Ciancio, D. J. (2005). Screening for secondary interventions: Concept and context. *Journal of Learning Disabilities, 38,* 494–499.

Foorman, B. R., & Moats, L. C. (2004). Conditions for sustaining research-based practices in early reading instruction. *Remedial and Special Education, 25*(1), 51–60.

Foorman, B. R., & Schatschneider, C. (2003). Measurement of teaching practice during reading/language arts instruction and its relationship to student achievement. In S. Vaughn & K. L. Briggs (Eds.), *Reading in the classroom* (pp. 1–30). Baltimore: Brookes.

Foorman, B. R., & Torgesen, J. (2001). Critical elements of classroom and small-group instruction promote reading success in all children. *Learning Disabilities Research and Practice, 16,* 203–212.

Friend, M. (2000). Myths and misunderstandings about professional collaborations. *Remedial and Special Education, 21*(3), 130–132.

Fuchs, D., Mock, D., Morgan, P. L., & Young, C. L. (2003). Responsiveness to intervention: Definitions, evidence, and implications for the learning disabilities construct. *Learning Disabilities Research and Practice, 18*(3), 157–171.

Fuchs, L. S. (1995). *Curriculum-based measurement and eligibility decision-*

making: An emphasis on treatment validity and growth. Washington, DC: National Research Council.

Fuchs, L. S. (2003). Assessing intervention responsiveness: Conceptual and technical issues. *Learning Disabilities Research and Practice, 18,* 172–186.

Fuchs, L. S., & Fuchs, D. (1998). Treatment fidelity: A unifying concept for reconceptualizing the identification process of learning disabilities. *Journal of Learning Disabilities, 13,* 204–219.

Fuchs, L. S., & Fuchs, D. (2006). A framework for building capacity for responsiveness to intervention. *School Psychology Review, 35*(4), 621–626.

Fullan, M. (2001). *Leading in a culture of change.* New York: Wiley.

Gambrell, L. B., Wilson, R. M., & Gantt, W. (1981). Classroom observation of task-attending behaviors of good and poor readers. *Journal of Educational Research, 74,* 400–404.

Garet, M. S., Porter, A. C., Desimone, L., Birman, B. F., & Kwang, S. Y. (2001). What makes professional development effective?: Results from a national sample of teachers. *American Educational Research Journal, 38,* 915–945.

Gersten, R., Baker, S., Haager, D., & Graves, A. (2005). Exploring the role of teacher quality in predicting reading outcomes for first grade English learners: An observational study. *Remedial and Special Education, 26,* 197–206.

Good, R. H., Gruba, J., & Kaminski, R. A. (2002). Best practices in using Dynamic Indicators of Basic Early Literacy Skills (DIBELS) in an outcomes-driven model. In A. Thomas & J. Grimes (Eds.), *Best practices in school psychology* (Vol. 4, pp. 679–700). Bethesda, MD: National Association of School Psychologists.

Good, R. H., Simmons, D., & Kame'enui, E. (2001). The importance and decision-making utility of a continuum of fluency-based indicators of foundational reading skills for third-grade high-stakes outcomes. *Scientific Studies of Reading, 5,* 257–288.

Good, R. H., Simmons, D., Kame'enui, E., & Chard, D. (2003, December). *Operationalizing response to intervention in eligibility decisions.* Paper presented at the National Research Center on Learning Disabilities Responsiveness to Intervention Symposium, Kansas City, MO.

Graden, J. L., Stoller, S. A., & Poth, R. L. (2007). The Ohio integrity system model: An overview and lessons learned. In S. R. Jimerson, M. K. Burns, & A. M. VanDerHeyden (Eds.), *Handbook of response to intervention: The science and practice of assessment and intervention* (pp. 288–299). New York: Springer.

Graves, A. W., Gersten, R., & Hagger, D. (2004). Literacy instruction in multiple-language first-grade classrooms: Linking student outcomes to observed instructional practice. *Learning Disabilities Research and Practice, 19,* 262–272.

Gresham, F. M., Reschly, D. J., Tilly, W. D., Fletcher, J., Burns, M., & Prasse, D. (2005). A response to intervention perspective. *School Psychologist, 59*(1), 26–33.

Grimes, J., & Kurns, S. (2003, December). *An intervention-based system for addressing NCLB and IDEA expectations: A multiple-tiered model to ensure every child learns.* Paper presented at the National Research Center on Learning Disabilities Responsiveness to Intervention Symposium, Kansas City, MO.

Hagger, D., Gersten, R., Baker, S., & Graves, A. W. (2003). The English language learner classroom observation instrument for beginning readers. In S. Vaughn & K. L. Briggs (Eds.), *Reading in the classroom* (pp. 111–144). Baltimore: Brookes.

Harn, B., Kame'enui, E. J., & Simmons, D. C. (2007). The role of the third tier. In D. Hagger, J. Klinger, & S. Vaughn (Eds.), *Evidence-based reading instruction for response to intervention* (pp. 161–184). Baltimore: Brookes.

Hiebert, J. (1999). Relationship between research and NCTM standards. *Journal for Research in Mathematics Education, 30*(1), 3–19.

Huberman, M. (1993). The model of the independent aRTIsan in teachers' professional relations. In J. W. Little & M. W. McLaughlin (Eds.), *Teachers' work: Individual, colleagues, and contexts.* New York: Teachers College Press.

Institute of Child Health and Human Development. (2000). *Report of the National Reading Panel. Teaching children to read: An evidence-based assessment of the scientific research literature on reading and its implications for reading instruction* (NIH Publication No. 004754). Washington, DC: U.S. Government Printing Office.

Jenkins, J. R. (2003, December). *Candidate measures for screening at-risk students.* Paper presented at the National Research Center on Learning Disabilities Responsiveness to Intervention Symposium, Kansas City, MO.

Justice, L. M. (2006). Evidence-based practice, response to intervention, and the prevention of reading difficulties. *Language, Speech, and Hearing Services in Schools, 37,* 284–297.

Kamps, D. M., & Greenwood, C. R. (2003, December). *Formulating secondary-level reading interventions.* Paper presented at the National Research Center on Learning Disabilities Responsiveness to Intervention Symposium, Kansas City, MO.

Kim, A., Briggs, K. L., & Vaughn, S. (2003). The classroom climate scale: Observing during reading instruction. In S. Vaughn & K. L. Briggs (Eds.), *Reading in the classroom* (pp. 83–110). Baltimore: Brookes.

Kovaleski, J. F. (2003, December). *The three-tier model for identifying learning disability: Critical program features and system issues.* Paper presented at the National Research Center on Learning Disabilities Responsiveness to Intervention Symposium, Kansas City, MO.

Lau, M. Y., Sieler, J. D., Muyskens, P., Canter, A., VanKeuren, B., & Marston, D. (2006). Perspectives on the use of the problem-solving model from the viewpoint of a school psychologist, administrator, and teacher from a large midwest urban school district. *Psychology in the Schools, 43*(1), 117–127.

Liu, K. (2009). *Development of an assessment rubric for the implementation of Response to Intervention (RTI) at elementary schools.* Ann Arbor, MI: Proquest.

Lyon, G. R., Fletcher, J. M., & Barnes, M. C. (2002). Learning disabilities. In E. J. Mash & R. A. Barkley (Eds.), *Child psychopathology* (2nd ed., Vol. 2, pp. 520–586). New York: Guilford Press.

Marston, D. (2005). Tiers of intervention in responsiveness to intervention: Prevention outcomes and learning disabilities identification patterns. *Journal of Learning Disabilities, 38*(6), 539–544.

Marston, D., Pickart, M., Reschly, A., Heistad, D., Muyskens, P., & Tindal, G. (2007). Early literacy measures for improving student reading achievement: Translating research into practice. *Exceptionality, 15*(2), 97–117.

McMaster, K. L., Fuchs, D., Fuchs, L. S., & Compton, D. L. (2005). Responding to non-responders: An experimental field of identification and intervention methods. *Exceptional Children, 71*, 445–463.

McMaster, K. L., & Wagner, D. (2007). Monitoring response to general education instruction. In S. R. Jimerson, M. K. Burns, & A. M. VanDerHeyden (Eds.), *The handbook of response to intervention: The science and practice of assessment and intervention* (pp. 223–233). New York: Springer.

Nias, J. (1989). *Primary teachers talking: A study of teaching as work.* London: Routledge.

O'Connor, R. (2000). Increasing the intensity of intervention in kindergarten and first grade. *Learning Disabilities Research and Practice, 15*(1), 43–54.

O'Connor, R., Harty, K. R., & Fulmer, D. (2005). Tiers of interventions in kindergarten through third grade. *Journal of Learning Disabilities, 38*(6), 532–538.

Peterson, D. W., Prasse, D. P., & Shinn, M. R. (2007). The Illinois flexible service delivery model: A problem-solving model initiative. In S. R. Jimerson, M. K. Burns, & A. M. VanDerHeyden (Eds.), *Handbook of response to intervention: The science and practice of assessment and intervention* (pp. 300–318). New York: Springer.

Pikulski, J. J. (1998). Preventing reading failure: Review of effective programs. In R. Allington (Ed.), *Teaching struggling readers* (pp. 35–45). Newark, DE: International Reading Association.

Reschly, A., Coolong-Chaffin, M., Christenson, S. L., & Gutkin, T. (2007). Contextual influences and response to intervention: Critical issues and strategies. In S. R. Jimerson, M. Burns, & A. VanDerHeyden (Eds.), *The handbook of response to intervention: The science and practice of assessment and intervention.* New York: Springer.

Simmons, D., Kame'enui, E., Beck, C. T., Brewer, N. S., & Fien, H. (2003). *A consumer's guide to evaluating supplemental and intervention reading programs grades K–3: A critical elements analysis.* Eugene: University of Oregon, College of Education, Oregon Reading First Center.

Snow, C., Burns, M., & Griffin, P. (1998). *Preventing reading difficulties in young children.* Washington, DC: National Academies Press.

Speece, D. L., Case, L. P., & Molloy, D. E. (2003). Responsiveness to general education instruction as the first gate to learning disabilities identification. *Learning Disabilities Research and Practice, 18*(3), 147–156.

Stoner, G., & Green, S. K. (1992). Reconsidering the science-practitioner model for school psychology practice. *School Psychology Review, 21*, 155–166.

Talbert, J. E., & McLaughlin, M.W. (2002). Professional communities and the aRTIsan model of teaching. *Teachers and Teaching: Theory and Practice, 8*, 325–343.

Tilly, W. D. (2003, December). *How many tiers are needed for successful prevention and early intervention?: Heartland Area Education Agency's evaluation from four to three tiers.* Paper presented at the National Research Center on Learning Disabilities Responsiveness to Intervention Symposium, Kansas City, MO.

Torgesen, J., Alexander, A., Wagner, D., Rashotte, C. A., Voeller, K., & Conway, T. (2001). Intensive remedial reading instruction for children with severe reading disabilities: Immediate and long-term outcomes from two instructional approaches. *Journal of Learning Disabilities, 34,* 33–58.

Torgesen, J. K., Rashotte, C. A., Alexander, A., Alexander, J., & MacPhee, K. (2003). Progress towards understanding the instructional conditions necessary for remediating reading difficulties in older children In B. R. Foorman (Ed.), *Preventing and remediating reading difficulties: Bringing science to scale* (pp. 275–298). Parkton, MD: New York Press.

Treptow, M. A. (2006). *Reading at students' frustrational, instructional and independent levels: Effects on comprehension and time on task.* Minneapolis: University of Minnesota Center for Reading Research.

VanDerHeyden, A., Witt, J. C., & Naguin, C. (2003). The development and validation of a process for screening referrals to special education. *School Psychology Review, 32,* 204–207.

VanDerHeyden, A. M., & Jimerson, S. R. (2005). Using response to intervention to enhance outcomes for children. *California School Psychologist, 10,* 21–32.

Vaughn, S., Linan-Thompson, S., & Hickman, P. (2003). Response to instruction as a means of identifying students with reading/learning disabilities. *Exceptional Children, 69,* 391–409.

Vaughn, S., Wanzek, J., Linan-Thompson, S., & Murray, C. S. (2007). Monitoring response to supplemental service for students at risk for reading difficulty: High and low responders. In S. R. Jimerson, M. K. Burns, & A. M. VanDerHeyden (Eds.), *The handbook of response to intervention: The science and practice of assessment and intervention* (pp. 234–243). Baltimore: Springer.

Vellutino, F. R., Scanlon, D. M., Sipay, E. R., Small, S. G., Pratt, A., & Chen, R. S. (1996). Cognitive profiles of difficult to remediate and readily remediated poor readers: Early intervention as a vehicle for distinguishing between cognitive and experiential deficits as basic causes of specific learning disability. *Journal of Educational Psychology, 88,* 601–638.

Vellutino, F. R., Scanlon, D. M., & Tanzman, M. S. (1998). The case for early intervention in diagnosing specific learning disability. *Journal of School Psychology, 36,* 367–397.

APPENDIX 13.1. RTI Assessment Rubric

Operational Definition
1. Tier 1 Instruction (in reading) is defined as the core reading instruction provided to all students in general education classes for a sufficient amount of time to meet grade-level instructional goals. In Tier 1 instruction, teacher teaches all "5 Big Ideas" as specified in NRP [NICHD, 2000] or relevant ones to specific grade level, using evidence-based teaching strategies.

Data sources for documenting the quality of Tier 1 Instruction:

☐ Classroom observation

☐ School schedule

☐ Teacher and student interviews

Level of Implementation	Descriptors/ Features
Fully Implemented	• Teachers explicitly teach all "5 Big Ideas" specified in NRP [NICHD, 2000] or relevant ones to specific grade-level (i.e., teaching phonological awareness might not be expected in Tier 1 after first grade); AND • Teacher teaches all students Tier 1 reading instruction daily for at minimum 60–90 minutes with most of the time spent engaged in grade-level-appropriate reading and writing activities. Teacher spends more than 50% of instruction time on explicit instruction of reading and writing. Many effective teaching behaviors identified in a chosen classroom observation checklist are present at the effective level during classroom observation; AND • Student appears on task 80% of time. (On task is defined as sitting in their seats properly, eyes looking either at teachers or at the instructional materials attentively, focusing on assigned reading or writing activities.) • Teacher and student believe instruction is appropriate.
Partially Implemented	Check those that apply (there may be more than one): _____ Teacher explicitly teaches some of the relevant "big ideas" OR _____ Teacher provides instruction less than the allocated time by teaching less each day or for 3–4 days each week; OR _____ Teacher spends 25–50% of instruction time on explicit instruction of reading and writing. Some effective teaching behaviors identified in the chosen classroom observation checklist are present during classroom observation at or above the level of partially effective; OR _____ Students appear on task 50–80% of the time; OR _____ Teacher and student are uncertain whether instruction is appropriate.

(cont.)

From Liu (2009). Copyright 2009 by Proquest. Reprinted by permission.

Not Implemented	• Teacher does not teach any of the "5 Big Ideas" explicitly; OR • Teacher teaches Tier 1 reading instruction for only a small amount of time each day or for 1–2 days each week; OR • Teacher spends less than 25% of instruction time on explicit instruction of reading and writing. Few of the targeted effective teaching behaviors are present during classroom observation at or above the level of partially effective; OR • Student appears on task less than 50% of time; OR • Teacher and student believe instruction is inappropriate.

Operational Definition

2. Universal Screening (in reading) is defined as using a measure (with appropriate evidence of validity and reliability) to assess all students' reading skills and identify students who score below predetermined benchmarks. Data from universal screening are presented in a manner that reflects an appropriate unit of analysis so that (a) teachers can identify students who need additional instructional support, or (b) schools can configure grade-level interventions.

Data sources for documenting the quality of universal screening:

☐ Document: Technical report or manual of the chosen screening measure

☐ Archival Record: the test dates, teacher roster, students scores on the screening measures

☐ Document: the test dates, students' scores, cut scores, or benchmark for the chosen screening measures

Level of Implementation	Descriptors/ Features
Fully Implemented	• The chosen screening measure has explicitly documented validity and reliability evidence; AND • The screening measure is administered to all students three times a year to identify students who need additional instructional support; AND • Data are gathered in a timely manner and displayed in a way that teachers can systematically identify students needing additional instructional support within each grade.
Partially Implemented	Check those that apply (there may be more than one): _____ The measure has face validity and some reliability evidence; OR _____ The measure is administered to all students once or twice a year OR only to some students; OR _____ Data are not gathered in a timely manner or not displayed in a way that teacher can easily identify students needing additional support.

(cont.)

Not Implemented	• The screening measure has no established validity or reliability evidence; OR • The measures are not administered to any students; OR • Data are gathered but not used for identifying students needing instructional support.

Operational Definition

3. Tier 2 and Tier 3 Intervention is defined as explicit and differentiated instruction for students who do not make progress with only Tier 1 instruction. It is supplementary to the Tier 1 instruction and is provided for a sufficient amount of time to improve targeted student's learning outcomes in the specific skill deficit areas (e.g., some of the "5 Big Ideas").

Data sources for documenting the quality of Tier 2 and Tier 3 interventions:

☐ Observation or record of school-based meetings (SST, RTI, or grade-level meetings)

☐ Classroom observation for Tier 2 and Tier 3 interventions

☐ Physical Artifact: School schedule and nature or programs/materials

☐ Teacher and student interviews

Level of Implementation	Descriptors/ Features
Fully Implemented	• Tier 2 and Tier 3 interventions are research-based and explicitly targeted to specific "big ideas" matching the identified instructional needs of students needing additional support; AND • The interventions are implemented with high fidelity and for sufficient amounts of time as specified by the program recommendations; AND • Teacher spends more than 50% of instruction time on explicit instruction of identified instructional big ideas, using evidence-based strategies. Most targeted effective teaching behaviors emphasizing differentiating instruction for low-performing students as identified in the chosen checklist are present at the effective level during classroom observation; AND • Student appears on task 80% of time. (On task is defined as sitting in their seats properly, eyes looking either at teachers or at the instructional materials attentively, focusing on assigned reading or writing activities.) • Teacher and student believe instruction is appropriate.
Partially Implemented	Check those that apply (there may be more than one): _____ The content of Tier 2 and Tier 3 interventions is not research-based or it is used to supplant Tier 1 instruction. _____ The interventions don't match the identified instructional needs of students receiving additional support. _____ The interventions are implemented with some fidelity, and/or not for insufficient amount of time.

(cont.)

	_____ Teacher spends more than 50% of instruction time on explicit instruction of the "5 Big Ideas." Some targeted effective teaching behaviors are present during the classroom observation at or above the level of partially effective.
	_____ Student appears on task 50–80% of time.
	_____ Teacher and student are uncertain whether instruction is appropriate.
Not Implemented	• The instruction is not explicit or does not have specific instructional emphases; OR • Teacher teaches Tier 2 and Tier 3 interventions for only a small amount of time each day or for only a couple of days each week; OR • Teacher spends less than 50% of instruction time on explicit instruction of the targeted "big ideas"; OR • Student appears on task less than 50% of time; OR • Teacher and student believe instruction is inappropriate.

Operational Definition

4. Progress Monitoring is defined as scientifically based practice that is used to assess students' academic performance and evaluate the effectiveness of instruction. Progress monitoring can be implemented with individuals or an entire class. Data from progress measures are presented in a manner that allows change over time to be visible.

Data sources for documenting the quality of progress monitoring:

☐ Document: Progress monitoring data

☐ Review of the technical adequacy of the chosen progress monitoring instrument

Level of Implementation	Descriptors/ Features
Fully Implemented	• Teacher selects progress monitoring measures that have documented validity and reliability evidence for monitoring progress on a specific skill that matches students' instructional needs; AND • Teacher uses progress monitoring measures to track student's progress in specific skills. They are administered weekly or biweekly at least three times to establish a pattern; AND • Progress monitoring data are collected on schedule and are used to inform instruction. The data are displayed in appropriate graphs so that the change over time can be visible.
Partially Implemented	Check those that apply (there may be more than one): _____ The measures have face validity or some reliability evidence for monitoring progress of reading. _____ Chosen progress monitoring measure is not designed to assess specific skill matching students' instructional needs. _____ Teacher administers the test, but not systematically or less frequently than monthly or only once or twice before changing the interventions.

(cont.)

	_____ Progress monitoring data are used to inform instruction. The data, however, are not collected on schedule or graphically displayed.
Not Implemented	• The measures have no established validity and reliability evidence for monitoring progress; OR • Teacher does not administer progress monitoring measures; OR • Progress monitoring data are not collected or used to inform instruction.

Operational Definition

5. Evidence-based decision making is defined as using data of the progress monitoring measures and program-specific assessments to judge the effectiveness of interventions to determine if intervention modifications are warranted.

Data sources for documenting the quality of evidence-based decision making:

☐ Teacher interviews

☐ Progress monitoring data and program-specific assessments

☐ Observations or records of school-based meetings

Level of Implementation	Descriptors/ Features
Fully Implemented	• Teacher systematically and regularly examines classroom data (e.g., data of program specific assessments) and data of progress measures. Teacher analyzes the graphs of progress monitoring data, focusing on students' levels of performance and rates of progress (slope); AND • Teacher analyzes specific instructional components; AND • Teacher determines whether to fade, continue, modify, or intensify the student's current instructional intervention based on the empirical data gathered.
Partially Implemented	Check those that apply (may be more than one): _____ Teacher informally and episodically reviews classroom data and graphs of progress monitoring data; OR _____ Teacher examines the instructional program in general; OR _____ Teacher changes instructional programs based mainly on random classroom observations.
Not Implemented	• Teacher does not review any classroom information or progress measures; OR • Teacher makes no reference to current instructional program; OR • Teacher provides unsystematic instruction.

(cont.)

	Operational Definition
	**6. Organizational Support** is defined as leadership, resources, administrative support, and professional training and collaboration to facilitate implementation of schoolwide programs.

Data sources for documenting the quality of organizational support:

☐ Teacher and administrator interviews

☐ Observations or records of school-based meetings

☐ Observations or records of professional training meetings

☐ Physical artifacts: school schedules

Level of Implementation	Descriptors/ Features
Fully Implemented	• There is clear and direct evidence of leadership directives, resource allocation, and administrative support; AND • Teachers receive multiple sessions of professional training and ongoing support to implement research-based instruction, assessment, and evidence-based decision making. The professional training is focused and interactive. Teachers collaborate with colleagues to identify students' needs and implement tailored interventions to address the needs; AND • Teachers collaborate to configure the schoolwide intervention programs.
Partially Implemented	Check those that apply (there may be more than one): _____ There is indirect evidence of leadership directives, resource allocation, and administrative support. _____ Teachers receive only initial professional training and have no ongoing support to implement research-based instruction, assessment, and evidence-based decision making. Professional collaboration occurs in isolated incidences. The extent of collaboration is limited due to issues of logistics and role responsibilities. _____ Teacher collaborate to configure the interventions only at the grade level or classroom level. There is no coherent schoolwide configuration of the intervention programs.
Not Implemented	• No evidence is available to show leadership directives, resource allocation, and administrative support; AND • Teachers receive no professional training and rarely collaborate; AND • Decision making is done by individual teachers.

PART V

Perspective from the Model Demonstration Coordination Center

Introduction to Part V

In 2005, the Office of Special Education Programs (OSEP) funded SRI International[1] to establish the Model Demonstration Coordination Center (MDCC), which is helping OSEP to consider "broad questions of interest about model demonstration such as, 'Are there common components of successful models?' or 'What project features promote scaling up of a practice/program?'" (U.S. Department of Education, 2005, p. 2).

Chapter 14 first describes the two major thrusts of the MDCC's work: (1) evaluation coordination, synthesis, and analysis activities and (2) efforts to identify the characteristics of an effective implementation–evaluation–refinement model demonstration process. We present the conceptual framework that guides the MDCC's work and then reflect on the earlier chapters in this book to highlight differences among the model demonstration grant-

---

[1]Located in Menlo Park, California, SRI International, formerly Stanford Research Institute, is one of the nation's leading not-for-profit research and problem-solving organizations, meeting the research, development, policy, and evaluation needs of federal, state, and local government agencies and private sector foundations and businesses.

ees related to four components of the conceptual framework: the models themselves; the implementation strategies grantees used to install their models in participating schools; characteristics of those schools, including their leadership, instructional practices, and culture; and the district contexts for their work. Lessons learned regarding the implications these differences have for successful implementation and model sustainability and expansion illustrate ways in which the MDCC is helping increase the value of OSEP's investments in model demonstration projects.

REFERENCE

U.S. Department of Education (2005). *Model Demonstration Data Coordination Center scope of work*. Washington, DC: Office of Special Education Programs.

CHAPTER 14

A Cross-Case Perspective on the Implementation of Model Demonstration Projects

Mary Wagner
Phyllis Levine

> The vision of schools as a community of leaders is not a
> fantasy. . . . Shared leadership expands the possibilities for
> school improvement, increases commitment, complicates
> decision-making, and makes for more effective education
> of children.
>
> —BARTH (1990)

In funding the work of the model demonstration projects that have been described in other chapters in this volume, the Office of Special Education Programs (OSEP) had a larger purpose than supporting the development, implementation, and evaluation of individual response-to-intervention (RTI) models. OSEP wanted to consider "broad questions of interest about model demonstration such as, 'Are there common components of successful models?' or 'What project features promote scaling up of a practice/program?'" (U.S. Department of Education, 2005, p. 2). This chapter begins by describing the Model Demonstration Coordination Center (MDCC)—

the mechanism through which OSEP sought to consider these kinds of questions—and its responsibilities in supporting the work of the model demonstration projects (MDPs). We then present the conceptual framework that guides the work of the MDCC in answering OSEP's evaluation questions. Those questions are identified, along with examples of how the MDPs' implementation experiences are being brought to bear in addressing them.

PURPOSES AND ACTIVITIES OF THE MODEL DEMONSTRATION COORDINATION CENTER

The MDCC was launched in 2005 to serve two major purposes: (1) coordinating each cohort's[1] evaluation and synthesizing and analyzing their findings to maximize the strength of evidence produced and (2) identifying characteristics of an effective implementation–evaluation–refinement process that moves a practice from early testing to being ready for sustainability and wider adoption. To achieve these ends, the MDCC did the following in support of the RTI grantees:

• Facilitated collaborative partnerships among the MDPs to create opportunities for learning and sharing ideas. Regular communication avoids reinvention and promotes trust. MDPs built on the ideas and tools of their colleagues to further their own work. The MDCC provided detailed notes of conference calls that served as a feedback loop and confirmation process and an ongoing documentation of the collaboration and joint problem-solving efforts. This book has grown out of this collaboration.

• Worked with the MDPs to establish consistent design elements across projects, including the target population, evaluation questions, and data collection methods and instrumentation to document student- and system-level outcomes.

• Negotiated agreements with the MDPs to document key features of their models, characteristics of the student sample, the organizational contexts for implementation and changes in these contexts over time, their implementation experiences, and model revisions made as a result of these experiences.

---

[1]A cohort refers to the set of grantees, funded in a particular year, that are addressing the same practice area. The four cohorts funded thus far have addressed progress monitoring within an RTI framework in elementary reading (2006–2009, the focus of this volume), tertiary behavior interventions (2007–2010), early childhood language development (2008–2011), and a tiered approach to improving secondary school writing (2010–2013).

- Supported cross-MDP documentation by suggesting common organizational and child assessment items and surveys, qualitative profile tools, and qualitative templates to describe the model specifications and the "story" of model development and implementation.

- Maintained a Web-based data system to track, enter, and process data efficiently across MDPs; minimize the burden on grantees; and make data accessible in real time for analyses and reporting.

- Developed and maintained the MDCC website that functioned as a common depository for MDCC- and MDP-generated data collection tools and measures, model descriptions, evaluation questions, contact information, and other information and resources relevant and accessible to individual cohorts. The website also contained information pertinent to potential grantees of future cohorts.

- Used a conceptual framework to study the model demonstration process and customized the framework for each new cohort.

Activities related to evaluation coordination, synthesis, and analysis and to use of a conceptual framework to identify characteristics of an effective implementation–evaluation–refinement process are described in more detail in the following sections.

Evaluation Coordination, Synthesis, and Analysis

OSEP asserted that it would learn more about the process and effects of its model demonstration investments if some consistent design elements were established across the MDPs. This was expected to increase the likelihood that differences between the implementation experiences and student- and system-level outcomes of the various models might more readily be attributed to the models themselves than to differences in the students served, for example. The MDCC worked with the MDPs to establish a common evaluation design, a consistent definition of the student population being served, a core set of evaluation questions MDPs would address in their individual analyses and that the MDCC would address in its cross-MDP analysis, and a uniform set of data collection methods and instrumentation to document student- and system-level outcomes.

Evaluation Design

The three MDPs proposed to rely on analyses of growth in reading proficiency (e.g., letter–word identification skills, oral reading fluency) to assess the effects of the models. However, the absence of a comparison group would make attribution of the growth that was measured to a model questionable; students might well have achieved the same growth under the "business as usual" conditions that normally occurred in the schools. Three design features were agreed to that would strengthen the evidence base for the models.

The MDPs agreed to obtain from their participating schools at least 3 years of pre-model-implementation state accountability test scores for third graders to serve as a baseline against which to assess the proficiency of third graders who experienced model intervention. If the models were effective, one would expect the growth in proficiency to increase with each subsequent year of model implementation. In addition, the MDPs agreed to take a baseline measurement of reading proficiency in spring 2006 in participating schools using the assessment tools they would incorporate into their models. Assessment results in the spring of each model implementation year could be compared with this baseline to identify any differences in the level of reading proficiency achieved by model participants versus earlier nonparticipants. However, this would not provide a baseline with which to assess whether greater growth in reading had been achieved.

To address this point, the MDPs agreed to delay implementation in one or more of their participating schools until the 2007–2008 school year and to measure the pre-model-implementation reading growth in those schools. Triangulating across these three data sources would paint a more complete picture of the efficacy of the various models than would have resulted from the originally proposed evaluation designs.

Student Sample Definition

The students for whom data were reported by the MDPs to the MDCC were first- through third-grade students in general education classrooms in each MDP's participating school. MDPs may have included other students in their work (e.g., kindergarteners, fourth graders), but data on those students were not included in the MDCC's cross-MDP analysis of the "core sample."

Common Set of Evaluation Questions

The MDCC and MDPs arrived at a set of evaluation questions that address the models' development, implementation, and outcomes. Each MDP was to address "Level 1 questions" in analyzing the experiences and results of its individual model. "Level 2 questions" (Table 14.1) are the focus of the MDCC's analyses; they mimic Level 1 questions, but rather than focusing on individual MDPs, they entail a comparative analysis of the three models to identify lessons regarding how differences in models might relate to differences in implementation experiences and outcomes.

TABLE 14.1. RTI Model Demonstration Project Evaluation Questions

Model development

1a. How do the core intervention components of RTI models differ?
1b. How do differences relate to the models' perceived:
   - Relative advantage
   - Complexity
   - Compatibility with the school and district contexts
   - Social validity?
1c. How do these perceived differences relate to the fullness/fidelity of model implementation and to establishing conditions supportive of sustainability?

Implementation

2a. How do RTI models differ with regard to:
   - Strategies for recruiting districts and schools and for introducing models
   - Professional development approaches
   - Approaches to ongoing support
   - MDP staffing strategies
   - Ways of learning from implementation experiences and adapting core implementation and intervention components?
2b. How do these differences relate to the fullness/fidelity of model implementation and to establishing conditions supportive of sustainability?

3a. How do participating schools differ with regard to key characteristics:
   - Children/families served
   - History with model-related practices
   - Organizational functioning
   - Staff and leadership
   - Resources relevant to model
   - Climate/culture
   - Support for the model?
3b. How do schools differ with regard to implementation outcomes—their ability to establish the following in support of implementation with fidelity and the potential for sustainability:
   - Staff knowledge, attitudes, and actions/behavior
   - Organizational structures, processes, and culture
   - External relationships
3c. How do differences relate to the fullness/fidelity of model implementation and to establishing conditions supportive of sustainability?

4a. How do model contexts differ with regard to:
   - District and state support for/alignment with model
   - District resources provided for model implementation/sustainability
   - Circumstances/authorities outside of the model that exert some control over implementation and/or sustainability?
4b. How do differences relate to the fullness/fidelity of model implementation and to establishing conditions supportive of sustainability?

(cont.)

TABLE 14.1. *(cont.)*

Outcomes

5a. How do models, districts, and schools differ with regard to:
- Individual-level outcomes
- System-level outcomes

5b. How do differences in core intervention and implementation components, destination organizations, and influences relate to differences in individual- and system-level outcomes?

Common Data Collection Instruments and Procedures

Addressing the evaluation questions at both Levels 1 and 2 required a variety of kinds and sources of data. To address model development and implementation questions, the MDCC negotiated an agreement with the MDPs that they would document key features of their models; characteristics of the student sample; the district, school, and classroom contexts in which the models were implemented; implementation experiences in each of the three implementation years; and revisions made to their models as a result of those experiences. To support that documentation, the MDCC developed school, teacher, and student survey questionnaires; qualitative district, school, and classroom profile tools; and qualitative templates to describe the model specifications and the "story" of the model development and implementation process. These were completed by each MDP. To address outcome questions, the MDPs agreed to use common oral-reading fluency (ORF) passages with each student in their sample and to administer the Stanford Achievement Test-10 (SAT-10) to second graders to meet OSEP's desire to have common data from a standardized measure of overall academic achievement.

Identifying the Characteristics of an Effective Implementation–Evaluation–Refinement Process

A second purpose of the MDCC was to look across the implementation experiences and the outcomes of the RTI MDPs and, eventually, across the full range of MDPs that OSEP funded in subsequent years to identify any patterns in relationships between variations in the models that might relate to variations in their ability to implement the models with fidelity, to achieve desired child- and system-level outcomes, and to poise the model for sustainability in its original sites and perhaps expansion to others. The MDCC was charged with identifying key variations across MDPs, using relevant literature to hypothesize ways in which model variations and implementation and outcome variations might relate and to scrutinize the qualitative and quantitative data from the models in light of those hypotheses in an effort to support, refute, or modify them. As each subsequent cohort of MDPs conducted its work, the number of models would increase and stronger evidence would emerge to inform the hypotheses.

To guide this analytical endeavor, the MDCC adapted a conceptual framework for understanding the implementation of interventions that has been developed by the National Implementation Research Network (NIRN) (Fixsen, Naoom, Blasé, Friedman, & Wallace, 2005). The NIRN framework specifies the key elements in the implementation process; the adaptation of this framework for the purposes of the MDCC's analysis of the RTI models is presented in Figure 14.1.

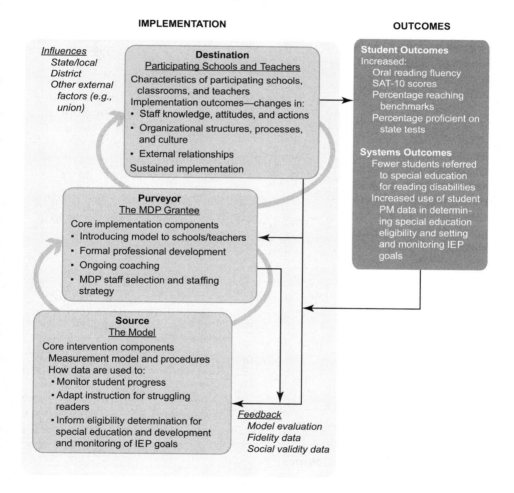

FIGURE 14.1. Conceptual Framework for Model Demonstration Implementation and Outcomes: Cohort 1. From Fixsen, Naoom, Blasé, Friedman, and Wallace (2005). Copyright 2005 by SRI International. Adapted by permission.

A CONCEPTUAL MODEL FOR UNDERSTANDING THE MODEL DEMONSTRATION PROCESS

Conceptual Model Elements

The conceptual model has four major elements. In the RTI MDP context, *source* is the model being implemented, which has "core intervention components" (i.e., the mechanisms through which the intervention is expected to produce desired outcomes). In the RTI model context, these were related to measurement (i.e., the use of progress monitoring tools to collect data on students' reading achievement) and to processes for using data to monitor student progress, adapting instruction to respond to student need and identifying students who may be eligible for special education services because of a learning disability. The *purveyor* of the model was the MDP grantee, which was implementing an RTI model in schools. Whereas the model itself had core *intervention* components, the MDPs had core *implementation* components in their process of bringing models to schools. These included strategies for (1) selecting demonstration sites and introducing the model to district and school administrators and teachers; (2) providing professional development in how to use the model; (3) offering ongoing coaching in support of implementation; and (4) MDP staff selection and staffing strategies (e.g., the characteristics of MDP staff who worked in the schools, how they were trained and supervised).

The framework posits that these actions of the MDPs were the mechanisms through which the RTI models were transmitted to participating schools (the *destination*) and the teachers in them, who were the intended implementers of the model. The schools in which the MDPs worked differed markedly, differences that could be expected to influence implementation experiences and student- and system-level outcomes, as well as the pace at which MDPs were able to reach them. Other potentially important factors were related to the teachers themselves, who differed significantly in demographics, background, skill, openness to change, and other important attributes.

A fourth element of the NIRN conceptual framework for implementation involves the model development context, or the *influences* on the implementation process. In the case of the RTI MDPs, influence occurred from factors within the state (e.g., the presence of a state technical assistance network or an RTI initiative) and district (e.g., being a "laboratory" district for an MDP university).

Conceptual Model Outcomes

In addition to its key elements, the NIRN model posits three *implementation outcomes* that would be expected to occur within the destination organization if implementation is successful:

(1) changes in adult professional behavior (knowledge and skills of practitioners and other key staff members within an organization or system); (2) changes in organizational structures and cultures, both formal and informal (values, philosophies, ethics, policies, procedures, decision making), to routinely bring about and support the changes in adult professional behavior; and (3) changes in relationships to consumers, stakeholders (location and nature of engagement, inclusion, satisfaction), and systems partners. (Fixsen et al., 2005, p. 12)

A fourth implementation outcome that is critical in the model demonstration context is the sustainability of the model after an MDP ends, an outcome that encompasses both the extent to which the destination organization maintained the core intervention components of the model and how well the model was positioned for expansion into other locations.

Because the NIRN conceptual model focuses solely on the implementation, not the results, of interventions, an element related to intervention outcomes needed to be added to reflect the full intention of the MDPs. The ultimate intention of the RTI models was to improve instruction, resulting in improved outcomes at both the student and system levels. Student outcomes involved increases in reading achievement, whereas systems outcomes focused on decreases in inappropriate referrals to special education of students whose difficulty in learning to read resulted from poor instruction, not from a learning disability. For students who did receive special education services for a reading-related disability, systems outcomes also included increased use of progress monitoring (PM) data in writing and monitoring measurable IEP goals.

Intervention and Implementation Adaptations

Finally, the conceptual model includes feedback loops between the purveyor and the implementation destination and between both of those elements of the framework and the source. A feedback loop also is evident between intervention outcomes and the purveyor's core implementation components and the model's core intervention components. These feedback loops are the "learning paths" through which experience with model implementation informs iterative adaptations in core intervention and implementation components. For example, MDPs made revisions to intervention or implementation components in response to changes in reading achievement and/ or systems outcomes. At the conclusion of the MDP's work, the adaptations to the core intervention and implementation components that were made, reflecting their experiences in model demonstration schools, were analyzed for similarities and differences and for relationships to intervention results.

APPLYING THE CONCEPTUAL FRAMEWORK
TO PM MODEL IMPLEMENTATION EXPERIENCES

Fleshing out the conceptual framework and the relationships embedded in it in order to identify characteristics of implementation–evaluation–refinement processes that move a practice from early testing to being ready for wider adoption clearly requires data from a larger and more varied set of models. However, the experiences of the RTI MDPs provided examples of the kinds of lessons the MDCC's analyses are generating, as illustrated in the following sections (see also Wagner & Levine, 2009). Examples relate to four components of the conceptual framework: the models (the "source"), the MDPs and their implementation strategies (the "purveyors"), the participating schools (the "destinations"), and the implementation contexts (the "influences").

Variations in RTI Models

The chapters in this volume describe a variety of differences in the RTI models, including characteristics of the measurement systems (e.g., skills assessed, frequency of measurement, instruments used) and the processes for using the data the systems produce (e.g., size and makeup of teams that used data to make instructional decisions). We asked whether there were configurations of the models that related to more positive implementation outcomes. To illustrate the kinds of lessons being generated in the MDCC's analyses, we focus on characteristics of one of the models' "core implementation components"—the PM measurement system.

The Minnesota, Oregon, and Pennsylvania models all included a technology component that, at a minimum, processed and displayed PM data for use by school-based teams to make instructional decisions. The Pennsylvania MDP team relied on a commercially available system, *AIMSweb* (Pearson Education, 2008), which is described as a system focused on "purely assessment, designed to measure and monitor the effects of any instruction" (Pearson Education, 2008). MDP grant funds provided access to the Web-based system and handheld devices for inputting data to schools implementing the Pennsylvania model.

In contrast, the Minnesota and Oregon teams relied on "homegrown" technologies. The Minnesota model had as a core component the "Office for Civil Rights (OCR) website" (see Marston, Casey, & Wallace, Chapter 8, this volume), developed by Minneapolis Public Schools (MPS) as a data warehouse that stores historical information for individual students on academic and behavioral performance, Tier 2 and Tier 3 interventions provided and student response, and summaries of IEPs and test accommodations, among other features (e.g., customized reporting capabilities, aggregation to school and district levels). The University of Oregon MDP incorporated use of *easyCBM*, a website developed by University of Oregon staff that makes available an extensive, research-based assessment system (see Alonzo & Tindal, Chapter 12, this volume) that enables educators to assess six aspects of students' reading abilities. These differences in technologies to support assessment have implications for the potential for the "reach," or scale-up, of the RTI models.

The long-standing MPS OCR website supported quick adoption and use of the Minnesota model in the implementation schools, and the experiences in those schools led to several adaptations and improvements in the website that supported use of the model more broadly in that district. However, the reliance of the Minnesota model on that district-developed website may be a limiting factor in its expansion beyond Minneapolis. Positive outcomes of the Minnesota model may encourage further adoption of PM and RTI approaches generally, but the specific measurement system and its related tools are limited to a single district.

In contrast, the measurement system used by the Pennsylvania MDP teams is commercially available, permitting wider adoption of that model beyond their implementing districts. However, the financial cost involved in subscribing to that system may be prohibitive for some districts in an economic climate in which program cutbacks are common. Use of the Oregon-developed *easyCBM* assessment system is free, and, as asserted in Alonzo and Tindal, Chapter 12, without explicit marketing it has fairly quickly acquired more than 38,000 individual teacher users who have assessed more than 320,000 different students using more than 1.1 million individual tests. Continued expansion of the assessment system to encompass higher grade levels and to add mathematics assessments is likely to make the system even more attractive to potential adopters of an RTI approach. In awarding future model demonstration grants, OSEP will attend to the technologies proposed for use and their implications for the ability of particular models to scale up after the conclusion of grant funding.

Variations in MDP Implementation Strategies

Readers of this volume will note a variety of differences in the "core implementation components" of the RTI models—that is, the strategies MDP teams used to install and maintain their models in implementation schools during the grant period. Strategies for staffing on-the-ground coaching and support activities illustrate another difference in MDPs that may have implications for model sustainability and the potential for expansion.

All MDPs provided professional development, though the timing, content, and intensity varied across the projects. Understanding that formal "trainings" are rarely enough to create change in teacher behavior (e.g., Showers & Joyce, 1996), the MDP teams also provided ongoing coaching support to teachers who were implementing the models, both individually and in teacher teams. The Pennsylvania teams provided coaching via university-based project team members who visited schools regularly to meet with principals, to observe teachers implementing tiered instruction, and to facilitate data-based decision-making team processes. They also maintained regular telephone and e-mail communication with school leaders and met regularly with district staff to report implementation progress and problem-solve as challenges arose. These MDP coaches gradually "faded" their support as the project progressed and school staff was more confident and better able to implement the core components of the model on their own.

The Oregon MDP team chose an explicit, empowerment-based coaching strategy that relied on volunteer staff from implementation schools to serve on school-based leadership teams. The RTI model also was implemented only in classrooms of volunteer teachers in each participating school rather than in all classrooms at targeted grade levels. Professional development in support of the model was largely provided by the district rather than the university, and ongoing coaching support to implementing teachers was provided by the school-based leadership teams.

The Minnesota MDP team established and funded a half-time RTI coordinator in each participating school to provide ongoing support to teachers in taking PM measurements and providing tiered instruction, to facilitate "job-embedded staff development" via teacher study groups, to support team-based instructional decision making, and to monitor fidelity of implementation. These coordinators were maintained in the schools with grant funds throughout the project, and the MDP team reported them to be critical to the successful implementation of their model in their demonstration schools.

Like other differences across MDPs, these differences in approaches to providing coaching support to implementing teachers could have implications for project sustainability and expansion. The reliance on outside trainers and coaches in the Pennsylvania model could conceivably restrict its scale-up if no other professional development agent could provide the support initially given by MDP staff. However, the presence in that state of the Pennsylvania Training and Technical Assistance Network (PaTTAN) and its involvement in designing, delivering, and refining the project's professional development and coaching support component ensured a source of support for model implementation throughout the state.

The principals in the Minneapolis schools that implemented the Minnesota model were successful in finding resources to continue to fund the half-time coordinator positions at the conclusion of the grant. The district also committed to funding some level of support for other schools within the district to permit expansion of the model districtwide. It is unclear, however, as schools and districts continue to face budget shortfalls, whether having a dedicated staff member in a facilitative role as a core feature of a model is sustainable over time. Gischlar and colleagues (Chapter 3, this volume) echo this concern regarding whether districts that wish to implement reforms without the funding provided through a model demonstration grant will be able to locate new resources or reallocate existing resources to provide the materials and professional development, among other resources needed for successful implementation. The MDCC is sharing this concern regarding financial sustainability with other cohorts of MDP grantees as they choose staffing strategies for implementing their models.

Variations in "Destination" Schools

The RTI MDPs were implemented in multiple schools within each of their partner districts, schools that differed markedly both within and across districts. Clemens and colleagues (Chapter 4, this volume) illustrate the differences in outcomes achieved in three implementation schools, with preliminary analyses indicating a generally positive trajectory in reading ability among third graders in "School B" and "School C," but not in "School A," and they speculated on possible reasons for the absence of positive student outcomes in "School A." Anecdotal data suggested an absence of strong principal commitment and leadership, significant deficiencies in reading among School A's third graders, less intensive training provided close to the beginning of implementation, and a clash between a long history of School A teachers managing their classrooms independently and the structured measurement and intervention team-based approaches that are fundamental to an RTI model.

The implication of such a clash between model requirements and the organizational context for implementation is well recognized in the extensive body of research on the diffusion of innovations, summarized and regularly updated by Everett Rogers (1962, 1972, 1983, 1995, 2003). The RTI models can be considered "innovations" in that they entail a set of practices that are new to the implementing schools and districts. Rogers contends that five characteristics explain approximately half of the variation in the rate of adoption of many types of innovations (Rogers, 2003). One of these characteristics[2] is compatibility—"the degree to which an innovation is perceived as consistent with the existing values, past experiences, and needs of potential adopters" (p. 240)—which "is positively related to its rate of adoption" (p. 249). MDCC analyses have generated lessons regard-

---

[2] Other characteristics include: relative advantage—"the degree to which an innovation is perceived as being better than the idea it supersedes" (Rogers, 2003, p. 229); complexity—"the degree to which an innovation is perceived as relatively difficult to understand and use" (p. 257), trialability—"the degree to which an innovation may be experimented with on a limited basis" (p. 458), and observability—"the degree to which the results of an innovation are visible to others" (p. 458).

ing how variations in several of Rogers's factors may relate to differences in implementation outcomes across MDP schools and districts. Here, we use variations in model compatibility to illustrate this process.

The contents of other chapters in this volume echo that of Clemens and colleagues in indicating marked differences in the compatibility of the MDPs' models with their "destination" schools. For example, the long history with PM and the problem-solving model of MPS meant that several building blocks that were needed to support the Minnesota model were already in place. The OCR website, a district training program for all new teachers on PM and the problem-solving model, a manual to guide their implementation, and school staff familiarity with the fundamentals of PM and data-based instructional decision-making were foundations on which to build. These core intervention components of the Minnesota model were highly consistent with the existing practices of the district, creating little incompatibility with previously introduced ideas.

In contrast, adopting the three-tiered model, with an emphasis on an evidence-based core reading program for all students, required a complete overthrow of the existing whole-language-based reading program in the Alliance School District. School staff, most of whom had had little or no training in providing or differentiating direct instruction in reading and who were reported by MDP staff to take no responsibility for the under-achievement of their students (see Kloo, Machesky, & Zigmond, Chapter 5), could well perceive the demands of the MP3 model as foreign to their environment; a hostile response, at least initially, could be expected and did in fact occur.

The schools in Eugene 4J School District, where the Oregon model was implemented, had a tradition of strong site-based decision making regarding curriculum, instruction, hiring, and staff development. Some 4J teachers perceived that the demands of implementing the new model simultaneously with the first district-imposed choice of reading curriculum were incompatible with this tradition. However, the long history of col-laboration between the district and the university and the MDP's strategy of beginning its implementation using volunteer staff in volunteer schools generated enough support for the model to allow the schools to "ease into" implementation. As the project progressed, these volunteer "early adopt-ers" became ombudsmen and spokespersons for the model throughout the district and more broadly.

The Lehigh University district partner falls somewhat between the Min-nesota MDP district's long-standing use of CBM and the problem-solving model and Alliance district's absence of exposure to evidence-based read-ing instruction before participating in the MDP. School staff in Lehigh's partner district was familiar with benchmarking assessments, and PM had been in use for special education students for some time. However, general education teachers largely did not use data for instructional decisions, nor did they systematically differentiate instruction to reflect students' RTI. To the extent that implementation progress is associated with perceived compatibility, MPS would be expected to have relatively fewer implementation challenges than other MDPs, and MP3 in Alliance School District would be expected to have the greatest challenges. This expectation is generally borne out in the evidence presented in other chapters in this volume. The importance of the compatibility of a model with its organizational context is now a topic of discussion between the MDCC and new cohorts of grantees as they evaluate potential partners for their work.

Variations in Implementation Contexts

The final component of the conceptual framework that guided the MDCC's work relates to the "influences" on the destination organizations, in this case the district contexts in which school implementation occurred. The MDPs worked in districts that differed in size (e.g., from fewer than 4,000 to more than 37,000 students), demographics (e.g., from 28 to 80% of students who were white, from 23 to 66% of students eligible for subsidized lunches), and resources (e.g., per-student spending ranging from just over $8,100 per year to almost $12,200 dollars per year). All districts, however, had schools that were failing to meet the academic needs of their students and had leaders who looked to the RTI models as having the potential to improve learning for all students in those schools.

This shared motivation to change played out in quite different ways across the districts, however, because of the different interplay of leadership styles, concurrent local pressures that sometimes competed and sometimes complemented the thrust of the RTI models, power struggles with teacher unions, and myriad other factors that made the implementation sagas told by the MDP teams take on something of the flavor of reality TV for those of us who heard them regularly firsthand. MPS staff were key partners of the grant team, so the district in many ways *was* the MDP. That didn't guarantee the Minnesota MDP a free ride in implementing their model; although only one school's implementation story is told in this book, two other schools participated in their project, and each presented its own challenges. Yet the central role of the district as a partner with the University of Minnesota and with the schools themselves and the ongoing presence of a coordinator whose primary job was to shepherd the change process in each school established a base of trust that supported the positive outcomes of their work. The deep involvement of the district in the project also fairly well guaranteed that the tools, experiences, and lessons of the model demonstration effort translated into strengthened assessment and instructional processes in other MPS schools.

A close partnership between Eugene School District 4J and University of Oregon staff manifested itself in a leadership team composed of two staff members from the district, representing general education and special education, and two university faculty members. These leaders not only successfully promulgated the RTI model in several elementary schools in the face of significant union resistance, but they also incorporated that work into a larger systemic change process focused on increasing equity, access to the general education curriculum, and effective instruction for all students. Curtis and colleagues (Chapter 11, this volume) detail a story of this wider district initiative as it first built on and then overtook the grant-funded RTI model, transforming it into a broader instructional intervention/progress monitoring (IIPM) model that included the core intervention components of the MDP (e.g., regular PM, tiered instruction) but also replaced the existing prereferral/referral process for special education eligibility determination with a more comprehensive special education evaluation system.

Chapter 3, by Gischlar and colleagues, details the implementation tale of the Lehigh University component of the Pennsylvania MDP team. Their implementation strategy focused on sustainability from the start, largely working within the existing resources of the district and schools in a thoughtful process that began with "training, modeling, and monitoring at the outset" (p. 74), proceeded through a tool- and procedure-generation phase to build district and school capacity, and concluded with a gradual fading of involvement to a handoff of all responsibility to the district and schools. A strong existing core program of reading instruction and an ongoing but underused assessment program served as a foundation on which to build in establishing school-based data teams and implementing the model, with a strong commitment throughout on the part of district leaders. By the end of the grant period, the RTI model was being implemented in elementary schools districtwide, and the district was one of only a few in the state that had been approved to use RTI as a basis for eligibility determination for students referred to special education evaluation because of reading problems.

The University of Pittsburgh component of the Pennsylvania MDP team faced a "perfect storm" of implementation challenges in their chosen district, where district leaders agreed that "an overhaul of the current reading instructional system was needed" (p. 105). The MDP team had no history of working with the district, there were virtually no building blocks in place with which to work in installing the model, and there was active, persistent resistance from many teachers and their union as they worked with district leaders to bring much-needed change to support improved reading performance. However, the MDP team reports being fortunate in working with a superintendent in the Alliance School District who had critical leadership skills and a commitment to "fundamental changes" in teacher roles and instruction, without which implementation would have been "impossible." In partnership with district leadership, by MDP staff accounts, the district was "transformed" through "top-to-bottom reform," improvements in student achievement were "dramatic," and by the end of the model demonstration grant period, plans were made for the model to be implemented districtwide in all elementary and secondary schools.

A somewhat surprising conclusion from these stories can be reached regarding the importance of district context and leadership. In several respects, the University of Oregon and University of Pittsburgh teams could be seen as facing the most challenging contexts for their work, with hostile teachers' unions being only one indicator. Yet the Eugene School District 4J and Alliance School District joined the Lehigh implementation district in having the grant-funded RTI models "go viral," spreading districtwide in broader systemic reform movements; the Minnesota model, too, is influencing practice in MPS through an active diffusion process. Clearly, a hostile environment makes reform more difficult, but it does not doom reform efforts to failure. In all four implementation stories, we saw that solid evidence of improvements in teaching and learning can overcome adults' sometimes long-held pessimism about their ability to truly help students. The MDCC worked with each individual model demonstration grantee with optimism regarding their ability to achieve full implementation of their models and positive outcomes for children and the adults who serve them.

CONCLUDING COMMENTS

The chapters in this book tell a positive story about the successful implementation of RTI models and their potential for improving reading outcomes for children, as indicated in what are self-described by MDP staff as preliminary analyses. These conclusions should be heartening to those in the business of bringing about change in adult knowledge, attitudes, skills, and practices as a way of bringing about positive change in children's knowledge, attitudes, skills, and practices. But Zigmond, Kloo, and Stanfa (Chapter 7, this volume) caution us not to declare victory over poor instruction and poor outcomes too quickly, and rightly so. Positive change is evident in teaching and learning, "but not enough, and not for everyone" (p. 197), as confirmed in the improvements noted in two of Lehigh University's implementation schools, but not the third.

More time and more research is needed to determine the full range and degree of effects of RTI for both adults and students, and several chapters in this volume suggest questions or topics that should be included in a continuing research agenda relative to RTI. More time also is needed to determine the full value of OSEP's investment in the model demonstration projects described here. The history lesson provided by Marston, Casey, and Wallace (Chapter 8) regarding Minneapolis Public Schools' involvement with curriculum-based assessment, tiered approaches to instruction, and the district's problem-solving model includes mention of receipt of an OSEP-funded model demonstration grant in the early 1990s and draws a direct line of descent to the current RTI model demonstration project. The OSEP investment in MPS almost two decades ago continues to pay off, as that base of research and implementation experience leads to continued improvements and expansions in policy and practice in this large urban district, affecting teaching and learning for more than 37,000 students each year. The MDCC staff cannot predict what the future will bring in the districts in which the RTI model demonstration grantees have worked, but will watch eagerly as it unfolds in those districts and in the sites where the grantees in the subsequent cohorts of model demonstration projects work on behalf of children and youths with special needs.

REFERENCES

Barth, R. S. (1990). *Improving schools from within: Teachers, parents, and principals can make the difference.* San Francisco: Jossey-Bass.

Fixsen, D. L., Naoom, S. F., Blasé, K. A., Friedman, R. M., & Wallace, F. (2005). *Implementation research: A synthesis of the literature.* Tampa: University of South Florida.

Pearson Education. (2008). AIMSweb assessment and data management for RTI. Retrieved June 12, 2010, from *www.aimsweb.com/index.php?mact=Glossar y,cntnt01,show,0&cntnt01tid=18&cntnt01returnid=18.*

Rogers, E. M. (1962). *Diffusion of innovations.* New York: Free Press.

Rogers, E. M. (1972). *Diffusion of innovations* (2nd ed.). New York: Free Press.

Rogers, E. M. (1983). *Diffusion of innovations* (3rd ed.). New York: Free Press.

Rogers, E. M. (1995). *Diffusion of innovations* (4th ed.). New York: Free Press.

Rogers, E. M. (2003). *Diffusion of innovations* (5th ed.). New York: Free Press.

Showers, J., & Joyce, B. (1996). The evolution of peer coaching. *Educational Leadership, 53*(6), 12–16.

U.S. Department of Education. (2005). *Model Demonstration Data Coordination Center scope of work.* Washington, DC: Office of Special Education Programs.

Wagner, M., & Levine, P. (2009). *The Model Demonstration Coordination Center (MDCC): Reflections on the first four years.* Menlo Park, CA: SRI International.

Index

Page numbers followed by *f* indicate figure, *t* indicate table